Siberia, Siberia

Valentin Rasputin

Siberia, Siberia

Translated and with an
Introduction by Margaret Winchell
and Gerald Mikkelson
Photographs by Boris Dmitriev

Northwestern University Press
Evanston, Illinois

Northwestern University Press
Evanston, Illinois 60208-4210

First published in Russian by Molodaia gvardiia as *Sibir', Sibir'* . . .
Copyright © 1991 by Valentin Rasputin. English translation copyright
© 1996 by Northwestern University Press. Published by arrangement
with Valentin Rasputin. All rights reserved.

Printed in the United States of America

First paperback printing 1997

ISBN 0-8101-1575-1

Library of Congress Cataloging-in-Publication Data

Rasputin, Valentin Grigor'evich.
   [Sibir', Sibir'. English]
   Siberia, Siberia / Valentin Rasputin ; translated and with an
introduction by Margaret Winchell and Gerald Mikkelson.
     p. cm.
   Includes bibliographical references and index.
   ISBN 0-8101-1575-1 (pbk: alk. paper)
   1. Siberia (Russia)—History. 2. Ethnopsychology—Russia
(Federation)—Siberia. 3. Siberia (Russia)—Environmental
conditions. I. Title.
DK753.R3713 1996
957—dc20
                                      96-7098
                                        CIP

The paper used in this publication meets the minimum requirements of
the American National Standard for Information Sciences —Permanence
of Paper for Printed Library Materials, ANSI Z39.48-1984.

For the nerpa and the *Epischura,*

for Amelia, Antonina, and Jane,

and for all other living things

whose well-being depends on us.

✤✤✤

Contents

A Note on Translation

For the transliteration of Russian words we have generally followed J. Thomas Shaw's *The Transliteration of Modern Russian for
English-Language Publications* (Madison: University of Wisconsin Press,
1967), using System I for personal and place names, except for those
with well-established English forms, and System II for words as words
and for bibliographical citations. Wherever feasible we have translated
rather than transliterated the names of places, buildings, and geographical features so that readers of this translation will grasp their meaning
the way readers of the original Russian do.

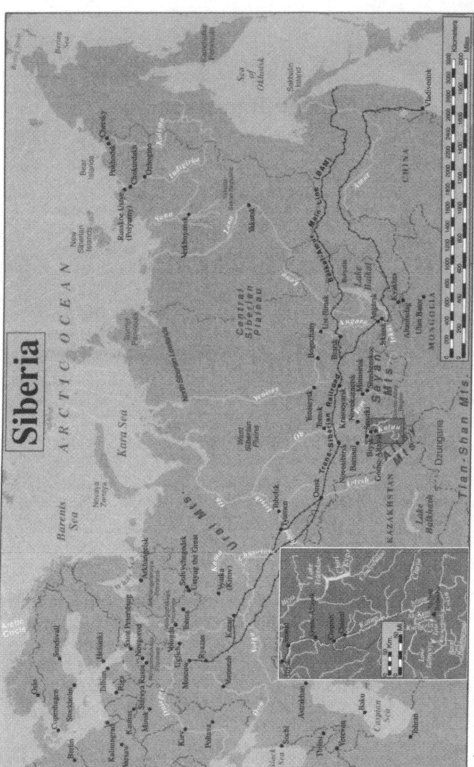

Map by Darin T. Grauberger and George F. McCleary, Jr., University of Kansas Map Associates

✣ ✣ ✣

Translators' Introduction: Valentin Rasputin Since *The Fire*

With the possible exception of Aleksandr Solzhenitsyn, who received the Nobel Prize in literature in 1970, Valentin Rasputin was the most gifted and influential Russian prose writer of the last thirty years of the Soviet era. During the two decades of his maturity and growing prominence in the pre-Gorbachev literary world (1965–85), Rasputin created at least a dozen masterpieces of shorter fiction (*malaia proza*) that have become what are known in Russian as "contemporary classics." The list includes five novellas (*povesti*)—*Money for Maria* (*Den'gi dlia Marii*, 1966), *Borrowed Time* (*Poslednii srok*, 1970), *Live and Remember* (*Zhivi i pomni*, 1974), *Farewell to Matyora* (*Proshchanie s Materoi*, 1976), and *The Fire* (*Pozhar*, 1985)—and several short stories that are deeply moving even when read repeatedly and that will provide pleasure and benefit for many years to come.

The distinguishing features of Rasputin's prose tales are the broad sweep of the tragic human events they depict, the penetrating psychological and social realism of his character portrayals, the vividness and rugged beauty of his nature descriptions, the profundity and provocativeness of the author's philosophical digressions, the persistence and integrity of his creative consciousness at work, and, above all, the ingenuity of his language. His lexicon and phraseology are deeply rooted in the fertile soil of Russian folk idiom. His protagonists speak a lively and colorful Siberian peasant Russian. His narration has an unhurried and majestic flow, reminiscent of his native Angara River. In reading any of Rasputin's novellas or short stories the reader gets an almost visceral satisfaction from every level of structure: isolated verb choice, sentence syntax, paragraph organization, chapter completeness, and the architectonics of the work as a whole. Rasputin is a master storyteller. There are no loose ends in his works. Moreover, his five novellas and best short stories, taken together, form an epic of Siberian village life in the twentieth century that spans several generations and chronicles the effects of two world wars, of revolution and civil chaos, of Stalinist terror and collectivization—and, more recently, of forced conversion from an agricultural to a logging and industrial economy, including construction of massive hydroelectric power plants and the flooding of once-populated river banks, in transforming a thriving rural culture almost beyond recognition.

Rasputin's exalted place in the history of Russian literature is, therefore, secure. He would be considered an outstanding writer had he created nothing other than *Live and Remember* and *Farewell to Matyora*. In view of his collected oeuvres, Rasputin ranks at least as high as his nineteenth-century forebears Ivan Goncharov and Nikolay Leskov; he is one of the few living Russian writers who could conceivably be awarded the Nobel Prize in literature.

Since the mid-1970s Rasputin has chosen a more direct means than belles lettres to speak out on issues of general human concern. Writing in the genres of the essay (*ocherk*), the prepared interview (*interv'iu*), the book preface (*predislovie*), and the anniversary commemoration, he has addressed a wide variety of topics while concentrating on the following: contemporary Russian literature, especially "village prose" (*derevenskaia proza*); the craft and obligations of the writer in society; the history of Russians in Siberia and their relationships with the indigenous Siberian tribes and with the central Russian (and Soviet) authorities in Saint Petersburg and Moscow; the dangers of destroying Lake Baikal and other precious natural resources and historical landmarks; and the restoration of Russian national consciousness, pride, and patriotism in an era when Russians are often blamed for the horrors of the calamitous Soviet experiment.

Rasputin's nonfictional writings usually appear first in a provincial Irkutsk newspaper like *Sovetskaia molodezh* (Soviet youth) or *Literaturnyi Irkutsk* (Literary Irkutsk) or in one of the national literary journals such as *Nash sovremennik* (Our contemporary) or *Moskva* (Moscow). Later they are published in book form. The most complete collections of his essays thus far are *Chto v slove, chto za slovom?*: *ocherki, interv'iu, retsenzii* (What's in a word? What's behind a word?: essays, interviews, book reviews) (Irkutsk: Vostochno-Sibirskoe knizhnoe izd-vo, 1987); and *Rossia: dni i vremena publitsistika* (Russia: days and times: essays) (Irkutsk: Pis'mena, 1993). Rasputin's longest work of nonfiction, translated here into English, is called *Sibir', Sibir'. . .* (Moscow: Molodaia gvardiia, 1991). It is the first volume in the author's long-term project of writing a personalized ethnohistory of his native Siberia since its original settlement by Russians beginning in the late sixteenth century. The opening and closing chapters discuss Siberia as a whole from initial conquest by Yermak's Cossack detachments to more recent times, about the peculiar physical and character traits of the Siberian Russian type, and about the gap between dreams and reality that has plagued the Russian experience in Siberia for most of the past four hundred years. Each of the six remaining chapters deals with particular parts of Siberia—Tobolsk, Lake Baikal, Irkutsk, the Gorno-Altay region, Kyakhta, and Russkoe Ustye—that, in Rasputin's view, provide ample reason for Siberians and Russians as a whole to feel at once proud and ashamed of their performance in this vast land. Rasputin's main message remains, as in his fiction, that Russians and all human beings should "live and remember."

During the Gorbachev years (1985–91) Rasputin, a famous cultural personage of high prestige and moral authority, was increasingly drawn into the arena of public affairs. In 1989 the Soviet Writers' Union elected him one of their delegates (*deputaty*) to the Soviet parliament (*S"ezd Narodnykh Deputatov*), in early 1990 Gorbachev chose him to be one of two writers (the other was Chingiz Aitmatov) in his inner cabinet, the Presidential Council (*Prezidentskii Sovet*), and for several years he has served as an active member of the governing board (*upravlenie*) of the Russian Federation Writers' Union. In all these capacities he appeared in the public spotlight more often than he wished (he is essentially a private, introspective person) and was asked to give speeches on a number of controversial topics, such as industrial development versus environmental protection, church-state relations in the Soviet Union (and, subsequently, in the Russian Federation), Russia's relationship to the West in the postcommunist era, the connection between freedom and responsibility, between words and deeds in Russia's developing democratic society, and the criteria that define a

3
+++

nation's authentic intelligentsia, or class of educated spokesmen. Closer to his heart, one supposes, were the writing and speaking assignments he undertook as a charter member of the All-Russian Society for the Preservation of Historical and Cultural Landmarks (founded in 1967) and of the society that, since celebrating the millenium of Russian Orthodoxy in 1988, has been organizing periodic celebrations called "A Holiday of Slavic Literature and Culture" (*Prazdnik slavianskoi pis'-mennosti i kul'tury*) in such ancient Russian cities as Novgorod and Smolensk. These events give Rasputin occasion to write on some of his favorite subjects, including environmental protection, historical preservation, and the unique mission of the Russian and other Slavic nations in the great family of humanity.

All this involvement in public affairs and the urgency of the issues facing Russia and the other parts of the former Soviet empire had decisive consequences for Rasputin's writing career and reputation. First, he did not publish any new belletristic works for nine years after *The Fire* (1985). During that period it was unclear from published interviews as well as from private correspondence and conversations whether he had stopped writing fiction altogether or was unable for some reason to complete stories to his own satisfaction. In an interview called "One Member of the President's Team," printed in the April 4, 1990, issue of *Literaturnaia gazeta* (The literary gazette) he said simply, "There is too little time for creative work." Second, while he was certainly no less prolific than in the late 1960s and the 1970s, Rasputin published exclusively nonfictional works from 1985 until 1994, most of which fell into the category of social commentary and polemics known in Russia by the untranslatable word *publitsistika*. Even the ethnohistorical discourses that constitute the chapters of *Siberia, Siberia*, while containing a wealth of fascinating information about this vast territory in both its historical dimension and present condition, are sprinkled with impassioned exhortations to his countrymen to learn about the deeds of their ancestors and to complete the rational, that is, reverent and conservationist, development of their Siberian homeland. This book, after the manner of Solzhenitsyn's 1990 essay on the past, present, and future of Russia as a whole titled "Kak nam obustroit' Rossii?" (How can we make Russia livable?), could easily be called "How Can We Make Siberia Livable?"

As a result of this shift from imaginative prose to *publitsistika* Rasputin is now known both in his homeland and in the West not only as the author of literary masterpieces but also, and perhaps even primarily, as an advocate of environmental protection and of the Russian people and nation amid the many conflicting factions that have emerged since Gorbachev's perestroika and the subsequent breakup of the Soviet Union. Public reaction to Rasputin's emergence as a polemicist and political figure was sharply divided. In the fierce ideological battle that took place among Russian intellectuals for the ear and allegiance of the people, he was both an active participant and a frequent target. His public policy positions can best be summarized as follows: Russia, in its desperation and haste to solve its urgent economic and political problems by adopting Western-style parliamentary and market mechanisms, should not squander its natural resources or mortgage them to foreign interests; and Russia, despite its grievous mistakes and the suffering and destruction it endured throughout the twentieth century, still has a sound cultural and spiritual foundation and a unique role to play in the world community. In other words, while the Soviet Union no longer exists and Russia, as the inheritor of most of its prerogatives as well as human and material assets, is not a superpower, it nevertheless has legitimate historical, geopolitical, and cultural claims to the status of a great nation. Russia, even as it draws closer to its neighbors and cooperates more and more in various international endeavors, should maintain its distinctiveness and independence. In short, the soul of Russia should remain Russian.

The key to understanding both the author's *Weltanschauung* and his art lies in chapter 16 of *The Fire*, in which the narrator, speaking for the hero, Ivan Petrovich Yegorov, and, presumably, for Rasputin as well, states that "each person's life has four structural supports: home and family, work, the people who share weekdays and holidays with you, and the land your home stands on. And each of these four is more important than the next. If one goes lame, the whole world tilts."[1] The issues of home and family are central to Rasputin's literary purview beginning with the short story "Vasily and Vasilisa" (1966) and continuing through the novella *Borrowed Time* (1970), in which the main characters are old people based on the author's grandparents. Work becomes an important element in his transitional period, the early

1970s, in the fictionalized travel sketch titled "Downstream and Upstream" (1972) and in the short story "French Lessons" (1973), which both contain a strongly autobiographical emphasis on growing up, meeting external and self-imposed expectations, and determining one's occupation in the outside world. Friendship ("the people who share weekdays and holidays with you"), especially among women, is an important subcurrent in his middle three novellas (Anna and Mironikha in *Borrowed Time*, Nastyona and Nadya in *Live and Remember*, Darya and her women neighbors in *Farewell to Matyora*) and in the short story "Auntie Ulita" (1985), which forms a kind of epilogue to *The Fire*. Male friendships are less well developed in Rasputin's work and are motivated primarily by blood ties (the brothers Ilya and Mikhail in *Borrowed Time*) or by mutual respect in the workplace (Kuzma and Vasily in *Money for Maria* and Ivan Petrovich and Afonya Bronnikov in *The Fire*). Male-female relationships, exclusively conjugal, are especially important in *Money for Maria* (Kuzma's loyalty to his wife, Maria), in *Live and Remember* (by far Rasputin's most moving, and passionate, romantic love story), and in *The Fire* (the mellowness and serenity of a couple long happily married). One's rootedness in one's place of origin ("the land your home stands on") gradually emerges as the dominant theme in Rasputin's fiction, somewhat muted yet in *Borrowed Time* in the nostalgia for childhood that Anna's daughter Lyusya experiences as she roams the countryside around her native village, growing stronger as Viktor in "Downstream and Upstream" and Andrey Guskov in *Live and Remember* make fateful journeys back to where they came from, and resounding tragically in *Farewell to Matyora* and *The Fire* as the heroes' homeland itself disappears under the waters of the rising Angara River.

Of these four structural supports, work holds special significance for Rasputin.

Work [for Ivan Petrovich in *The Fire* and, by implication, for everyone, in Rasputin's view] is performed not only in the name of His Royal Highness the Belly . . . . Work is what remains after you're gone. You are no longer there, you yourself are already becoming work for others, but those who come after you will still be reminded of you for a long, long time by your work . . . . And so it is, especially if your work flows into a useful river. There are two rivers, one with a useful current and the other with a useless current, and community life [*obshchaia zhizn'*] moves toward whichever of these is the more powerful.[2]

Rasputin's own work is his writing, and the building blocks of his aesthetics are formed by his views on language, both spoken and literary, and on the role of the writer in history and society. For him, language is the chief repository of a nation's collective consciousness and value system. In his works "language encompasses everything—national character, experience, history, philosophy, beliefs, aspirations, and hardships over the long haul. And a nation's spiritual health, its moral condition is captured first and foremost in the common people's language."[3] The liveliest and most telling forms of speech lie in common sayings, proverbs, folk songs, tales, and anecdotes: "Folklore, more fully and extensively than anything else, lays bare a people's soul."[4] Rasputin acknowledges Russia's enormous debt to such early transcribers of its oral literature as Mikhail Maksimovich (1804–73), Pyotr Kireevsky (1808–56), and Vladimir Dal (1801–72): "Folklore recordings . . . transmit living native speech . . . . They are the sanctuary of a language [*eto zapovednik iazyka*]."[5] It is then the task of scholars and writers to plumb the depths of this multivoiced linguistic abyss and to describe or reproduce it in their works.

The creative writer plays a crucial role in keeping alive a nation's memory of its past, of its language, and of its most worthy ideals: "[the writer] must sense in himself the entire historical and spiritual experience of his people, their historical path into the future, and be able to distinguish in the present between the traits of the temporary and those of the eternal."[6] The contemporary Russian writer has a rich tradition to draw on and to emulate. Rasputin says: "If you want to find out what Russians were like in the nineteenth century, look for them and their soul in the works of Gogol, Leskov, Dostoyevsky, Tolstoy, Fet, and Tyutchev."[7] It is no accident that Rasputin and Solzhenitsyn agree almost exactly on their lists of favored literary forebears. Of twentieth-century authors Rasputin especially venerates the prose of Ivan Bunin and Viktor Astafiev. And like Solzhenitsyn he believes it a writer's duty to expand the reader's vocabulary by having characters speak in natural intonations and by employing idiomatic expressions in his own narration:

I don't think there's anything wrong with dialectisms and older words that have for some reason gone out of general use showing up in an author's language. . . . Let the reader look them up in a dictionary; he has nothing to lose. . . .[8] Only someone who has lost his generic memory [*rodovaia pamiat'*] could argue that a word originating at the dawn of a nation or in the depths of its history should remain in those depths and not lay claim to literary competence simply because it is alleged to have become incomprehensible. If you can't understand it, then figure it out, find its meaning, hunt down its roots, and plunge into the swampy milieu of its source; if you think the word is covered with mold, wash it off and place it where it begs to go, and then you'll see how it begins to dance and speak. Why must the majority of people with healthy, undamaged hearing accommodate themselves to the deaf majority who use worn-out, bloodless speech and consider this the contemporary standard?[9]

Again like Solzhenitsyn, Rasputin argues that folklore, both archaic and contemporary (i.e., anecdotes), peasant speech, and the works of great writers past and present are the richest and most reliable sources of linguistic vigor and inventiveness for the living author. In his words, "it would do no harm and it's not too much to expect us to preserve the Russian language to the thirtieth and fortieth century. A nation is alive as long as its language is alive."[10]

As a Russian and, therefore, an inheritor of the tradition of Pushkin, Gogol, Dostoyevsky, Tolstoy, and Bunin, Rasputin, not surprisingly, holds an exalted view of the role of the writer in history and society. The writer is not a sorcerer or an entertainer but rather a culture-bearer, a teacher, a healer (*vrachevatel'*), a conscience, and, above all, a patriot. Possessing extraordinary talent does not deprive the writer of his freedom of self-expression, or even of self-contradiction, but it places a heavy burden of responsibility on his shoulders—to his ancestors (he must be worthy of the tradition), to his contemporaries (he must articulate their deepest longings), and to posterity (he must be comprehensible and relevant to them). Talent itself is mere potential—it can be used destructively, squandered on fleeting, momentary issues, or applied to more permanent and sacred tasks like preserving a culture, resurrecting a people's self-respect, and pointing the way toward a worthy future. Rasputin writes that "we [i.e., writers] are the bearers of Russia's strength and her pain, of her language [*slovo*] and her spirit."[11]

In Rasputin's view of literature, genres fall into a distinct hierarchy. The novella, the staple of village prose, is the genre that most adequately and completely conveys the agonies of the Soviet period of Russian history and the spiritual and cultural foundation on which the future of Russia might be based. Rasputin pays his respects to village prose as a whole not only for fulfilling its retrospective obligation to chronicle the breakdown of rural life but also for pointing out "the spiritual and moral values that, if we plan to remain a people and not just a population in the future, will not harm us even on asphalt."[12] And he has written about the particularly important contributions made to Russian literature by Fyodr Abramov, Sergey Zalygin, Vasily Shukshin, and Viktor Astafiev. What they have in common, in his view, is the ability "to locate precisely the nerve endings on that enormous body which we call *the people* [*narod*]."[13] Using the only instrument at their disposal, language, these writers were able to forge "a spiritual commonality" (*dukhovnaia obshchnost'*)[14] with their readers and to give them "moral direction" (*nravstvennaia napravlennost'*).[15]

While great works of imaginative literature produce the deepest and most permanent impact on the reader, writers feel obliged under certain circumstances to use a faster means of communication. In Rasputin's words, "the long-term therapeutic effect of imaginative literature on the human soul . . . can, unfortunately, arrive too late."[16] Russian writers speak out on issues when they sense that their country is heading for trouble and some drastic action is necessary. Writers, scholars, and other intellectuals from all wavelengths along the political and ideological spectrum make direct appeals to their countrymen—sometimes from the podium or the stage, sometimes on radio or television, but most frequently in print, in a popular journal or in a mass-circulation newspaper. A common technique is the open letter, either written and signed by one individual or collectively by several well-known public figures. Rasputin's signature on two collective letters ("A Letter from the Writers of Russia" and "A Letter to the People"), which appeared during the chaotic aftermath following the breakup of the Soviet Union, did little more than tarnish his reputation. He much preferred to speak for himself in the form of essays and prepared interviews, in which the style and ideas were unmistakably his own, born of pain and thoughtfulness, and he didn't have to apologize for the excesses of fellow signatories. While post-Soviet events made him less sanguine than before about the influence that writers could bring to bear on the course of events with their essays and public speeches, he did not regret having put so much energy into this kind of nonfictional writing. Toward the beginning of glasnost he wrote:

The writer who follows the dictates of his conscience not only cannot afford at the present time to ignore *publitsistika* but cannot manage without it.[17] . . . Just try under present circumstances to wash your hands of it and argue that you have no time, that you're busy creating some eternal message that will be heeded not only by your contemporaries but by your descendants as well. . . . We are forced [by circumstances] to resort to bare-bones language, not embellished by any literary imagery, in our call for common sense [*blagorazumie*] and justice.[18] . . . *Publitsistika* is motivated by impatience, by the desire to produce a quick and fair result—by its very nature it is the most active, open, and mobilizing genre. . . . Even those who sit in spacious [government] offices are forced to read it and take it into account precisely because the writer is expressing not just his own but also a widely held point of view [*obshchestvennaia tochka zreniia*].[19] . . . Thus *publitsistika* today is not a parochial activity but the duty of every writer who is not indifferent to the fate of his homeland. The times themselves demand *publitsistika*.[20]

The cornerstone of Rasputin's concept of the writer, and of his *Weltanschauung* in general, is his patriotism. "The artist's worldview," he writes, "is first and foremost fidelity to his homeland, its fate, its well-being, and its ability to stand up for itself [*protivostoianie*]."[21] *Patriotism*, for Rasputin, "is the most all-encompassing word. . . . Everything else is part of it: conscience, and duty, and truth, and goodness, and faith, and individuality, and citizenship."[22] In Rasputin's view, there are only two pitfalls that the artist must avoid at all cost: indifference to his homeland and contempt for its shrines. Rasputin is a key figure in his country not only in the movement to save the natural environment but also in the effort to preserve and restore Russia's cathedrals and historical landmarks, especially in Siberian cities such as Irkutsk, Tobolsk, and Kyakhta. He believes that there must be an inextricable link between past, present, and future generations. A proper understanding of how our ancestors lived, why they treated the land and each other the way they did, what they believed, and how their beliefs were put into action—this is how we properly define who we are, how we are to behave, and how we can leave the planet conducive to an abundant life for our children and grandchildren. During his year (1990–91) as a member of Gorbachev's Presidential Council, he made speeches advocating a total ban on the industrial pollution of Lake Baikal, the world's largest freshwater lake, and the complete separation of church and state in the Soviet Union, that is, an end to government-sponsored antireligious propaganda and to interference by public authorities in religious affairs. The kind of faithfulness to one's place of origin that Rasputin advocates is not so much Russian nationalism—at least when defined as something sinister or threatening—as it is what he calls "the Siberian's patriotic consciousness" (see Chapter 8).

Rasputin is, first and foremost, a writer and a Siberian patriot. He speaks on behalf of Russia as a whole primarily when he is confronted by anti-Russian slogans and sentiments. Indeed, he has manifold connections with Russia that include language, history, ethnicity, and culture. He speaks of Russia, especially northern Russia (the Novgorodian dominions before Ivan the Terrible's time), as his ancestral homeland (*prarodina*). "Homeland [*rodina*]," he says, "is not just your place of birth but also where your ancestors and forebears came from" (see Chapter 5). But he most emphatically identifies himself as a Sibe-rian and even uses the slightly derogatory Siberian term for European Russia—*Raseya*—which associates the latter with *rasseiannyi* (scatterbrained, absent-minded) and connotes impracticality and misguidedness. Rasputin proudly joined other Russians in the 1980s to mark five hundred years since the victory at Kulikovo Field over their Tatar oppressors in 1380, one hundred fifty years since Pushkin's death in 1837, and one thousand years since Prince Vladimir adopted Orthodox Christianity as the official religion of Kievan Rus in 988. Yet even in his essay "Kulikovo Field" he draws a comparison between European Russian peasants and their Siberian counterparts that is distinctly favorable to the latter. Siberians, in his view, are more decisive and resourceful, more acutely observant of their surroundings, more doggedly persistent in pursuit of a goal, more imperturbable, more

11
+++

ruggedly individualistic, and have a more highly developed sense of self-esteem than their counterparts in European Russia. Siberians developed these traits because they were very far removed from the centers of power, had greater freedom in a land without serfdom and a gentry class of overlords, and were forced to cope with the extraordinary harshness of nature in the wilderness. The main task of Siberian patriotism is to save the land itself, to save Siberia's natural resources from senseless and uncontrolled exploitation.

What Rasputin means by his homeland can best be visualized as a set of concentric circles, each of which denotes a spatial-geographical-ecological entity, superimposed on two separate temporal-historical continuums. One continuum extends backward in time from today's Siberia through the four hundred years since Yermak's Cossack detachments first crossed the Urals, to northern Russia before its absorption into Muscovy, and on back to medieval Kievan Rus; the other encompasses Siberia before the Russians arrived, the archaeology of its indigenous populations, and the geology of its natural features. At the center of the concentric circles, the center of Rasputin's geographical, ecological, and spiritual universe, lies his "little homeland" (*malaia rodina*) in the middle reaches of the Angara River. This core is surrounded, in turn, by Irkutsk Province (including the city of Irkutsk, the taiga, or subarctic evergreen forest, and Lake Baikal), then Siberia as a whole (which, for better or worse, is an integral part of Russia), and finally the world, the planet as a whole. Missing from this scheme, at least until its very existence was threatened in 1990–91, was any particular loyalty to the Soviet Union as such. Siberia is, for Rasputin, "the lungs of the planet earth" (see chapter 1) and Lake Baikal "a barometer for the problem of our interrelations with nature, . . . the summation of our moral and spiritual problems."[23] Rasputin follows in the footsteps of early Soviet (roughly 1917–28) conservationists such as G. A. Kozhevnikov and V. V. Stanchinsky, who emphasized nature's fragility and warned of the possibilities of an ecological collapse.[24]

Rasputin was born and raised in a peasant family in close proximity to nature on the banks of the Angara River. The land on which his childhood home once stood now lies submerged under a reservoir created after construction in the early 1960s of the huge Bratsk dam and hydroelectric power plant. Along with the land, the dam also destroyed the agricultural way of life that nurtured Rasputin's ancestors for three centuries. Concerning his *malaia rodina*, Rasputin writes:

Our "little" homeland gives us much more than we can imagine. . . . The nature of our native region is engraved in our souls forever. For example, whenever I experience something akin to prayer, I see myself on the banks of the old Angara River, which no longer exists, alongside my native village of Atalanka, the islands across the way, and the sun setting beyond the opposite bank. In my lifetime I have seen many beautiful things, those made by human hands and those not made by human hands, but I will die with this picture before me; for there is none other so near and dear to me.[25]

This feeling of closeness to one's place of birth and childhood experiences is the main source of a person's identity and the meaning of life. "From the time we are born we drink in the salts and scenes of our homeland; they influence our character and organize the cells of our body in their own manner. For this reason it is not enough to say that they are dear to our hearts—they are a part of us, the part that is formed by the natural environment. Its ancient voice is obliged to keep speaking inside us."

And in Rasputin's view, it is primarily writers who speak for Siberia—poets, novelists, historians, and ethnographers. Each age must have chroniclers (*letopistsy*) who correctly discern the dominant trends of their native region and write works in whatever genres are most effective (the topical essay [*publitsisticheskii ocherk*], the novella, or ethnohistory, for example) in raising the social and patriotic consciousness of their fellow countrymen.

While Rasputin as a writer acknowledges the importance to himself of the entire Russian literary legacy, especially of Dostoyevsky and Bunin, he sees himself as following also in the tradition of Siberian literature, whose chief representatives have always been acutely sensitive to the connections among art, nature, history, morals, and education. The founder (*raschinatel'*) of Russian literature in Siberia, according to Rasputin, was Kiprian, the first Orthodox archbishop of Siberia, who lived in Tobolsk in the seventeenth century, during the early years of the Romanov dynasty. Kiprian compiled the first Siberian chronicles and labored tirelessly to raise the moral standards of the earliest Russian settlers in Siberia and to establish the practice of looking after their spiritual and intellectual as well as physical needs. Rasputin calls Kiprian Siberia's first enlightener (*prosvetitel'*) and keeper of memories (*pamiatovatel'*). Rasputin also claims an affinity with the early nineteenth-century pioneers of Siberian Russian literature such as the poet Pyotr Yershov and the historical novelist Mikhail Zagoskin. The Siberian literary forebears he regards most highly, however, are the regionalists (*oblastniki*), the men of letters of the second half of the nineteenth and early twentieth centuries who campaigned long and hard for the rational development of Siberia. Their main emphases were education, abolition of the exile system, equitable and mutually advantageous economic relations with the mother country, quality migration to the area, and humane relations with the native populations (see Chapters 1 and 8).

Since the late sixteenth century, Siberia was governed by often tyrannical and rapacious rulers from European Russia. Consequently, instead of becoming an independent, sovereign nation, as did the United States when the North American colonies broke away from England, it remained a colony of the Russian Empire and later of the Soviet Union. Instead of becoming a model for national expansion and equitable integration into Russia as a whole, Siberia remained essentially a storehouse of raw materials—fur, timber, gold and other precious metals, and, more recently, coal, oil, natural gas, and water—to be raided for the benefit of compatriots west of the Ural Mountains and for export to foreign countries.

Siberians' consciousness of their colonial status and continual exploitation gave rise in the nineteenth century to a kind of patriotic feeling that became known as Siberian regionalism (*oblastnichestvo*). The leading regionalists were the historian Afanasy Shchapov (1831–76), the explorer Grigory Potanin (1835–1920), and the writer/ethnographer/archaeologist Nikolay Yadrintsev (1842–94). These scholarly activists advocated greater cultural, economic, and political autonomy for Siberia, at times even calling for Siberia to break away from Russia and form an independent nation. Yadrintsev, whose most famous works are *Sibir' kak koloniia* (Siberia as a colony, 1882; 2d ed., 1892) and *Sibirskie inorodtsy: ikh byt i sovremennoe polozhenie* (Siberia's indigenous peoples: their way of life and present situation, 1891), spent nine years in prison and exile for espousing "Siberian separatism" (*Sibirskii separa-*

tizm). Rasputin calls Yadrintsev "one of Siberia's finest minds and a true, remarkable patriot" and refers to his *Siberia as a Colony* as "a thorough and profound study of our region" (see Chapter 8).

The nineteenth-century regionalist scholars occupy an important place in the development of a distinctive Siberian historiography founded two hundred years earlier by Gerhard Friedrich Müller, "the father of Siberian history."[26] They exemplify a distinguished though minority trend in Russian historiography, sometimes called "the federal school," which emphasizes the differentness of each nationality and major component of the Russian Empire, the centripetal forces in Russian history, and the positive value of customs and institutions emanating from outlying areas such as Ukraine, Belarus, and Siberia. Shchapov believed that federal (i.e., decentralized) government was the only proper form for an empire the size of Russia. While these "federalists" were often reviled by official historians (e.g., in the nineteenth century Sergey Solovyov attacked the Ukrainian Nikolay Kostomarov) and occasionally banished from their academic posts or even arrested, their "provincial" point of view remains valid and deserves at least untrammeled coexistence with the more canonical historiography that extols the virtues of centralization, supranationality, and imperial control. The validity of this view of Russian history was underscored when the Soviet Union disintegrated into separate national states in 1991, which some regarded as the last of the European empires forced to grant independence to its colonies.

Rasputin's patriotism follows in this tradition. The connection between the Siberian regionalists and separatists of the nineteenth century and Siberian writers of more recent times—Zalygin, Astafiev, Aleksandr Vampilov, and Rasputin—was rarely explored by Soviet scholars, an exception being Nikolay Yanovsky in *Pisateli Sibiri* (Writers of Siberia, 1985). The West, too, has not given adequate attention to this subject, and ignorance of it has led to common misperceptions about Rasputin's beliefs. Siberia, as he sees it, is a salad of nationalities and religions not unlike the United States. Its population is a relatively harmonious mixture of Russians, Ukrainians, Poles, an array of Paleoasiatic, Tungus-Mancu, and Samoyed indigenous tribes, and a smattering of Jews, Germans, and other groups who emigrated from Europe. The character traits of all true Siberians, regardless of ancestry, make them well suited for living in and making use of the resources of their majestic, forbidding land. Rasputin's Siberian patriotism is an outcome of his pride in the accomplishments and adaptability of his predecessors, compatriots, and neighbors in Siberia and of his pain at the sight of irreplaceable natural treasures being defiled and destroyed by outsiders from European Russia and elsewhere in the former Soviet Union.

In Rasputin's view, the nineteenth-century Siberian regionalists achieved many of their most cherished goals for the rational development and enlightenment of their native region: Siberia's first university was established in Tomsk; the mass exile of criminals to Siberia was curtailed; Siberia was able to feed itself and produce an agricultural surplus, even exporting butter and cheese to foreign countries such as Denmark; increased emigration of peasants from Russia, Ukraine, and Belarus strengthened Siberia's population base and added to its class of agricultural yeomen; and the Europeans in Siberia coexisted more or less amicably with the native populations, who continued to pursue their traditional, often nomadic and shamanistic ways. If Yadrintsev were to visit Siberia one hundred years after his death, he would approve of the multiplicity of Siberian universities, Siberia's own branch of the Academy of Sciences, and its large cities, industry, and railroad network.

He would, however, be appalled at the submersion of fertile lands, the chemical pollution of the black earth, the ravaging of virgin forests, and the construction of hydroelectric dams on Siberia's major rivers. For Siberia, the past hundred years, especially since World War I, have essentially been wasted. Siberian agriculture has been destroyed, some of its native peoples are near extinction, its resources are being exploited by the central authorities, its educational system is superficial and narrowly specialized, and its people are leaving to find a better life elsewhere. Siberia's nineteenth-century patriots had placed their hopes in institutions of local self-government that would be responsible for regional development. Their hopes were dashed by the devastation of Russia's civil war, the collectivization of agriculture, and the relentless removal of Siberia's nonrenewable and partially renewable natural resources. Ministries and government agencies have mercilessly destroyed the Siberian countryside. Even local authorities are unable to stop them. Siberians have had to accept a few crumbs from the sumptuous table of the former Soviet, now Russian ministries. Siberia plays the role of a Third World, developing country for Russia and for multinational corporations: it merely supplies raw materials. A society that cannot moderate its appetites, that devours its resources at such a maddening pace, is a society with shaky moral foundations. And although Siberia is no longer a bottomless well, the ministries continue to treat Siberia like a colony, like a barge laden with riches headed for Europe or East Asia. The Siberian land has been tyrannized by ministerial autarchy, by the radical reconstructionists whom Rasputin calls "reversers" (*povorotchiki*), and by the seasonal workers (*sezonniki*) and roughnecks (*arkharovtsy*) he so vividly portrays in his novella *The Fire*.[27]

Small villages in Irkutsk Province and the taiga form the setting for all of Rasputin's major fiction. This is the locale he has most frequently called his "little homeland," the part of the world that he is from and that remains in him as an essential component of his being, of his soul. But since his home village of Atalanka was relocated to another site, on higher ground above the rising waters of the Angara River, Rasputin has gradually broadened the definition of his "little homeland" to include other parts of Siberia: Irkutsk, where he has lived with only occasional interruptions since 1954; Lake Baikal, near which he has done much of his writing and whose survival he has been promoting continuously in his main civic role as an environmentalist; and more distant parts of Siberia in the north, west, and south. In his novellas, he developed an image of the East Siberian peasant village as a once coherent, harmonious, and productive rural culture that has been gradually and unmistakably undermined and destroyed by the incursions of Soviet rule and rampant modernization. Even before he finished writing *The Fire*, Rasputin had embarked on a venture no less challenging and formidable than the novellas that made him famous, that is, the study of Siberia as a whole. This quest, which includes examination of the written record, travel to remote places in all four corners of Siberia, and serious thought about the vast changes that have occurred, especially in his own time, has resulted thus far in the present volume and continues unabated.

Chapter 1 of *Siberia, Siberia*, titled "Siberia without the Romance," provides the framework for the book by introducing those themes that relate to the four-hundred-year experience of Russians in Siberia as a whole. It begins with a discussion of the word *Sibir'* itself and of the great variety of associations, some historically justified, others quite fantastic, that this name has evoked through the centuries. In general, those who live in Siberia permanently perceive it quite differently from outside observers, either from foreign lands or from other parts of Russia. Outsiders viewed Siberia in the eighteenth century as a source of mineral wealth and territory ("our Mexico and our Peru"), in the nineteenth century as a vast frontier begging to be settled and cultivated ("our United States"), and in the twentieth century as "a source of colossal energy" and "a land of unlimited opportunities." Those native to the region, regardless of ethnic background, regard Siberia as their homeland, "a homeland that, like every other, needs love and protection, perhaps even more protection than any other place because it still has something left to protect."

The obscure and often contradictory accounts of the Cossacks' armed penetration into the land beyond the Urals in the 1580s, of their battles with the Tatars of the Siberian khanate, and of the year of Yermak's death or even the exact form of his name illustrate how unconcerned Russians have been about the details of their own country's historical record. The heroic feats of these detachments of Cossack warriors have been immortalized primarily in Russian oral tales and songs in which Yermak ranks alongside Stepan Razin, the Don Cossack leader of a huge peasant insurgency, as one of Russia's most highly revered folk heroes. By the middle of the seventeenth century, an astonishingly short time considering the vast distance, rugged terrain, and severe climate, Russians had reached the Pacific Ocean, thanks primarily to a series of extraordinary explorers, including Semyon Dezhnyov, Yerofey Khabarov, Vasily Poyarkov, and others, many of whom were born in the same northern Russian town, Ustyug the Great. Rasputin calls these men of almost superhuman fortitude "the crossbows [*samostrely*] of the Russian spirit." He surmises that these first waves of Russians in Siberia must have been driven by something more than the chance for material gain or else their progress across the continent would have been more gradual; there were enough sable and ermine at each stop along the four-thousand-mile route to last a long time. In Rasputin's view, "national pride [*narodnoe samoliubie*] provided no small amount of the energy for this mighty upsurge." He sees in this relentless movement to the east, with all its dangers and deprivations, a kind of Russian manifest destiny, which he calls "the will of history itself [*voleiz"iavlenie samoi istorii*], bending down low over that region at that time and picking out daredevils to test and prove the capabilities of the downtrodden Russian people, who were, in a widely held view, half asleep."

In Rasputin's opinion, the most important phase in the development of Siberia was accomplished by the peasants who followed the Cossacks and explorers into that uninhabited virgin land and "were plowing up the steppe or clearing the taiga to make fields, sowing and harvesting crops year after year, raising children, adding to the number of families there, and making a land of hardship, by now already theirs, accessible and fit to live in." It was primarily these "dirt farmers" (*khlebo-roby*) who settled Siberia and made it Russian. "The peasant was the one who finally grafted Siberia onto Russia, completing with his wooden plow the immense undertaking—immense in scope and in consequences—begun by Yermak with the aid of weapons." Siberia was conquered by those who could feed it.

The Russian settlers, through intermarriage with the indigenous peoples and through adaptation to the harsh circumstances, gradually evolved into a distinctive physical and character type, as different from their ancestors and countrymen in European Russia as North Americans are from their European forebears. Typical Siberian Russians have a slightly Asiatic look (*aziatchina*) and "keen powers of observation, a heightened sense of self-respect that does not accept anything alien or coercive, inexplicable changes in mood and an ability to withdraw into themselves to some unknown private recesses, a raging passion for work alternating with bouts of wanton idleness, and also a touch of cunning mixed with kindness, a cunning so transparent that it can be of no advantage whatsoever." The unwillingness of Siberian Russians to accept coercion stems from their being descendants of "freedom seekers" (*vol'nookhochie*), people who went to Siberia to escape authority, "fleeing restrictions and repression and seeking freedom of all sorts: religious, social, moral, occupational, and personal," or "to escape punishment by hiding in remote areas far beyond the Urals."

According to Rasputin, the most important factor shaping the character of Siberian Russians is neither their ethnic origins nor the reasons their ancestors went there in the first place, but rather the land itself. "Thus a Siberian is not only a thick skin accustomed to inconvenience and freezing cold and not only stubbornness and persistence in achieving goals (qualities that the local conditions produced), but also a certain fatedness, a deep and solid rootedness in this land, a compatibility between the human soul and the spirit of nature." Rasputin's concept of character development is a kind of geographical determinism. He calls this "the genetics of the land" (*genetika zemli*). In his words, "the genetics of the land is just as primordial and fixed as the genetics of the blood." While Rasputin understands the feeling of exploitation by European Russia that motivated some of his antecedents to strive for Siberian independence from the mother country, he himself is not a Siberian separatist. He believes that once Siberia had been "grafted" onto Russia, it became a necessary and permanent part of that nation, not just needing Russia for its own development but forming an essential part of Russia. In fact, Rasputin, like his older contemporary Solzhenitsyn, believes that the center of Russian civilization will someday be located in Siberia. And while he himself, a native of Irkutsk Province, is partial to the East Siberian taiga and to the region around Lake Baikal because of their exceptional beauty and bountifulness, he believes that each part of Siberia is important for a particular reason, including the historical events that both Russians and their indigenous neighbors experienced there and what each place lends to a full appreciation of the concept of Siberia as a whole, as a distinct entity today.

As he delves into the history and examines the present condition of various parts of Siberia, Rasputin's attachment to them grows. In an interview in the newspaper *Sel'skaia zhizn'* (Country life) (January 27, 1992, p. 3), in which he explains the aims of *Siberia, Siberia*, he uses the term "little homeland" in reference to the actual place of his birth and childhood and also to Siberia as a whole. "My purpose," he says, "was to show reverence for this powerful land, for my little homeland of more than seventy million square kilometers, to say a good word about its gatherers, builders, and caretakers [*radeteli*], and to appeal to my countrymen to come to the defense of Siberia against its despoliation [*razgrablenie*] by foreign and domestic speculators." The places that Rasputin covers in the six central chapters of *Siberia, Siberia* represent four distinct corners of the vast territory of Siberia: its western edge (Tobolsk), its south-central border (the Gorno-Altay region), its northeastern shore (Russkoe Ustye), and its southeastern heartland (Lake Baikal, Irkutsk, and Kyakhta). Each locality exemplifies not only a particular set of geographic and climatic conditions but also a specific mixture of population and pattern of historical development. Each place played its own role in Siberian history and deserves not only acknowledgment of its achievements but also careful preservation or restoration because of the unique contribution it could make to the well-being of Siberia (and of Russia) in the future.

The main themes of Chapter 2 are: (1) Tobolsk as "the father of Siberian cities" and the first capital of Siberia (until 1839); (2) Siberia as an inseparable part, a colony, of Russia; (3) the incompleteness of the early historical record; (4) Archbishop Kiprian as the first teacher and chronicler of the Russians of Siberia, as the arbiter of their morals (which tended to be corrupt in this frontier region), and as the founder of Siberia's written history, recorded in Russian (*raschinatel' ee porusskoi pis'mennosti*); (5) Tobolsk as the birthplace of Gavriil Batenkov (the only participant in the Decembrist Uprising of 1825 who was originally from Siberia), Pyotr Yershov (author of the verse tale *The Little Humpbacked Horse* [*Konek-gorbunok*, 1834]), Potanin, and Yadrintsev; and (6) Tobolsk, paradoxically, as an example of Russians' negligence in regard to their own historical landmarks and of a vigorous grassroots campaign for their restoration.

The main emphases in Chapter 3, titled "Lake Baikal," include: (1) the sacredness of Lake Baikal to all the peoples who have lived on or near its shores; (2) the breathtaking beauty of nature in its pristine state; (3) the uniqueness of the fauna in Lake Baikal, including the freshwater seal (nerpa) and the oilfish (*golomianka*); (4) the sense of the numinous, of divine tranquility, imparted to humans through their contact with the lake ("And when Baikal finishes storming and raging, once again it wears a peaceful face and God's heavenly grace [*bozh'ia blagodat'*]"); and (5) the ecological danger and damage brought on by human activity, the greed and shortsightedness of uncontrolled economic development. Communing with nature near Lake Baikal is, for

Rasputin, quite literally a religious experience. The magnificence of this place provides evidence for the existence of the human soul and of the Creator. In his words:

Beside Baikal it's not enough to contemplate the way you usually do; there you must think in a higher, purer, stronger manner, on a level with its spirit, not feebly, not bitterly. When something great touches us, we are capable of merely raising questions; it is only through questions that we seek, that we hail the language that we didn't manage to recognize.

Maybe nature stands between God and human beings. And until you unite with nature, you won't move forward. It won't let you. And without its preliminary involvement, without its accompaniment, your soul won't come under the protection it covets.

And finally, the agonizing thirty-year fight to save Lake Baikal from industrial pollution has persuaded Rasputin that the role of writers is at once essential yet not sufficient in forming public opinion on ecological questions. Some victories have been won: no new plants have been built on the shores of Lake Baikal since the 1980s, a few efforts have been made to dilute the effluents before they are dumped into the lake, and more and more of the shoreline is being designated as nature and wildlife preserves (*zapovedniki*). Yet the pulp and cellulose conglomerates at the south end of the lake and on the Selenga River (in Buryatia), which empties into Baikal, continue to churn out their wastes, and it is by no means clear that they will be closed or redesigned for less harmful production in the foreseeable future despite Soviet government decrees of the glasnost period, which may no longer have any force. For Rasputin, the patriotic writers' duty is clear: they must continue to lobby for the protection of Lake Baikal, even if they turn away, at least for a time, from their original artistic calling. In his words, "Some writers, who existed for the purpose of creating odes, and some scientists who were also confused about the reason for their existence, and then the common folk, stirred up by the writers and scientists, began to raise the question, Won't we destroy Baikal? And they arrived at an answer: Yes, we will. Over our dead bodies." Yet Rasputin is not certain that the environmentalists, even with public opinion on their side, will be able to overcome the still formidable inertia of ministerial autarchy and of the colossal size of production, however obsolete, at these plants.

Chapter 4 describes Irkutsk, where Rasputin has maintained his primary home for most of his adult life. Here he stresses (1) one's sense of homeland as a source of strength and identity ("We always remain in our homeland at heart"); (2) people's need for knowledge and a sense of history, "a sense of closeness to the acts and destinies of their ancestors, . . . an inner comprehension of their responsibility for the place granted them in the vast, general continuum that allows them to be what they are"; (3) the necessity for preserving the few stone and wooden buildings that remain from earlier times; and (4) the importance of the Russian-American Company, which was located in Irkutsk, and of the progressive branch of the merchant class in the development of Siberia. Rasputin writes that the merchants of Irkutsk "combined serving God and Mammon quite well, better than anywhere else: frequently rolling in money, Siberian industrialists could afford to fork over fat sums for the good of their native land as well as for their hometowns without any detriment to their pocketbooks." Rasputin explains that Siberian Russians probably inherited their inventiveness and aesthetic instincts from their distant ancestors in the northern regions of European Russia, especially Arkhangelsk, Vologda, Ustyug the Great, and Novgorod.

The main themes in Chapter 5, titled "The Gorno-Altay Region," are: (1) the indescribable beauty of the Altay Mountains, particularly Mount Belukha, Lake Teletskoe, and the Katun River. "For each of us," writes Rasputin, "they [i.e., these natural features] may well be the last recollection, on the eve of massive transformation, of a land that allows us, if we work at it properly, to glimpse paradise on earth"; (2) small dams on the tributaries of the Katun might not be harmful, but huge dams and heavy industry will be catastrophic for the jewels of nature in this region; (3) while each locality has its own fauna and flora, its own predestination, as it were, Siberia as a whole remains a single, vast land; (4) the Siberian peasants, especially those of Old Believer origin, were more free-spirited than those of European Russia; (5) the Old Believers (schismatics) were always prepared to make sacrifices, even to move on, when their autonomy and way of life were threatened; and (6) the Russians of Siberia, as a rule, were not cruel or oppressive to their indigenous neighbors. Points relating to the author's worldview in this chapter include the suppositions that God created human beings so there would be someone to admire his handiwork; that the earth should know its organizers and poets and then it will also know its own worth; that the concept of homeland has several dimensions, including where you were born and where your ancestors came from; and that we carry within us an indelible trace of all that has happened to our people in the past. In his words, "we are the repositories of all their synods and schisms. As a tree builds up annual growth rings, it adds not simply a record of time passing but the character of the times as well; in a Russian, every scar and every stroke of the Russian people's fate repeats itself like an echo and a reflection." Lake Teletskoe, still in an unspoiled state, reminds Rasputin that, despite the widespread destruction of nature in recent times, "there still are some heavenly spots left on earth [*est' na svete eshche blagodat'*]." And finally, the extraordinary life and career of Nikolay Smirnov, a longtime forest ranger in the nature preserve at Lake Teletskoe, reminds the author that honest work is therapeutic, a great healer for the earth itself as well as for people: "Why should the land lie fallow? It ought to work, just like human beings, and it will be better off as a result."

The town of Kyakhta, the subject of Chapter 6, was vital to the Empire until bypassed by the Trans-Siberian Railroad in the early twentieth century. Kyakhta, located on the border with China, supplied tea to all of Russia, was a place where people of diverse religions and cultures intermingled, and represented Siberia's (and Russia's) "window on the East." This human diversity was also reflected in the peculiar mixture of architectural styles in Kyakhta: Chinese-type country houses standing beside typical Russian Orthodox churches and log cottages. It was also a point of embarkation for the geological and ethnographic expeditions of Potanin and Yadrintsev and the home of some of Siberia's most highly enlightened and generous merchant families. Indifference in Soviet times to the glories of Kyakhta's past was tragically symbolized when authorities paved over a historic graveyard to build a soccer stadium where "present-day youths chase a ball on the bones of their grandmothers and grandfathers."

Chapter 7, titled "Russkoe Ustye" (which means Russian Estuary), deals with the inhabitants of a cluster of small but remarkably durable settlements in the tundra of northeastern Siberia where the Indigirka River empties into the part of the Arctic Ocean known as the East Siberian Sea. On the basis of their archaic language and folk legends, Rasputin argues that the ancestors of these hardy Russians most likely arrived at that remote spot not by land, as did most Russian settlers in Siberia, but by the North Sea route more than four hundred years ago, leaving the dominions of medieval Novgorod to escape the tyrannical rule of Ivan the Terrible during the expansion of Muscovy into the once independent northern Russian lands. The feats of these pioneers not only in making such an inhumanly dangerous trek but also in surviving the polar conditions in their new home defy the imagination. They were, evidently, people of deeds and abilities rather than of words. They established viable communities on the permafrost and learned to coexist with the nearby indigenous peoples, the Yakuts and Yukagirs, but without extensive intermarriage or intermingling. In this way, they preserved their ethnic Russianness (*russkost'*) better than their countrymen in other parts of Siberia. In Rasputin's words:

They were tiny islets of Russian culture, dotlike "birthmarks" on the canvas of the tundra, but they stood their ground, held out under conditions they were unaccustomed to, and displayed a dignity and wisdom in their dealings with the aboriginals that, above all else, say something about the heart and nature of the numerous Russian people, which make them great. Moreover, they also preserved their ancient inner core, with all its poetry and prose, so completely that we can only marvel.

In this chapter Rasputin pays tribute to the people of Russkoe Ustye and their ancestors, a unique and remarkable strain of the Russian ethnos that because of their isolation from the rest of the country and from the outside world retained a large part of their native ways, customs, language, etc., and thus remind us even today of what Russians must have been like in an earlier era. He calls the culture of Russkoe Ustye "the last echo of Russia's ancient language and way of life." This group of Russians survived because they had moved there in search of freedom and learned to live under the harshest of conditions; they grafted themselves onto the delicate arctic nature and became one with it. For them, Russkoe Ustye, "the outer limit of survival and sorrow . . . had become the Promised Land." Even on religious matters these people adapted to their surroundings; they were both Russian Orthodox and pagan at the same time. In Rasputin's words:

Christianity was for the salvation of the soul, while the old religion concerned the maintenance of the belly (by the way, in Russkoe Ustye the word *zhivot* [stomach, belly] has not lost its original meaning of *life*). Out there, in the middle of nowhere, one faith was considered all the more insufficient. And besides, Christ didn't have time to bother with driftwood or molting geese, so the Indigirka dwellers apparently relieved him of worrying about such trifles.

Rasputin sees his role as a continuation of the efforts of Russian ethnographers in the nineteenth and early twentieth centuries, particularly of Andrey Birkengof and Vladimir Zenzinov; that is, to record as much as he can of the language and culture of the people of Russkoe Ustye while it lasts. In his words:

You wish that others could hear and enjoy this speech before it's finally too late. For in a little while the sounds of bygone times will be heard no more and the valve will shut forever, that valve in Russians that rises slightly from time to time over the narrow, imperceptible opening through which we hear the coherent whispering of our ancestors, who know they will be understood. But as soon as there is no one left to understand them, nothing more will be said. . . .

Let's listen to the Russians of Russkoe Ustye some more, before they fall silent.

Chapter 8, titled "Your Siberia and Mine," concludes the book. While this chapter is based to some extent on Rasputin's 1984 article of the same title, here the emphasis is different. Its main themes are: (1) how far Siberia needs to go to fulfill the hopes and expectations of late-nineteenth-century patriot-regionalists like Yadrintsev and Shchapov; and (2) while criminal exile to Siberia was abolished and Tomsk University established (followed by numerous other universities and scientific research centers in the Soviet period), Siberia is still treated like a colony: it is exploited for its abundant natural resources, ravaged ecologically, and left to languish with a lower standard of living than in much of the rest of Russia. In Rasputin's view, Siberia is worse off in many respects than it was one hundred years ago: "Siberia needs to be developed. But it needs development, not the highway robbery concealed by this beneficial concept. . . . The guest-worker system, no matter how many people it provides, is suitable for worthless territory unfit for habitation but not for Siberia, which deserves a better fate, which is capable of giving humankind an abundance of all the essentials." The plight of the indigenous peoples of Siberia, the Voguls, Ostyaks, and Evenks, for example, is particularly desperate because "oil, gas, power plants, clear-cut forests, chemicals, and smoke drive them out of their ancestral territories and deprive them of their ancestral occupations." Rasputin fears that these native Siberians may be doomed to extinction. In his words, "the primitive Siberians over whom the local boosters rightfully shed compassionate tears felt significantly safer under the czar than under the Ministry of Energy and the petrochemical industry." If the haphazard, rapacious mining of recent times continues unchecked for one or two more decades, "Siberia will vanish into thin air." Rasputin calls current practices "tyranny . . . not only in relation to society but also in relation to the land."

Despite the bleak picture he paints of Siberia today, Rasputin ends on a somewhat optimistic note, placing his hopes for the future mainly on the growth and strengthening of institutions of local and regional self-government (*samoupravlenie, oblastnaia duma*) and on a moral and spiritual regeneration that he thinks may already be happening among Siberians themselves. In his words, "a new kind of person might appear, individuals who, in view of the catastrophe with which our activities threaten them, will find saving, affirmative routes to take and won't confuse destruction with creation. . . . Siberia is waiting for just such people to be its saviors, builders, and guardians [*spasitel', stroitel', khranitel'*], tirelessly peering into the faces of all who ride and walk by, wondering if they aren't the ones, if they aren't bringing deliverance."

When Rasputin visited the University of Kansas and traveled briefly in the upper Midwest in March 1985, he had just submitted his last novella, *The Fire*, for publication in *Nash sovremennik* (it appeared in the July 1985 issue) and was already at work on the most ambitious writing project of his literary career: a multistage review of the history and present condition of Siberia as a whole. A year or so later, the contours of his plan were clear enough to be sketched briefly in an interview for the May 30, 1986, issue of the magazine *Knizhnoe obozrenie* (Book review), in which Rasputin said, "I am working on a journalistic book [*publitsisticheskaia kniga*] about our precious Siberia [*o zapovednoi Sibiri*]. It will consist of essays about nature around Lake Baikal, in the Gorno-Altay region, and in Yakutia, and about Siberia's older cities, such as Tomsk, Tobolsk, and Irkutsk. It will include ruminations on historical and cultural masterpieces. Its tentative title is *Siberia, Siberia*. The publishing house Molodaia gvardiia plans to publish it in its series called The Fatherland [*Otechestvo*]."

Rasputin stressed in this interview that his motives were at once literary, patriotic, and environmentalist in character and therefore in keeping with the writers' tradition in his country. In his words, "Russian literature always, at all times, has responded to the needs of the Fatherland. Today, like never before, we are faced with the urgent task of adopting a diligent and protective attitude toward nature. Each writer working in our common literary field has a plot of land on which he is able to produce the maximum benefit." In the early stages of this project Rasputin made extended trips to the places in Siberia that he intended to write about. He would keenly observe the lay of the land, the customs of the inhabitants, the remnants of pre-1917 Russian civilization, and the changes wrought since the Revolution by Soviet power, by industrial development, and by contact with the outside world. He was particularly attracted to those parts of Siberia populated by the Russian religious schismatics known as Old Believers (*starovery, staroobriadtsy, raskol'niki*; in Siberia, *kerzhaki, semeiskie*), especially in the Gorno-Altay region, primarily because he admired their work ethic and their dogged adherence to high moral principles; to those towns that produced or attracted Russian Siberians who were notably civic-minded and patriotic in their activities, including Tobolsk, Kyakhta, and Irkutsk; to those settlements that were unusually successful in preserving venerable customs, such as Russkoe Ustye; and to those regions with geographical features, gems of nature, that are unquestionably worth saving, namely Lake Baikal and the Gorno-Altay region.

When the separate sections of this work began to appear in print in 1988 and 1989, they were no longer identified as essays (*ocherki*), which is the usual genre designation for his polemical pieces, but as "chapters from the book *Siberia, Siberia*." Their contents also demonstrated the author's erudition and showed that he had done voluminous research into Siberian history and buttressed his own insights and travel impressions with the observations and authority of his predecessors, some of Russia's most illustrious explorers, chroniclers, ethnographers, and writers. In this book, more so than in his previous writings, Rasputin draws on all the resources of his academic training (he received a broad humanities education, emphasizing literature and history, at Irkutsk State University in the late 1950s) and of his reportorial experience (he worked as a journalist for several newspapers in Eastern Siberia in the early 1960s). The ethnographic strengths of this book remind us of how skillfully Rasputin described the way of life of the Tofalar people in *A Land Next to the Very Sky* (*Krai vozle samogo neba*) in 1966 and of how acute his powers of observation of nature and of human behavior have always been. When in his thirties, he had such extraordinarily keen eyesight that he was able to write in miniature form, using extremely hard, razor-sharp lead pencils and crowding more than one thousand words onto scraps of paper no larger than file cards, composing in a hand so minuscule that it could not be read by anyone else's naked eye. He used this method not to keep what he had written a secret, but to discipline himself in the writing process. While his eyesight has weakened over the years (he now wears glasses for close work), his attention to detail and descriptive thoroughness remain undiminished.

While each chapter of *Siberia, Siberia* is a self-contained unit, understandable and informative on its own terms (they could, perhaps, be read in any order), they fit together like the pieces of a mosaic, like a puzzle whose outer dimensions have been defined, whose main internal forms have been assembled, but that is still missing a few parts (e.g., a chapter on Tomsk). *Siberia, Siberia* occupies a place in Rasputin's oeuvres comparable to that of key nonfictional works written by several of his illustrious Russian literary forebears, for example, Karamzin's *Letters of a Russian Traveler*, Goncharov's *The Frigate Pallada*, Tolstoy's *Confession*, Dostoyevsky's *Notes from the House of the Dead*, Chekhov's *Sakhalin Island*, or Solzhenitsyn's *The Gulag Archipelago*. Each of these works provides in its own way a detailed, fascinating, and highly personalized account of a journey made by a major Russian fiction writer—either to a series of places far removed from one another, from one human encounter to another within a rather confined space, or back and forth through the labyrinthian passages of his belief system and own soul. Each departure from conventional narrative prose fiction played an important role in its creator's development. The writers valued them as highly as their belles lettres. And these works served their authors well, becoming as permanent a part of the Russian literary record as their novels, short stories, and dramas. Rasputin's *Siberia, Siberia* is a case in point, a genre different from his earlier imaginative prose and polemical essays. It is written not for the fickle tastes or amusement of a sated modern audience but for the most patient and thoughtful of the author's countrymen, who are as deeply troubled as he about the fate of their nation, for those of us who share his concern for the survival and perhaps even future renaissance of Russian culture, and for posterity.

To what did Rasputin devote his energies after publication of *Siberia, Siberia*? The years 1993–95 represented still another turning point in the career of this remarkable writer. Seeing no clear solutions to Russia's monumental problems—political, economic, ecological, spiritual—and no evidence that his efforts in the public arena had done much good, Rasputin turned away from politics. He stopped actively associating with political movements and parties, although he continued to work for environmental protection (especially of Lake Baikal) and for historical preservation and restoration (including reconstruction of the Church of Christ the Savior in Moscow, which was destroyed on Stalin's orders in 1931). In 1993 he published *Russia: Days and Times: Essays* (*Rossiia: dni i vremena: publitsistika*), written during the late 1980s and early 1990s. A new edition of his collected works in three volumes (*Sobranie sochinenii v trekh tomakh* [Moscow: Molodaia gvardiia]), whose third volume contains *Siberia, Siberia*, appeared in 1994. And, most important, he began to write fiction again. Three short stories—"Senya is Coming" (*Senia edet*), "Young Russia" (*Rossiia molodaia*), and "In a Certain Siberian Town" (*V odnom sibirskom gorode*)—appeared in July 1994 in the journal *Moskva* (Moscow). They are perhaps overtendentious but show flashes of Rasputin's apparently undiminished literary gifts. When in 1995 "Woman Talk" (*Zhenskii razgovor*) was published in the May issue of *Mir zhenshchiny* (Women's world), "In the Hospital" (*V bol'nitse*) in *Nash sovremennik* (no. 4), and "Into That Very Same Ground" (*V tu zhe zemliu* . . .), also in *Nash sovremennik* (no. 8), Rasputin's admirers and critics alike rekindled their shared hope that he would yet produce literary masterpieces reminiscent of his novellas in their narrative sweep and power.

In addition to fiction Rasputin also started composing a series of biographical sketches, which he referred to as "portraits of Siberians." An offshoot of *Siberia, Siberia*, they demonstrated the author's continued dedication to the cause that remained closest to his heart: the fate of his unique, magnificent, and long-suffering native land.

Valentin Rasputin. Photograph by Anatoly Panteleev, St. Petersburg

1

✤✤✤

Siberia without the Romance

This vast expanse bears the common name *Siberia*, which will
probably stay with it forever because nothing other than Siberia
can ever come of it.

Vladimir Andrievich,[1] *specialist on Siberian history*

The word *Siberia*—and not so much the word as the concept itself—has long sounded like a warning bell announcing something vaguely powerful and imminent. In the past its tolling grew
muffled whenever interest in Siberia suddenly dropped off and then
became louder again when interest rose; now it rings continually with
ever-increasing forcefulness. Siberia! Siberia! . . . Some people hear
confidence and hope in this resonant sound; others hear ominous
human footfalls in a faraway land; still others hear nothing in particular
but listen with the vague sense that the changes coming from this
region might bring relief. Even those who have never been here and
who remain distant from its life and concerns inevitably feel Siberia
inside themselves. Siberia itself has become a part of the lives and concerns of a great many people, if not as a physical, material concept then
as a moral one that promises an unclear but much desired renewal.

In the eighteenth century Russians said, "Siberia is our Mexico and
our Peru." In the nineteenth century they said, "It is our United States."
In the twentieth, "Siberia is a source of colossal energy," "a land of
unlimited opportunity." As we can see, humanity's arsenal of technology is changing, our needs are changing, and the way we characterize
Siberia is changing, too. Siberia has everything, from virgin mineral
wealth lying on or near the surface to processible wealth buried deep in
the ground. It has obliged every age, and all assessments of it, from the
earliest rumors to the most recent substantiations by economic experts,

have invariably abounded in superlatives. But even now, when Earth can feel the symptoms of asphyxia, we are already turning to Siberia, calling it "the lungs of the planet." Even now . . . It's not hard to figure out what humanity's prime and permanent necessity will be in thirty, forty, or fifty years and in what way Siberia could verily become a force of healing and salvation.

We are used to the language of comparison, but no comparisons will tell us anything about Siberia. We can merely juxtapose the results of developing it, the work of human hands, and that's all. There is nothing in the world that we could place in the same rank as Siberia. It seems capable of existing as a self-sufficient planet; it contains everything in all three realms of nature—on the ground, under the ground, and in the air—that a planet ought to have. We cannot categorize its actual life, so varied and diverse, using known concepts. With everything bad and good, discovered and undiscovered, finished and incomplete, reassuring and inaccessible that exists within it, Siberia remains Siberia, a land that has its own name, lies in its own spot, and has molded its own character, which is unlike anything else. Its spirit hovers over it from region to region and end to end, seemingly undecided, even today, whether to embody good or evil—it all depends on how human beings behave here. During the four hundred years that have passed since Russians conquered Siberia, it seems to have simply remained a giant that they have tamed and made to look presentable in places but have never managed to fully awaken. And we would like to hope that this awakening, this spiritual realization of its own self, is yet to come.

The word *Siberia* has never actually been deciphered; its exact etymological meaning has not been found. To outsiders who know about Siberia only through hearsay, it is a huge, austere, and wealthy land where everything seems to have cosmic proportions, including the same frigidness and inhospitableness as outer space. And they see native-born Siberians as a product of enigmatic nature rather than as a product, like they themselves, of the enigmatic human race. To those of us who were born and live in Siberia, it is our homeland, nearer and dearer to us than anything else in the world, a homeland that, like every other, needs love and protection, perhaps even more protection than any other place because it still has something left to protect. And the parts about Siberia that scare others we find not only normal but also essential: we breathe more easily in the winter during a hard frost than during a thaw; we feel peace, not fear, in the wild, virgin taiga; mighty rivers and unmeasured expanses have formed our free and restless souls. Differing views of Siberia—a view from the outside and a view from within—have always existed; although they have shifted, fluctuated, and drawn closer to each other, they remain different even now. Some people are accustomed to viewing it as a rich province and envision the development of our region as the rapid, high-powered removal of its riches; those who live here and feel patriotic toward this land have always regarded its development as more than the exploitation of natural resources and industrial expansion. It includes this, too, but within reasonable limits, so as not to completely squander the riches that will become priceless tomorrow and that even today are moving out ahead of all the others, as the lucid mind not intoxicated with industrial zeal understands. These riches include the air produced by the Siberian forests, which we can breathe without harming our lungs; pure water, which the world is experiencing a huge thirst for at this very moment; and land that is not contaminated or exhausted, that could adopt and feed far more people than it feeds at present.

Humanity could in effect turn over a new leaf by leaning on Siberia and a few other areas that are as yet untrammeled. One way or another, the human race will have to solve major problems very quickly if it intends to go on existing: what to breathe, what to eat and drink, how and for what purposes to make use of human intellect. The earth as a planet is coming to rest more and more heavily on four pillars, not one of which can now be considered reliable. And even if the root meaning of the word *Siberia* is not *salvation*, Siberia could still become its synonym. Then the colonization of Siberia, which lagged behind that of North America and for which old Russia was criticized for a long time, would turn into a great advantage; and then Russians could feel, with justification, that they had fulfilled no small part of their cleansing mission on Earth.

But here is a chance to do justice to our national character. Steadfastness in
all their undertakings and tirelessness in carrying them out are the qualities that
distinguish the Russian people. And if I had room to elaborate on my hypothesis,
then I could show that an enterprising spirit and consistency in following
through with whatever they undertake have always been the main reason
for the Russians' achievements.

Aleksandr Radishchev,[2] "A Word about Yermak"[3]

Although Siberia is located on the same landmass as Europe and is partitioned off from it only by the Rock—the Ural Mountains—which can certainly be considered surmountable, it was nonetheless opened up for civilized humanity almost one hundred years later than America.

Vague rumors about Siberia had circulated throughout the world since antiquity, of course, and naturally Russians, especially the tireless Novgorodians, hunted, fished, and traded in its domains, penetrating Siberia both by land routes and from the northern seas, but because they regarded these activities as ordinary, they did not report their unauthorized penetrations to anyone and simply passed along their experience to their sons. The Novgorodians were familiar with Yurga (as the northern lands east of the Urals were called) as early as the eleventh century and perhaps even earlier. The word *Siberia* first appears in Russian chronicles[4] at the beginning of the fifteenth century in connection with the demise of Khan Tokhtamysh,[5] the same Tokhtamysh who, after the Battle of Kulikovo Field during the reign of Dmitry Donskoy,[6] set fire to Moscow but held power for only a short time and was killed, as a result of internecine feuding, in "the Siberian land."

The rumors about Siberia that arose periodically in Western Europe during ancient times were so full of fables and fairy tales that they scared off some people and made others smile in disbelief even back then. Relying on such rumors, Herodotus notes in his *History*, apparently having the Urals in mind: "At the foot of some high mountains dwell people who are bald from birth and have flat noses and oblong chins." But later he cannot help having some doubts: "The bald ones say—which, incidentally, I do not believe—that some people living in the mountains have goats' feet and others living beyond them sleep six months out of the year."

Foreigners in ancient and medieval times can be excused for believing that the depths of Asia were inhabited by monsters with dogs' heads or even with no heads at all, with eyes and mouths on their bellies, but there is actually a Russian written source from the sixteenth century, the same century in which the Russian government began to annex Siberia, that, in describing the country beyond the Urals, repeats the old tales in which the people there ostensibly die for the winter and come to life again in the spring. This is not surprising: a few years ago in West Berlin someone asked me, "What do people in Siberia do during the winter?" The questioner actually supposed that in our part of the world all you can do during the winter is sleep.

Pyotr Vyazemsky,[7] a man of letters and a friend of Pushkin, makes an intriguing comment about opinions of this sort: "If you want an intelligent person, a Frenchman or a German, to blurt out some nonsense, make him render a judgment on Russia. This is a subject that will intoxicate him and immediately cloud his mental faculties." These words are all the more applicable to Siberia. And you don't even have to go to Europe: for a long time Siberia "intoxicated" and "clouded" the minds of its own brethren, its fellow countrymen, who uttered (and sometimes still utter) such stuff and nonsense in their views on Siberia that now we can only regret that no one ever took it upon himself to gather them all, for the sake of amusement, into a single book. But this nonsense was not always harmless and sometimes manifested itself in decrees that had to be carried out.

Even today, just as in ancient times, people continue to search for miracles that don't fit the scientific conception of order in the world. We must assume that Siberia is one of those areas where the human spirit of contradiction and doubt has suffered considerable disappointment in its time: here, too, things are essentially the same as everywhere else.

The conqueror of Siberia, as we know, was Yermak Timofeevich. The fact that Yermak himself and his band of warriors were all Cossacks signified a great deal. *Cossack* [in Russian, *kazak*] is a Tatar word that translates as daredevil, bold spirit, someone who has severed ties with his social class. The Cossacks arose in Rus[8] shortly after the Tatar yoke was thrown off and became a distinct group during the sixteenth century, when the Russian people were increasingly subjected to feudalism and serfdom. Those who did not want to endure any sort of yoke, including a paternal one, fled to the Wild Field[9]—the lower reaches of the Don and Volga Rivers—where they founded their own settlements, elected chieftains called atamans, established laws, and began a free, new life that was not subordinate to any khanate or czardom. Later on the Russian Cossacks were still forced to submit to the czar's rule (otherwise they could not have survived), but in the sixteenth century this had not happened yet; at that time the Cossacks were their own masters. The czarist authorities, playing on the Cossacks' patriotic feelings, could use them against their restless southern neighbors, against Turkey and the Crimean and Nogay Tatars, but they could also send punitive expeditions against them for unauthorized actions or as a result of diplomatic maneuverings with those same neighbors; relations between Moscow and the free Cossacks were always complicated, especially at the beginning. One good thing about this arrangement was that if any serious danger threatened Russia, the Cossacks considered it their duty to rise to its defense no matter where the danger came from, be it nearby Turkey or distant Lithuania. Historians have argued recently that on the eve of his Siberian campaign Yermak Timofeevich took part in the Livonian War.[10]

The Cossacks played an exceptional, almost supernatural role in conquering and opening up Siberia. Only a special class of people— daring, desperate, and not crushed by the ponderous Russian state— could do what they, by some miracle, managed to do.

When discussing the figure of Yermak, I find it hard not to pause and pay tribute to our Russian negligence and forgetfulness. Between the overthrow of the Tatars and the reign of Peter the Great,[11] Russia's fate held nothing more important or monumental, more fortunate or historically significant than the annexation of Siberia, whose expanses could have accommodated old Rus several times over. Our imagination freezes in confusion before this fact alone, as though getting stuck just beyond the Urals in the deep Siberian snows. In contrast we know everything there is to know about Columbus, the discoverer of America: where he was born, what he did until his hour of "stardom," when, down to the month and day, he embarked on his first voyage, and on his second, third, and fourth, when he reached the American coast, when his flagship, the Santa Maria, landed on a reef and what happened then . . . Columbus nothing! We remember more about the

Yermak

emperors and patricians of ancient Rome than about Yermak. All right, he couldn't have kept a journal the way Columbus did, and there was no quick-witted historian at his side, as there was at Nero's when he planned his murders, but in Yermak's case there wasn't a single soul who understood the significance of this figure and the greatness of his campaign. Only afterward did we come to our senses, when it became clear that we didn't know either Yermak's real name or his ancestry, that there was no recollection or record of the year in which he went into battle against Kuchum,[12] how many Cossacks made up his detachment and what kind of aid the Stroganovs provided, whether he reached Isker, the capital of the Siberian khanate, in one crossing, as the well-known historian Ruslan Skrynnikov[13] believes, or whether he had to go back across the Urals after wintering there and then gear up all over again. We are forced to question the accuracy of the Stroganov Chronicle[14] precisely because it was commissioned by the Stroganovs and might exaggerate that family's role in the annexation of Siberia. We look just as skeptically on another document, the *Sinodik*—the roster of Cossacks fallen in battle—which was compiled forty years after Yermak's death by Kiprian,[15] the archbishop of Tobolsk, based on the stories told by surviving participants in the campaign: in the interests of the local church the Right Reverend Kiprian no doubt wanted very much to make Yermak a saint and for that reason would not have hesitated to embellish or omit any facts from Yermak's biography that were not appropriate for canonization. Not for nothing is it said that whoever controls the present also controls the past.

And so for a couple of centuries now we've been trying to guess whether it's true that Yermak, as the folk songs have it, went on periodic sprees like Stepan Razin,[16] roaming up and down the Volga and Don Rivers before going to Siberia, and profited from getting his hands on merchants' caravans and even on the czar's. Or, for the sake of greater glory, do the common people, mixing up virtues, endow their hero with attributes he never had? We argue over whether *Yermak* is a nickname or a truncated form of the name *Yermolay*. Or maybe it comes from *Yeremey*, or *Yermilo*?

Regarding Siberia's first hero and his feat, we are obviously on safest ground when following the well-known trails blazed by history. The revised versions proposed by present-day scholars are not convincing enough to accept without reservations. Thus there is practically no basis for whitewashing the part of Yermak's biography that pertains to gang life on the Volga when they try to prove that Yermak could not have engaged in the indecent "thieves'" trade ["*vorovskim*" *remeslom*]. His comrades-in-arms might have, but not Yermak. Isn't it safer in this instance to rely on folk memory and folk intuition, which rarely erred in assigning such heroic traits as these? In addition, considering the times and morals back then, it's hard to imagine that a man who spent at least twenty years in the Wild Field and became an ataman would have insulated himself from the customary occupations of the Cossack outlaws. As the song puts it:

Dreaded Czar, he said, accept respectful greetings from Yermak.

As a gift I offer you the whole Siberian land,

Yes, the whole Siberian land: grant a pardon to Yermak!

And so Yermak and his comrades caroused up and down the Volga and took part in skirmishes and battles; by that time the Stroganovs, a famous merchant clan, had settled on the eastern fringes of the Russian czardom, along the Chusovaya, Kama, and Lysva Rivers in the Ural Mountains, had established profitable enterprises for salt production, agriculture, trade, and other activities there, and, not content with what they'd already acquired, had obtained permission from Ivan the Terrible to expand into the lands along the Tobol and Irtysh Rivers. Granting such permission cost the Terrible Czar nothing, for those lands did not belong to him: Khan Kuchum, who had united the Siberian tribes and sown the seeds of Islam among them, was lord and master there. Thus the Stroganovs, on one side, looked longingly at the rich expanses that ostensibly belonged to them but in fact did not, while on the other side Kuchum, gathering strength, began harassing the outlying settlements more and more often. Under those circumstances it was only natural for the Stroganovs to turn to the Cossacks for help.

Now we will never know who took the initiative—Yermak himself, when his sins forced him to flee the Volga region, or in fact the Stroganovs, finally resolving to take serious action concerning their neighbor to the east—just as we will never know whether Yermak had any doubts about making the difficult and dangerous march into Siberia, but it would have been a shame if someone other than Yermak had taken on Kuchum. Yermak, a man of the common people, was extremely well suited for this role, as if the people themselves had sent him to Siberia and then rewarded him with fame. He, along with Stepan Razin, became permanent favorites of the Russian people, the embodiment of their ancient, freedom-loving aspirations. But while Stepan Razin sought liberty by leading a rebellion on the lands of old Russia, Yermak opened up fabulous new lands that seemed to have no limit and no end, flinging the doors wide open for freedom.

He set out on his campaign to the territory beyond the Urals in 1581 or, according to other hypotheses, in 1579 or 1582. During the

41
+++

tricentennial celebration of this event, one of the Russian journals observed:

Yermak's feat, the conquest of an entire realm with a handful of Cossacks, was, of course, astonishing. No matter how superior to a bow and arrow a rifle might be, we still must not forget that locusts can extinguish whole bonfires that block their path, even though multitudes of them perish. The Cossacks numbered only five units of one hundred each, while the enemy counted themselves in the thousands and would have saved themselves by putting up a stubborn defense had not the head of the brave Russians been the outstanding commander and administrator Yermak and had the internal bonds that linked the Siberian tribes been stronger. Glorifying Yermak's feat, we also can't help being astonished that it was a man of the common people who manifested the law of history that moved Rus eastward into Asia and that has continued to lead it in that direction down to the present. Yermak took the first solid step beyond the Urals, and others followed after him.

And those others accomplished a feat no less astonishing.

No! Everything that the Russian people could do in Siberia they did with uncommon energy, and the result of their labors deserves astonishment because of its magnitude. Show me another people in the history of the world that could cross an expanse greater than the expanse of all Europe in a century and a half and establish a firm foothold there! Everything the Russian people did went beyond its powers, beyond the historical order of things.

Nikolay Yadrintsev[17]

It's a mystery why Yadrintsev, the famous Siberian writer and scholar of the nineteenth century, says that it took the Russian people a century and a half to cross Siberia and establish a foothold there. This obviously applies to "establishing a foothold," to occupying Siberia in all its breadth and might, to figuring out where to till the soil, where to hunt game, and where to dig mines.

According to the old sources, Yermak captured Isker, the capital of the Siberian khanate, in the fall of 1582 and perished in an unequal nighttime battle in August, 1585, after which the surviving members of his detachment were forced to withdraw; yet in 1639 Ivan Moskvitin,[18] a government servant[19] from the Yenisey region, set up a winter encampment on the shores of the Sea of Okhotsk and Russians reached the Pacific Ocean, while in 1648 Semyon Dezhnyov[20] sailed across the strait that separates America from Asia. This defies comprehension! Anyone who can even vaguely imagine those great and deadly distances can't help shaking his head in disbelief. Traveling only by river (for there were no roads) and dragging canoes and heavy loads across portages from one body of water to another; wintering in hastily built log cabins in unfamiliar places among hostile indigenous nomads while waiting for the ice to break up; suffering from cold, hunger, disease, wild animals, and blood-sucking insects; losing comrades and strength with each move; using not maps and reliable information but rumors that could easily prove to be pure invention; often numbering just a handful of men; and not knowing what lay in store for them the next day or the day after that, they kept pressing forward, farther and farther to the east. Only after them would winter quarters appear along the rivers, and wooden forts, and crude maps, and written copies of "oral histories" [*zapisi "rasprossnykh rechei"*], and experience in dealing with natives, and plowed fields, and saltworks, and simply notches on trees to point the way—the earliest explorers were doing it all for the first time, and everything was a dangerous, uncharted novelty. And nowadays, when we don't hesitate to call every step and every deed done by the builders and subduers of Siberia a marvelous feat, it wouldn't hurt to remember and it wouldn't hurt to try to imagine a little more often what it must have cost our ancestors to take the first steps and perform the first deeds.

He trudges through the Tobolsk forests and endless snows with a heavy arquebus across his shoulders, which was issued to him from the voivode's[21] storehouse for the duration of his journey. He is searching for new river valleys rich in sable and drawing sketchy maps. He crosses immense snowy expanses on skis, races along on a shaggy bay horse, leading another one by the reins, and sits at the helm of a wide, flat-bottomed boat with a rawhide sail flapping over his head. Danger lies in wait for him. He hears a black-feathered arrow sing as it approaches him. He doesn't spare himself in "close" (hand-to-hand) combat [*v "s"emnom" boiu*], and at the end of a life filled with hardships, his wounds are impossible to count. He sleeps on the snow, feeds himself any way he can, goes for years without seeing fresh bread, and often eats pine bark and "any old foul thing" [*"vsiakaia skverna"*]. The government hasn't paid him his salary—in money, bread, and salt—for many years. "Gearing up" [*"podnimaias'"*] to search for new rivers and lands, he buys everything with his own money, signing agreements with crushing terms and running up debts he can never repay.

This is a portrait of one of the first explorers drawn by the well-known writer Sergey Markov[22] at the beginning of his essay on Semyon Dezhnyov. And it is by no means a complete list of the hazards that lay in wait for the "prospector" [*"dobytchik"*] and "profit seeker" [*"pribyl'shchik"*] on their long journeys. Add to this the unfairness and greed of such voivodes as Pyotr Golovin, a *stol'nik*[23] in Yakutia. Add the duplicity and behind-the-back actions of local princelings, who were totally unreliable; the "floggings" [*"pravezh"*], "inquiries" [*"rozyski"*], and denunciations on the part of informants, whom even the smallest collection of Russians could rarely do without; and the struggle, sometimes reaching the point of battle, with defectors from their detachments, as occurred between Khabarov and Polyakov or between Dezhnyov and Stradukhin —and all this on top of the harshness of nature in Siberia. They endured shipwrecks, and vanished without a trace, leaving not a single record of their activities behind, and wintered time and again in places we now know to be the sites of record-breaking cold, and lost their minds during the long arctic nights. . . . What more can be said?! Siberia exacted its tribute from them in full measure. They began their journeys as Cossacks strong both in body and spirit and ready for all sorts of deprivations, even one-tenth of which they could hardly have foreseen, and finished them, those who managed to finish, as men with a special superhuman fortitude and strength, men before whom the earth beneath their feet had to yield. Apparently no one like them came along afterward; they were what might be called the "crossbows" [*"samostrely"*] of the Russian spirit, for this was largely a spontaneous, grassroots movement undertaken at their own risk, with which the government's and even the voivodes' decrees could not always keep pace. We do not have enough imagination to visualize their exhausting feat; our imaginations are not equipped to walk the same long routes that these heroes took on their treks through Siberia.

What led them eastward? What forced them, scorning torments

and dangers, to be in such a rush? One reason is usually given: a craving for profit, a need to find new lands where the natural riches, especially furs, were still untouched, and a desire to serve a voivode or the czar by coercing more native peoples into paying tribute. All this did motivate them, of course, but if these were the only reasons, then the first Cossack explorers would not have been in such a hurry. In those fifty or sixty years that it took them to get from the Irtysh River to the Pacific Ocean, ermine and sable were not yet wiped out in the "known" part ["*provedannaia*" *chast'*] of Siberia, while the wooden forts that the Cossacks hastily put up on their way east were meager and few in number and provided no safety. It would seemingly have made more sense to build a proper foundation, to store up plenty of victuals and other provisions, to make the rear areas, as we say nowadays, secure, and then to move onward slowly and surely. But no, they were in a big rush. Just try to imagine them enduring a quiet and sensible life sitting in one spot if nomads told them that up ahead lay the great Yenisey River, then the great Lena River, where a numerous and talented people (the Yakuts) lived, and then the rivers all simply ran off into the distance to meet the sun. No, it was not in the Russian character to calmly sit still awaiting instructions; it wasn't in the Russian makeup to be prudent and cautious, abandoning their inborn "just maybe" ·[*avos'*]. We can be certain that the Cossacks were driven not only by self-interest and not only by the spirit of competition, by a desire to get there first—a more noble reason—but also by something greater. It was like the will of history itself, bending down low over that region at that time and picking out daredevils to test and prove the capabilities of the downtrodden Russian people, who were, in a widely held view, half asleep. National pride provided no small amount of the energy for this mighty upsurge.

We don't usually erect monuments to cities that distinguish themselves. But it would be only fair if somewhere in the expanses of Siberia, say on the same Lena River where the most active "frontiersmen" ["*zemlesvedyvateli*"] gathered in the middle of the seventeenth century, we acknowledged and underscored Siberians' noble recollection of Ustyug the Great [*Velikii Ustiug*], now a decaying town that produces accordions. But at that time Ustyug the Great, which once rivaled Novgorod the Great itself, was still a big name, and it confirmed its greatness through the likes of Semyon Dezhnyov, Yerofey Khabarov, Vasily Poyarkov, Vladimir Atlasov, Vasily Bugor, Parfyon Khodyrev, and many, many others who achieved fame for their courage along Siberia's rivers, portages, and seas. All of them came from Ustyug the Great. This is not merely amazing; it seems unbelievable. What an oddity! How did so many of them get their start there, in the cradle of seafarers and discoverers, and how did they develop their backbone and strength of spirit?! To have produced only Dezhnyov, who discovered the "Bering" Strait, would have been enough for the town to be proud of itself for centuries. Any capital would consider it an honor to boast of Khabarov's "odyssey" had he been born there. And what about Atlasov, the conqueror of Kamchatka?! And Poyarkov, who "found" the immense territories of northeastern Siberia! And for all we know, Ustyug may have been the home of the legendary Penda, who set out from the "gold-rush" town of Mangazeya[24] and penetrated the Lena River region ahead of everyone else. Wasn't Ustyug also the birthplace of Pyotr Beketov, one of whose expeditions inspired the following comment by Johann Fischer in *A History of Siberia from the Discovery of Siberia until the Conquest of This Land Using Russian Weapons:*[25] "He achieved his aim with such a small number of men that it seems almost unbelievable that Russians could have been that courageous."

It's also worth noting at this point that twice in the course of one decade (in 1630 and in 1637) Ustyug the Great, along with neighboring Totma and Solvychegodsk, sent large groups of single girls to distant Siberia to become the "womenfolk" [*v "zhonki"*] of Russian men in government service. After that, how could Siberians not feel bound to the town by blood and not bow down to it in heartfelt gratitude from afar?! They should also bow down to all of northern Russia, to the dear old land of Novgorod, Vologda, Arkhangelsk, and Vyatka, which is where the artisans and plowmen who followed on the heels of the Cossacks came from and where the initial migration to Siberia began.

Siberia was fated to enter the flesh and blood of Russia, and that is exactly what happened. Yermak, by quickly driving a sharp, knife-like wedge into the Siberia of the khans, deprived it of its former power; the first Cossack explorers, by racing across Siberia from one end to the other and quilting it with armed wooden forts, seemingly sewed it onto Russia. But Siberia was settled and made Russian not by warriors or government servants, not by hunters, fishermen, or tradesmen, but by dirt farmers. Those motivated by profit rolled in and out like the tide, seeking furs and mammoth ivory, gold and other precious metals, and, after wiping out or hauling off the riches, after ravaging Siberia's forests and Siberia's mineral wealth to the extent that the means available then allowed, the seekers of quick fortune would head home and spread dark rumors about Siberia, calling it a dead, impoverished country unfit either for success or for a comfortable life. That's how it always is: the robber never says thank-you to the victim. Even during the nineteenth century some of our better minds, discouraged by what they considered too small a productive return from Siberia, declared that Siberia, feeding on the juices of Russia, knew only how to sap the strength of its nurturer. Meanwhile, the farmers who had followed the Cossacks into that uninhabited virgin land were plowing up the steppe or clearing the taiga to make fields, sowing and harvesting crops year after year, raising children, adding to the number of families there, and making a land of hardship, by now already theirs, accessible and fit to live in.

This quiet, inconspicuous labor, pleasing to God, as people used to say, was the deciding factor. In the end, Siberia submitted to those who fed it. Just one hundred years after Yermak's campaign it began to manage on its own grain alone, and after another hundred years it didn't know what to do with so much. Curiously, the opponents of constructing a railway across Siberia in the nineteenth century put forth as one of their main arguments the fear that Siberia would use such a railroad to flood Russia with its cheap grain, while Russia, they claimed, would have no place to market its own.

The peasant was the one who finally grafted Siberia onto Russia, completing with his wooden plow the immense undertaking—immense in scope and in consequences—begun by Yermak with the aid of weapons. And we must admit that Russia acquired Siberia more easily than anyone might have expected. Its acquisition was like a great stroke of good fortune, or, to use the Siberian expression, an unprecedented lucky break [*fart*].

Siberia, Siberia

> We ought to be fair to Siberia. For all the shortcomings that have taken
> root there because of the constant influx of various, often highly impure elements
> such as dishonor, selfishness, secretiveness, and mutual distrust, Siberia is distin-
> guished by a special breadth of spirit and thought, by a true magnanimity.

Mikhail Bakunin[26]

> A Siberian's mind is completely engrossed in material gain and keenly
> interested only in routine, practical goals and concerns. These cold calculations
> and mercenary passions have crushed every predisposition toward the ideal,
> even public-spiritedness, that the population contained.

Afanasy Shchapov[27]

If we could gather all the opposing opinions together, it would be clear that non-Siberians speak better, and often with rapture, of Siberians than Siberians speak of themselves. And this, too, is in character for Siberians. They prefer to be unfair by exaggerating their faults rather than their merits, and they won't hide their disappointment in their fellow countrymen and in their homeland, which they would like to see become better, closer to perfection.

After ending up in an unfamiliar natural environment, after finding themselves surrounded by aborigines, the native inhabitants of these regions, and after confronting new terms of existence in many aspects of life, Siberians naturally had to be different from their kinsmen living in the old part of Russia. Just as the European in America turned into the Yankee type, so, too, did the Russian in Siberia become transformed into the Siberian type, acquiring distinctive characteristics in psychological makeup and even in physical appearance.

As soon as you cross the Urals, you find faces with Asiatic features. It is widely acknowledged that the Russians who went to Siberia turned out to be superb colonists from the very start. True, they did attempt to establish slavery here as well, using North America as a model, with the intention of drawing on the local population for raw material; their attempts, however, not only came to nothing but were a big flop, condemned by the government, by public opinion, which was just arising, and by the practices of the simple peasants who had migrated here.

Concerning the government, it must be said that in all serious disputes between Russians and non-Russians, the authorities, as a rule, sided with the latter. That's how it was under Peter the Great as well as under Catherine. This did not, of course, prevent the voivodes and their men from mercilessly humiliating and fleecing non-Russians, but the simple peasant who settled in a new place next to a Buryat or a Tungus had no trouble entering into friendly relations with him right away, passing along his experience as a plowman and an artisan while picking up his neighbor's skills in hunting and fishing, along with his knowledge of local conditions and nature's calendar. Not suffering in the least from elitism (Russians never seem to), the settlers began to establish family ties with the aborigines and got so carried away that this practice alarmed both the government and the church. As early as 1622 Filaret, the patriarch of Moscow, sent a reprimand to Kiprian, the archbishop of Siberia:

It hath come to our knowledge both from voivodes and from lower-ranking officials who formerly served in Siberia that many of the public servants and other residents of Siberian towns are living not by Christian customs but in accordance with their own vile lusts: many Russian men . . . reportedly take pagan Tatar and Ostyak and Vogul wives and dwelleth in sin, while others live with unbaptized Tatar women and committeth foul acts with them . . .

The church, incidentally, was not consistent in its demands, forbidding mixed marriages with one raised finger while allowing them with another on the condition that those of different faiths convert to Christianity. The parties of single girls sent out from the Russian provinces from time to time to become wives could not have sufficed for the whole vast region; Russian peasants, moreover, had the right to make their own choices. Therefore it is not surprising that the farther you go into the heart of Siberia, the more mixed marriages you find and the more often you see Asiatic features on Russian faces. In Eastern Siberia, for example, nearly every third or fourth face has broad cheekbones and slanting eyes, which give female beauty new contours and an expressive freshness that sets it apart from the tired, washed-out look of European beauty. The Siberians who resulted from blending Slavic impulsiveness and spontaneity with Asiatic naturalness and self-absorption did not, perhaps, stand out as a unique character type, but they did acquire some noticeable traits, both appealing and unappealing, such as keen powers of observation, a heightened sense of self-respect that does not accept anything alien or coercive, inexplicable changes in mood and an ability to withdraw into themselves to some unknown private recesses, a raging passion for work alternating with bouts of wanton idleness, and also a touch of cunning mixed with kindness, a cunning so transparent that it can be of no advantage whatsoever. It's possible that all this is not yet fully formed, for every feature reveals two sides that have yet to combine into a single whole. We must assume that nature needs more time than it has had so far to complete what it began, but it obviously performs this task with a certain amount of pleasure.

When discussing the character of Russian Siberians, I must emphasize that common freemen[28] were the ones who shaped it from the very outset. The colonization of Siberia was above all a popular movement, and groups of "freedom seekers" [*otriady "vol'nookhochikh"*] made their way out here ahead of those whom the government sent "by choice" [*"po vyboru"*] and "by decree" [*"po ukazu"*]. The people who came to Siberia were fleeing restrictions and repression and seeking freedom of all sorts: religious, social, moral, occupational, and personal. Those who were at odds with the law headed this way to escape punishment by hiding in remote areas far beyond the Urals; others sought fair communal laws to counteract administrative oppression; still others dreamed of a wonderful land without any laws whatsoever. Righteous individuals walked side by side with shady characters; hard workers rubbed shoulders with empty souls and crooks. The religious schism of the seventeenth century[29] brought to Siberia tens of thousands of the strongest people, extremely steadfast in character and spirit, who refused to acknowledge innovations in church and state and who preferred to withdraw from the world into an impregnable wilderness. Even today our forests still harbor settlements where the inhabitants have remained the same in language, customs, beliefs, clothing, and means of livelihood as they were three hundred years ago. We can marvel at the fanaticism of these people, but we must also marvel at their steadfastness and tenaciousness, which exceed our usual understanding of these concepts. Everything came together in Siberia—and the community of Old Believers, noted for their pure, strong morality, offset the brotherhood of exiles and criminals, who abided by laws of a completely different kind. Yadrintsev notes:

The reason these villages bear the stamp of olden times, the reason they display strength and order, is that religious dissenters make up the bulk of their population. The same orderliness, the same prosperity in everything, can also be seen in other settlements of schismatics throughout Siberia, whether in Eastern or Western Siberia, wherever they may be. The very appearance of the inhabitants is different, as if they constitute a special breed. Beautiful, plump women with white faces and fresh complexions wearing neat, colorful jumpers, neatly groomed, respectable-looking old folks, handsome lads—everything exudes orderliness, cleanliness, and prosperity.

Now, too, descendants of the *semeiskie*, as Old Believers living east of Lake Baikal are called, arouse special interest and respect even among Siberians: their background, as a rule, makes them excellent workers and reliable friends.

There were always a lot of folks going back and forth to Siberia. At times it resembled a revolving door—with all the inevitable behaviors people display when merely passing through. This is still true to a large extent even today. The vast multitudes constantly rolling into Siberia's celebrated construction sites like breakers, with the noise, music, and impressive might that breakers usually bring, vanish quietly and unobtrusively after a few years as if seeping into the sand. Then come more breakers and more multitudes—and another ebbtide of hidden, receding rivulets that leave provincial areas with a tiny fraction of the new arrivals. The explanation for this rests squarely with the prevailing attitude toward Siberia: take its riches as quickly and as cheaply as possible. Concern for the welfare of those who live under Siberian conditions, a topic of much discussion, occasionally slips several notches, but no one ever wants to take this slippage into account and start it a few notches higher.

Living in Siberia, needless to say, is not easy. Its climate, having grown more capricious in recent decades, continually comes up with surprises, as when melting snow starts dripping on New Year's Eve or when a winter snowstorm hits in June, and has hardly gotten any milder. Since time immemorial the harshness and bleakness of these parts have strictly weeded out colonists and conquerors of every sort. In order to become acclimated and to remain here, you must have the spirit of a Siberian—not momentary bursts of enthusiasm but a state of constant readiness for all kinds of annoyances and surprises and a knack for overcoming them without expending too much energy. This spirit does not necessarily have to originate in Siberia; it can develop anywhere but must be in keeping with Siberia and enter its general atmosphere by following a parallel course. There are people whose family trees have been growing in Siberia for several generations, but who have never actually become Siberians—the longer they live here, the more keenly they suffer in a land that is alien to them—and there are those who seem made for Siberia and who, once they get here, adapt without any particular difficulty. Thus a Siberian is not only a thick skin accustomed to inconveniences and freezing cold and not only stubbornness and persistence in achieving goals (qualities that the local conditions produced), but also a certain fatedness, a deep and solid rootedness in this land, a compatibility between the human soul and the spirit of nature. Siberians are rarely unfaithful to their homeland; the urge to move from place to place that has become epidemic everywhere is less noticeable in them and is confined, as a rule, to the boundaries of their native region. The land of our forebears, which lives in each of us as a primordial component, exists in Siberians as a more demanding passion, perhaps because it was gained with great labors, the memory of which has not yet been lost in the passing of generations.

Human beings could not have lasted here very long without the stubbornness and persistence that Siberians are often criticized for. The first inhabitants, the founders of villages and towns, had to literally battle with the taiga for every clump of land in Siberia's interior. If they slackened their efforts even slightly, the forest would attack the plowed strip that had been taken away from it. The taiga stood like a wall, while high above the taiga hovered mountains whose snowcaps never came off. The long winters wore down people's mental stamina and the short summers required twice the normal amount of physical energy. Light frosts could suddenly strike without rhyme or reason in the middle of summer and wipe out what they'd intended to harvest in the taiga and in their gardens and fields; during the winter starving animals would visit villages, kill livestock, and attack human beings. In warm weather they were oppressed by blood-sucking insects: mosquitoes, midges, and also *mokretsy*, tiny, barely visible malicious flies that swooped down in swarms during bad weather. Cattle, pestered by midges, grazed only at night; during the day they stood tethered close to smoking fires. People worked with horsehair nets pulled over their heads, which made it hard to breathe, and also smeared themselves with tar as an added precaution. And all these practices from our grandfathers' day have come down to us as well: when I was growing up in the 1940s and 1950s, you couldn't go outside on the lower and middle stretches of the Angara River for even two minutes without a net. We wound and wrapped rags around ourselves from head to foot in nearly 30°C [86°F] heat (no one cared about getting a tan) so that— God forbid!—not a single patch of skin would show. We tarred our- selves like devils and stuffed grass into the tops of our knee-high moc- casins and boots, plugging all entrances and exits, but it didn't do much good: we still went around with puffy eyes and our arms and legs were all eaten up and covered with bloody welts.

Concerning our mosquitoes, Sommier,[30] an Italian who visited the land beyond the Urals at the end of the nineteenth century, writes: "If Dante had traveled in Siberia, he would have invented a new form of torture for his criminals, using mosquitoes." The mosquitoes seem to have changed little here during the three hundred years before Som- mier's visit and the one hundred years since; during the twentieth cen- tury they adapted better than human beings to the smoke and industri- al waste and all the other changes in their domain.

In order for the early settler to stand his ground and not lose heart, he had to have more than strong muscles. He also had to have a strong spirit, the spirit of proud resistance and unflagging stubbornness: I'll hold out no matter what. I won't leave—I'm stronger than everything, no matter what.

"Didn't God mold this land into Siberia at the very end of creation, when he began to have doubts about the human race?" That's what a Siberian might have thought back then in mournful arrogance as he looked around from the middle of his field at the unfriendly distant prospects unfolding before him.

Add one more affliction to Siberians' past misfortunes: vagabonds. Siberia is well known as a land of hard labor and exile, where a vast empire not founded on the rule of law dumped people for any offense, large or small, assuming that this was of benefit to an underpopulated area. For some reason we have come to believe (no doubt on the basis of memoirs, which common criminals don't write) that practically the only offenders sent here were political exiles. Siberia, incidentally, was lucky to get the political exiles it did, from Decembrists[31] and Polish insurgents to Marxists and Bolsheviks, although they themselves, to be sure, did not feel lucky to end up here. But good is good in whatever circumstances it may be done, and for our land, benighted and little studied at the time, their endeavors in the arts, sciences, and cultural life and simply in moral and individual education were an enormous blessing. The mere presence of the Decembrists, who were scattered in exile all across the expanses of Eastern and Western Siberia, had such an influence on the intellectual community, which in many places consisted of a few minds isolated from each other, that, first, it became a true community of intellectuals and, second, it acquired goals that eventually led to the opening of Tomsk University.

But Siberia for the most part was inundated with common criminals. In some spots they outnumbered the local inhabitants, and naturally could teach them nothing but their own trade. It wasn't even a matter of corrupting morals; native Siberians were staunch enough not to succumb to corruption. The main trouble stemmed from large numbers of such people roaming the countryside. Supervising them was completely useless. Escaping from the place they'd been deported to was far easier than surviving afterward on the open road; for this reason those who decided to run away were prepared to do anything: to rob, steal, murder. We are the ones who now lament their ruinous fate when we sing the plaintive song about a vagabond who "walks up to Baikal and makes off with a fisherman's boat," but our ancestors shed bitter tears on their account. They kept weapons handy to defend themselves not only against wild animals but also against the shady characters who might rap on the window at any moment and demand whatever they felt like demanding. After this should we be surprised at Siberians' distrustfulness and secretiveness, at their supposed coldness and unfriendliness? Yes, they are distrustful, cold, and wary, but only at first, only until they've gotten to know you and concluded that you bring no harm—then they'll bare their souls, and the Siberian who seemed on the verge of turning you away from his doorstep will welcome you and regale you like his own brother, without superfluous words and unnecessary feelings but in a friendly, hospitable way, showing the kind of sincerity and cordiality that reflect the joy people ought to take in one another's company in this world.

Siberian hospitality is legendary. The legends might exaggerate somewhat, but they arose and live on for good reason.

The towns and villages along the rivers lay far apart from each other, were not large, and contained one and the same circle of people. That is why Siberians, whose back-breaking tasks and long hunting and fishing expeditions in the taiga made them yearn for a fresh face, knew how to appreciate human contact and make the most of it. It was like a holiday for them. And even their relationships with each other, with their neighbors and fellow villagers, were notably solid and earnest. Trivial matters didn't lead to petty quarrels and grudges; when they were friends, they remained friends, and when they were foes, they stayed foes, going all out and not stopping halfway.

It was harder to make do without mutual assistance and a communal spirit here than in any other place, and, oddly enough, the communal spirit got along beautifully with the Siberians' secretiveness and individualism: one was for ties with the known, familiar world and the other for everything that seemed foreign and suspicious, of which Siberia had more than its share. When hunters left their winter shacks in the taiga, they would always set out dry kindling, matches, salt, and food—they never knew what straits the people who came after them might be in. This law was strictly observed for centuries and began to disappear only in very recent times. When locking up for the night, Siberians did not forget those same vagabonds who'd caused the old-timers so much suffering—they'd put a jug of milk and a loaf of bread in the window they'd cut in the solid plank fence for that very purpose: Have a bite to eat, traveler, and move on. In the beginning they did this out of compassion but later in order to turn the hand of evil away from their farmsteads. And Siberians would customarily give their last kopeck when strangers, hiding their eyes, went around the cities and towns from house to house and cottage to cottage collecting money "to help a friend escape" [*"na pobeg tovarishchu"*].

But it was Siberia itself that most influenced the character of Siberians, as the land, the world they lived in and whose air they breathed, as the homeland that gave them birth and sustenance. Each individual reflects his ancestral home just as "whole peoples reflect their fatherland" (Shchapov).

The only kind of grandeur, of mightiness, that can overwhelm us are those that stand out sharply and unnaturally amid everything else, making any comparison sad and crude. When, however, everything in the surrounding natural environment is consistently and proportionately on the same large scale, this, in turn, elevates human beings as well. The genetics of the land is just as primordial and fixed as the genetics of blood. In view of nature's greatness and unabating triumph, human beings couldn't help feeling strong and significant, and the sparseness of population reinforced this outlook. The gigantic efforts they expended in order to tighten their hold and to survive in this rugged land made them inclined to respect themselves, as if they stood just as tall as everything around them, even taller. The whole world alongside them breathed an austere dignity and freedom, a concealed depth and strength, and in its outward tranquillity a coiled tension could be sensed; Siberians, quite naturally, adopted this spirit, and, when superimposed on their ancestors' elemental love of liberty, it became set, probably a bit more firmly than was necessary. It's not true that Siberians are unsociable, but their sociability bears the stamp of rivalry and competition when dealing with equals and of protectiveness toward unequals. Both attitudes manifest themselves spontaneously, without role-playing or prior thought, but Siberians always remember that they are Siberians and let everyone know it. Pride in their place of birth sometimes reaches the point of arrogance. Now, of course, this quality has weakened considerably, but it hasn't been lost altogether.

Another important point is that Siberia never experienced serfdom, which crushed people both morally and physically, deprived them of self-sufficiency, and had an oppressive effect on their attitude toward work and toward life in general. Siberians got used to relying on themselves. Land was abundant; you could take and cultivate as much as you wanted, as much as you could handle. The yoke of government bureaucracy, which weighed heavily on the cities, reached the country-side as weak, ineffective orders that experienced peasants were in no hurry to carry out. For them the Russian proverb "Trust in God, but don't slip up yourself" [*Na Boga nadeisia, da sam ne ploshai*] had a practical, literal meaning. And indeed Siberians were not known for deep contemplation and piety (except, of course, for the schismatics); a calculating intelligence prevailed over feelings, not for personal gain but because this was part of the old-timers' very make-up. It would seem strange to look for the softness and slackness typical of Russia's steppe dwellers in this "fireproof" spirit [*v . . . "ogneupornom" dukhe*], born of constant resistance and tempered by deprivation. But I say this not to make the Siberian a model of virtue, but simply to show what he had in him and what he lacked. He would even crane his neck and peer into the sky as if gazing at a powerful neighbor, dreaming confidently of finding a way to harness it for himself and his household needs.

You can say that in all their qualities, good and bad, fortunate and unfortunate, Siberians exemplify what could become of people who stayed one step ahead of restrictive laws for a long time.

But when reflecting on Siberians as a branch of Russia that stood out thanks to selectivity and local conditions, we should not forget that the settlers were spread across an enormous territory and came from a variety of social groups and for those reasons alone could no longer share one manner and one style. The Altaians, who trace their roots to the stern schismatics, and the inhabitants of the Lake Baikal region, whose ancestors were sent there to work in the mines, and the direct descendants of free Cossacks who live on the banks of the Yenisey bear little resemblance to one another. And that is why any attempt to single out some general feature common to all Siberians will have exceedingly fuzzy outlines.

Rather, it is the ability to resist being reduced to a simple formula and to remain a thing in itself that makes this land Siberia and these people Siberians.

We sometimes like to say, and not without pride, "Siberia is more Russia than Russia."

These words, which appeared long ago and have become a popular saying, carry no hint of opposition or argument. Siberia and Russia are a single whole. Siberia doesn't exist without Russia, and there is no need to present evidence to prove this. Our saying means something else. Perhaps out of false patriotism, or perhaps based on observations that have shifted in our favor, we would like to believe that certain qualities in Russians have been better and more fully preserved in Siberians. We claim no credit for this—it just turned out that way— and our feelings can't possibly have no basis whatsoever. Back in the nineteenth century Semyon Kapustin[32] noted:

> The Siberian peasant represents the Russian as he was in ancient Russia, before the appearance of servitude, slavery, and serfdom;[33] the innate characteristics of the Russian farmer developed freely in Siberia.

In this connection we can recall that every foreign influence, be it French or German, that periodically swept through the Russian capitals[34] like a conflagration and reached Tomsk or Irkutsk only after crossing thousands of versts on horseback would inevitably become covered with Siberian hoarfrost and adopt a strong Siberia "dialect." We can cite the traditional distrustfulness of Siberians, who were not about to suddenly start fulfilling the directives that kept coming one right after another without looking them over carefully to see whether or not they would do them any good. And we can observe, on taking a close look at Siberians, that despite all the damage done to their character in recent decades, they still remain within the bounds of sincere relationships and a more or less healthy moral code, a great boon in this day and age. But most important, Russians (like any other nationality that retains its primordial ethnic mix), who feel fully Russian and fully human only amid the part of Mother Nature that created them and who are at a loss wherever their connection to it has been destroyed, still have the opportunity, for the time being, to live amid their native steppes and native forests in Siberia. But I must caution that this opportunity decreases and shrinks with every passing year, and if the reversal of Siberian rivers[35] is ever actually accomplished, it will undoubtedly disappear altogether.

Of course today's Siberians are no longer what they were even one hundred years ago. The "Siberian breed" has been heavily diluted and seems destined to become merely a geographic concept in a very short time. Nothing passed through Siberia without leaving its mark, be it exile and hard labor or the mass migration of peasants between the emancipation reform[36] and the beginning of World War I, when four million people moved to Siberia—almost as many as its existing population. Only strong, well-established moral standards, with a little help from dear Mother Nature, could make Siberians out of them in the course of a few decades. Equally important, the immigrants came here to live permanently and were forced to reckon with the local laws, written and unwritten, whether they wanted to or not. But when the new "conquest" of Siberia began twenty or thirty years ago and mighty waves of recruits poured in to work on construction projects, this obstacle no longer stood in their way. Young people came here primarily to work at some building site that, after they'd finished their business, learned a trade, and earned enough money to support a family, they could leave at any moment, which is usually what happened and still happens today. Those returning from Siberia might even retain the warm feeling toward it that they take back with them, but they don't change their casual, detached attitude toward the land where they happened to work temporarily and that simply never became their own.

And faced with a huge number of temporary and seasonal people, native Siberians have been forced to step aside. They plow and build and fell trees and mine ore, their share of the labor involved in the changes taking place in Siberia is much greater than newspapers and magazines would indicate, but they do everything in the wake of others, carried along by powerful economic and industrial currents. Acting out of their feelings and sense of duty as Siberians, they seem to instinctively choose jobs in which they can more easily and effectively look after the land that is kindred to them.

Present-day Siberians have changed drastically both in the country and in the city. But they are still Siberians, and the more they needed their distinctive qualities to provide strength and security in life, the more they long for these qualities once they are lost (the heroes of the books and films by Vasily Shukshin[37] can be cited as examples). But this is precisely what offers hope: they will hang on to what is left of their "core instincts" with characteristic stubbornness and persistence.

Siberia, Siberia

> Creating Siberia is more difficult than creating anything else under the blessed sky.
>
> *Ivan Goncharov*[38]

Cold and wild expanses! . . .

How long ago were these words first spoken, and did someone actually say them or did they always hover soundlessly and imperiously over Siberia like a ghost, dropping anguish and alarm on the wayfarer? For if someone actually said these words, it was a wayfarer flinching in advance at the thought of the vast distances and painful ordeals he would soon have to overcome. He crossed the Urals, stopped at a border marker covered with heart-rending farewell inscriptions written by convicts and by ordinary folk who expected nothing good up ahead, and then moved on, but the impression left by the inscriptions and reinforced by his own sorrow held him in its grip for a long time. Verst after verst slipped slowly and tediously behind him, and his eyes fell on one and the same landscape, which looked dreary and lifeless and which contained the rough, wearying road that made him think of the road to hell. And also traveling this road were columns of unfortunate wretches, ragged and frightened, sometimes prisoners, sometimes immigrants seeking their fate; here, too, a red-faced daredevil coming from the opposite direction would frighten him for no reason with a few nasty words. Everything was like the reverse of normal human life, and everything seemed to be in a foreign place that could never warm up or be regarded with affection and that was impossible to picture as someone's beloved homeland.

In this frame of mind the wayfarer traveled for a day, then two, then three, noticing, however, through his glum thoughts that the scanty forest along the roadside had given way to steppe. But the steppe, too, froze in monotony for a long time, and it seemed endless, incapable of arousing warm feelings. He could only be patient with it and wait to see what would come next, hoping to find relief for his jaded gaze in a worse but at least new landscape.

And relief actually did come. Waking as if out of a deep sleep, the traveler suddenly noted with surprise and delight that the occasional groves that had made him weary, and the pine and larch forests that were emerging from the impassable environs with growing frequency and boldness, and the land itself, gradually losing its level contour, were beginning to excite him more and more all the time, raising in him an increasingly perceptible reaction to what seemed like a primordially ordained encounter. And he no longer understood—he refused to understand—how he could have looked at his surroundings with indifference, what had happened to make him turn away from this rare beauty.

Anton Chekhov, who crossed Siberia in a horse-drawn carriage at the end of the nineteenth century while traveling to Sakhalin Island,[39] was bored all the way to the Yenisey River. "Cold plains, crooked birch trees, puddles, lakes here and there, snow in May, and the dreary, uninhabited banks of the tributaries of the Ob—that's all my memory manages to retain out of the first two thousand versts" [about 1,320 miles]. And even women: "The women here are just as dull as nature in Siberia." But on reaching the Yenisey, he exclaimed, "Never in my life have I seen a river more magnificent than the Yenisey." And he continued on his way enraptured with the gloomy, endless taiga and with the tales that worldly-wise people told him about hunting and about life.

Forty years before Chekhov another Russian writer, Ivan Goncharov, took a trip around the world[40] and passed through Siberia going in the opposite direction, starting from the Sea of Okhotsk. After the rich, lush beauty of the tropics, after China and Japan, he could hardly stand the frigid, bare expanses of Northeastern Asia at first. But not far from the Lena River he, too, came to life. And even the wintertime appearance of the great river, covered with snow and ice and lifeless at that time of year, aroused in the tired traveler a fresh feeling of sincere emotion and delight that he, calling himself a romantic, retained as he continued his journey.

In both cases this is just the way it had to happen. From whichever direction you approach it, Siberia is in no hurry to reveal itself, and it placed its finest creations with love and good taste in its heartland. What constitutes its finest creations, incidentally, is still an open question. No two people will share the same opinion. For me, an inhabitant of central Siberia, the best places are right around Lake Baikal, the Sayan Mountains, and the Yenisey River; an Altaian will assure you that they lie in his region, in the Altay Mountains; and a Chukchi will say that they are located on the shores of the cold northern seas. Our place of birth is dear to each of us, which is another characteristic of the Siberian: fervent patriotism. The subject at hand, however, is not local opinion but an overview, as objective as possible, of Siberia as a country created by Nature.

Of one thing I am certain: the very same landscape that our traveler considered dreary and joyless on entering Siberia would be transformed to such an extent on his return trip, becoming so relevant and attractive and capable of strongly affecting his aesthetic sense, that he would start looking around in bewilderment, thinking, "This can't be. Why, it's probably a different road." No, the road is the same and the landscape is the same, altered, perhaps, only by a change of season, but the traveler is no longer the same. He has now been to Siberia, he has seen many things that struck his imagination, and his impressions of Siberia have opened up inside him some new and glorious expanses that he'd never even suspected were there before.

Siberia has the virtue of not startling or astonishing you right away but of pulling you in slowly and reluctantly, as it were, with measured carefulness, and then binding you tightly once you are in. And then it's all over—you are afflicted with Siberia. After malignant anthrax [*sibirskaia iazva*, literally, "Siberian ulcer"], which apparently doesn't exist anymore, this is Siberia's most famous disease: for a long time after being in this land a person feels hemmed in, sad, and mournful everywhere else, tormented wherever he goes by a vague and agonizing sense of his own inadequacy, as if he's left part of himself in Siberia forever.

Everything in our neck of nature is mighty and free; everything stands apart from similar phenomena in other places. In Western Siberia a plain is not just a plain—it is the largest, flattest plain on the planet; swamps are not just swamps—even from an airplane they seem to have no boundaries and no end. The taiga in Eastern Siberia is an entire landmass, which, by the way, is suffering the most frightening disasters of its life because of logging and fires. The rivers—the Ob, the Lena, the Yenisey—can rival only one another. Lake Baikal contains one-fifth of all the freshwater on the earth's surface. No, everything here was conceived and carried out on a full and lavish scale, as though the Most High began creation of Earth with this land, starting at the Pacific Ocean, and made it massive and flashy, not scrimping on material; only later, after suddenly realizing that he might run out, did he begin to cut back and make do.

But this concerns size and volume. What can we say about Siberia's beauty? Is it even possible to express in words anything remotely worthy, for example, of Lake Baikal? Any words, any comparisons would be just pale, feeble shadows. If there were no mighty Sayan Mountains close by to match it, no Lena River originating not far off, and no Angara carrying Baikal's water to the Yenisey, you might conclude while standing on the shore of this miracle/lake and gazing down on its nearest contours and water, on its colors and luminosity, which make your soul not merely melt but freeze in a deep swoon, you might conclude that Baikal was accidently dropped from some other planet, wealthier and more joyful than ours, where it was in complete harmony with the native inhabitants. You get the same feeling when you look at Lake Teletskoe in the Altay Mountains. The Gorno-Altay region is very often compared with Switzerland, the model of European beauty. Nature there does not simply live but reigns limitlessly and with absolute power, and, as though ashamed of its heights—its distance not above sea level but above human perception—it magnanimously begins to descend, bringing down its riches with majestic ease so that their cheering, inviting tones might ring out like divine sounds made visible. It's no accident that the Altay Mountains were precisely where Russians spent two centuries on end searching for the mysterious Belovodye, a legendary land created as an earthly paradise where they could live in complete happiness. They searched for it and, in their view, found it, then brought their fellow countrymen from European Russia, from the Urals, and from the plains of Siberia and began building houses and tilling the soil—this means there was something special, something out of the ordinary, in those parts that made people regard them with blessed hope. And everything there could have been like paradise, except that human beings let nature down, making their way into the deepest wilderness with their habits, laws, and institutions.

The Minusinsk District in the Krasnoyarsk Territory, on the southern border between Eastern and Western Siberia, is also called a Siberian Switzerland. If a little corner of Siberia has ended up—heaven only knows how—in Switzerland or somewhere else in warm Europe, then there is an explanation: a mix-up occurred, and by pure luck the piece meant for Europe found itself here. Siberia is Siberia all around, but in the Minusinsk Basin cantaloupe and watermelon ripen splendidly and tomatoes grow so large that even southern varieties can scarcely compete with them.

Incidently, we have quite a few such sprinklings of a seemingly non-Siberian nature. There is a short stretch along the Snow River [*Snezhnaia reka*] near Baikal where, growing alongside the larch and Siberian pine, you find immense poplars and blue spruce, relics from an earlier age. You're better off not even starting a discussion of Baikal. It has altogether too much of everything, from the simplest plants to large animals, existing as unique species that occur nowhere else, and those that do occur elsewhere have no business being in this part of the world, according to the laws of nature. Where they came from and how they got there are a mystery. Scientists, as they continue to discover new species, continue to be puzzled. Not everyone knows that certain heavenly spots on Baikal have more days of sunshine per year than do the southern health resorts (I recently read in a respectable publication that after Davos, Switzerland, Irkutsk receives more sunlight than any other place in the world), or that the water, always cold and icy in the lake proper even during summer, warms up to more than 20°C [68°F] in the bays. And you can't help concluding that all these exceptions, both explicably and inexplicably successful, were made for one reason: they were created with the deliberate purpose of suggesting what humankind should do, in which direction to transform Siberia should it seem niggardly and inhospitable.

Nature in Siberia, like everything else here—the people, the land, the climate—cannot be as uniform as peas in a pod. Imagine just the distances that would have to be discussed to convey a general idea of their extent. And only in winter does everything in nature freeze from one end to the other in a single ponderous, inaccessible thought. White plains lie bare and cold, mountains jut calmly out of the snows like abandoned border barricades and bend under their weight, the taiga slumbers in a puffed-up pattern of frost, and the rivers and lakes are covered with ice. Everything is directed inward; everything is bewitched by a single gigantic, protective force. At this time of year you can clearly see how legends arose in the past not only about people who went to sleep for the whole winter but also about words that froze in the air before reaching the ear and that were capable of thawing out in the springtime warmth and resounding on their own, far from the person who had spoken them.

In Siberia it's easy to succumb to such a frame of mind.

Spring in our parts is not spring in the usual sense but a good two months of winter simply swinging back and forth—warm/bitter cold, warm/bitter cold—until it finally takes a turn toward steadily warm weather. And then everything all around races to thaw and bloom, to bud out and turn green. At the northern latitudes summer comes like a gunshot: just yesterday the land lay ravaged and bare and was still merely preparing for change, while today a simultaneous sprouting has already begun to peep out everywhere, and tomorrow summer will erupt in full glow. And it will begin to blaze with a vivid, reckless beauty that can't look back, for summer is as hurried as winter is sluggish. At the very beginning of August it is already rounding the bend and autumn comes to pay a friendly call, making itself at home. This is what summer has to live with: a cold spring hems it in on one side and autumn on the other.

To make up for this, autumn is usually long and mild. Of course, no two years are the same and anything can happen—sometimes even this season doesn't manage to stick around—but when it comes early, more often than not it will make a late retreat, giving all living things in nature, exhausted from their labors, a chance to rest up and bask in the sun. And it is not unusual for buds to swell a second time during autumn, fooled by the unseasonal warmth, and for mountain slopes to bloom with wild rosemary, a gnarled bush dearly loved by Siberians that is not much to look at but that blossoms so selflessly, so joyfully with violet or rose-colored abandon. And the forests blaze, burning low, for a long time, inflamed with a broad scattering of fall colors that are especially pure and radiant here, filling the air to a considerable height with their iridescence.

Burn, blaze, glow, flame—these words don't come from a passion for fire terminology. That's just the way things are in Siberia. The lazy, sated beauty of southern climes is not characteristic of nature in Siberia, which, I repeat, must hurry in order to have enough time to bloom and fade, bearing fruit, and it does this with measured swiftness and short-lived but vivid celebration. We have a type of flower that doesn't grow west of the Urals and that we call simply Siberian globe flowers [*zharki, ogon'ki*, literally, "bonfires, little lights"]. When they blossom in July, the clearings in the taiga light up with a lush, festive glow, and nothing can dispel the impression that they give off a heat you can feel.

And so there is swiftness at one time of year and sluggishness at another, with uneven and unstable transitions at their boundaries—that's what Siberia is. Impetuosity and torpor, openness and secrecy, vividness and restraint, generosity and concealment, which by now appear in concepts that apply not only to nature—that's what Siberia is. And when you reflect on these two almost opposite principles and recall how large, varied, and unsimple Siberia is, you rush to heed its restless call with the same impetuosity and come to a halt with the same restraint: Siberia!

Altogether too much is bound up in this word nowadays.

And how you wish to extract something from this immense, complex tangle of contradictory hopes and aspirations that are linked to Siberia, how you wish to obtain from it, like a magic pearl, one simple and obvious certainty: that in one hundred and two hundred years people approaching Baikal will stop in their tracks at its primordial beauty and pure depths, and that in one hundred and two hundred years Siberia will still be Siberia—a land suitable for habitation, conducive to noble aspirations, and preserved intact, not a devastated lunar landscape dotted with the remains of petrified trees.

In every spiritually mature individual the outlines of his homeland are duplicated and alive. We Russians automatically carry within ourselves the antiquity of Kiev, the greatness of Novgorod, the pain of Ryazan,[41] the sanctity of Optina Monastery,[42] and the immortality of Yasnaya Polyana[43] and Staraya Russa.[44] The dates of our country's victories and losses flicker in us like the burning bush. And in this sense we have long felt Siberia within ourselves as the reality of the future, as a reliable and imminent step in our forthcoming ascent. What this ascent will become we can only vaguely imagine, but through the contours of random scenes we dream that it will be something new and different, an age when human beings will abandon labors that are unnecessary and harmful to their existence and, having learned a lesson from the bitter experience of recent times, will finally start taking care of the land—not in words but in deeds—that they have been lucky enough to inherit.

This will be the true fulfillment of Siberia. And this is what Siberians, the inhabitants of a young and glorious land, ought to be like, for their land has a right to its own future.

1987

2

❖❖❖

Tobolsk

Tobolsk lives within each Siberian, whether he's ever been there or not, the way Moscow lives in every Russian and Kiev in every Slav. Kiev is the ancient capital of *byliny*[1] fame, Moscow the fair and foremost first capital, and Tobolsk the eastern courtier of relatively recent greatness who governed a vast, northern land of midnight. Acquired and erected through the daring of Russians and kept alive through sheer boldness, it was Moscow's left hand, but my, what a long arm it had and what a lot it raked in for Moscow! Kiev has Vladimir's Hill, Moscow has Beautiful Hill[2] near the Kremlin, and Tobolsk has Holy Trinity Point [*Troitskii mys*], a promontory thirty sazhens [about 210 feet] long at the confluence of the Irtysh and Tobol Rivers where scenes of sweeping grandeur, magnified ten times in the Siberian manner, unfold before the eye, allowing you to see for a great distance. And they unfold precisely in the direction that Tobolsk was placed to look—to the east.

Tobolsk came into being at the time when Rus, with the annexation of Kazan and Astrakhan, was just beginning to become Russia. But the lands along the Volga River all the way to its mouth had always seemed to belong to Russia, destined by nature itself to be ruled by one hand; these "borderlands"[3] had simply not been appropriated yet, which was merely a matter of time and strength. But off in the distance nature had erected a boundary—the Ural Mountains—that was all too noticeable. We must assume that this also played an important role in holding back Ivan the Terrible, who stopped just beyond the Volga. Unaccustomed to the title of czar, he still called himself the grand prince of all Rus as well. But an empire was not far off. And the appearance of Tobolsk—and with it the quick seizure of so many eastern nations and languages that scribes, when naming the parts of the sov-

ereign's autocracy, must have run out of ink—the appearance of Tobolsk served as a gate that was strong for protection yet wide and well
aimed for conquest. Historians, as a common matter of course, usually
do not give any weight to Tobolsk's role in increasing Russia's territorial
might, but it did indeed bring in a goodly amount. Even before the victories of Peter the Great, his father, Czar Alexis, could have called himself emperor based solely on his acquisitions in Siberia. And didn't
Asian Russia cover more territory than European Russia during Peter's
reign, too? Yet after the greatness of his achievements, you could only
look across the Urals from Moscow and Petersburg and shut your eyes;
the Chuds, or primitive Siberians, as the voivodes called their subjects
whenever they took a census, were still primitive. And only Tobolsk,
from its vantage point on Holy Trinity Hill [*Troitskii kholm*], had to see
and know everything; to find out and to guess; to build and acquire; to
demand and promise; to rule and be held accountable; to attend to
rations and provisions, government servants, peasant farmers, artisans,
furs [*miagkaia rukhliad'*, literally, "soft stuff"], and ores; to take stock
and keep watch; to administer capital punishment and show mercy;
and to conduct diplomacy with local princelings across the entire
expanse of a vast region as well as with foreign rulers beyond its
boundaries.

It was the capital of Siberia, the father of Siberian cities. Only
Moscow and Tobolsk could receive ambassadors and dispatch diplomatic delegations. Everything that took root in Siberia—chronicles,
schools, books, the theater, scholarship and crafts, Orthodox Christianity, the exile system, bribery and corruption, government informers, and so forth—all this and much more began in Tobolsk and spread
to the interior only afterward. It was first in everything. In 1593 it
received the first exile, the Uglich Bell, which had proclaimed the
assassination of Czarevitch Dmitry.[4] More than three hundred years
later, after the February Revolution in 1917, it received the last Russian
emperor and his family. By the time Nicholas II was banished, Tobolsk
had long since lost all independence and gone to seed,[5] and its glaring
impoverishment was ideally suited for a dynasty fallen from power.
Some kind of destiny or fate was at work here, some cold and painfully
exacting justice. But that same fate spared Tobolsk the ultimate sin and
disgrace of murdering the imperial family.

By looking at Tobolsk, at its history and customs, at the hodge-podge of people who settled there, at its appropriate division into Upper Town and Lower Town, and at its flights and falls, we can put together a nearly flawless portrait of the Russian character in Siberia, which was gradually becoming Siberian in its distinctive features but didn't succeed before merging with the character of Russia proper again, losing its unique traits along the way. Tobolsk's most recent history merely bears out the condition of present-day Siberians. Character, naturally, ripens best in a country's heartland, where crops and crafts also come to fruition, but just as the results of these labors used to be displayed at trade fairs, so, too, did character traits show through more noticeably in towns, where life was a bit livelier and more open.

We should probably begin the story of Tobolsk with the fact that, although it was first in everything in Siberia for a long time, Tobolsk itself was not Siberia's first Russian town. It appeared too late, though just barely. And at this point, like it or not, we must go back to Yermak.

No other historical figure seems to have left as many unanswered questions as Yermak. He turned out to be a true Cossack in this regard, too, having covered his tracks well. The debate over his name, his motives, and the details of his campaign began in the eighteenth century, continued in the nineteenth, and hasn't ended even now. And the harder historians try to arrive at the truth, the more they confuse things. The date of the beginning of his campaign keeps changing, as does the date of his death; even the circumstances of his death itself have been altered more than once. Sometimes they deny that the Stroganovs aided and abetted Yermak; sometimes they acknowledge it. Different historians, working from different assumptions and different sources (the disagreement among the Siberian chronicles is like the uproar of drunken Cossacks bursting into reminiscence, interrupting each other and cutting each other off), different historians attach significance first to one battle, then to another. They mix up casualty figures and confuse Tatar and Russian names. The dead rise from their graves and take part in battles, while distinguished figures vanish who knows where. And so it goes, with no end in sight.

And here is Yermak himself. The church calendar listed no such name, so his, therefore, must have been a nickname. But where did it come from? Did it sound like his real name, or did it actually derive from the common cauldron called a *ermak*, dating back to his youth, when the future conqueror of Siberia was supposedly the camp cook for a band of Volga Cossacks, or did it come from some other source? No one seems to dispute the notion that he went off on his campaign as Yermak. But the Tatar language also contains this word, meaning a passage or a military breakthrough. And if you agree with Pavel Nebolsin,[6] a nineteenth-century historian, that before Yermak's triumphant breakthrough he had spent some time on the Chusovaya River and knew the routes across the Urals, then couldn't he have clashed with Tatars during brief incursions before his conquest and received his nickname for military daring from them? Be that as it may, this conjecture won't make things any more confused than they already are, and if truth sighs one more time in disappointment, we won't be able to hear it anyway.

We dispute everything. We've all known since childhood from reading Karamzin[7] that Kuchum's capital city, which Yermak occupied, was called Isker or Sibir. Eventually the name *Isker* somehow began to die out by itself as *Sibir* became more common; people started assuming that the former referred to something else entirely. All right, Sibir it is. Etymologically, the town that gave its name to the entire landmass beyond the Urals meant center or meeting place. No sooner had historians established this than they began correcting themselves: it wasn't Sibir but Kashlyk—that's what the chronicles said. And that town was ostensibly so small that the three or four hundred Cossacks in Yermak's detachment who were still alive after the battle couldn't find room to winter there and went off to the mouth of the Tobol River to Karacha's[8] encampment, where they spent three whole winters. If that is so, then whom did the Tatar *murza*[9] Karacha besiege for several months early in the spring when both Yermak and Ataman Meshcheryak[10] were listed among the besieged occupants of Kashlyk (Koltso[11] had been killed by then)? Having no intention of getting into an argument with the historians, who, when they lack documentation, ought to have a sixth sense that can penetrate the centuries, I still can't help noticing what a taste they've developed for revisionist interpretations of the story of Yermak, continually proposing more and more new versions that seem constructed on the sands of the Irtysh. No matter how often one chronicle contradicts another, nowhere—and historians are forced to admit this—do they mention a winter's stay with Karacha. Where do scholars get this idea? Probably from a desire to tie up the loose ends in their scheme of things, which makes them pay too little attention to what has become established fact.

In just the same manner the main battle at Chuvash Point, for which Kuchum had plenty of time to prepare, making tree entanglements, building a rampart, and assembling a numerous host (the Cossacks nearly faltered on the eve of battle at the sight of Kuchum's army), for some reason this central engagement has now become an insignificant episode, a mere adventure, historical smoke without fire. The Cossacks delivered a volley at the start of battle, the Ostyak princelings turned tail, and Kuchum, who had been following the battle from a hilltop, lost no time in taking flight after Czarevitch Mametkul[12] was wounded, opening the way to his capital. The Cossacks supposedly suffered almost no losses. The statement "It was a vicious fight; they hacked away at each other, grabbing each other by the arm" is considered an exaggeration. And again this runs counter to the evidence Yermak's Cossacks left in the *Sinodik*, the roster of the dead given to the church so that prayers could be said for the salvation of their souls. Scholars claim that the *Sinodik* was compiled forty years after the event and therefore the Cossacks couldn't have remembered much. They didn't remember where they'd experienced the most important twist in Siberia's fate, at Abalak or at Chuvash Point? Why, even rotting bones wouldn't forget such a thing or mix up the facts. All the more so when the *Sinodik* was written in Tobolsk and Chuvash Point was right there under their noses, one and a half versts [a little more than one mile] away.

But historians have already started picking up and passing around the following notions from book to book: it wasn't Yermak who deprived Kuchum of his Siberian troops but Kuchum who handed them over almost voluntarily; the fighting came later; and we can't trust any part of the Cossacks' memoirs. This is what introducing a fascinating novelty into history means.

Slightly less than one hundred fifty years ago Nebolsin observed with wise irony:

It must have been plain dumb luck! Only a simple Cossack, a Volga Cossack, could have come up with the happy thought of going to Siberia. Luck must have helped him get to Siberia, helped him conquer the Tatars, kept him from starving or freezing to death, helped him take possession of Siberia, helped him hold out there for three years, kept him from letting it slip through his fingers, helped him point the way for others, and made all of posterity honor his memory . . .

No, this is way too much luck!

You can't help recalling the words of another lucky Russian: "It's not all luck—why, you've got to have some brains, too, for God's sake!"[13]

However that may be, no matter how many victims the victory at Chuvash Point cost, it did open the way to Isker/Sibir/Kashlyk. According to previous information, the Chuvash conflict took place on October 23, 1581; in the current amended version it occurred on October 26, 1582. Without getting into the debate over the year, for which Ruslan Skrynnikov, whom we are quoting, gives the most persuasive evidence for revision, we will, nonetheless, stick with the original day, since it was revised on the grounds that Yermak entered Kuchum's town on October 26 and had to have fought on the same day because there was nowhere else he could have been for three days. Nowhere else he could have been? Let's not forget the custom of "fighting to the death" [*"stoianie na kostiakh"*], after which the warriors buried their fallen comrades, regrouped, and took measures to guard against surprise attacks. Yermak was in a foreign land, he could receive information only "by word of mouth" [*ot "iazykov"*], that is, from captives, and before moving on to Sibir, which he could reach only by rowing roughly fifteen versts [about ten miles] upstream, he must have taken a careful look around and prepared for the next extremely important step without making a mistake or yielding to the intoxication of victory.

Yermak must have taken a good look around, and he could not have helped noticing another point of land, called Alafey's Hill [*Alafeevskaia gora*] by the Tatars and subsequently named Holy Trinity Hill by the Russians, which stood close by, at the confluence of the Irtysh and Tobol Rivers. Moreover, there was a settlement located there, where one of Kuchum's wives lived. Having passed it many times, by water and by land, during his three years in Siberia and being "very intelligent" ["*vel'mi razumen*"], he could not have helped looking at it and thinking, "Two rivers right in front of your eyes and only a short distance to a third, the Ob—what a great place to put a fort." We can surmise that Yermak found the site for Tobolsk even before it was conceived and named; the place itself was just asking to be chosen and begging for a building.

And when in 1587, two or three years after Yermak's death, Danila Chulkov,[14] the voivode's chief administrator, sailed downstream from Tyumen, which had been founded a year earlier, thus becoming the first Russian town in Siberia, he knew where he was heading. His barks perched on the steep bank near Alafey's Hill, and his Cossacks set to work unloading them without scouting around. Among those approximately five hundred (this figure is repeated so often when calculating medieval troop strength that it is automatically taken to signify a multitude, the way the Tatar word *tiumen'* means one thousand), among those five hundred or so who arrived with Chulkov and carved out Tobolsk were Yermak's companions, veterans of his campaign. From that time on, the history of Siberia began almost invisibly to keep pace with outside events; it recalls that after the Cossacks unloaded their vessels, they got right to work taking them apart and then dragged the sides and bottoms up the hill to start building a fort.

But its beginning is just that—almost invisible. Without giving any explanations, Pyotr Slovtsov,[15] a Siberian historian, for some reason states that Tobolsk's foundation was laid in 1586; then the town supposedly changed location the following summer and rose on the spot where it now stands. As a scholar searching for historical truth, Slovtsov was meticulous and strict, reprimanding the very fathers of Siberian history, Müller[16] and Fischer,[17] for inaccuracies and omissions, and he was ready to flog the living daylights out of the composer/ chroniclers from Irkutsk and other places who, instead of writing chronicles, kept stationhouse records of the arrivals and departures of officials and warehouse accounts of caravan traffic. There probably was some basis, however obscure, for starting the chronology of Tobolsk with its move. But there were also grounds for not insisting on this interpretation. In either case, Tobolsk traces its lineage from 1587, a period in which we would not have such a hard time finding beginnings and endings nowadays were it not for several fires that burned Siberia's leading old town to the ground.

During that first summer Chulkov's band of warriors put up a fort, made it secure, and raised a small church within its walls in honor of the life-giving Holy Trinity, whose name came to designate both the hill and the entire cape, burying their old appellations. No, as the Cossacks erected their little fort they couldn't have helped sensing the triumphant and grateful proximity of Chuvash Point: "inasmuch as the accursed infidels were vanquished and defeated there . . . this town of Tobolsk took the place of Sibir (Isker) as the reigning town." Much later, when the citadel of white stone was completed, one of the Decembrists would remark that no town was more picturesque than Tobolsk. And that is true to this day. In Siberia, at least, there is not and can never be a lovelier town until real architecture, in defiance of modern designers, returns.

But Tobolsk was "picturesque" from the very beginning, even before the appearance of Saint Sophia's Cathedral [*Sofiiskii sobor*], the Rentereya, as the treasury building was called, and the entire ensemble of buildings inside the citadel walls. Only not to such an inspired height, not to the point of spiritual perfection, of a complete amalgamation of human and nonhuman creations, of a thrusting pressure in the chest when you look upward from the Irtysh—ah, a living legend, pure and simple! Rather, it was picturesque because of the beauty and inspiration of nature that human beings skillfully captured, not quarreling with the creator. Even in its wooden state of completion that work of human hands must have reminded everyone of a crown, however modest, lacking gilt and luster and not as majestic as it would be later on but displaying its authority with sufficient eloquence. When the crowned city became affluent and famous, it also replaced its crown. What a pity that after the old crown was removed, it couldn't have been kept in a storehouse, where we might feast our eyes on its design and on the way it sat above the town. The architectural monuments from those times (which none in Siberia can equal—those that remain intact, like the tower from the wooden fort at Bratsk, for instance, are half a century younger) will give you some idea of what fortress buildings similar to those that might have been in Tobolsk were like, but they won't tell you anything about Tobolsk itself. Everything in that town, even the most ordinary structures, must have stood differently and looked different—more striking and impressive—because they stood high and majestic and reigned for a long distance, the way television towers, having seized power, reign today. Quite recently, by the way, and with great difficulty the residents of Tobolsk, acting together, forced this new ruler of our hearts and minds out of the citadel, where the T.V. tower had picked a spot for itself, scaring the populace by threatening not to broadcast from any other place. Only from the citadel, so it could look down from above on Saint Sophia's Cathedral and its belfry. But when they moved it, nothing happened—it now broadcasts from a cemetery. Sometimes it even shows Holy Trinity Point in closeup, where the restored courtyard of Saint Sophia's soars like music, like a fairy tale, like a miracle.

The Tobolsk of Danila Chulkov did not last long; built hastily, with everything crowded together, it played its part, which consisted of establishing a firm foothold in the Siberian steppe; as soon as that was accomplished, it had to give up its spot for a more spacious and, we must assume, more "picturesque" fort. But near the end of the very first summer, by all accounts, even before construction was finished, it was given a chance to take revenge for the deaths of Yermak, Ataman Ivan Koltso, his closest comrade-in-arms, and the many Cossacks who perished not in honorable battle but as the result of treachery and deception. For all the various views accompanying Yermak's campaign to this day, there are some events that everyone agrees on, indicating unquestionable authenticity. When Koltso returned from Moscow after delivering the news to the czar that Yermak had taken Siberia, *Murza* Karacha murdered him along with his detachment of forty men in a completely and utterly base manner: he persuaded Koltso to join forces with him against a Kazakh horde that was supposedly oppressing him, thus playing on the feelings of the Russians as they tried to make peace with him, and at the very first opportunity he slaughtered every last one. And Yermak perished after believing some cleverly started rumors about a group of Bukhara merchants, whom he decided to intercept so they wouldn't reach Kuchum. No matter what the circumstances of Yermak's death or what his final moments were like, there is no doubt that he was tricked, lured away from his men, pursued by a huge force,

The Tobolsk Citadel

and attacked in the middle of the night. All the legends obediently become true stories in this regard.

And now came the Russians' turn, thanks to a stroke of luck, to answer perfidy with perfidy and get rid of their most dangerous enemies in one fell swoop without a lot of drawn-out, complicated scheming. By that time Kuchum had lost his kingdom once and for all through internecine warfare and was traveling from one nomadic encampment to another with his clan, a mass teeming in the Asian manner and more numerous than an army; now and then he went around collecting tribute and making his usual dangerous secret raids. A diarchy, if not actually a triarchy, had sprung up along the Ob, Irtysh, and Tobol Rivers. Voivode Vasily Sukin[18] had established a stronghold in Tyumen, Seid-khan[19] was in Isker, and Karacha was roaming the steppes. For that reason when Karacha appeared at Prince's Meadow [*Kniazhii lug*] near Tobolsk along with Seid-khan and five hundred warriors (five hundred again!) and they began to amuse themselves with a falcon hunt, Chulkov, the town's chief administrator, had every reason to doubt that this was indeed a place for hunting falcon. "Oh, sports! You bring peace!"[20] was still an unknown precept four hundred years ago and they were perfectly capable of bringing war in the guise of a sporting event. In such situations God prudently steps aside, and the Devil gave Chulkov an idea for outwitting the Tatars. Outwardly their relations were fair; until that day the chief administrator had tried to get along without any clashes. He sent his ambassadors to Prince's Meadow with an invitation asking the distinguished guests to attend peace talks. After ensuring their safety, or so they thought, with a bodyguard of one hundred crack warriors, the Tatars accepted. They stationed the rest of their troops just outside the fortress walls. The guests were asked to comply with the customs of their hosts and come to the table unarmed. Whether fooled by the small number of Russians inside the fort, or by their guileless faces and warm words, or by the conceit that there was no lad alive who could outsmart a crafty easterner, the Tatar commanders let down their guard; they removed their weapons themselves and ordered the members of their horde who accompanied them to do the same. Karacha's heart must have belatedly skipped a beat when he saw his old enemy, Ataman Meshcheryak, from Yermak's detachment, sitting at the table, a man with whom he could never make peace. But Meshcheryak, in his turn, must also have had a premonition and begun to count his final hours. The old heroes, veterans from both sides, were simultaneously leaving the stage after catching a glimpse, without Yermak, as it happened, of someone else's scene, for new dramatis personae were now taking over their roles.

The culmination of this gripping tale can be viewed as all too Russian, involving a practice that has not disappeared even today. They filled a goblet and gave it to the khan. Saddled with Islam, which forbids alcohol, he was forced to decline. They poured a drink for Karacha, but he declined, too. The words that ensued are familiar to us: "Aha! If you're this finicky, you've probably got treachery on your mind!" (Nowadays they would have said, "This means you don't respect us!") "To hell with you! Tie them up, lads!" The Russians fell on them and bound them and then settled accounts with the bodyguards. But four hundred members of the horde still stood outside the fortress gate. As eyewitnesses recalled four hundred years ago, Yermak's last living comrade, the brave Ataman Meshcheryak, laid down his life in the hand-to-hand combat that followed. But Karacha and Seid-khan were dispatched to Moscow where, as was customary then and as had happened with many of Kuchum's captured sons, nephews, and wives, they were rewarded with estates and jobs in government service.

To each his own: death to the victors, honors to the vanquished.

However badly Chulkov may have behaved by resorting to a shabby trick, he did obtain peace. The Tatars left Isker again, this time for good, the diarchy came to an end, and the land beyond the Urals went to the Russians once and for all. Just as Russia was drawing closer and closer to the Time of Troubles,[21] Siberia's troubles were fading away; a well-organized force like that of Kuchum and his successors no longer existed farther to the east.

The Time of Troubles is precisely when Russia must have first properly appreciated not only the economic but also the political benefits of acquiring Siberia. The new might of Siberia was gradually entering the body politic as a whole and becoming irreplaceable. When the Polish army was advancing on Moscow, the Siberian Cossacks had gone off to the Yenisey River. As Prince Pozharsky[22] assembled a home guard, he wrote of his plans to the Siberian voivodes, and, after realizing those great plans of his and liberating Moscow, he sent them a triumphant epistle, seeing unshakable support for the fatherland out there, beyond the Urals.

Writing to "the Siberian voivodes" meant writing to Tobolsk, which had ceased to be subordinate to Tyumen and become Siberia's leading town very quickly, just seven years after Chulkov's men pounded in the first peg. In 1596 it was presented with a seal for the entire Siberian domain, which was expanding with unprecedented speed. This territory was governed by a voivode and his deputy. One ran military affairs, while the other was in charge of civilian matters, although in reality they had to toil and moil at everything combined; the voivode's duties increased with each addition to his domain. And what didn't they have to contend with?! The defense of the wooden forts that had already been built and the construction of new ones; patrolling old routes and exploring new lands; supplies; armaments; the collection of tribute and the cultivation of public lands;[23] the summoning and settling of peasants; the recruitment of Cossacks, among Tatars as well as Russians; the demand for single Christian girls as wives for the men in government service; first an imperial order to catch fugitives and return them to Russian estates, and then a law allowing them to go free if not caught within six years; commerce and customs; relations with non-Russians inside their realm and relations with neighbors outside it; incentives and penalties; churches and public houses; government informers and quarrels—what *didn't* give the first Siberian voivodes a headache, especially when the times were so harsh that no one's head sat securely on his neck to start with? Following Nebolsin's lead, we, too, certainly ought to speak well of them. Nebolsin writes:

When reminding ourselves of the way our first Siberian voivodes lived, we are very sorry that we can't present the reader with descriptions of magnificent palaces, ceremonial entrances, delicious feasts, romantic incidents, and luxuriant nature, which the Russian rulers in our Siberia, imitating the Spanish generals in America's Siberia, might have enjoyed. Our chroniclers were stingy with these descriptions, and besides, Siberia itself offered very few tasty morsels in this regard. . . . Our voivodes led a wretched life. Their lot was endless labor, endless trouble, and endless deprivation.

History has not always been fair to Siberia's administrators. Listening to it, you'd think that thief after thief and swindler after swindler sat in power and ran the show like a petty tyrant. We've had enough of this, and then some. Like a wealthy, simpleminded aunt, Siberia's sole purpose was to be robbed blind at all times under the guise of benefaction until it would finally wise up—but certainly not by everyone in succession. The concepts of honor and duty existed in those days, too. And if morality in all its righteous strains had not yet been dug out of the Siberian snows completely, had not materialized from the northern twilight in full form, then it must have called people to account in an exacting manner over and above the written laws by using its own salient features, which appeared with the birth of the first human being. There can be no doubt about this if you look on morals and manners as belonging to a particular locale, fashioned out of local materials, but back then moral standards came mainly from Moscow and showed what shaped ethical behavior in the foremost capital.

Although their names are muffled and indistinct, it is still possible to glean from history the names of voivodes and governors to whose activities Siberia has been indebted from the very beginning for the organization of its life and power. Boyar Suleshov[24] and the Cherkassky princes[25] belonged to the group of voivodes who remained largely in obscurity only because fame likes to feed on crime rather than on good deeds. To the list of governors—Soymonov,[26] Speransky,[27] Muravyov-Amursky,[28] Despot-Zenovich,[29] Chicherin[30]—we'll also add Prince Gagarin,[31] who rendered considerable services to Tobolsk and Siberia that were unfortunately canceled out later on by an ignominious death: he was executed for bribery and corruption. If you try to compare the previous reigning "nephews" who came to govern "Auntie's estate" to the present ones, you'll be forced to admit with chagrin that in the immoral times of old they took bribes only for themselves and couldn't carry much back to European Russia, especially since there was a rule requiring the inspection of a voivode's carts when he left Siberia. The present rulers, with a few exceptions, don't take anything for themselves but will spare nothing for others; the more they hand over for plundering and desecration, the higher they'll rise as they advance in their careers. In Siberia the secret bribe has turned into an open, wild squandering of natural resources that the thieving voivodes never dreamed of. Judge for yourselves whose morality is preferable.

But this is still far in the future. Let's return to the early days of Tobolsk, when it had just come into God's world. It came in a Cossack's homespun coat, but turned out to contain the bloodline of a capital, rising, as they say, from rags to riches. Not only did its title need to be in keeping with the royal seal; it also had to have the proper appearance for its status. By clambering up Holy Trinity Hill, Chulkov could not have chosen a more appropriate spot for Siberia's capital. But after perching there, Tobolsk fidgeted for a long time, turning round and round on that hill, unable to settle comfortably and majestically on it once and for all; during its first hundred years it was rebuilt six times entirely of wood before they began to use stone. Three of those times fires were a contributing cause. The log fort built by the first chief administrator lasted just seven years and did not seem secure to the voivodes, Merkury Shcherbatov and Mikhail Volkonsky; they tore it down and rebuilt it to suit themselves. Voivodes changed every two or three years in those days, and when Shcherbatov and Volkonsky departed, Tobolsk fell under a new axe once again; in 1606 it migrated to "the other hill" [*drugoi bugor*] to the extreme western end of the point. It was built out of logs for the last time in 1679 and stood for one whole year: then savage flames licked it away, along with its churches and five hundred houses. Only after that did they set about erecting the citadel in the form in which it has been partially preserved to the present day. Pavel, the metropolitan of Siberia,[32] went to the czar at that time, Fyodor Alekseevich,[33] with hat in hand, asking permission to build with stone, and permission was granted. Then they built the town not only more solidly and handsomely but also more quickly. Saint Sophia's Cathedral was completed in 1686, the Church of Our Lady [*Bogorodskaia tserkov'*] in 1690, Znamensky Monastery [*Znamenskii monastyr'*] in 1691, and Holy Trinity Church [*Troitskaia tserkov'*] the same year as the monastery; shortly afterward they enclosed St. Sophia's courtyard with a fence two sazhens [about thirteen feet] tall that contained six towers and a sacred gate and put up a two-story house for the metropolitan (which is no longer standing). And all this when, according to the czar's injunction, they had to look for workers in the immediate area and attract peasant farmers "without burdening them and without interfering with the cultivation of public lands." It's true that several experienced master metallurgists were sent from Moscow at Pavel's insistence, but that was all the skilled help they got. Everything else had to be sought on their own private lands: they had to find workers, train them, obtain materials and support, and indulge anyone who showed a flair for precision and beauty.

They began with a willing spirit, and it was precisely under Peter the Great that the buildings housing power and trade ensued. Government Hall [*Prikaznaia palata*] and Merchants' Square [*Gostinyi dvor*]—the latter a series of shops in the form of a fort with a tower in each corner—were built inside the citadel even before the reign of Prince Gagarin. But these already represent the creations and the era in fortress architecture of Semyon Remezov,[34] a local middle-level government servant better known for his "sketchbooks," on which we base our impressions of Siberia's distant past. The story of Remezov—historian, writer, architect, artist, and geographer—deserves separate treatment, but the mere recollection of this name makes us automatically heave a sigh over posterity's attitude toward our great ancestors, the pioneers and establishers of cities, arts, crafts, and trades. Remezov died a pauper, and his grave has been lost; Tobolsk, one of whose main thoroughfares bears the name Rosa Luxemburg—and as if that weren't

83
+++

enough, it also has a Rosa Luxemburg Lane—Tobolsk couldn't find a corner for Remezov until recent times. In Irkutsk, in Tobolsk, and in many other cities you can't track down any reference to their founders; the educators, reformers, and benefactors have been forgotten. All of Europe—Europe nothing! the whole world knows Philipp Strahlenberg,[35] the Swedish captain who was taken prisoner after Poltava and served his term of exile in Tobolsk, made a map of Siberia, and wrote a book about Russia after returning to his native land. And now imagine this: what if Remezov had ended up in Sweden, as good or bad luck would have it, and had brought back a map of that country like the one he drew of the whole of Siberia, down to the last parcel of land? Would anybody give him credit for this now, especially when the services he rendered his own fatherland have been buried under a thick layer of oblivion and lack of culture?! We want Tobolsk to remember and even mark with the material flourishes of commemoration the names of Captain Strahlenberg, and the Croat Juraj Križanić,[36] who labored over his Slavic union in that town, and the German Müller, the first author of Siberian history, and other famous outlanders, should they come to light, but above all not to lose one iota of the names and acts of its own great countrymen, whether a homegrown poet or architect, a home-grown Decembrist, or a coachman who compiled a chronicle.[37] Unfortunately, our own origins still serve not as a help but as a hindrance to our sense of pride.

But we've digressed. Tobolsk is not Moscow or Kiev or Novgorod, but so much in it is striking and memorable and so many names and events in its history remain hidden that tugging on a single thread is like walking down one street and ignoring all the side streets, knowing you must return to them whether you want to or not in order to assemble even bits and pieces of the general picture. The citadel was not built right away, when they built the Upper Town; neither the Lower Town nor the city's noble lineage, its capitalness, appeared in a flash; and its glory, notoriety, and eminence did not take root in a single decade or century or begin to fade afterward in one big shift of direction. For these reasons we won't be able to follow Tobolsk's chronology in a straight line no matter how hard we try. When Count Speransky sent the historian Slovtsov, who lived in Tobolsk, a gift of a watch and a Bible, he wrote, "Here you are, time and eternity." Distinguishing

Tobolsk's time from its eternity is not at all simple. To do this you would have to pronounce the verdict that despite the poverty and wretchedness of Tobolsk's present condition, all its eternity remains in the past.

Drawing from its eternity, whose existence no one can deny, we have fleetingly mentioned the Uglich Bell, the first and most unusual exile, which pointed the way toward what was not exactly Siberia's best function—to be the site of mass banishment and hard labor, which lasted more than three centuries and then kept on going. . . . Hundreds, thousands, even millions followed the mournful, crowded path of outcasts into the dark interior beyond the Urals, giving Siberia an everlasting bad name as a dismal land of forced labor incapable of offering either refuge or comfort. For a long time they all passed through Tobolsk or stayed in Tobolsk. If its memory is impartial, if it doesn't rely on the standard textbook line of recognition and nonrecognition, then the city must, in its own unspoken roster of the dead, say prayers for many, many great Russian martyrs.

Kiprian, the first archbishop of Tobolsk and Siberia, their first enlightener and keeper of memories, had not yet become the head of our diocese, even though it was established in 1620 under his direction. After the Time of Troubles and like no period before or since, the powers of church and state came together in a single house, the House of Romanov, which understood full well the significance of Siberia for Russia. Not by accident did Patriarch Filaret,[38] the father of the new dynasty's first czar, send to Tobolsk a close proxy entrusted with a crozier from himself and a gilded cross from the czar engraved with the words "Sibir, the reigning town" and remain attentive to it from then on. More than one hundred fifty years later Catherine the Great would present the eastern "reigning town" with an absolutely superb symbol of royal favor, her imperial throne, which she evidently sent after getting new furniture. But we haven't come to that period yet.

The very first gift was made by Boris Godunov.[39] Nowadays few people remember the imperial throne and the engraved cross for Kiprian's chest, but all Russians whose paternal consciousness has not died for good undoubtedly know about the Uglich Bell, which announced the murder of Czarevitch Dmitry and was dispatched to Tobolsk, with an "ear" ripped off, as punishment.[40] It arrived at the destination ordered by Godunov in 1593, while a great many citizens from Uglich, who had risen in revolt when they heard its peal, were dragged off, some with torn nostrils, some with severed tongues, to Pelym,[41] which was created soon after Tobolsk. We must assume that when Voivode Lobanov-Rostovsky[42] received the movable exile from Uglich, he was more than a little perplexed about what to do with it, but then decided that it could still celebrate church services even with its "ear" cut off and ordered it to be raised in the newly built Church of Our Savior [*tserkov' Spasa*]. Its fate after that, like the fate of many who ended up in Siberia against their will, remains dark and mysterious. During the nineteenth century, three hundred years after the death of Czarevitch Dmitry, the town of Uglich asked that the bell be sent back to its native soil for the anniversary celebration; after much arguing and haggling, the residents of Tobolsk returned it, but first they cast an exact replica as a keepsake and built a chapel for it in the citadel, where it hangs to this day. But consciously or unconsciously they'd forgotten a long-standing reference to one of the devastating fires in the seventeenth century in which the Uglich Bell melted completely. If this is true, then during the nineteenth century Uglich triumphantly turned out to meet a copy of the rebel, while Tobolsk kept a copy of a copy.

The authorities in European Russia broke an "ear" off the Uglich Bell, tore out the tongues of the Uglich citizens who colonized Pelym, and slit the nostrils of Fyodor Soymonov, comrade-in-arms of Peter the Great during his seafaring days and future governor of Tobolsk. And yet we still place the responsibility for morality on Siberia, where the most nimble, freedom-craving public, acknowledging neither God nor the Devil, flocked along with the Cossacks as well as followed in their wake and where hard-core undesirables with no urge to go there, treading on the heels of the aristocratic families who had destroyed one another during the sudden changes of power, were later driven from all over Russia.

Siberian morality greatly concerned the archbishop of Tobolsk as he tried to assert the true faith. Kiprian's last name was Starorusennikov; his native town was Staraya Russa, in the Novgorod area, which Fyodor Dostoyevsky later selected as the location for his work.[43] From time to time certain individuals found employment in Siberia, including pastoral employment, who were so impressive and biographic that sticking only to their brief Siberian period without taking a look at their prior life would mean saying too little about them or saying nothing at all. Once you've assigned Soymonov the role of governor of Siberia, just try not to pause in amazement at his fate—not a single Russian historian has omitted it—so capricious and amazing (and venerable) it was, having in addition that rare feature in those days, a happy ending. Another such outstanding figure was Archbishop Kiprian. He had committed a sin against Russia that lay on his conscience: during the Time of Troubles the Novgorod authorities, choosing the lesser of two evils to avoid swearing allegiance to Władisław IV,[44] had decided to invite Karl Filip, the son of the Swedish king,[45] to take the throne and had sent Archimandrite Kiprian to Sweden with the mission of bringing back a new Varangian. The Swedes did not decline the invitation but demanded that Novgorod the Great break away from Russia. The secret envoy could hardly have had the authority to decide the fate of Novgorod, which had been a free city at all times, but he objected to the very idea of tearing it away from Russia. The Swedes tortured him, demanding to know certain state secrets, starved him, and kept him unclad in the freezing cold, but they couldn't get anything out of him. When the Romanovs ascended the throne,[46] Kiprian was allowed to go home. He appeared before the czar and fell to his knees, asking forgiveness not for himself but for Novgorod; along with his city, he, too, received a pardon, recognition, and proximity to the ruling family.

And so before seven years had passed, he'd jumped out of the frying pan into the fire, from Sweden to Siberia. After Novgorod, where the rule of law had long been in force, Tobolsk seemed to Kiprian utterly corrupt. The Cossacks drank heavily, gambled (exiled Lithuanians had brought dice games with them), did not observe religious fasts, kept womenfolk in every place they were sent to serve, and bought and sold them like delicacies from the garden. Kiprian hadn't had time to look around and be horrified before he received a reprimand from Filaret: "It hath come to our knowledge . . ." What had come to the knowledge of His Holiness was that the Cossacks were wedding girls who showed no sign of the cross not only in their hearts but not even around their necks, disregarding the first principle of Christian norms. It was up to him to correct the accepted customs concerning morals, insofar as possible, with the strongest measures.

In addition to this, Kiprian entered the pages of Siberia as the founder of its written history, recorded in Russian. Almost forty years had gone by since Yermak's feat, the last of his comrades-in-arms were living out their final days in fortified towns around Siberia, and yet it had never occurred to anyone to write down their recollections and compile a list of the participants in the campaign. This was done through Kiprian's efforts in 1622. Thus the *Sinodik*, the roster of the Cossacks fallen in battle, came into being, and every year since then glory and memory have been rendered to Yermak and his fellow warriors, each individually, "with a cry" [*klikom*]. One hundred years ago a merchant from Kyakhta named Nemchinov bequeathed several thousand rubles to Saint Sophia's Cathedral in Tobolsk, with the interest on the endowment to be used for celebrating a requiem for Yermak twice a year for all time, never suspecting that "all time" would quickly come to an end.

Kiprian has remained in our memory as the insistent compiler of the *Sinodik*, and his attempts to correct Siberian behavior have been completely forgotten. Yet this was harder than questioning Cossacks. It was harder than conquering Siberia; this Siberia, if we can believe writers old and new, from the Frenchman abbé Chappe[47] in the eighteenth century to Anatoly Rybakov[48] in the twentieth, was actually never conquered at all. I must add, for my part, that if this is so, then Siberia extended its mighty arm to the whole country long ago, since moral standards in Moscow are not one whit better today but, according to our observations, are in fact worse there than in Yakutsk or Krasnoyarsk, unenlightened places in terms of the latest amusements, which make the sins of the Tobolsk Cossacks, though crude and in keeping with the spirit of their times, look like innocent fun. In this regard we can't help recalling that even during our lifetime not only the sons of Arbat Street were sent to Siberia during the 1930s, but the daughters of the Arbat were sent there as well, right up to the 1980s—the last time so as not to spoil the chaste spirit of the Olympic Games for foreign visitors.[49] And isn't it disgusting, after this, to read about the licentiousness the well-behaved children of the Arbat encountered in the lower reaches of the Angara among the descendants of Kuchum and Yer-mak?! As a native of those parts, I can attest that all kinds of sins may be ascribed to my fellow countrymen, including an ignorance leading to assertions that Pugachyov's rebellion[50] took place with the help of the Bolsheviks, but not those sins that Rybakov depicts with such rel-ish. Does he do this to butter up the reader who wants something of this sort and is conditioned to hunt for such things, or to take revenge on the sites of slave settlements, which are about as much to blame as a mare, breaking wind from pulling too hard, is to blame for the inhu-mane burden heaped upon it?

Here is a good place to cite one of Slovtsov's observations:

From time immemorial the residents of Russia proper have slandered him [the Siberian (Rasputin)] in diverse ways, even accusing him of using the art of black magic to evoke evil spirits, just as in our day shallow observers, with the exception of the prudent Lieutenant Wrangel[51] and his companions, call the reasonable, frugal, well-comported Siberian a boor, a loafer, and a profligate. While letting all three of these attributes pass without comment as applicable to the riffraff among the Russian deportees, we would not be able to listen to the same criticisms without indignation should someone take it into his head to ascribe them to the indigenous class of Siberians.

But we're not about to exaggerate Siberia's virtuousness either; let every land and every age be saddled with its own sins. "You're a fool!" is not logic but abuse. Archbishop Kiprian no doubt had good reason to be outraged and found plenty to correct in the local inhabitants. We don't know if he achieved any noticeable results during his three years in Siberia; the number of families worshiping different gods probably declined, while everything else simply disappeared out of sight into the darkness. But he did leave behind a strong, well-prepared, and stable cathedra that summoned the many-faced Siberian populace to the bosom of one faith and morality. In any case, one hundred years later the Russian Orthodox Synod had to compose an appeal to church members, above all to the women of Tobolsk, who couldn't bring themselves to start families with Swedish prisoners of war. The church leaders thought they simply couldn't make up their minds, but after the appeal it became clear that the women didn't want to—that's how they'd been raised. What was this—the cost of a Christian upbringing? Or ignorance again? Let's try to compare this with today's enlightened passion for taking up with foreigners of every stripe in order to escape across the paternal borders, and let's consider which is better.

And yet many scenes relating to daily life and to the handling of power now seem wild and strange and incomprehensible.

Johann Gmelin,[52] a naturalist who participated in the Saint Petersburg Academy of Science's Siberian expedition of 1733–43, describes one such custom in his book, which for some reason has never been translated in Russia from the German original (I have taken excerpts from Aleksandr Pypin's *A History of Russian Ethnography*).[53] According to this custom, which we somehow never happened to hear about before, the bodies of all those who passed away in Tobolsk from unnatural causes or without receiving last rites were apparently hauled to a shed outside of town and buried together once a year, on the Thursday before Trinity. Gmelin proved to be not only a serious scientist but also a serious observer of morals and manners; he was no abbé Chappe, who observed the eclipse of Venus in Tobolsk in 1761 and who, in relating his subsequent impressions of Siberia, mixed up and mocked everything on Russian soil. We have to believe Gmelin. He was the one who witnessed wild drunkenness in Irkutsk and Tobolsk, but for us this is certainly nothing new. "Such holidays truly do seem devoted more to the Devil than to God, and these spectacles set a very poor example for the numerous pagans in the region, since they see that supreme happiness for Siberians consists of drunkenness."

During the rule of Tobolsk's Governor Gagarin, a certain Yegor Laptev, who had intentionally started a fire, was discovered in Solikamsk (at that time the province of Siberia went beyond the western spurs of the Urals). In order to teach the arsonist a lesson once and for all, they buried him alive.

According to archival reports about punishments, perhaps the most persuasive measure was flogging with "a nautical cat-o'-nine-tails" ["*morskie koshki*"]. Single girls were flogged, and married women, and government servants, and tradesmen. The documents give no explanation as to what a "nautical cat-o'-nine-tails" was and why it had such an effect on the sensibilities of the residents of Tobolsk. For diversity's sake, it's true, they were also edified with cudgels and lashes and sticks.

Empress Elizabeth[54] abolished capital punishment, while Catherine the Great ordered that every instance of corporal punishment be reported to the province's central office—but who in Siberia would ever bother with a petty detail like that?!

In Tobolsk people were punished with floggings and horrendous fines for growing beards and wearing Russian dress (German dress was required) decades after Peter the Great.

In 1750, on instructions from the police chief at the central office, the bodies of two Old Believer women who had died on the way to Siberia and which, according to the rules back then, should have been simply committed to the earth without a Christian burial, were bound with ropes, dragged all over Tobolsk, and thrown into a ditch outside of town. After this, why should we be surprised at reports coming in from every corner of Siberia for more than one hundred years that Old Believers were committing mass self-immolation? "In 1679 up to 2,700 souls of both sexes, including children, came together from various places in Siberia at Beryozovka on the Tobol River and made a holocaust of themselves." In 1687 about 400 souls cremated themselves in a cathedral in Kamenka, near Tyumen; in 1722 an unknown but huge number did the same thing near the settlement of Karkinaya on the Ishim River; in 1724 some 145 souls set fire to themselves outside of Pyshma . . . and so forth. And so it went until the end of the eighteenth century, even cropping up here and there during the nineteenth.

The Schism was a great tragedy for the Russian people and constitutes a special subject in itself. Concerning the customs in Tobolsk that make you shudder today, you might have some excuse if they'd occurred in this form only in Siberia. But no, all of European Russia was surfeited with them; they were actually brought to Siberia from there.

Montesquieu wrote that you had to flog a Russian to bring him to his senses. We'll leave these words to the silent conscience of the French philosopher, especially since he didn't know Russia and based his opinions about it on hearsay; anyone who wishes to can also find countless examples of barbarism in Montesquieu's country during his lifetime. But can't we simply disregard this aspect of his comment? Isn't it better to look more closely at the great Frenchman's offensive remark and try to find some common sense in it? For practically all of Russia's history, with a few short exceptions, education was a third-rate affair, the laws were harsh and unjust, moral standards were distorted by the necessity for hidden opposition to the law, and the imperial suit of armor weighed down the common people, who constantly lived on the brink of physical and moral exhaustion. The sovereign governments, deposing and eliminating rather than continuing each other, undermined faith in the blessed sanctity of the body politic and forced individuals to build fortresses within themselves. Giving his neighbor the shirt off his back probably promoted morality, but when someone living in Russia noticed that the number of neighbors was growing larger and larger, that his impulses were taken as an obligation, and that meanwhile he still had only one shirt, he took it off without enthusiasm and squinted in disbelief as he listened to sacred commandments turned inside out. The conviction arose among educated people that Russia's very fate forced it to make sacrifices, but for what purpose they were unable to offer any coherent proof. "The Heavenly King in the guise of a slave"[55] blessing Russia long remained the country's symbol, its consolation and its hope, until representatives of the Enlightenment took that image away, too. And no one knows how long Russia has been standing with its legs wide apart, split between its own and foreign soil, now leaning on one leg, now on the other, rushing from extreme to extreme as if it doesn't suspect that it can actually stand on both legs, since it has grown two of them, as long as it doesn't forget meanwhile that the right leg is the supporting one, the one that bears all the weight. Otherwise the whole idea of a separate people and their national character is lost.

But now it's time to rise to the surface of modern-day Tobolsk, which just recently celebrated the 400th anniversary of its founding. It threw a gala celebration, observing all the usual rituals, inviting guests, the sons and daughters of whom it could be proud, rendering remembrance to the past and hallelujahs to the present. The city has grown and spread out, putting on weight in industry, in number of residents, which surpasses one hundred thousand, and in housing figures. The anniversary celebration followed the standard formula despite the fact that, although it's hard in an age of demographic explosion to avoid making a virtue of additional population, this is the same as some middle-aged guy bragging about his weight.

Even during its last celebration one hundred years ago Tobolsk had to dust off its official, full-dress uniform of a retired hero with extra care. The governorship had been taken away from Tobolsk in 1839 and transferred to Omsk, the main highway ran south of it—and the Siberian capital was shunted aside. But the Siberia of one hundred years ago did everything it could to keep Tobolsk from noticing its deprivation. Deputations arrived from Kyakhta, Irkutsk, Krasnoyarsk, Omsk, and Tomsk, all thriving towns then, with splendid gifts and sincere homage for the prime creator of Siberia. Throughout the entire vast land the press gave Siberia's glorious old town its due, and meetings and conferences were organized, collections taken up, books published, and streets named, all in its honor. The Siberia of one hundred years ago was far more integrated, compact, and kindred than it is now when, thanks to high speeds, distances have shrunk. Another illustration of this was the opening of Tomsk University, to which the entire region beyond the Urals responded with the magnanimity reserved for a general holiday or a general victory.

You can say that Siberia didn't even notice Tobolsk's recent celebration, just as it didn't notice the anniversary dates for Tyumen, Irkutsk, or Tomsk. It had no time, what with oil, coal, hydroelectric power plants, timber, metals . . . Siberia takes orders not from local administrations but from departments in Moscow where history, culture, and a sense of patriotism mean nothing when it comes to quotas. The 400th anniversary of Tobolsk turned out to be an event of no more than local significance. And in terms of local significance (and this is not the fate of Tobolsk alone) what a bad time all those Chulkovs, Poyarkovs,[56] Sukins, and other voivodes' administrators and boyars' sons[57] picked to undertake construction of their forts: local authorities were already up to their ears in work, but no, now they had to get sidetracked by trivia, by an anniversary celebration. They had to organize, orchestrate, ram everything through the bureaucracy . . .

This happens everywhere from the Urals to the Pacific: Siberia has no time for Siberia. It has no time for old Tobolsk, no time for the remains of Fort Kuznetsk, which has been squeezed so hard by indus-

trial Novokuznetsk[58] that tears ooze out of its rock, no time for
Yeniseysk, for Kyakhta, for Selenginsk, for the surviving groves, for
archaeological burial grounds, for what is precious and unique. And by
now the sole masters of our land hear the sounds of Siberia the way
they want to: *sebe beri, sebe beri, se'beri*[59]—take what you can, take what
you can, take it all. . . . Carry it out, haul it out, look alive before somebody else gets there first.

Immediately following a rush of pride over its newly restored
white-walled citadel, Tobolsk, still laid out in two parts, Upper Town
and Lower Town, must then have felt its heart sink the same thirty
sazhens [about 210 feet] as Holy Trinity Hill rises when it looked at its
Lower Town. With the destruction of the simple old drainage system, a
result of the unprecedented level of today's technical competence, the
groundwaters have risen, all summer the streets lie under a swamp
covered with green duckweed, the wooden houses are buried in mud
and beginning to rot, a fate that even the house of Pyotr Yershov,[60]
author of *The Little Humpbacked Horse*, has not escaped, and the smells
hovering over the area just below the wall make you ponder the origin
of the complicated word *aroma* [*blagovonie*: *blago* means good or
blessed; *-vonie* derives from *von'*, stench].

I was in Tobolsk in May, and the festivities were scheduled for
June. Then they had to be postponed. During that spring of 1987, the
Tura, Tobol, Irtysh, and Ob Rivers all kept splashing water out of their
banks and flooding their settlements and towns. Our bus left Tyumen
and set off down the Tobolsk Highway as though traveling along a strip
of embankment; floodwater stood all around, stretching far into the
distance on both sides, and kept rising higher and higher. In Tobolsk
sandbagging along the Irtysh was going on round the clock; on May 20
the water level surpassed eight and a half meters. Arkady Grigorievich
Yelfimov, the young chairman of the city's Executive Committee, who
had come to that post six months earlier from the construction industry, grabbed naps at odd moments, mobilized all suitable vehicles
belonging to local enterprises to help sandbag, and was constantly
dashing from the telephone to the riverbank to the sandpits, doing
everything possible to save the Lower Town. But a secret thought, contrary to the task at hand, must have occurred to him more than once:
To hell with this. Let everything be swept away once and for all, and

then, you see, they'll fork over some money for a natural disaster. Neglect had reached such a state (and no one pays attention to this warning mark) that it was probably easier and cheaper to build anew than to patch and repatch.

But they held back the water, saving the Lower Town from yet another inundation, and then, with the same haste in which the head of the city had walled off the old buildings to protect them from the Irtysh, he had to enclose them with new Potemkin fences so that their indecency would not disturb any anniversary gazes. Everything, literally everything, needs renovation and repair, but there was only enough money for fences, and now the next centennial celebration is rather a long way off.

Tobolsk has grown in recent times with the discovery of the Tyumen oilfields, the laying of a railroad, and the construction of a petrochemical conglomerate close by. The conglomerate put up blocks of new apartment buildings for its workers in the upper part of the city, which of course look just like all the other socialist subdivisions around the country, built a major road many kilometers long from its housing complex to its factory workshops and named it after Dmitry Mendeleev,[61] a native of Tobolsk, erected its own monument to him, seemingly taking the great scientist away from the old town, and now stands proudly and independently: See how wonderful I am! I have strength, power, youth, and money. You can't argue with me! But even the conglomerate is beginning to complain that the Ministry of Energy is putting pressure on it and not fulfilling its promises. Whoever neglects others deserves to be neglected, too. As they pump huge profits out of the Tyumen land, which includes Tobolsk, the oil and gas magnates won't earmark even the tiniest portion to help fill that land's empty cultural/historical stomach.

Even in colonies it is customary to give something back. . . . In what way is Siberia worse than a colony?!

This is a good place to recall once again the Siberians of old. After growing so rich from furs and gold, mining and commerce that their dear native land became too cramped for them and they'd moved their households to Petersburg or Moscow, they knew how to maintain their feelings of indebtedness and guilt regarding the place of their birth and enrichment. And every time support was needed to build the cultural and spiritual life of their homeland, to protect and encourage its arts, sciences, and crafts, they would pay so that Siberia would not remain "the northern land of midnight" [*"polunoshchnaia strana"*] forever, so that it would not simply send its best minds and hearts off to the spiritual energy field of Russian society but would be enlightened from within. Not all moneybags were that bright, but quite a few of them certainly were. Some contributed to picture galleries, libraries, and schools; others gave money for learned and technical societies.

And now let's compare them with the present-day emigrants from Siberia, with those all-powerful ministers who are indebted to our region for their education or elevation. All right, what benefaction does Siberia receive from them? They have no time to be benefactors. That's just icing on the cake. They seem bent on getting revenge for their origins, vying with each other to see who can take the most and give the least, whose industry will turn Siberia into a played-out slagheap the quickest. If only they were also forced to give a little something for the so-called social necessities—not for the good of Siberia but simply for the good of their departments, so that they would have some place to spend the night and something to amuse themselves with before getting back to pumping oil and gobbling up coal. If it were possible to operate even half the mines and derricks, the felling sites and conglomerates with robots, which could be propped up against a wall for the night without any fuss and would not be subject to occupational illnesses so that no one would have to build any apartments or facilities for preventive health care, then they wouldn't think twice about starting a profitable reconstruction of native Siberians. Even now Siberians get along with so little while giving so much that they aren't far from being robots already.

No, it is the Messrs. Sibiryakov, Lushnikov, Demidov, and Trapeznikov[62] who are to blame. They did a poor job of enlightening Siberia, weren't sufficiently patriotic, made too little progress, and here is the result: decades later Siberia's present-day bigwigs have no concern for it; all they care about is timber, oil, and coal. Of course the comrade ministers and the ministers above them can counter that the Messrs. Sibiryakov had their own private pockets to dip into, whereas their pockets belong to the nation as a whole and parentage and friendship mustn't enter in. But here even political logic, along with patriotic feeling, breaks down. So, then, Siberia is no longer part of the nation? Why are you acting on behalf of the nation when you climb into its granary but on your own when it comes to making payments? Where and who is a fair mediator between taking and replacing? What nation has one?

It's certainly true that the Messrs. Sibiryakov didn't make much progress, that they didn't succeed in enlightening Siberians.

At the risk of taking the reader a very long way from Tobolsk, I nonetheless want to bring up Sundsvall, an industrial town in the north of Sweden. Not for the sake of comparing it to Siberia's industrial towns; these are birds of a different feather that don't lend themselves to comparison. Looking for similarities between Sundsvall and, say, Bratsk on the grounds that both are blue-collar towns is like looking for similarities between a lump of anthracite and a nugget of gold; they have nothing in common except that both started out as rocks. All you'll find is differences.

Sundsvall has three cellulose conglomerates, a woodworking factory, a machine factory (which, incidentally, supplies the equipment for Bratsk's timber-industry complex), an aluminum plant, and a chemical plant. The population stands at one hundred thousand. Neither the conglomerates nor the factories are visible. They feed the town but don't wield power there the way such enterprises do in Russia and don't proudly put their buildings and smokestacks on display. Sundsvall was a successful trading center in the old days and liked to adorn itself though architecture; today's modernity in the town's construction is amazingly respectful and formal regarding the distant past, just as the attitude toward the elderly in that nation is generally elevated to the rank of a national virtue. Old folks are given so many privileges and are surrounded in society by an atmosphere of such favored treatment that young people seriously dream of retirement. Something similar, I believe, occurs in municipal architecture as well: until a new building stops being new, no matter how it is executed or what feelings it evokes it goes through something like a test period that might end only when it is repaired for the first time.

I traveled around Sweden with a journalist and translator named Malcolm Dixelius, a longtime acquaintance of mine who worked in

Moscow for several years and who has been to Siberia more than once. Sundsvall is his hometown; his parents live there. For that reason, when we were still in Stockholm planning our itinerary, we drew the first line along the eastern seaboard to Sundsvall. And as soon as we got there, Malcolm, knowing my keenest interests, took me straight to the rows of warehouses in the old trading district that were being converted into a cultural center. We spent about three hours there talking with artists and restorers; I also met one of the leaders of the municipal government and one of the local residents interested in those labors. At that time a children's library had already moved in and final preparations for a display depicting the town's history were under way. I asked questions, they explained everything in detail, and I became more and more convinced that the whole town was preoccupied with the fate of those warehouses.

Then we walked around them; there was nothing special about the way they had looked in their former official capacity. They were just like any other warehouses standing close to a pier, with the difference, of course, that they didn't resemble Russian ones: they didn't leak or have gigantic padlocks on the gates. They had been built in such a way that they didn't spoil the view of the town from either land or sea, and yet they weren't built to be museums either. And when they began to stand empty and became dilapidated, the same fate awaited them as awaits warehouses everywhere. Or rather, the same fate should have awaited them. But the distant past has a completely different meaning for the Swedes than it does for us; they don't attach any educational or historical significance to it in order to use it as proof for convincing someone of something. For them the distant past is their ancestors' world, no part of which is subject to judgment without dire need. The citizens of Sundsvall are proudest not of the cellulose conglomerate or of the chemical plant but of a twelfth-century relic located in a church on their Alnön Island: a wooden chalice that served as a baptismal font. If the conglomerate burned down, it would be a disaster for those townspeople who would lose their jobs, but if the sacred object from Alnön Island should suffer any damage, that would be a tragedy for everyone. After the font was shipped to Paris for an exhibit and cracks appeared in it, I was told without irony that cracks appeared in the heart of every Sundsvall resident as well.

In deciding the fate of its commercial warehouses, the town was not stingy and chose the most expensive design for their restoration, in which the warehouses would all be linked by a glass gallery and become a single renovated building. In addition to the children's library and the display on town history that I've already mentioned, it would house a picture gallery, a display on wildlife conservation, a reading room, and several cultural organizations. By now, of course, all these have moved into their new quarters, joined together to form a single center, and are open to the public, and the expenditure of one hundred million kronor is a thing of the past. I must point out that the government paid for part of it, the town paid a share, and part of the money came from private donations.

After viewing the warehouses, Malcolm Dixelius and I went to have lunch, discussing as we sat at the table the role of culture in the fate of peoples and individuals. The reader needn't worry: I won't go so far as to describe the menu. I refer to this lunch only because after it we had to change our plans quickly. What Dixelius asked me held no great significance for him, and I am grateful to the impulse that made him inquire:

"Do you know anything about Captain Strahlenberg?"

"You don't mean my 'fellow countryman,' who was taken prisoner after Poltava and spent his time in captivity in Siberia, in Tobolsk?"

Malcolm began to laugh.

"But he's my fellow countryman, too. Thanks to Strahlenberg and his comrades in misfortune, you and I are closer than we supposed. Did you know that this captain's map of Siberia is located here, in our town?"

As on those occasions when you involuntarily cry "ouch," the words simply burst out of me from surprise:

"That can't be!"

Malcolm left for a moment and went to a telephone. Two minutes later he announced:

"They're waiting for us. I won't presume to pass judgment on Siberia, but the map of Siberia is intact."

"What about his book?"

"Preserving the book was probably easier because it came out in more than one copy. The map drawn by Strahlenberg's own hand, though, is of great value. But Strahlenberg seems to have made it into the encyclopedias of world knowledge not for his map and not for his book but because he discovered some ancient rock paintings somewhere in your country."

"The Tomsk Hieroglyphs [*Tomskie pisanitsy*] on the Tom River, not far from present-day Kemerovo."

"Have they been preserved?"

"Yes. But I don't know what condition they're in. I've never seen them. I've heard they're planning to set up a nature preserve there."

We drove outside the city limits and passed on our right one of the cellulose conglomerates that looks no worse architecturally than the new music hall in Irkutsk. There we turned left, then turned once more and found ourselves on a low hill in front of an ancient castle. No less surprising than the news about Strahlenberg's map being in Sundsvall was its location: in the archives of Merlo, which belongs to the cellulose conglomerate's joint-stock company, SCA. How extraordinary for cellulose manufacturers! I was beginning to understand that country less and less all the time. In Russia we would have lost no time repulpifying it, as a class enemy, into a few grams of cellulose for the tire industry.

A likable, rather short man of middle age came outside to meet us—he turned out to be the archivist. Archivist? Why, certainly: if you have archives, you've also got to have an archivist. Jan Öström, as he was called, led us into a conference room, where the map hung on a wall. He took it down and carefully spread it out on the huge table. We bent over it together, trying to find Tobolsk, Irkutsk, the Tom River, the Lena River, and Lake Baikal. I examined the half-familiar naive contours with the same feeling with which we might peer into the living faces of direct ancestors who preceded us by almost two centuries. According to that map, Siberia was still a mysterious, fairy-tale land, vast and unmeasured. How I wished I could have been there then!

"Do people in Siberia remember Captain Strahlenberg?" The archivist must have had to ask his question more than once, for I didn't hear him.

"Yes, they do. But he's better known in our country by the name Tabbert because he became Strahlenberg only later, after returning to his homeland."

"Yes. He took the name of his native town. Do you want to look around the archives?"

I did. But as I moved from exhibit to exhibit, from the Bible of King Charles XII to ancient manuscripts, from sacred object to sacred object, I experienced a kind of depression and shame: now here are technocrats for you! And by then I was not surprised when they told me that several years ago the aluminum factory in Sundsvall decided to expand its plant, but the city demanded guarantees that the expansion would not bring any additional pollution along with it. The company couldn't make such guarantees and gave up the idea of reconstruction. It, too, probably has its own archives containing items of cultural value.

You can't help agreeing with the great thinkers: a country's attitude toward culture can make any nation fall just as far as it can help it rise.

And now I'm standing on Chukman Point, to which the Cossacks' legs automatically carried them during the very first hours of Tobolsk's existence without knowing that this is actually the choicest spot for a look around and that it offers "the best view" of Western Siberia. I put "the best view" in quotation marks only because it was noticed long ago but now seems to have received the stamp of approval from the guidebooks and handbooks, which rank it as a local attraction. The view actually is as far-reaching and wide, as all-encircling and free as if the generous bend in the Irtysh had been put down below to make you fly. For what is it when you are carried farther and farther away without interference, with joy and wonder, if not flight? And as the Irtysh winds in a sweeping, overflowing arc, coming out around Podchuvashi[63] and dropping behind Holy Trinity Point, it, too, resembles flight—uninterrupted, mighty, and imperiously calm—into the deep verdure of the sky. What else can you take this boundlessness for if not the sky?!

And I climbed to the top of Chukman Point and Panin Hill several more times to feast my eyes on Western Siberia, and the Lower Town, and the citadel on the right, and Summit Road [*Vershina*] on the left, a street lined with medieval wooden houses, almost all of them still intact, that lies in the ravine alongside Kurdyumka Creek, which flows down into the city. Summit Road also looks like a boom amid the clouds in the sky, ornamented with wisps of melted cloud in imitation of regenesis. Only here could the question have arisen that residents of Tobolsk are fond of asking, What do we have more of, water, greenery, or wood? And the answer: sky.

After gaining victory over Kuchum at nearby Podchuvashi, Yermak could not have failed to climb Chukman Point. He must have climbed it, for how could he have refrained from taking a look from an elevated spot to see what kind of country would unfold before him, where it would lead, how it would feel to the eye? One hundred fifty years ago a plain, austere marble obelisk enclosed by a heavy chain was erected on that site in honor of Yermak, with a short, addresslike inscription on its base: "To Yermak, the conqueror of Siberia." Beyond it, at the heart of a knoll, a park dedicated to the conqueror of Siberia was also laid out in the nineteenth century; now it is pretty much neglected, colonized by conquerors of weeds.

But on the right, on the right, across steep Nikolsky Road, stands the citadel with Saint Sophia's Cathedral, whose five domes together with the belfry look like teats gathering in heavenly food. Whether seen from the side or from below, the whole ensemble of Saint Sophia's courtyard, with the renovated towers and wall, the archbishop's house and Merchants' Square, the churches and bell tower, is nothing less than a magical vision, a happy sigh and a human thank-you for the sun and the earth. Human—and yet you have to make a real effort to believe that all this was built and restored by human hands and not sent down from heaven. We habitually say "fixed in legend," "set in stone," "frozen in the past". . . . But how this frozenness shines, breathes, and lives, how magically and how much doth it declaim! Siberia was carved out daringly, freely, and beautifully not for lodging travelers but for time everlasting, not for a guest-worker way of life but as a heavenly kingdom on earth. . . . This is the spot where its fate was revealed, and the Tobolsk citadel enjoined Siberia's fate to be lofty and bring glory.

Down below lie the lacework and sprawl of the old part of town. Filled with sluice gates and precipices, knots and holes, it has burned down many times, floated a great deal, and turned dark over the years. The high waters of the Irtysh lie rearward, Kurdyumka Creek runs near the hill in front of it, and flashes of water gleam here and there in the middle of the streets as if the whole town were afloat from one end to the other, like goods and chattels loaded on rafts and waiting to set sail. Among the dark, old wooden residential buildings are splendid merchants' mansions, schools, and offices, all built of stone, and the commanding presence of those churches that have managed to hold out. And if you peer closely, you see that, why, no, it's not floating, it's standing on the ground—cars are scurrying around down there, people are walking about—but it has been abandoned and resettled just recently and the residents haven't had time to deal with the destruction, drain off the water, reestablish life. And axes are banging away as they build new fences—people are settling in again, recalling where things used to be, putting the picture back together. After all, this is the most "picturesque" town in Siberia!

Half of Tobolsk is located there, half its history, half its life.

You can walk down Nikolsky Road to the lower historic district and leisurely stroll through the days of old. Everything there belongs to the distant past; objects of recent vintage look like little patches on the common canvas, and there aren't many of them. You can still find the section where the free peasants and foreigners exempt from state obligations used to live [*sloboda*], with its special spirit, its own style, its own laws. At one time Tatars, Poles, Germans, Lithuanians, and Swedes all lived there in separate communities, trades and handicrafts developed among them, and commerce descended from the citadel to that part of town. I am not the first to note that they probably couldn't have settled in a worse spot—a muddy swamp flooded regularly by the Irtysh—but this shows you the nature of those who lived in Russia: the impossible was actually possible. Whether for beauty's sake, or out of rivalry, out of defiance or homage, how could they have helped nestling up against Holy Trinity Point?! They must have suffered from their own stubbornness, from fire, from the damp, yet they grew ever more firmly embedded there and loved the Lower Town for its martyrdom, for the freeness of its origins and life, and for its democratic character. When you view the citadel from below, beauty is gathered together in a supreme orderly principle, a single whole, but when you look at the historic district from above, beauty spreads warmly throughout its streets and courtyards, finding more and more places to receive new bows. If the Upper

Town is the crown of the tree, the Lower Town is its roots. They are like two sides of the same coin. Neither can exist without the other. And rust on one side will eat through the other side, too.

In comparison with Russia proper, Siberia is not as rich in great names who hail from there. In the old days people used to say "those who have left" [*"vyshedshie"*]. They left to go to the capital cities and become famous in their endeavors there. What can you do?! Siberia has no choice but to be proud of exiled schismatics, anarchists, Decembrists, Poles, and only then of its own great figures. Thus Tobolsk contains the graves of several Decembrists, including Aleksandr Muravyov and Ferdinand Volf, who moved there in 1845 after serving their sentences near Irkutsk, Wilhelm Küchelbecker (Pushkin's friend Kyukhlya), Aleksandr Baryatinsky, Stepan Semyonov, Flegont Bashmakov, and Semyon Krasnokutsky. Mikhail Fonvizin's house is still standing. Only one of the Decembrists was a Siberian by birth rather than by exile. He was Gavriil Batenkov, from Tobolsk. Vasily Perov,[64] the artist, was also born in this town. And poet Pyotr Yershov, author of *The Little Humpbacked Horse*, and historian Pyotr Slovtsov, who both came from Tobolsk, actually remained there; to them we must add the mightily talented Semyon Remezov, who did the same thing even earlier. Just imagine what Tobolsk would have been like without those sons who didn't desert it either in their glory or in their vale of tears. How much would Siberia have lost if Grigory Potanin,[65] also a native of Tobolsk, Nikolay Yadrintsev, archaeologist Aleksey Okladnikov,[66] our contemporary, and others had left?

In the Lower Town, right in front of the citadel, stands a long, squat, two-story building whose fame is very likely unrivaled in all of Siberia. Now it houses a health clinic, but it was built in the eighteenth century by the Kornilievs, a family of merchants. It was sold later on, following a fire in the governor-general's palace inside the citadel, and then served as the residence of the governor-general, who at that time was Aleksandr Alyabiev, father of the composer.[67] The future great composer was actually born in that house. It was remodeled at the beginning of the nineteenth century and became the province's main secondary school, where Batenkov studied and where Ivan Mendeleev, father of the great chemist, was the principal. During Mendeleev's tenure as principal, one of his pupils was Yershov, who himself subsequently became principal and under whom, in his turn, the fourteenth child in the Mendeleev family studied the basic sciences and went on to devise the periodic table of the elements. Everything in Tobolsk, a small town, was closely interwoven among the well-known families. Dmitry Mendeleev's mother came from the Korniliev clan, the same ones who built the house that became the school and who started a publishing business in it, issuing the first literary journal in Siberia under the title *The Irtysh Turning into the Hippocrene.*[68] Slovtsov, it's true, held an unflattering opinion of it:

A periodical work called *The Irtysh Turning into the Hippocrene* was published in 1790 and 1791. But didn't the Hippocrene actually turn into the Irtysh? Instead of concerning themselves with reporting the current news in Siberia, or presenting excerpts from local history, or describing trade, agriculture, and economic life in general, the publishers started out by aping philology and banal poetry.

Tobolsk was held strictly accountable for its art from the very beginning. In the museum of a local theater you'll find this passage, taken from a chronicle:

During the spectacle of a comedy presented in Tobolsk on May 8, 1705, the Feast Day of Saint John the Apostle, a cruel storm in the form of a thundercloud aroseth and smashed the whole top of a cathedral from the altar upward, including its dome and cross. As a sign of the Lord God Almighty's wrath at the creators of comedic spectacles, at that very hour the hills on Marketplace Road slid nearly three sazhens [roughly nineteen feet] down a smooth place.

The "comedic spectacles" ["*igrishcha komedianskie*"] were still going strong more than two centuries later. In the era of the playbill we read:

Sunday, 7 February 1926. The first production of the sensational hit of the season will take place. Exclusive subject matter. Since the play depicts certain residents of Tobolsk as well as historical events from the time when the former czar and his family were here, this production holds exceptional interest for Tobolsk. *The End of the Romanovs* [*Konets Romanovykh*]. A drama in five acts. Written by M. Volokhov and P. Arsky.

After this event several churches saw their crosses and domes topple during "a cruel storm"; half of them stand decapitated even today.

Concerning exclusive subject matter, worshipers of the sensational are currently drawn to it again just as in the 1920s.

Now that we find ourselves near the theater, we must say a word or two about the building itself. Vivid, joyous beauty always arouses either admiration or irritation. In Tobolsk, and above all in the Lower Town, there are a good many festive buildings in baroque style, in Siberian baroque, and even, as specialists call it, in local baroque that exhibit an unexpected play and theatricality of form. If living quarters and churches were carefully embellished in a theatrical manner, then the theater in Tobolsk had to have been singular, unlike its counterparts anywhere in the world. When it was still under construction people wrote that a poor provincial town (which Tobolsk was at the end of the nineteenth century) had no business acquiring a tower like that. And it actually is a tower. A wooden one. And not just one but several, all running into each other, grabbing each other, and joining together to form a common tower city with hip roofs like crowns over the main building and the additions; it is capped with turrets and spires, decorated with gingerbread trim, and holds up its entrance with patterned columns. Nothing in Siberia springs immediately to mind that could hold a candle to such elegance, such imagination, such showing off. Perhaps the wooden patterning in Tomsk, but there the design is richer, in keeping with the city; it flaunted itself during the town's heyday, when Tomsk was vying with Irkutsk for capital status in Siberia. Tobolsk had been completely shunted aside by then. But Tobolsk wouldn't be Tobolsk if even in poverty it didn't remind everyone of its existence with a grand and beautiful gesture. And despite all that is said about Tobolsk's theater—that it is garish, overloaded with detail, and creates a carnival atmosphere, that its contours contain nothing of value—let's remember that it wasn't built in the sixteenth century and it wasn't built to be a university. We ought to thank the theater for remembering and replicating the most distant past, for adorning itself in imitation of the fairy-tale days of old, and for displaying the Russian spirit as vividly, lavishly, lightly, and intricately as a Bilibin[69] illustration. After one look at it, your soul straightens up freely and a smile surfaces. Theater begins with the theater building, with the walls that welcome the audience.

This was one of the last distinctive strokes added to the architectural visage of the town. Apparently all that appeared after the theater was the mansion of the Kornilovs, a merchant family, near Marketplace Square [*Bazarnaia ploshchad'*]—it, too, did not lack a pretentiousness that the capital cities, still alive and functioning, would have been considered outdated. Then began a physical rather than a moral aging, a using up and dying out of what had been gained. That's why the theater has needed repair for a great many years and can't wait any longer. Architecture, as happened everywhere, began to draw everything in square meters, the Remezovs and Cherepanovs (the Cherepanovs were Tobolsk architects, builders, and chroniclers descended from a family of coachmen) disappeared, high-ranking civil servants without any sense, let alone Russia, in their heads proliferated, the need for master craftsmen dropped off, and the new style of life demanded the substitution of political agitation for spirituality and craft for art. While constantly talking about the fine future, no one laid a single stone for the foundation of that future or even kept pace with the present; out of the poverty and the wealth, the scarcity and the grandeur, which they jumbled together, they extracted a gruel that maintains nothing but the belly . . .

As Tobolsk was finishing up the re-creation of its citadel, restoring it to its former appearance, the city seemed to be at a loss: What next? The work is endless, the entire Lower Town is crying for attention, but the workshops that specialize in restoration have little clout and master craftsmen are in short supply; they might as well be donating their labor for what they get paid. If the residents of Tobolsk knock on other doors, they find the same thing everywhere; if they knock on their own doors, everyone is busy with food-and-warmth concerns and has no time for history, no time for the distant past. Life has long since taken on a conveyor-belt quality with ever accelerating speed, and whatever you don't manage to throw onto the conveyor belt today you won't be able to get anywhere tomorrow. This blind, gluttonous line is racing past old Tobolsk, racing who knows where, demandingly urging everything onward, and it is constructed so cunningly that you can only pile things onto it without daring to take anything off. It is still possible between sprints to show sympathy for the historic town as it perishes, but no one has the time to help it, or the money, or the energy. Later, later. . . . This refrain has started to sound like rock music.

I'd heard about Tobolsk's Good Will [*Dobraia volia*] before; unlike the vast majority of the informal organizations that have filled public life in recent years, it appeared even before perestroika. It appeared and, despite the suspicions it aroused, for patriotic movements always breed suspicion (we are more accustomed to accepting group violence than group potential or group aid, which is instantly transformed into aiding and abetting and to which everything under the sun is tacked on), despite the mistrust and the outcries, it did not disappear. In such cases there has to be a leader, someone in charge. Since our intelligentsia would much rather lead discussions than act, the leader turned out to be Lyudmila Nikolaevna Zakharova, an engineer who had moved from Omsk to Tobolsk more than ten years earlier to help build the petrochemical conglomerate. Coming from Omsk gave her decisiveness and initiative; Omsk residents had treated their antiquity like a vestige of the accursed past and had destroyed it, but in Tobolsk Lyudmila Nikolaevna found a town that seemed like something out of another world whose existence she'd never even suspected. She'd fallen in love with it and sensed how amenable it was to the soul, how protective of paternal faith, how much its walls and streets had to say. In time she'd taken a closer look and seen that not only demolition and theft but also apathy, negligence, incidentalness, and the habit of making do spiritually with the bare minimum were destroying Tobolsk to no less an extent than they'd destroyed Omsk, only at a slower pace. Something had to be done. To test public response, Zakharova put an ad in the newspaper asking the citizens of Tobolsk to meet at a certain time and place for the first *subbotnik*[70] devoted to restoring the distant past. And they came. If government authorities had made a similar appeal, people would most likely have been suspicious, accustomed as they are to distrusting the powers that be in anything that goes beyond the here and now, but this was an appeal practically from themselves, from a sincere and inexperienced heart. It turned out that they, too, were heartsick for the same reason, that they, too, suffered because of the neglect of historic structures and the sluggish playing around with restoration. Schoolchildren came, and college students (Tobolsk has a

teachers' training college which, oddly enough, bears the name of Dmitry Mendeleev and not Clara Zetkind[71]), workers came and bone carvers,[72] grandmothers with grandchildren, and employees of the regional museum and the House of Pioneers.[73] First they became "parishioners" of the Church of the Archangel Michael [*tserkov' Mikhaila Arkhangela*], using picks and crowbars to chip away the dirt that had accumulated inside and turned rock-hard over the decades in order to make an exhibition hall once it was restored. Then they went on to rescue Yershov's house, creating a museum named after him, and then Fonvizin's, transforming it into a museum on political exile. They compiled a register of historic wooden buildings and got to work on a vacant lot piled high with construction debris, where they put in a park. And after work came the samovar. Now that Good Will has demonstrated the trueness of its name, it has been given one of the square towers in the citadel to use temporarily and also to repair. Sitting around the samovar, they read aloud and discuss the city's past, sing songs, and meet with tourists visiting Tobolsk.

Of course compared with what Tobolsk requires today—and it requires major financial allocations rather than crumbs, a significant increase in the capacities of the restoration workshops, and municipal and regional leaders more highly qualified in their attitude toward the historic town—compared with all this, the "manual" contribution [*"ruchnoi" vklad*], let's call it, of Good Will is not as great as we would like it to be when placed alongside mechanized production, but even this tiny bit brings enormous benefit. Its main benefit lies in showing how things ought to be done. We shouldn't wait around for some do-gooder to come along and deign to notice that next to the oil lies the ancient town that years ago turned this land toward Russia; rather, we should act and educate by example so that such people can't help appearing.

We seem to have no other option.

Lower Tobolsk looks prosperous only around Marketplace Square. The commercial and administrative centers moved down there back in the nineteenth century, and now it contains a wide network of streets, splendid mansions, and asphalt; the department store in the shopping arcade generates a lot of bustle and noise; and Saint Zachary's Church [*Zakhar'evskaia tserkov'*], a model of local baroque, is encased in restorers' scaffolding. Not far away stands the governor's house, where the czar's family was held under arrest after the Revolution, with a military parade ground beside it. Opposite is the palace of the Kornilovs that I mentioned earlier, which was built shortly before the Revolution. Today the Communist party's district and executive committees are located in the governor's house, the Kornilovs' residence contains a bank, and the Church of the Annunciation [*Blagoveshchenskaia tserkov'*], in which the emperor prayed, was demolished back in the 1950s so as not to remind anyone of the superfluous. "Russia can't be grasped by reason . . ."[74] To be assured of this once more, all you have to do is take a leisurely stroll down the Street of Peace [*ulitsa Mira*], where named and unnamed buildings are present and absent and have extended their architectural styles—classical, baroque, eclectic, and primitive—to contemporary society.

From Marketplace Square you can climb 198 wooden steps up Saint Sophia's Street, which at various times was called Pryamskoy Street,[75] Trade Street [*Torgovyi vzvoz*], and Market Street [*Bazarnyi vzvoz*], looking back at the Lower Town as you go, to the arch of Dmitry's Gate [*Dmitrievskie vorota*], where one of the citadel buildings, the Rentereya [*Rentereia*] or Swedish Hall [*Shvedskaia palata*], stretches out across its top. Why Swedish? Because it was built according to Semyon Reme-zov's blueprint by Swedish prisoners of war. Beyond the gate you are immediately transported to a different world where there is not one whiff of Siberia, like some place you might find in medieval Europe. The gate's steep-walled stone passageway, deep as a canyon, seems designed to lead only to a dungeon. Even nowadays legends continue to circulate about the underground passages leading from the gover-nor-general's palace that were later made habitable by bandits, but the tunnel from Saint Sophia's Street takes you to the open expanse and light of Holy Trinity Hill; you come out facing the citadel's western wall, next to Saint Sophia's Cathedral. The first thing you see on the old masonry is a mosaic portrait of Semyon Remezov, the Siberian archi-tect, designer and builder of the citadel, chronicler, cartographer, artist, and poet, which was executed in our time, when memory began to return.

What is enclosed by the walls and now called the citadel is really only half the citadel: Saint Sophia's courtyard with Merchants' Square added on. The other half, the administrative center, was located in Lit-tle Town [*Malyi gorod*], on the western extremity of Holy Trinity Hill. The two halves were joined by the solemn transition of the Rentereya, which was designed as a repository for public funds. But by all accounts the Rentereya served in this capacity for only a very short time. Aleksandr Radishchev, who was detained in Tobolsk for six months on his way to exile in Ilimsk,[76] discovered that the Rentereya had already become a depository for archives, where he became engrossed in reading about Siberia's history, later composing "A Description of the Region Ruled by the Governor-General of Tobolsk" and "A Description of Trade with China."[77]

The Rentereya stretched out across the top of steep Saint Sophia's Street even during the time of Governor Gagarin. Before that Remezov, who held the post of the stone citadel's chief builder, had erected Government Hall in Little Town, along with Merchants' Square. Merchants' Square is currently being restored, while Government Hall became part of the governor-general's palace back in the eighteenth century.

Tobolsk attained its greatest power in the eighteenth century, beginning with the division of the Russian territories into provinces. The Tobolsk, or Siberian, Province alone encompassed as much as the other four put together, stretching from the Great Novgorod to the Great Ocean and including the Vyatka, Perm, and Orenburg lands, as if by going all the way to the ocean and spreading out it had begun to extend its authority beyond the Urals. That "as if," as far as we can surmise, would have serious consequences later on.

The first man to be appointed governor of Siberia was Prince Matvey Gagarin, who had served as a *stol'nik* in his youth under Peter the Great and then become voivode of Nerchinsk, a judge in the Siberian administrative office, and commandant of Moscow. At that time Petersburg was still under construction[78] and, like the Baikal-Amur Main Line[79] in our day, it was built by the entire country; building with stone was prohibited everywhere else, for Petersburg didn't have enough master craftsmen. Only Gagarin, thanks to his closeness to the emperor, managed to get an exemption for Tobolsk. Construction of the citadel was completed during his rule. It wasn't completed according to Remezov's plan—according to his design, Tobolsk's citadel would not have lagged far behind Moscow's Kremlin—but it did attain the result that we perceive as a finished architectural ensemble. Under Gagarin trade expanded, crafts developed, reports came in from all over about the discovery of ores, of silver and gold, new islands were discovered in the Arctic Ocean in the Far North, and the subjects of Dzungaria asked to be taken under Siberia's wing. It was nothing for Gagarin, using the manual labor of the captive Swedes, to simply divert the course of the Tobol River two versts [about one and one-third miles] to one side to prevent it from washing away the hill where the citadel stood. Tobolsk minted its own Siberian coins. Siberia was resembling less and less the little-known country that others still considered it even on the eve of the new century.

The sudden retribution of Peter the Great and the ignominious death of Prince Gagarin remain fraught with mystery to this day. We can only speculate about what aroused the awful wrath of the sovereign. "Bribery and corruption" ["*za likhoimstvo*"] are probably far from being the only causes. Yes, Matvey Petrovich loved luxury and splendor; when taking up his new post, he'd sailed from Verkhoturye to Tobolsk in a vessel trimmed with red cloth. Rumors more tenacious than the actual evidence—and they cast a spell to this day—asserted that when the prince went out, his horses clattered down the roadway in silver horseshoes and the rims of his carriage wheels were also studded with silver. But he himself liked to give lavish gifts. He would hand out several thousand rubles in aid to the Swedes, then send gold receptacles to the Kievo-Pecherskaya Monastery, then present the Tobolsk Cathedral with a priceless miter "decorated with a gold cross containing diamond chips and adorned with 40 golden engraved pieces of enamel and 778 precious stones, including 8 emeralds, 532 diamond chips, 31 large rubies, and 3,131 pearls." Peter imposed severe penalties for bribery and corruption and was also quick to punish, but surely not to the extent of ordering the body of the celebrated governor of Siberia, who was hanged before the College of Justice, to be left on the gallows until the rope rotted. And when the rope rotted, rumor again has it, they picked up the corpse and hung it on a chain. This was something above and beyond punishment; this required guilt for something more than cupidity. Having no proof, historians imply that during the inquest "the tongues of ingratitude, backbiting, and spite were loosened in Siberia . . . and some asserted that Gagarin was plotting to break away from Russia" (Slovtsov).

Isn't this precisely where we should seek the solution to the riddle of Peter's retribution? Gagarin would hardly have "plotted" anything, but the great lord and governor could certainly have barked in his usual stentorian voice in the presence of a tale-bearer who happened to turn up at the right time, "We are a nation unto ourselves!" He might also have repeated these words when displeased with some new command. And this would have proved sufficient to be sentenced for a substitute crime, while the true charges remained hidden. Is it pure coincidence that shortly after Gagarin was recalled to Petersburg Siberia was divided into provinces, and that during the reign of Elizabeth and the provincial governors secret commissions were set up? Russia could no longer even contemplate life without Siberia, Siberia had made the government dependent on easy income, and its generosity contributed greatly to our general negligence.

Let's try to think of something more pleasant and instructive about Siberia's governors than bribery and corruption. Let's recall Fyodor Ivanovich Soymonov, who took up the governorship forty years after Gagarin. He, too, had been a favorite of Peter the Great, who'd saved his life when he was young. During the era of Biron,[80] Soymonov had been tried on false charges, his nostrils had been slit, and he'd been sent to Siberia to serve a life sentence of hard labor. For altogether too long Rus had been in the habit of making those elevated under one ruler into criminals under the next. Soymonov was pardoned when power changed hands; he was located with some difficulty near Okhotsk, given back his decorations and estates, and dispatched to Tobolsk as governor.

We won't even begin to enumerate the fruits of his activities in Siberia. Let's believe the historians when they say that his accomplishments were significant for those times and had to do with education, provisioning the common folk, organizing means of communication, easing the plight of the schismatics, and so on. But here is what Soymonov left behind of his written labors: "A History of Peter the Great"; "A Brief Explication of Astronomy"; "Information on Siberian Markets"; "Siberia—A Gold Mine"; "A Description of the Caspian Sea"; "A Description of the Art of Navigation,"[81] etc.

Another of Siberia's governors, Dmitry Bantysh-Kamensky,[82] was the author of the five-volume *A Dictionary of Memorable People from the Russian Land.*[83]

Aleksandr Despot-Zenovich considered his primary activity the protection and sponsorship of culture and the press.

And Alyabiev, the composer's father! And Speransky! And Muravyov-Amursky!

Yes, there were real people in your day . . .[84]

I set off with Boris Eristov, a research assistant at the Tobolsk Regional Museum [*Tobol'skii kraevedcheskii muzei*] and an expert on the city's distant past, to take a look at Isker. This town, the Tatar capital of Siberia on the banks of the Irtysh and the headquarters of Kuchum, from which he governed his domain and to which he hauled a vast amount of tribute, disappeared long ago. The town is no more, but I wanted at least to look at the place where it had been and to imagine how it had stood, from which direction Yermak had entered it, and what he'd seen before him. And although I knew that the Irtysh (whose name comes from a Turkic word meaning burrowing animal) was washing away Kuchum's Hill [*Kuchumov kholm*], too, and that most likely very little of it remained, I was anxious to see even that "little bit."

Driving down the Irkutsk Highway, we passed Saint John's Monastery [*Ivanovskii monastyr'*], whose first building was erected in the middle of the seventeenth century, then went several more versts along some fields and stopped before a patch of woods. The Irtysh lay to the right, beyond the fields. There was no road leading in and no reminder of Isker anywhere. Only historians and eccentrics still remember it, and now people rarely ask about Suzga, Kuchum's beautiful wife, to whom Yershov dedicated his narrative poem. As history feeds itself, it, too, cultivates its own arable land, and a whole layer of soil has been turned over during the last four hundred years, burying Kuchum's kingdom completely. And there is every sign that it won't take much for a new layer to form on top and cover Tobolsk's bygone might forever, even in memory.

We followed a path along the edge of some woods, where we picked up ticks from the birch trees, which we then spent about three days pulling out of our skin. All that now remains of the Sibirka River, which once flowed up to Isker, is a dense swampy forest where the channel used to be. The forest turned sharply to the left, but we went straight, heading across an unplowed field toward the Irtysh. And when we came out, we seemed lifted up, and the gently sloping, mighty Siberian land unfolded far, far into the distance, about thirty versts [roughly twenty miles], filled with verdure and old river beds, low banks and islands. Standing before a scene like that, you feel your own muteness with special sorrow; such rapture has no tongue. The streams of sensitivity are apparently drying up in us, too, just as the

Sibirka dried up, and only through dim, weakened impulses can we try to guess where and before what they might spurt up and fill us with radiant passion. Doesn't the very same thing happen when we pause before the works of human hands, before the crowning creations of our ancestors, guessing that they are worthy of rapture? And rapture has grown scarce! We can clean out the channel where the Sibirka used to flow, but where will we get moisture if the sources have been plugged up and turned into desert? Often, too often, our admiration has a mechanical force to it, as if when seeing something that is customarily admired, you give yourself a command and start working the little pump.

We walked along the high bank of the Irtysh and came to the steep ravine beyond which Kuchum's Hill used to rise. Two and one half centuries ago the historian Müller found a hill fifty sazhens [about 190 feet] wide on this spot; one hundred years ago Mikhail Znamensky[85] a Tobolsk artist and student of local lore, measured only fifteen sazhens [about ninety-five feet]. Now even the starting point of their measurements has vanished underwater. Znamensky drank ice-cold water from the Sibirka and stood over Kuchum's famous well, which he'd dug in case of siege. Today everything has sunk into the underworld. Not even part of the hill remains any more; there is only a slight drop toward the Sibirka from the northern side. Just as time sweeps away events, so water and wind sweep away the places on earth where those events occurred, and the louder and more vividly they resounded in history, the more pitiless is the result.

Isker was doomed to extinction when Tobolsk was founded and Russians moved in; the Irtysh merely carried out the sentence. And what fate now awaits Tobolsk? Is it possible that some other people will show up, build a new town, and hand Tobolsk over to the Irtysh or some other force? Is it destined to exist? Or have the newcomers, young and energetic, unburdened by any memory of what happened on this land, already arrived, popping up next to Tobolsk and squeezing it closer and closer to the precipice? The distance from Isker to Tobolsk was fifteen versts [about ten miles]. These people are right beside it. Doesn't this mean that their pitiless encroachment will be that much swifter?

Or will they nonetheless manage to live peacefully side by side?

Or will it share the fate of the house that belonged to Znamensky, the very man who looked for Isker a hundred years before us? They demolished his house, put up a new one in its place, and nailed onto the completely new building the same old memorial plaque: "M. S. Znamensky, the famous artist and democrat, lived here." This is another possible outcome for the historic town.

What awaits you, Tobolsk, famous, glorious old capital of Siberia?! Will we muster enough strength, courage, persuasiveness, memory, and volunteer spirit to save you?

1988

Lake Baikal

Baikal-Amur Main Line (BAM)

BAIKAL-LENA NATURE PRESERVE

BARGUZIN NATURE PRESERVE

Davsha

Baikal Mountains

Kirenga

Lena

Hare Islands

Chivyrkuisky Bay

Holy Nose Peninsula

Barguzin

Sarma

Barguzin Bay

Barguzin

Khuzhir

Uzur

Sarma

Olkhon Island

Small Sea

Turka

Seaside Mountains

Kamenka

Angarsk

Irkutsk

Sandy Bay

Kika

Selenga

Uda

Selenginsk

Trans-Siberian Railroad

Kultuk

Baikal Shoreline RR

Listvennichny (Listvyanka)

Ulan-Ude

Slyudyanka

Baikalsk

BAIKALSK NATURE PRESERVE

Khamar-Daban Mountains

Lake Gusinoe

Novoselenginsk

Temnik

Selenga

Chikoy

Khilok

RUSSIA

MONGOLIA

Kyakhta

Altanbulag

Selenga

0   50   100   150   200   250   300   Kilometers
0   50   100   150   200   Miles

Map by Darin T. Grauberger and George F. McCleary, Jr., University of Kansas Map Associates

3
❖❖❖

Lake Baikal

The Lord looked and saw that the earth had turned out
unfriendly. . . . What if it took offense at its creator?! . . . And
to keep it from harboring a grudge, he up and flung at it not some
old mat for its feet but the actual measuring scoop for his bounties,
with which he measured how much everything would get from
him. When the scoop landed, it became Baikal.

I don't recall when or from whom I heard this proud,
unsophisticated legend about the creation of Lake Baikal. Or maybe I
heard it not from someone else but from my own self when incantations were repeated to me during one of my unconscious meditations
on this miracle, but every time I walk up to Baikal, I hear these words
inside me over and over: "The measuring scoop for the Lord's bounties
fell to earth and became Baikal."

Scientists believe this happened approximately twenty million
years ago, altogether too long before the appearance here or anywhere
else of the first human being.

This is precisely what's incomprehensible: Baikal was there, but
human beings weren't, so there turned out to be no one to admire it
and marvel at it. But this is terribly foolish. We've gotten used to thinking that everything on earth—its beauties and bounties, all the laws of
nature—exists for us, that everything was created for us and intended
for us, and we've begun to forget that the human race, like many other
things, is a product of Nature, a fortunate coincidence of circumstances. And yet our self-centered but sincere bewilderment is also
justified: How is it that people, the only creatures capable of higher
enjoyment and comprehension, did not exist, while objects of delight
existed?! Why was this? If nobody was able to appreciate and compare
them, if no one's head would spin and no one's heart stand still at their

Lake Baikal

beauty and marvelousness, then no one's mind would make an attempt to discover the reasons for them! But everything probably happened in its own good time, and as soon as the Earth ripened to the point of producing fruits and beauties, human beings appeared, too. And wherever it broke free of coldness, wherever it began covering itself with forests and grasses, people moved in to settle.

As a consolation, we can assume that Baikal did not exist in its completed form until after the appearance of the human race. Until then it was merely making preparations, gradually forming, filling up and coming alive, covering and coloring itself with shoreline. The process of formation hasn't ended even today. The lake is constantly shifting, trying to get comfortable, and sometimes, as happened during the extremely powerful earthquakes at the very beginning of 1862 and in 1959, this can be quite dangerous for humans. It is growing, at the rate of two centimeters a year, its shores are expanding like those of the World Ocean, and some suspect that, dissatisfied with its fate, it even aims to become an ocean.

One more curious point: when Russians first set foot in Siberia and moved rapidly eastward, they rushed right past Baikal. By all accounts, they came out at the Pacific Ocean before they reached the interior "glorious sea." One of the first Russians to drink Baikal's water (he is considered the first, but there are vague reports about predecessors) was Kurbat Ivanov, a *piatidesiatnik*[1] who, before crossing the watershed in 1643 from the upper reaches of the Lena River, succeeded in putting the Lena, Kolyma, and "other dog rivers"[2] on a map while he was in the Far North. Kurbatka Ivanov, a Cossack from Tobolsk, was somehow not of high enough stature to be called the father of Siberian cartography, but what can you do? You can't just close your eyes and hope he'll go away. Baikal also received its first outlines from his hand. "An Inventory Based on Sketches from the Kuta River Upstream along the Lena to its Highest Point and along the Side Rivers That Flow into the Lena River and How Far by Ship from River to River and How Far across Plowed Areas and Oral Histories from the Tungus Princeling Mozheulka about the Bratsk People and about the Tungus and about Lama and about Other Rivers"[3]—this is the title of the work that the *piatidesiatnik* sent to Pyotr Golovin, a *stol'nik* in Yakutsk, when he completed his expedition and that nowadays requires some clarification.

Kurbat Ivanov collected his "oral histories" in the upper reaches of the Lena River by questioning Mozheulka, an Evenk princeling, and among the Evenks Baikal was called *Lama*. When a detachment of Russians sailed across the lake to Olkhon Island, they encountered "Bratsk" people—Buryats—among whom, in their turn of tongue, Baikal had its actual present-day name. But Kurbat Ivanov believed that the name he'd heard first sounded more authentic, and he used it to indicate Baikal in his description and on his map. Thus until the end of the eighteenth century Baikal existed sometimes under its own name, sometimes under the name *Lama*, and sometimes as *Dalay*, indicating the sacredness of its water, until one name became rightfully established once and for all.

Where this name originated, from which quarter and which people, is disputed to this day. Similar sounding words meaning a big, magnificent body of water exist in the Yakut and Buryat languages, and even Arabic turns out to have one, but if you look for it, you'll find something even farther away, as if a single call were prepared for Baikal, as our future savior, in every mode of expression, large and small. The

Chinese have *bei-hai* (northern sea). Scholars lean toward the Yakut variant: Yakuts lived near Baikal until their exodus northward, and even now their language retains *baig"al* (sea). The Buryats probably acquired this word from them. But didn't the ancient Yakuts, in turn, acquire it from someone who lived there before them, from the same Kurykans, a people of Turkic origin, who left traces of habitation at Baikal back in the late Neolithic Period? Or from someone else? Niko-lay Spafary,[4] the Russian envoy to China, who visited Baikal in 1675, notes: "And in their native tongues all the foreigners—the Mongols and the Tungus and others—all call the Baikal Sea *Dalay*, which means *sea*. . . . And the name of this Baikal does not appear to be Russian; its name [comes from] the name used by the foreigners who lived in those parts."

One thing certainly came down from the distant past: every people that took refuge on the shores of Baikal revered its water as sacred and invested it with the utmost God-bearing power. The Buryats have holy places, which they continue to revere in a vague way, scattered all along most of the shoreline; an especially large number of them are located on Olkhon Island. Practically every big hill or cliff there is a place for communing with Burkhan, the principal spirit of Baikal. True, this does not prevent present-day Buryats from making their sacred island a huge dump or from turning the sacrificial sprinkling of revered rocks with "fire" water ["*ognennaia*" *voda*] into a drinking bout, but in our time, unfortunately, this is common not only among Buryats. In this practice they are equals among equals, carelessly and senselessly perpe-trating an outrage against their native land and adapting ancient holy days and popular beliefs for the worship of other gods. . . .

Using the past in the name of inculcation or even comparison is usually a useless and senseless pursuit; we'll listen to testimony about how our ancestors regarded Baikal only out of curiosity, not to learn any lessons.

In *Notes on the Russian Embassy to China, 1692–1695*, Evert Ides,[5] a European, writes:

I should point out that when I left Saint Nicholas Monastery [*monastyr' sv. Nikolaia*], which is situated at the mouth of the Angara River, and sailed out onto the lake, many people warned me with great fervor and begged me, when I ventured into that ferocious sea, to call it not a lake but *dalay*, or sea. They added that a great many distinguished people who headed out onto Baikal and called it a lake, that is, stagnant water, quickly fell victim to violent storms and ended up in mortal danger.

Benedykt Dybowski,[6] who explored and studied Baikal, writes (in 1686):

Baikal, which the natives call "the sacred sea," is imbued with a wonderful charm; something legendary and mysterious along with a certain inexplicable fear are connected with everyone's conception of this lake. Each time we made ready to head out onto the lake, people predicted an inevitable accident.

The superstitions, like the legends, are tenacious; if you ever get caught in a gale on Baikal, just try making fun of the local stories about all-powerful sea spirits who seem to release squall after squall and destructive gusts one more savage and dangerous than another as if shaking them out of their sleeves. If you can make fun of them at a time like that, then more power to you; you can do anything.

The legends, incidentally, link Olkhon Island with the name of Genghis Khan: that is where he allegedly found eternal rest. This is a case when you would prefer to cast doubt upon a legend, knowing how many corners of Asia lay claim to the great conqueror's remains. But even while doubting, you still want to argue that if the master of many lands had taste and if this were his last wish, why not Olkhon?! If you could choose a place of eternal grandeur for your eternal refuge, if you could look for a spot next to the gods, what more could you possibly want?! All you have to do is walk out to the cliff called Sagan-Khushun on the northern extremity of the island and, standing on the precipice, turn your gaze in all four directions, sense that you are simultaneously amid the elements of sky, water, and earth, feel a rush of air on your face as if from a quick movement, hear the sometimes powerful, sometimes lulling splash of the waves, see that the antiquity in the rock beside you is not fading and that it rises out of the earth in plants that have vanished everywhere else; all you have to do is give in to this mood and realize that below this abyss there is no division into days and weeks, into arriving and departing lives, into events and results, that there is only an endless, all-encompassing flow arranging inspections for which one and the same thing, plunging alternately into light and darkness, reports countless times. . . . All you have to do is visit this place, and no matter who you are, you're a captive. . . .

124
+++

The discovery of Baikal, or rather its appearance, did not make any special impression on the first Russian explorers. They left no testimony of a personal nature about it: they were more concerned with ore, sable, and grievances. Either the great toiling pioneers of the seventeenth century found it overwhelmingly wondrous or else it wasn't customary at that time to express feelings in writing. But people of an artistic bent, once their turn came, couldn't help being stunned by Baikal. We must bear in mind, however, that three centuries ago the Russian language was not a very flexible tool for picturesque descriptions, for creating half shades and half-tints, and that you often heard groaning where a vivid depiction should have appeared. But here, too, we can pass judgment only from our own narrow perspective; it is perfectly possible that back then words, not surrounded by the props of definitions and fine distinctions, possessed a broader expressiveness than they do now and that readers sensed their drift the way we intuitively continue to hear it in speech.

The very first hymn to Baikal was sung by Archpriest Avvakum,[7] the fanatical leader of the Schism in the church. On returning from exile in Dauria in the summer of 1662, he describes it this way:

High hills and exceedingly high rocky cliffs are all around it—over twenty times one thousand versts and more have I dragged myself and nowhere seen any like unto these. Atop them are bed chambers and sleeping benches, gateways and pillars, stone fences and courtyards—all wrought by God. Onion groweth upon them and garlic—larger than the Romanov onion, and exceedingly sweet. There, too, doth grow God-cultivated hemp, and in the courtyards beauteous grasses both colorful and surpassingly fragrant. Exceedingly many birds, geese, and swans swim upon the sea, covering it like snow. It hath fishes—sturgeon, and salmon, sterlet, and omul, and whitefish, and many other kinds. The water is fresh and hath great seals and sea lions in it: when I dwelt in Mezen,[8] I saw nought like unto these in the big ocean/sea. And the fishes there are plentiful: the sturgeon and salmon are surpassingly fat—thou canst not fry them in a pan, for there will be nought but oil. And all this hath been wrought by Christ in heaven for mankind so that, resting content, he shouldst render praise unto God.

One decade after Archpriest Avvakum, Nikolay Spafary complains:

The Baikal Sea is invisible to both the old and the present-day physiographers because they describe other small lakes and swamps but have left no memoirs about Baikal, which hath such tremendous depths.

To fill in this gap, Spafary stayed on at Baikal for almost a month and gave the lake its first intelligent and lively description, listing rivers, bays, and safe havens for mariners, describing the forests and the occupations of the local inhabitants, marveling at the abundance of fish, and explaining why Baikal can be called both a lake and a sea. "And it hath exceedingly clear water—the bottom is visible for many sazhens—and the water is exceedingly healthful for drinking," writes Spafary.

Anton Chekhov picks up this refrain two centuries later: "You can see through the water as if looking through air; its color is a soft turquoise, pleasing to the eye."

There are so many rapturous responses to Baikal that they would fill more than one book. A hundred times as many remained unrecorded, and these responses, organized into music, sound forth at those times when people must answer to heaven, offering up a wonderful song of human thanksgiving. Paying homage to Baikal was a universal practice for a long time, although for some the lake affected mainly their mystical feelings, for others their aesthetic feelings, and for still others their practical side. People were dumbfounded at the sight of Baikal because it didn't fit their conceptions: Baikal lay where something like that should have been impossible, it was not the sort of thing that should have been possible anywhere, and it did not have the same effect on the soul that "indifferent" nature usually does. This was something special, unusual, and exceptional.

In time Baikal was measured and studied, in recent years with the aid of deep-sea instruments. It acquired definite dimensions and characteristics and began to be compared according to them. Scientists sometimes liken it to the Caspian Sea, which is the only inland sea with more water than Baikal, but the Caspian contains salt water; sometimes they compare it to Lake Tanganyika, regarding it as Baikal's twin on the opposite side of the planet because it has the same crescent shape, similar depths, and a huge number of endemic species. They've calculated that Baikal holds one-fifth of all the freshwater on the earth's surface and that the human race could live on Baikal's water alone for at least forty years without restricting its use. They've explained its origin and conjectured as to how species of plants and animals existing nowhere else could have originated and been preserved in it and how species found many thousands of kilometers away managed to end up there. Not all these explanations and conjectures tally even with each other. Baikal is not so simple that it could be deprived of its enigma; yet based on its numerical parameters, it has been assigned a fitting place among other great wonders that have already been measured and studied, as well it should. And it stands alongside them solely because Baikal itself, alive, mysterious, and majestic, not comparable to anything and not repeated anywhere, is aware of its own place and its own life.

How and with what can its air and water, its beauty, actually be compared? And is this beauty? We won't insist that nothing in the world is finer than Baikal: each of us regards his own region as beloved and dear, and the Eskimo or the Aleut considers his icy wilderness the crowning glory of nature's perfection. From the time we are born we drink in the salts and scenes of our homeland; they influence our character and organize the cells of our body in their own manner. For this reason it is not enough to say that they are dear to our hearts; they are a part of us, the part that is formed by the natural environment. Its ancient voice is obliged to keep speaking inside us. It is meaningless to compare the ice caps of Greenland with the sands of the Sahara, the Siberian taiga with the steppe of Central Russia, or even the Caspian Sea with Baikal, giving preference to one or the other; we can merely convey our impressions of them. All these have their own splendid beauty and their own amazing vitality. More often than not, attempts at comparisons of this type arise from our unwillingness or inability to see and feel the singularity and perfection of a particular scene.

The normal concept of beauty fits Baikal least of all. What we take for beauty is an impression of a different type, like something that hangs above the horizon of our sensitivity. No matter how often you've been to Baikal, no matter how well you know it, each new encounter is unexpected and requires effort on your part. Each time you seemingly have to raise yourself to a certain height again and again in order to be on the same plane, in order to see and hear it.

Not everything, as we know, has a name. It's impossible to give a name to the regeneration that occurs in people when they're near Baikal. There's no need to remind anyone that for this to take place a person must have a soul. And here he stands and looks around, is filled with something and carried off somewhere, and can't understand what's happening to him. Like a fetus in its mother's womb, he passes through all the evolutionary stages of human development and, spellbound by the ancient, mighty unfolding of this miracle, he experiences the timeless tidal feeling of the powers that created humankind. Something in him cries, something exults, something plunges into peacefulness, something becomes orphaned. He feels both anxious and happy beneath the penetrating, all-enveloping eye, parenting and inaccessible; he becomes filled now with hope stemming from recollections, now with inconsolable bitterness based on reality.

All of us know the wonderful song "Glorious Sea, Sacred Baikal," written in the nineteenth century by the Siberian poet Dmitry Davydov[9] from the viewpoint of a convict who has run away from his captors and is sailing across Baikal. It contains these words: "Sensing liberty, I've come to life." This is just what we experience at Baikal, as if we've momentarily broken out of the torture chambers of slavery we've created into unrestricted freedom before going back to them once again.

FROM "A BAIKAL DIARY"

January 17th. Listvyanka, at the source of the Angara. Baikal rose up, then froze. Yesterday, when I arrived, there was still open water—the wind had just recently broken up the weak ice and swept it away—but today it's covered over once and for all. The huge ice field looks like a patchwork: the blocks of ice haven't ground together yet, and water splashes out and pushes up fragments at their points of juncture. Near the Angara it presses against the ice with a muffled grumble, dissatisfied and unaccustomed to there being no exit where it used to get out.

The day is sunny and bright. I recall that in the number of hours of sunlight per year Baikal has a head start on every European health resort. The sunshine shatters and smokes as it falls on the gelid blue mass. The forest stands on the hill in sensitive numbness; people move about slowly and sluggishly. The ice sheeting casts a spell over everything. A dog barks at an ice wall pushed up near the shore. The mountains on the opposite shore look bulky. Even the air has frozen along with the water.

Duck-winterers swim in a dense flock near the edge of the ice at the Angara's source. For them, too, this is fresh and new. They are carried away, then swim back and run into the ice again; leaving a trail, they move along the stationary ice belt near the shore at fixed intervals, disappearing one after another in dives. Their take-offs make the air chir.

I stood on the observation platform at the river's source for probably an hour. A wedding party took pictures. They drove up, started slamming car doors, and began cussing joyfully as they assembled. Foul language instantly makes young people look ugly. No one marveled at the ice or at the sunshine or at the ducks surfacing nearby; no one even seemed to glance at the Angara or at Baikal. Cars stopped; people got out, performing the customary ritual and making the usual motions with their feet and tongues, plunging into the bliss of the landscape without eyes or souls.

As I walked away, I also recalled that Aleksey Martos,[10] who passed this spot almost 170 years ago during his travels through Siberia, noted in his diary the local inhabitants' barbaric custom of using guns to kill ducks that were just as trusting of people as these. Now such practices have apparently disappeared altogether. Maybe human beings have actually become better, but they still have such a long way to go . . . I don't feel like continuing. Nature stopped all creatures on one level but set human beings free—and just look at what they've done with their freedom!

January 18. Here's "once and for all" for you: Baikal is open again. There was no wind during the night, and it wasn't especially warm, but when I got up this morning, the Angara stretched far into the sea, and the pure band of water, completely lacking ice, lies calm and somehow victorious as it broadens out into Baikal like a funnel. And only near the shore is there an ice ledge, where some kids are chasing a hockey puck. This is Baikal showing its true nature: I'll cover myself when I want to and open up when I want to.

. . . It blazes wonderfully at sunset when the sun has already departed and streaks of evening glow are flaming in the west. Baikal seems illuminated not from above but from below—by the sun, which has gone underwater and shines through it up to the surface. The soft purple radiance did not drown when the sunset burned out, as if Baikal had gathered it up like warmth to hold in reserve and will keep giving it back until the morning sun comes up anew, the way it gives back summer's warmth until spring comes again.

Beyond the point and the hill the Angara grows dark toward the rear, but Baikal keeps on blazing and blazing. . . .

January 20. It's begun to freeze again. The ice is so smooth and thin that you can't distinguish it from the water when you look down on it from the shore. Only by the sun's reflection can you tell the difference: the sunlight slides around and scatters all over the ice but lies in the water of the Angara like a narrow, drooping verst marker.

There is another "scene" this evening. The whole sky on the Angara side seems curtained off by a thick, gray cloudbank, and there are also stormclouds on the opposite side, over the Khamar-Daban Mountains; the setting sun (it has already set) catches their edge, striking one central spot—as if even the sun were just barely covered on top by thunderclouds. All of Baikal is wrapped in a blinding radiance, everything is splashed with sunlight, but a wall of fog   noving in from the mountains. The fog advances from one side, from the Khamar-Daban Range, crowding out the light, while from the other side, from the Angara, comes the darkening shadow of twilight, and the tapering strip of sunshine grows brighter and brighter—it blazes, melts, sparks.

February 17. The white, deserted field of Baikal, which you can't keep your eyes on in the sunlight, is blindingly white and deserted, has no horizon, and turns into sky in a bright whiteness. You can tell that this is the sky only from the faded patterns and subsiding color high overhead. There is a kind of excessiveness, inaccessible to us, in the white plain of snow that we can't penetrate because our vision lacks something. We are blinded without a dark object to rest our gaze on and become lost; we slip on the annoying alienness of this excess and quickly turn our eyes away.

Yesterday was also a bright day, but there was a wind that blew not away from the Angara, as usual, but into the Angara, raising mist. Today is completely still. The water on the Angara has a smooth blue surface unusual for winter and is studded with ducks that fly across it with a pure, stippled sound when they've drifted away. This music makes the river ring.

I went down to the ice and walked out across it onto the sea. The snow hasn't blown away yet; it is hard and crusty but has patches of ice like blue glass through which you can see the water stirring. The snow is rough and granulized. It doesn't crunch underfoot but makes a swishing sound and is pleasant to walk through.

Baikal didn't seem to notice me at first. But then the fun began! First something would crack, then give a sudden groan, then explode right under my feet so that once or twice I barely refrained from jumping back. A noise like thunder might arise somewhere off to the side but then fly at me or race by very close, scaring me. I know perfectly well that it's safe, for I walk on the ice every winter and experience the same rapturous terror each time. I know that various laws of nature make this happen, but I don't want explanations. I want to think that Baikal, playing with us and scaring us, arranges this cannonade for human beings.

February 18. This morning the mountains are clearly defined, like a Rockwell Kent painting, close and visible in such detail that you could even sharpen your eyes on them. They catch fire beyond the point as the sun rises, but the immense snowfield below lies in a jacket of porous blue. Melted sunshine keeps sliding farther and farther down the mountains and flows out onto the field; the boundary between the dry blueness and the dry reddish burning is plainly visible. It moves closer, and behind it, where everything was clear just a moment earlier, a light, misty haze springs up—like steam. Sunshine gradually floods the whole field, rolling out from behind the point, and the mountains are gradually blocked and blinded as the bright twilight advances.

There is a breeze from the Angara, not at all strong, but I can't see the Angara because of the fumes drifting in from Irkutsk. The water beneath the breeze is an inky black and the sky, blackened by smoke, looks unhealthy. The sun is white, spread out, and dishevelled. On the opposite side, to the east, the sky is deep, summerlike, and light blue.

All this together, all in one hour.

July 3. Baikal Harbor. A week of rain. I kept sitting around in the city, waiting it out, and yesterday I couldn't stand it and came here, counting on breaking the bad weather with my arrival. Nothing of the sort happened, and today it's pouring again, so furiously that you don't even want to stick your head outside.

Around lunchtime I went into the entryway to get something I needed. A swift was lying on the floor, barely moving a wing. I tried to warm it up and feed it, but I was too late. It died in half an hour. This evening Fedya, a kind, weak fellow suffering, as many here do, from the "Russian" disease, for which he was transferred from ship to shore duty, dropped by on his way home from work and said that a great number of birds, after getting wet and losing strength, were falling into the Angara and drowning. He'd picked up nine swifts while walking from Molchanovskaya Hollow to the carpentry shop. They'd warmed them up at the shop, and then he let four of them go.

We went outside together at dusk and stopped a water truck so Fedya could ride the rest of the way. As he was getting settled, the driver told us that during the day he'd picked up thirty birds lying in the road; now they're flying around in his shed until the sun comes out.

A week of rain, but my little spring, which used to gurgle across the yard in summers past, simply hasn't come to life.

July 13. This morning it's light and clear, and suddenly five minutes later I can't see the riverbank right under my nose or the water or the sky—fog. Half an hour later it's clear again. And in this clarity, when you can distinguish each tree on the opposite bank forty kilometers away as if looking through binoculars, a white chimney of fog rises from the Angara, blown out neatly, with no breaks, and stretches who knows how far into Baikal. But the sky above it is full of stormclouds, seething, twisted, thunderous.

September 22. And again, like last year, we have warm weather; summer comes later and later and moves back farther and farther, shortening autumn. Today the temperature was over 20°C [68°F]. I'm in a mood that has appeared for the first time, one I've never experienced before. The woods blaze with a bright withering, everything all around is fading or has already faded, is aging or getting ready to hibernate; soon everything will freeze up and go into hiding, but I have no sense of anguish or of parting—on the contrary, I feel uplifted and grateful for life. This comes either from the sunshine, from the warmth, or from my proximity to Baikal, or from being at that crossing point in age when you feel as though you're looking down from a height followed by a slope so cunningly made that for a few more years you'll think that you are continuing to ascend and that your powers are increasing. But that's tomorrow; today there is a total and successful match-up with your own self, a sense of coziness and freedom—as if you've heard and fulfilled something said to you without words: If that's you, then do this. . . . You wouldn't have done it yesterday, and you won't do it tomorrow, but today, having turned your back on everything alien, you are capable, perhaps for the only time in your life, of accomplishing a great deal. . . .

November 17. Still, limp weather, snow and warmth; every day the temperature is above freezing. As if nature has grown languid and soft, unable to make a decisive movement.

Now it's evening. The soft grayness of the water, the soft whiteness of the snow. And the deep soft sky, half of it clear and half of it ruled on its western slope into long, even stripes with cooling, stretched-out cloud marks between them—like notations on staff paper. And moving toward it from above, without pressing or pushing in at all, is a little crescent moon, sonorous, delicate, and sharp. There's a faint, intermittent twinkling above the horizon; somewhere over there they must be hearing music.

I looked and saw the moon reflected in the depths of the sky: two little crescents, one behind the other, bowing in identical fashion to the scattering of cloud. And it's not reflected in the water. The water is no longer gray but dark and dense, not admitting the sky. And only later does a meandering lunar path just barely show, like a wetting on something hard, like a warming on something cold.

Although his propensities for good and evil mature and develop, a person remains a child his whole life. He doesn't succeed in reaching adulthood during such a short span of time and doesn't want to. You stand before Baikal small and weak, though still regarding yourself as not the worst specimen of what constitutes the human race; you try to understand that Baikal is in front of you and you in front of it; you strain yourself in excruciating appeals to see, understand, and give it meaning—and you back away: it's useless. Beside Baikal it's not enough to contemplate the way you usually do; there you must think in a higher, purer, stronger manner, on a level with its spirit, not feebly, not bitterly. When something great touches us, we are capable of merely raising questions; it is only through questions that we seek, that we hail the language that we didn't manage to recognize.

Maybe nature stands between God and human beings. And until you unite with nature, you won't move forward. It won't let you. And without its preliminary involvement, without its accompaniment, your soul won't come under the protection it covets.

Baikal stretches 636 kilometers from south to north; alternately contracting and expanding, it is between twenty and eighty kilometers wide; its shoreline is about two thousand kilometers long. It is the deepest lake in the world: the deepest abyss found so far reaches a depth of 1,637 meters, but this could be surpassed at any moment, for Baikal does not lie still; underground storms occur beneath it daily. In learned circles some scientists recently advanced the opinion that Baikal was bottomless: since its water is less mineralized in the deep zones than in the upper layers, they concluded that a permanent, powerful spring of extra-fresh water exists at the bottom of Baikal that can come from nowhere else but the upper mantle of the planet, more than seventy to eighty kilometers from its surface. This version was immediately picked up by other scientists, if I may call them that, who were at the disposal of Baikal's industrial polluters and who struck in unison: It's impossible to poison Baikal, the Earth's mantle will prevent this from happening, so rev it up, boys! And the good old boys, with the approval of science, rolled up their sleeves and got right to work.

In the size of the area it floods, Baikal is comparable to such countries as Belgium, Denmark, or Holland. Were it not for those good old boys who have set up shop on Baikal, you could drink its water without ever using it up, rake in its gifts without taking them all, and feast your eyes on it without getting your fill. It lies within sovereign shores for which all the patterns, colors, and charms in nature, all the magnificence it has contrived, seem to have been specially chosen. Based on the way they see and understand Baikal, the human beings that flock to it and attach themselves to it are divided into an indigenous breed of people and a branch that is moved with unusual ease by petty or mercenary passions.

Baikal's western shore is mountainous almost everywhere; there the Seaside and Baikal Ranges [*Primorskii i Baikal'skii khrebty*] come close to the water. The middle part of the eastern shore slopes more gently and is well-positioned for the big rivers, of which the Selenga alone carries almost half the inflowing water. When looking at the outlines of Baikal, you automatically begin to conjecture about its distant and relatively recent past: the Olkhon group of islands and Holy Nose Peninsula [*poluostrov Sviatoi Nos*] simply beg for a connecting link, which then must have sunk; or, just the opposite, you can visualize a single strait between the present-day Chivyrkuisky and Barguzin Bays, where a narrow dividing land bridge could have risen later. In the latter instance this is probably what actually happened, when the tireless architect of Baikal made a simple and—like everything simple—ingenious adjustment by adding two deep, roomy, rich pockets in the form of bays, without which Baikal's shape would have looked a good deal coarser. Concerning the first instance, the well-known scientist Gleb Vereshchagin[11] discovered an underwater mountain range extending from Olkhon to the eastern shore and named it the Academy Range [*Akademicheskii*]. And how could you not jump at the bait and conclude that in its geological past the Lena River, like the Angara, originated in Baikal when its upper reaches are, all told, only eight kilometers away?! Eight kilometers—a mere stone's throw! But running through these carefully counted kilometers is the watershed of the Baikal Mountain Range, on whose other side this legend no longer sounds so alluring. A lively mind, after spotting how close the Irkut River comes to Baikal on the south and then all of a sudden turns sharply aside as if reacting to a shout, will inevitably find that the Irkut used to be a tributary of the lake/sea until the earth, in due course, reared up in front of it and forced it to forge another path. And an artistic mind will make up a beautiful, romantic story about how Father Baikal intended to give his only daughter, the Angara, in marriage to the Irkut, but in the dark of night the willful daughter fled from him to the mighty Yenisey. Baikal threw a rock to stop her, which became the Shaman Rock[12] at the source of the Angara, but he was too late, and the distressed Irkut had no choice but to go away empty-handed.

According to legend, the one the Angara preferred should be indisputably mighty, but in reality it is the Angara, when merging with the Yenisey, that carries more water, which gives us the right to think that the Angara does not empty into the Yenisey, but the Yenisey into the Angara.

Baikal is as embellished with legends as its ice with lacy hoarfrost and its water with ripples. When people encountered Baikal a song would begin to sound forth of its own accord: words would form, derived from the mysterious depths of the origin and behavior of "the glorious sea" and, accompanied by the noise of the wind, the lapping waves, and the view all around, would be continually strung together until they formed, like a new tributary, an exhalation of gratitude.

In addition to beautiful legends Baikal also has some sad ones. One of these arose from a fact that was true one hundred years ago, when Ivan Chersky,[13] a Polish exile who studied Baikal, was making a description of the lake. He counted 336 large and small tributaries feeding Baikal. A good deal of water has dried up since then, but this indestructible, almost biblical figure continues to be heard in all the artistic and scientific tales about Baikal. And no one lifts a finger to correct it in accordance with the living waters.

Chersky, it's true, committed one pleasant blunder in the nineteenth century that in our time has turned into a plus. He plotted twenty-seven islands on his map of the lake. Baikal somehow managed to hide three more islands from him, or else Chersky didn't consider it necessary to count them as such. The number twenty-seven remained firmly in the memory only of specialists, while among the various amateurs it began to "float" and "dive" depending on their own calculations: suddenly they would declare that Baikal had six islands, then stop being stingy and give it fifty. And it is only quite recently that, apparently through the meticulousness of biologist Oleg Gusev,[14] all the i's have finally been dotted: there are thirty, a figure that can't be changed until new cataclysms occur.

But islands, tributaries, points, gulfs, and bays are, after all, right there in plain view. What does this say about the lake's depths?! The Siberian branch of the Russian Geographical Society began its activities in the middle of the nineteenth century by announcing, after the expedition of naturalist Gustav Radde,[15] that Baikal was exceptionally poor in fauna. Nothing could be simpler than making such "discoveries." In that same century, at the end of the 1860s, two other Poles—Dybowski and Godlewski[16]—literally gasped when, ignoring the Geographical Society's verdict, they took a look into Baikal's womb using the means available then. In a letter to the Society's scientific section they reported:

It is strange and incomprehensible how the view based on the superficial observations made by the first natural scientists over the past hundred years concerning the poverty of lower forms of fauna in Baikal could have prevailed for so long and how it could have become firmly established in the scientific world and found constant confirmation in the accounts of the naturalists who traveled there with the scientific aim of studying Baikal's fauna. This is all the more amazing since the single fact that millions of omul[17] and other fish are caught every year should have led to the logical conclusion that fish can't exist without food and that billions of lower animals are essential for such a huge quantity of fish to grow. . . . In short, the wealth of animals is so great that you can say without any exaggeration that Baikal is teeming with more life than you are ever likely to encounter in southern seas.

By the time a permanent scientific research station was opened at the lake in 1925, 760 species of plants and animals were known to exist in Baikal. By 1960, when the station became the Limnological Institute, that number had jumped to 1,800, and by the end of the 1980s it exceeded 2,500. In the animal world almost two-thirds of these are endemic—species not found anywhere except in Baikal. The "census" of Baikal's "population" continues to be taken; writing down all the names will probably go on for a long time. If Lake Tanganyika, likewise interesting for the uniqueness of its inhabitants, supports life for only the first one or two hundred meters, below which lies a dead zone, Baikal, as deep-sea devices have confirmed, is populated all the way to the bottom of its tremendous depths. "The first thing we saw when we landed on the bottom of Baikal at a depth of 1,410 meters was a silt floor covered with hillocks and a bullhead lying there, carefully looking us over. Not far from it a gammarid crayfish was crawling in leisurely fashion," writes Aleksandr Podrazhansky in his book *I See the Bottom of Baikal!*[18] Podrazhansky was a member of the research group that submerged itself in Baikal during the summer of 1977 using two Pisces, a device of Canadian manufacture. They brought back more riddles for the scientists: Where did those hills in the stationary layers of the lake come from? And why does the Baikal oilfish [*golomianka*] move vertically, like a load on a cord, when rising and descending?

This oilfish is a total mystery. A small semitransparent fish with iridescent tints, it is 50 percent fat and, considering its vast quantities, could have been caught for food had it not preferred a solitary existence. Only a blizzard can cast it ashore, and then the local residents, back in the early twentieth century, would scramble to gather up the fish in order to render their fat, which has extraordinary healing properties. But that's still not the whole story of the oilfish: the real miracle is that it's one of the few viviparous fish, which give birth to live offspring. All others spawn, just as nature arranged it, but the oilfish, as if having a premonition that in the future fish would have no place to spawn because human beings would turn all the rivers into sewers and dumps, begged for permission to multiply in a more reliable way. And it didn't miscalculate. Neither did the nerpa, a northern freshwater seal that got into Baikal no one knows how or when (here there's no comparison: Lake Tanganyika has the crocodile, but Baikal has the sweetest of creatures, the nerpa) and that doesn't need to cast a sweep net: it gulps down oilfish one at a time and is always satisfied.

After the oilfish, Baikal's second miracle, to which it owes its exceptional purity, is a crustacean called the *Epischura*. Baikal wouldn't be Baikal without this whiskered copepod, which is scarcely perceptible to the eye and amazingly numerous and hardworking, managing to filter all the water in Baikal ten or more times a year. This creature with a passion for cleanliness won't tolerate any foreign objects, whether washed into the lake by the rivers, thrown overboard from ships, or victims of a disaster. It is pointless to search two or three days later for anything lost in Baikal. The *Epischura* selflessly rushed to attack the toxic discharges from the cellulose plants, too, but this delicacy proved beyond its powers, and it began to perish.

Science will never know how many species of plants and animals lived in Baikal during more fortunate times. They are now starting to disappear one after another.

Only the winds remain the same.

Like a gigantic animal, Baikal breathes deeply, powerfully, and fitfully, now abating, now making a lot of noise while greedily sucking in streams of air. Baikal's winds are swift and unexpected. Don't be deluded by their innocent names, which derive from the names of rivers and sound like song: *sarma, kultuk, barguzin, angara.* God forbid that you should end up dancing to this "music" on open water. Local residents aren't about to beg, "Hey, Barguzin, stir up a swell . . ."[19] They know that this wind, like the "mountain" wind, the *sarma,* is capable of raising a swell up to six meters high. And then save yourself any way you can! Thousands and thousands of prayers for the dead have been sung in the handful of churches scattered around Baikal; sometimes, after the lake exacted large amounts of tribute, they could be heard for weeks on end.

Sarma is also a little river in the southern part of the Small Sea [*Maloe more*] (between Olkhon Island and the western shore), but the wind that tears out of its narrow opening resembles an avalanche. An old set of prerevolutionary sailing instructions for Baikal, trying to educate the reader, says: "This wind, which rages especially often in the autumn, is noted not only for its horrifying strength and duration (winds exceeding forty meters per second [more than eighty miles an hour] that blow for twenty-four hours and longer are not uncommon here) but also for raising whole clouds of watery spray that quickly turn to ice in the air." The *sarma* tears heavy cargo ships loose and tosses them out into the sea; in the winter it rolls trucks across the ice to any place it pleases and then turns them over; it rips roofs off houses, flinging them around. Its record of fatalities includes many different things. After sailing vessels, after flat-bottomed boats and wind-propelled cargo ships, after all the single-masted, flat-bottomed means of navigation [*plavsredstva*], as we would say now, that could take up to six thousand poods [216,000 pounds] of cargo on board and that still fell easy prey to the waves, all hope rested with steamboats: surely these could make headway against any swell. But they, too, would give up before Baikal's winds, cutting their cables and abandoning barges full of people and cargo to the mercy of fate. As recently as 1902 there were two major shipwrecks on the Small Sea in which the steamboats *Potapov* and *Aleksandr Nevsky* lost hundreds of victims.

It would be a different matter if the *sarma* alone were that kind of wind and if, when discussing accidents, we had to look only at the past. But no, even today the wind is capable of wreaking all sorts of havoc when, with no warning in the weather forecast, it suddenly bursts down the mountains through the narrow river valleys. And if one wind is joined by another and then by a third, if they raise a violent commotion over Baikal by tossing heads of water from side to side, if a swell starts twisting into a coil, then it's all over. But as people were advised in the distant past, "it is almost impossible to estimate all the mishaps involving mariners that have occurred on Baikal and would be inappropriate here" (from the journal the *Siberian Herald* [*Siberskii viestnik*] for the year 1821).

But after this quotation it is worth retelling one Baikal "odyssey," all the more so since it happened back in the eighteenth century, a time sufficiently distant from us. This story holds a certain interest because of the cat-and-mouse game Baikal played with some seafarers for its own amusement and because of the particulars of the deprivations that fell to their lot.

Thus we read:

The vessel was 11 sazhens 2 1/4 arshins [about twenty-nine feet] long and its cargo consisted of lead bound from the works in Nerchinsk to those in Kolyvansk. . . . On July 31 it reached Baikal [from the Selenga River (Rasputin)] and was blown off its true course by a strong wind. On August 1 it set sail to continue its journey but was becalmed near Sandy Points [*Peschanye mysy*] [it had now reached the western shore (Rasputin)]. On the 2d this vessel encountered another head wind by the Goloustnoe Winter Camp and the crew, fearing violent weather, dropped anchor in a safe place. On the 3d a favorable wind arose [bearing the name *obetonnyi*, which has now dropped out of use (Rasputin)], and the mariners, after hauling their drags and mooring lines out of the water, hastened to take advantage of it, but at that moment the wind intensified and the vessel was flooded with water. On the 4th they pumped the water out and moved the vessel to a deep stream, where they spent the night in anticipation of a favorable wind. On the 5th they had just managed to get under way when, below the Incense Winter Camp [*Kadil'noe zimov'e*], they once again encountered mountain weather, which not only carried the vessel into the middle of Baikal but also tore off the lifeboat fastened to it. On the 6th they headed for the northwestern shore of Baikal. There, three versts [slightly more than two miles] from Sandy Points, mountain weather caught them by surprise and carried the vessel to Ambassador Monastery [*Posol'skii monastyr'*] [on the eastern shore (Rasputin)], to the so-called Women's Peninsula [*Bab'ia karga*]. They stayed there four days, and the people on board, for want of other food, were forced to be content with the remaining dregs of kvass. In the end, when even this wretched fare gave out, they decided on August 11 to lash the ship's oars together and send three comrades on them to Ambassador Monastery to solicit help in such a dire situation. The emissaries returned in the lifeboat that had been torn off the vessel on the 5th, which they had found ten versts [almost seven miles] from the monastery. They brought back about three poods [about 108 pounds] of bread and a few fish. When a favorable wind sprang up they set off again for Larch Point [*Listvennichnyi mys*], but three versts away they encountered a wind so strong that it smashed the rudder and carried the vessel to Kultuk, to Mishikha Creek [the farthest point on Baikal's southwestern tip (Rasputin)]. There the mariners spent seven days in grievous distress, living solely on the roots of dog rose growing on the shore, from which they all became extremely exhausted and several succumbed to illness. Seeing that they would inevitably perish, they mustered their last bit of strength and, raising the sail no higher than one sazhen [a little more than six feet], headed for the Karginskoe Winter Camp. On arrival their vessel, smashed by waves and uncaulked in many places, was flooded with so much water that they couldn't pump it out, and they had to drag it to shore, where on August 26 it was completely smashed apart by intensified mountain weather.

Now there's a lake for you. And that's where you get the prejudices of the benighted local inhabitants who entreated travelers starting out across Baikal to call it nothing other than a sea.

When the steamboat *Heir to the Czar* [*Naslednik Tsesarevich*] suffered an accident in 1860, the people managed to get onto barges, which floated on Baikal for a month and a half until they froze fast in the ice. In keeping with the ignorant and superstitious state of society, each incident of this type used to be described in detail; nowadays people gasp and sigh a little, then forget.

"Almost all the large hollows around Baikal produce wind." This certainly comes as no surprise, but these words, taken from Gusev's observations, are followed by a truly strange statement: "Even the points of land and the clouds at Baikal can create wind." Many times I have experienced not merely a puff of air from a point but a penetrating wind that vanished as soon as I left the point behind. The explanation turns out to be simple: the air around the point warms up unevenly, and this sets it in motion, creating movement that is by no means gentle. Clouds also produce wind: "When the air above the lake falls under the shadow of an onrushing cloud, it instantly cools, becomes heavier, and races off in the direction away from the shady spot, to where the sun is warming the air as before" (Gusev).

And when Baikal finishes storming and raging, once again it wears a peaceful face and God's heavenly grace. During the summer it will lie motionless in a glassy blue or start playing in gentle ripples as if nothing has happened; during the winter, when the water is open, *sokui*— huge, whimsical ice figures on the rocks and bushes that have washed in—bear witness to "what happened." Baikal freezes late, later and later all the time in comparison with the past; in recent years it hasn't frozen in the southern part until late January or early February. One hundred years ago the first bad winter weather often came in December. And by late April the ice is already beginning to break up and scatter around the lake, gradually freeing the water farther and farther northward. And then all of Baikal's spirits, good and not so good, congregate above the water and start deciding whose turn it will be to raise a ruckus on Baikal.

FROM "A BAIKAL DIARY"

August 27, 1988. The beginning of an expedition with Paul Winter, the American composer and originator of ecological jazz. This is not his first visit to Baikal; he's been here in winter and summer, with his concert band and with American defenders of nature, of whom Mark

Dubois sticks in my memory, a tall, determined guy who amazed the residents of Irkutsk by going around in all kinds of subzero weather with a bare head. Dubois achieved national fame in his homeland when, while trying to save his native river from dam builders, he chained himself to a rock in its canyon and obtained first the interest of the press and then the salvation of the river.[20]

Paul Winter plans to compose a large work about Baikal in which he is counting on the nerpa to take part. He uses the sounds of nature and the voices of animals in his music; whales have answered his saxophone and wolves have picked up and continued his melodies. While on Baikal he hopes to record the voice of the nerpa. And naturally you can't plunge into the element of Baikal from the tiny tourist oasis in the town of Listvennichny [also called Listvyanka], where party after party of foreigners pours out; you have to be tossed around on it, to smell and listen to your heart's content.

For our trip we rented from the steamship line a vessel called the *Baikal-3*, an impressive fellow of a tugboat that had worked without a breather for more than ten years while the Baikal-Amur Main Line was under construction. Now that the toil of building BAM is over, the multiplied Baikal fleet has to keep an eye out for, and often even snatch away from each other, any kind of work, down to carrying picturesque groups such as ours who hunger for Baikal.

Our group is picturesque not only in its composition, although in this regard, too, it presents an unusual phenomenon: among us are four Japanese (journalists and employees of the company that issues Paul Winter's records); a film crew from Novosti Press Agency making use of the opportunity to photograph Baikal and the famous composer; Boris Pereverzev, a Moscow friend of Paul's and promoter of his music in our country; and, waiting for us to take him aboard in Sarma, the stomping ground of the Baikal wind I mentioned earlier, Semyon Ustinov, a scientist from Irkutsk specializing in hunting and game and an expert on Baikal without whom our journey would have lost half its value.

If you arranged us, the representatives of various countries, in a single row—and we did line up in a single row on deck when our vessel was casting off from Listvennichny—and tried to tell from our faces and figures what had brought us together on this unwieldy old tub that was meant to pull barges or rafts, then you'd have to conclude, for a lot of reasons, that a comedy was being filmed on Baikal, something like a new *Volga-Volga*.[21] Each of us taken individually might have seemed ordinary and serious enough, but all together we formed a company, seemingly selected by an experienced directorial eye for our contrast to one another, whose appearance alone brought a smile and made any observers try to guess from which quarter this crowd would launch into a funny number.

After setting sail we almost turned back. I was urgently summoned to the captain in the deckhouse, where Galina Vasilievna, the chef/cook responsible for our cuisine, stood whiter than snow, having learned at the last minute that among the family entrusted to her were two vegetarians, one of whom didn't even eat fish, while the other didn't even drink tea. And these, of course, were not Soviet citizens.

The comedy commenced.

"What am I going to feed them? What?" exclaimed Galina Vasilievna, in shock. "I've got meat, canned goods, tins of Yugoslav ham. No, transfer me off this ship. I'm not going. I'd never have agreed to this if I'd known!"

I had to use firmness. One of them doesn't drink tea? Let him drink water. Let him go on a binge drinking from Baikal; it won't hurt him. One of them doesn't eat fish? Let him eat Canadian waterweed. What in the world is that? Algae. The whole bottom of the lake is covered with waterweed. You can feed all of Japan with it.

The Canadian waterweed set Galina Vasilievna's mind at rest. Anything from abroad, even if it's on the bottom of Baikal, inspires us with confidence.

As I went below, I heard the warbling of a nightingale. It was so exuberant, so enthusiastic that I automatically stood still, looking around and trying to remember where I was, afraid of believing it and of scaring the bird away. It turned out that Paul had put on a cassette of bird songs. They were in the bar, talking about whales. Five years ago Takeshi Hara, one of the Japanese passengers and senior editor of the newspaper the *Daily* [*Mainichi*], wrote a book about whales, which is called simply *The Whale*[22] and enjoys great popularity in Japan. Hara is certain that before his book appeared, only about 10 percent of the Japanese public were against the use of whale meat for food, whereas now no less than half oppose it. The provincial areas of Japan, you see, have traditionally been accustomed to this food and giving it up is not a simple matter.

Boris Pereverzev interpreted, showing interest in the conversation. Galina Vasilievna, bustling around near the electric samovar in the corner, kept stopping in her tracks as she listened and glancing stealthily out of the corner of her eye at the other Japanese passenger, the one who didn't eat fish, probably suspecting him of eating whale. He was sitting as motionless as Buddha and looking at Baikal, where the waves were picking up.

From whales the conversation turned to wolves. Paul talked about how the world's attitude toward wolves as harmful and dangerous animals is gradually changing. Perhaps his music, especially "Wolf Eyes," where the song of his saxophone is joined more than once by the voice of a wolf, has even played a certain part. During a concert Winter gave at the U.N.,[23] the huge hall, after hearing "Wolf Eyes," began to howl, imitating the animal. The lights had been turned out, and the diplomats, either recalling something in the dark or forgetting themselves, howled enthusiastically and in harmony.

The samovar boiled, splashing out water. Galina Vasilievna sat beside it glued to her chair. The howling diplomats had done her in. She was filled to overflowing with impressions after just one hour, while we were in for ten days of Baikaling together.

But her fears concerning the vegetarians turned out to be greatly exaggerated. Instead of tea Paul was perfectly happy to gulp down plain old hot water, making us recall each time we watched him that his father had lived to be a hundred, while his mother swims with whales in Hawaii at the age of seventy-six. The Japanese vegetarian had brought along a supply of packets containing something almost like birdseed, and out of curiosity we helped him peck away at the sweet mixture inside. Galina Vasilievna's concoctions, incidentally, also turned out to be excellent.

August 28. Rain. A damp whiteness of sky, a cold mounding of water, and branches of shoreline spreading out in the fog. The rain splashes off the canvas of the sea as though bouncing off dry land.

We stopped at Sarma to pick up Semyon Ustinov. Paul Winter, constantly glowing from some kind of inner harmony, began to glow even more after embracing Ustinov. There is practically nothing in Baikal and in the surrounding taiga that Ustinov isn't familiar with. Reading his books about bears and elk is pure pleasure. A big man reared by the taiga, into which he has been regularly disappearing for several decades, amazingly calm and goodnatured, with a frame trimmed to the bare essentials and therefore light on his feet, rising and carrying himself without effort, he remains one of a handful of examples of the Siberian on whom nature did not economize.

On the very first day, after listening to Ustinov, Hara referred to him as an art critic of nature.

Paul, unable to let a moment go to waste, put on a cassette with recordings of cranes. Ustinov immediately recognized the Siberian cranes. The tragedy is that there are fewer and fewer of them all the time. The cormorant has completely vanished from Baikal; only the Cormorant Islands [*Baklan'i ostrova*] in Chivyrkuisky Bay continue to indicate the site of their former numerous nesting places. The black stork has become an extreme rarity. The scoter is vanishing from the lakes to the north. You won't find the gray goose, the bustard, the bean goose, or the swan goose on Baikal anymore. And all this has happened within the last few decades.

To distract us from our bleak mood, Paul began telling the story of how he once flew to his place in Wisconsin with four Siberian crane eggs, which he planned to add to the nests of some American cranes. Suddenly he heard a peep from under his seat, where the incubator was. The Siberian fledglings had decided to make their appearance in God's world in midair. After receiving the first two newborns, Paul had no choice but to thrust them into the hands of the passenger sitting beside him. Simultaneously horrified and delighted, the man held them until Paul finished carrying out his obstetrical duties and settled the family in its cradle.

A Japanese thousand-yen bill, it turns out, has a picture of a crane on it, which, in Hara's opinion, evokes sympathy and love for animals.

. . . In Khuzhir, the largest town on Olkhon Island, there is no longer rain but a light drizzle, a fine wet sifting. We bought bread and traded some vodka for an omul; it was already dusk by the time we'd sailed to the other side of the island, circling its northern extremity. Around midnight Paul, having gone up on deck, improvised "a lullaby for Baikal." It was very quiet, the searchlight picked out part of a cliff in the darkness, waves were splashing against it, and the melody seemed to rise out of the noise of the waves, which seemed to continue it.

August 29. Uzur, one of the most ancient human settlements on Baikal. A cut in the mountains, and a fairly wide one, that lacks a stream, along with a small town containing a meteorological station and research stations belonging to two institutes in Irkutsk. Steep mountain walls on both sides. It's not at all surprising that the tastes of ancient human beings and of Irkutsk scientists should coincide: there is probably no more heavenly spot on Olkhon than this. Warm, sheltered from the wind, cheerful rain or shine, and all decked out in a pine forest as though drawing you in to see if it's just as beautiful farther on, at the heart of the island.

This morning we went over to Uzur in a launch, which a young Buryat standing on the shore in rubber boots helped us haul ashore; he was Anton Irshov, a lab assistant at one of the research stations. After looking the place over, Paul took his instrument and walked toward the rock wall on the left; ten minutes later we began to hear a melody coming from that direction, which was joined by an echo on one side, intercepted on the other side, and carried out to Baikal. It was a desperate kind of call, seemingly repeated for the first time since the days when there was not a single living creature here except for the mountains, and the mountains, catching and reinforcing the sound, announced their readiness to receive life.

Another Buryat, an elderly man named Innokenty Badeevich Ishutov, came up to us, attracted by the exotic landing party loaded with gear. The Muscovites began questioning them about whether Buryats still actually burn corpses. Both of them confirmed it: yes, they do, when the old folks themselves request it. They pick out a dry tree trunk ahead of time, which is later sawed down, made into a sort of shell, and lined with brush, and then the body lying inside the shell is committed to the flames.

The nerpa was what interested me. The skeleton of one was lying on the shore. News of the mass destruction of the nerpa had been coming in from various quarters of Baikal recently. The same thing was happening to the seals in the Baltic and in the North Sea. Scientists hastily explained the cause: an infection. But infections don't just come out of the clear blue; they need conditions favorable to them, and unfavorable to the nerpa, that foster disease. Trying to escape it, the seals crawl onshore, seek the protection of humans, scream, and finally grow stiff. Anton added that if you walk along the shore, every kilometer you'll find one or two carcasses that have been cast up by the sea.

In order to reach Sagan-Khushun, a sacred place for the Buryats, we got the local supply manager to lend us a small truck, then piled onto it with all our bag and baggage and set off past virgin pine forests and the virgin cover of a steppe dotted with bunches of nettles. We passed two sheepfolds and, when it looked as though we were about to fly down a precipice, came to a stop. Here is the spot I picked for the peacefully resting Genghis Khan. This is where I would bring sinners of every kind, so that they could see what sort of world they are making war on; weak souls would find comfort here, the ailing recovery, and for those who are excessively healthy with arrogance and conceit—off with their heads.

It's hard to look at Baikal from this cliff, so overflowing is it with strength, power, sky, and water, so splendidly fenced in on the sides where the mountains stretch into the distance, so splendidly laid out as a mighty, mysterious waterway running down the center. Feelings fall into confusion and the mind grieves at the sight of this scene.

We followed a narrow footpath, which hung above an abyss for the last few meters, to a cave. Now, at the end of August, there are snowdrops on the path. The cave is spacious and seems made of two rooms, a front hall and a side room on the right with a hole up to the sky. There are no traces of a hearth, and the cave is clean; in antiquity sheep were probably driven here in bad weather, while people hid out in it even before that. Mystical signs, a mystical spirit. Paul asked Ishutov to sing something in the Buryat language, then picked up the ancient tune on his saxophone, and this made the sense of unreality even stronger.

When we were climbing back up to the truck, Boris Pereverzev asked me if I believed in the transmigration of souls. In other places you can permit yourself not to believe, but here it's better to be cautious. Here you can't help feeling drawn in and carried away into something different from what you are; here you have a suspicion that someone is attentively watching over you.

After lunch we weighed anchor and set off through strong waves and black, gloomy upswells of water for the Hare Islands [*Ushkan'i ostrova*]. The closer we got, the more clearly and distinctly Big Hare Island [*Bol'shoi Ushkanii*] stood out in the shape of a huge sturgeon swimming toward Holy Nose Peninsula.

August 30–31. On the islands. They're called the Hare Islands, I assume, because of the chain that is not long—it has only two bends—but quite intricate: here is Baikal's richest breeding ground for the nerpa, around Baikal the nerpa, based on some mysterious similarity in appearance, was called a rabbit, and in Siberia a real rabbit, which bears no relation to the nerpa, is a hare.

The Hare Islands are one of the wonders of Baikal. The lake has many wonders, some of which give rise to amazement because of their inexplicability; others evoke respect through their grandeur and abundance; others cause intoxication through the unusual influence of seemingly ordinary figures; and still others elicit reverence, from a desire to touch, absorb, and be inspired. The Hare Islands attract everyone: scientists who marvel at their peculiarities and origin and who try to get to the geological beginning of Baikal by following the late "trail" of this archipelago; tourists ready to pilfer the marble pebbles with amazing colors and shapes that lie all along the shores, the way they steal stones from the Colosseum; and nature lovers who gawk at the huge anthills as tall as a person and also at the white anthills made entirely out of marble crumbs, who wet their feet in the natural marble baths at the southern extremity of Big Island. But the Hares are most famous for the nerpa; here, on the "baby hares" [*ushkanchiki*]—three small islands—is the "beach" where dozens and hundreds of them climb out onto the rocks and warm themselves in the sun. For this reason we couldn't possibly skip the Hares: if there were any place to get a close look at the "heroine" and try to listen to her, this was it.

The first morning our ship dropped anchor across from a meteorological station, and a boat immediately left shore and sped toward us. Aleksandr Timonin, a hydrologist who has worked at the station a good ten years, had no objection whatsoever to accompanying us to Round Island [*Kruglyi*], the "baby hare" the seals particularly like.

We could spot it about five kilometers away in the direction of Holy Nose. All of us without exception wanted to go, but the motor on our launch kept stalling. Besides, it would only serve to scare the seals away rather than seek their company, so Timonin had to make three trips. Paul, the sound producer, the cameraman, and the director headed out first.

All this equipment—for filming, listening, recording, reproducing, duplicating, and so on—made our expedition picturesque and gave it a special luster. The equipment could do everything, it seemed to me, right up to inventing an image by itself, filming it by itself, and then touching it up by itself. And it cost an outrageous amount of money. Watching them load it into the boat, I couldn't help thinking about the values of our world. Human beings were insignificant objects during this operation; those departing worried least of all about how they would jump into the boat without miscalculating, but they handed over and received cameras, tripods, microphones, and some kind of nickel-plated cases of cyclopean construction with such gentleness, with such a stopping of the heart along with a great many "carefuls," that God have mercy and save us all.

Ustinov and I arrived at Round Island with the second group and traveled in a perfectly human fashion, saying no prayers for any eyepieces. We docked at the north end, got out carefully, and just as carefully, so as not to accidentally scare off the sweet little creatures obligingly lying on the rocks in a state of bliss, followed a footpath to the island's southeastern tip. We didn't have far to walk; the small island was pretty modest. For the last few dozen meters we hunched down as we crept along, and I peered at the boulders on the shore, trying to guess which one of them would start to stir first, but I should have been looking at the water. Seals were surfacing nearby; sometimes five or six heads would bob up at once, swimming like black balls, alternately hiding and appearing. One of them crept up quite close and, thrusting itself out of the water, suddenly sneezed just like a person, got embarrassed, and vanished. Paul came over and gave me his binoculars, through which I could see how the nerpa moved through the depths, ripping through the water like a torpedo at enormous speed.

We sat there waiting for about an hour and a half, but the seals expressed no more desire to dry off than they had before. A slight breeze began rising from below, and the bay was covered with crinkles. Paul turned to his last resort: he stood up straight and began to play

"Glorious Sea, Sacred Baikal," which should have made the lowliest crustacean appear before us no matter who performed it. The seals did not appear.

We had better luck the second day. Sunshine had a greater effect on them than "Glorious Sea," and without any particular wariness they began to straddle the boulders they themselves had polished, comically moving their flippers up and down and pushing themselves higher and higher in spurts. Observing them posed no difficulty for either the equipped or the unequipped eye. Paul had managed to conceal a microphone right next to them and the recording went on for hours, but it produced nothing more than puffing and the smack of waves against the rocks.

But Paul was satisfied with even this much. He had seen the nerpa, become closely acquainted with it, you might say, and confirmed his decision to use it in a fairy-tale story that would sound forth in music bewitched by this beauty.

. . . Now onward. Our itinerary goes like this: the Barguzin Nature Preserve, where Semyon Ustinov once worked for five years, so that they know him there, he knows them, and they'll help us get to know it; then, on the way back, the recently created Baikal-Lena Nature Preserve on the western shore, where the same Ustinov now works as the deputy director for scientific research. After that we'll go back to Olkhon, not for omul this time but for the Buryats' distant past, and our most unpleasant stop will come at the end: Baikalsk, where there's a cellulose complex, the impressions of which should be softened by Baikal itself during the three or four hours it will take us to sail across to Listvennichny.

September 1. We headed for Davsha (in the Barguzin Nature Preserve) at night, when the ship had already started to rock slightly. The forecast was for an *angara*, a northerly wind that can cause trouble if you're out on the water. I was awakened in the middle of the night by a crashing and rumbling; a gale was tossing and tearing at our vessel, something was rolling around up above, producing a loud thunder that ran back and forth, something was creaking painfully. And something was rolling around inside me with the same unpleasant sounds. Until then I'd had no idea what seasickness was all about, even though I'd been in a number of scrapes right here on Baikal, but this time we made each other's acquaintance. I suffered until dawn, then crawled with difficulty, clutching the bulkhead, to the deckhouse. The news is that we never made it to Davsha because our vessel, afraid of exposing its side when crossing to the eastern shore, was forced to head north, straight into the wind. I can't see the shore; swells are splashing everywhere. These weren't even swells but mountains coming one after another; the ship would cut into them, rise up with a leap, and then bury itself heavily in the watery precipices. Water washed over the whole upper deck and splashed against the windowpanes of the deckhouse. Later, when the shoreline began to appear, it, too, looked like dashing waves.

And what waves! Three and a half to four meters high. This happens often enough! But the first mate explained that that's the limit for navigation on Baikal.

It began to calm down around ten o'clock. The rolling of the waves became more even, but every two or three minutes such a whopper would suddenly pile up that you wanted to scream for help.

We lay side by side in a row until twelve o'clock.

September 2. Corpses Point [*Mys Pokoiniki*]. On Baikal there are two Corpses Points and two towns with this unlyrical name. One is on Chivyrkuisky Bay and the other here. According to legend, this name had stuck but was carried over onto the maps only later, after the inhabitants suffered mass food poisoning attributed to sturgeon. Whether this is true or not is hard to say. Sturgeon have now become as great a rarity in Baikal as Nessie in her mysterious lake. But here the name most likely came from Corpse Creek [*rechka Pokoinitskaia*], which has some basis for its appellation: it comes to life only in the spring and summer after the rains, then keeps drying up over and over again.

The meteorological station stands not on the point but in a beautiful sharp bend in the creek where there's a deep meadow. Here lies the forest conserve of the Baikal-Lena Nature Preserve, the largest at Baikal, with 660,000 hectares of land and 120 kilometers of shoreline. A most comforting thought: here the water is patrolled for a distance of three kilometers from shore, whereas if some thief crawls out of the Baikalsk Nature Preserve and gets one step away from land, the law is powerless.

The Baikal-Lena Preserve is not completely developed yet; its boundaries have merely been determined. In Russia it's standard practice in matters of conservation for officials to take their time. Two years have passed since they announced the decision to create two national parks at Baikal, one on the Buryat side and one on the Irkutsk side, but in both places they're still not even out of the starting gate. Not long ago Olkhon was free territory, then its northern part became a game reserve, and now it's a national park, but putting up signs doesn't change a thing, and Olkhon remains what it always was. People chop down trees there just as before and pull up medicinal herbs, those who aren't too lazy, while columns of cars pour across on the ferry without any restrictions whatsoever.

Oleg Gusev is the man we have to thank for the Baikal-Lena Nature Preserve. Not him alone, but him above all. Sometimes good endeavors also meet with success. He spent years measuring and describing, going around to various offices, demonstrating the need, and—who could have thought it possible?—it worked!

. . . And suddenly a fiery sphere appears on the horizon up ahead on the way to Olkhon—a scarlet glow with a green ray. The glow keeps growing wider and wider above the Small Sea until it turns into a rainbow, still spherical but becoming long and rising into the sky. And only after ten minutes or so does the other end of the rainbow appear on the western shore.

September 3. Khuzhir again. We arrived early this morning, visited the regional museum, assured ourselves, based on material from the joint Soviet-American archaeological expedition that made excavations on Olkhon, that Americans and Siberians are close cousins, having rubbed shoulders with each other at one time, and then spent the whole day preparing for an evening of Buryat songs, sung, of course, around a campfire. The producer was dying to see a shaman, and he got to see one: an undersized, fidgety man who allegedly practices on the sly. Some schoolgirls would sometimes put on performances; we went to their teacher and she agreed to talk her girls into performing for us and to bring them back that evening.

A campfire means omul roasted on a spit. We got permission to build a fire in a forested area (it's a national park!) and hauled in some firewood. Then we set out at dusk for Shaman Hill, a holy place for Buryats about 1-1/2–2 kilometers from town.

Baikal lay tranquil, as though in a dish; seagulls sat high on the water, welded to the lake. Visibility was so great you believed you could see all the way to the end, to the rows of mountains on each side. Even the air stood still; it didn't breathe but floated in its skin, which you could feel after the rain.

From this upper Shaman Rock we descended in the same solemn march to the sacred cliff that the path to the cave ran through. Shamans used to enter the cliff from one side and, performing a miracle, come out the other. Our shaman, adopting the role with unusual and suspicious willingness, started to explain the distant past; Paul listened attentively, Boris Pereverzev stood with his notepad ready. But the shaman, not saying anything that made sense, got lost and confused, and it became clear what kind of shaman he was. On the way back up the hill some boys who'd appeared out of the clear blue took two of the girls aside and ordered them to follow. As it turned out, these two girls with Russian faces had somehow learned several Buryat songs, while the other three girls—Buryats—didn't know their own language.

And when it got dark and they tried to sing, nothing came of it. An old Buryat woman was there, too, the grandmother of one of the girls; she remembered bits and snatches, would start singing, and then falter. Finally our shaman flatly declared that on this hill you weren't supposed to utter even ordinary words without performing the sprinkling ritual first.

But as luck would have it, we'd forgotten the necessary liquid back on the boat. And the boat, as luck would have it, had left the pier and anchored far out in the roadstead. We sent a car to signal it, but that took over an hour, during which the girls stood up several times to do the *yokhor* (a Buryat round dance), holding hands and trying to move around the fire, but no one knew the words; the inner columns of flame chirred above their feeble movements. The shaman shouted at them imperiously; the teacher's son, a boy of about four, stared at all this with his mouth open in fright.

The vodka finally arrived. The shaman hurriedly started sprinkling the fire, dipping his fingers into a mug, let Paul sprinkle a little while, then drank the rest and became even more animated—and by now nothing could hold him back. They tried to sing again and again were unsuccessful. It ended by our being treated to omul on a spit, which alone turned out wonderfully well because Semyon Ustinov was in charge of it, and we began edging away to the sound of the shaman's cries.

Baikal lay in solid darkness, gleaming dimly under the gloomy sky. We felt especially ashamed of all this buffoonery in front of Baikal.

After returning to the boat, we suddenly realized that Paul wasn't with us. He showed up half an hour later. Earlier in the day he'd spotted a poster announcing "A Party for Young People" and had dropped in on the way back to see what it was. "And what was it?" I tried to get out of him. He didn't reply immediately or willingly, and his face looked dark. Primitive rock music had been blaring, while boys and girls twitched and jerked. He didn't ask, What is this doing here? and there was no need to answer.

But an answer did come. When Paul's saxophone began to sing in the darkness from a hill, all of Baikal responded: the echo rang out pure, powerful, and wide. The genuine answering the genuine.

September 5. We arrived in Baikalsk early this morning. Rain. Clouds of smoke from the pulp plant press against the land and water and spread like a dirty fog across Baikal.

Against this background Paul played a song of protest, which he'd performed in the Grand Canyon a month earlier at an Indian reservation suffering because of uranium mines. Later, not ashamed of using fine-sounding words, he said that the Grand Canyon and Baikal not only resemble each other, but that their fates should resemble each other's, so that they will serve beauty and joy forever.

Every last one of us lined up in a row on deck, gazing at the plant, and we looked at it for a long time with the kind of stoniness that arises when consciousness refuses to understand what has happened.

This is the feeling of all who write about Baikal: no matter how much they say about it, they've merely dipped their toes in its water, looked at its majestic outstretchedness from the very edge, clumsily poked their noses into its life. Grigory Galazy, director of the Limnological Institute for thirty years and now director of the Baikalsk Museum, recently published a book called *Questions and Answers About Baikal*[24] in which he gives nearly a thousand answers to a thousand questions, but many more thousands of questions concerning Baikal probably still remain. Just as there is yet another element beneath its aqueous element—alluvia up to six kilometers deep have accumulated over millions of years—so there are thicknesses and thicknesses of virgin territory beyond the layer of the known. What could be simpler than the surface shape of Baikal, its geography, all that yields to vision and calculation? But scientists kept making corrections here, too, until very recently. Sometimes Baikal itself undertakes these corrections, as happened in the nineteenth century when an earthquake in one fell swoop caused a steppe north of the Selenga River measuring two hundred square kilometers to vanish underwater, forming Gap Bay [*zaliv Proval*]. But more often than not people walked its shores and sailed its waters without noticing. And its grandness, enthronedness, preciousness, which affect the imagination and the soul—these certainly aren't mineral deposits that you can count, but they, too, seem designed, along with the mineral reserves, for the whole span of time that human beings will exist near Baikal, and they don't reveal themselves in an instant. Baikal is greater now and will always be greater than any library devoted to it or any feelings and representations.

Time and again you suddenly realize: no one has written about Chivyrkuisky Bay, where the water warms up in the summer to the same temperature as water in southern climes, where the soft patterning of shore is dotted with hot springs, and where rocky islands stand guard at its entrance, pining for the cries of cormorants. Olkhon, where you can find everything—taiga and cliffs and steppes and deserts—within eighty kilometers, has not been examined from end to end. No one has paid a call on Sandy Bay, where by the will of the creator bell-towers of rock rise along its edges and seem poised to strike someday with a heavy stony peal, raising mighty forces from the deep. And the lakes near Baikal remain on the sidelines, but one of them, Frolikh, to the north contains yet another mystery: a red fish called the Frolikh char [*davatchan*]. No one has walked the whole length of the Baikal Shoreline Railroad [*Krugobaikal'skaia zheleznaia doroga*], built at the beginning of the twentieth century in harmony with Baikal and now abandoned; no one has marveled at the numerous tunnels,

The Baikal Shoreline Railroad

viaducts, and bridges over raging streams that Baikal has completely domesticated over the decades, as if that's how things were when it was created.

No, not everything about Baikal can be described; you have to see it. But when you see it, when you're constantly beside it, opening yourself up to it, you become aware of the feebleness and futility of your powers of perception. What is pouring into you cools and darkens before it has time to reach the main thing, some kind of light bulb capable of illuminating and bringing together the whole perceptible domain. The answering reflections are intermittent, like sheet lightning, and indistinct, now reaching a point of passionate agitation, of enthusiasm, of triumphant music, now dimming unexpectedly to a faint smolder. But if you start blowing vigorously on these smoldering reflections, you can't fan them into flames. And then come thoughts about the all too striking disparity between us: Who are we if not bugs in comparison with the great works of life lying and soaring before us? Are we really allowed to count the hieroglyphs stretching many versts across its pages and to figure out the sounds resonating above the world? We hear only what we take enough pains to hear.

But later on, as if out of nowhere, without any summons, something will suddenly light up inside you as a scene that your memory didn't retain, that perhaps you are seeing for the first time, only you have no doubt that it belongs to Baikal; it smells of its breathing, will come to life with its colors and last for minute after minute, will draw you along its shore, will open up farther and wider—and you'll believe that it's not you who has remembered Baikal but Baikal who has remembered you and summoned you for friendship and conversation, that it finds protection in all who are drawn to it.

Who would have thought that we, small and disparate, coming into the world for a fleeting instant, would actually be needed for protection?!

The first portent of disaster, like the harmless cloud creeping out of a narrow valley by which an experienced person can unfailingly predict the approach of "mountain" weather, appeared at Baikal back in the early 1950s, when the catches of omul, the famous Baikal fish, began to dwindle. Had the lake been fished out? There had always been so many omul and the local inhabitants had gotten so used to them that they couldn't even begin to imagine life without omul. Overfishing did occur, of course, in the starvation years during and after World War II, when they extracted up to one hundred thousand centners [about 5,500 tons] for the state alone and no one knows how many for themselves, but this couldn't have cleaned out Baikal. Over the years the real reason became apparent. After the war loggers had set to work clearcutting the taiga around Baikal without any restraint, floating timber down the rivers where the omul went to spawn, polluting them, clogging the bottoms and banks with wood, and blocking the omul's means for continuing its kind. In this way they completely exterminated the Barguzin strain (there had been four populations of omul, then three remained; the fourth was cultivated elsewhere for commercial purposes). It goes without saying that the omul was not the only one to suffer; the abundance of fish, which enraptured everyone who saw Baikal, from Archpriest Avvakum to Fridtjof Nansen, and which was as commonplace to the local folk as the undiminishing countlessness of stars in the sky, suddenly seemed to have been undermined and was being undermined more and more every year.

The causes are clear, so get busy and take measures! What could be simpler!

But when in our country did anyone come to his senses before a disaster struck, while the disaster was only sending out warning signals? No, those in charge must invariably wait until it has fattened up, hardened, and grown from a mere trifle into an enormous problem, a worthy opponent, and then meet it with pealing bells, do circle dances around it as though they're at a carnival, find the most comfortable place possible for it, and make sacrifices. Moreover, they put things off until a second disaster and a third, so lovingly nurtured by the guardians' noninterference, show up to join the party. Only later, when they finally find themselves in a choke hold, Bang! comes a government decree: Not one step back! And they dillydally for a few more years so that the battle will unquestionably be not for life but for death, no less so than the Battle of Stalingrad, then walk away, trying to deceive the enemy, to their own grave—and anon a government decree! And then it's a matter of who will outmuscle whom. . . . That's the way we do things in our country.

This is just what happened at Baikal.

So the omul is depleted—aw, that's too bad! Now no one had time for omul, no one had time for sturgeon: a high-stakes game had begun at Baikal. After the dam for the power plant at Irkutsk went up, the level of the Siberian sea rose one meter. This circumstance suggested an idea to a certain N. Grigorovich, a bold engineering mind from the Hydroelectric Energy Project, who proposed lowering Baikal below its previous level—to make it feel the hand of humankind! All they had to do was put thirty thousand tons of ammonite at the base of the Shaman Rock at the source of the Angara and blow it into the air, and the liberated Baikal would take off for the Angara's hydroelectric stations—the greatest in the world—without impediment. That its water already turned turbines was considered insufficient. The backers of this plan calculated that lowering the level of Baikal by only one centimeter would provide so much electricity that they could smelt eleven thousand tons of aluminum. And if they lowered it several meters? Why, that's a whole sea of aluminum! Sheer abundance! Communism!

Commissions began scurrying around: Should they blow it up or not?

And Grigorovich would have given the Shaman Rock, which was blocking the path to communism, a good whack if Siberian scientists hadn't resorted to an extreme measure, intimidating the zealous engineer and his supporters with the likelihood of an unforeseen geological upheaval, after which a huge swell from Baikal could easily sweep away all that had been built up and made habitable along the Angara for three hundred years.

As with every revolution, the revolution in science and technology could not get along without overthrowing the old authorities and erecting new ones. This time they tackled the very foundations of nature. They found the view of water as the basis of life antediluvian; water became a mechanical mover of technological progress, a means of flushing, cooling, and transporting. With such a turn of affairs they couldn't let Baikal be a sponger any longer. The cleanest water in the world with the highest content of oxygen and the lowest content of mineral salts: Isn't this not water but gold? That's just the kind we need.

The decision to put pulp plants on the shores of Baikal was made back in 1953. By that time the Americans had sneaked up on a new rayon cord, known by the brand name Super-super, whose fibers had an unprecedented breaking length and which would be used in tires for high-speed aircraft. We, naturally, needed cord of similar quality, too, but only extra-clean water with a minimal dose of mineral substances was suitable for washing the cellulose from which it would be made. Only three sources met this requirement—Lake Ladoga, Lake Teletskoe in the Altay Mountains, and Baikal. We can assume that what decided Baikal's fate in the end was a most insignificant and unlikely thing concealed in assonance. The plant in Florida that produced the new product belonged to the Buckeye Cellulose Company. Competition is competition: you have Buckeye [*Bakai*], we have Baikal. It was not known whether we would beat the Americans in cellulose, but we would certainly beat them with Baikal. The strong in this world sometimes exhibit weaknesses of this sort; for them nothing human is off-limits.

After a site had already been picked at the mouth of the Solzan River on the south end of Baikal, they had a chance to move the cellulose complex to Bratsk, where a power plant was under construction, which even the minister for the timber industry himself was inclined to do. But the planners objected. "We don't care about the cost!"—this song, it seems, was not yet sung on every street corner in those years, but its spirit was hovering overhead. Fish look for the deepest water, planners for the best site. Bratsk couldn't compare with Baikal: it had bloodsucking insects, taiga, remoteness, whereas Baikal had picturesqueness, omul instead of flatfish, and a good supply of cheerfulness. Its name alone aroused eagerness and enthusiasm in the planners' hearts as they bent over their sheets of Whatman paper. And if we ever have to erect a monument to the escort that voluntarily set about conducting Baikal to the place of its demise, then in the foreground should be B. Smirnov, the tough chief engineer at the Siberian State Institute for Planning Pulp and Paper Enterprises, a man prepared to destroy anything: in the discussion that unfolded with the lake's defenders, this figure acted like a drill sergeant, yelling at writers and scientists as if they were new recruits.

Builders appeared at the site of the future Baikalsk in 1958. Its construction was publicized as a crash project for the Young Communist League. A little later work also spread to the Selenga River, where they began erecting a complex to make cardboard out of cellulose. In one book on Siberia I recently ran across a rhyming slogan that the "crash project" [*udarnaia*] flaunted back then and that would be a shame not to quote:

Hey, Barguzin, stir up a swell!
Admire our strength and our savvy:
We're building a plant and we'll build one more plant
In the wide taiga river valley!

Taiga? What the hell were they talking about?! It was the most heavenly spot, not far from the railroad, in the warm sunny valley of a small stream.

A lot of things are now blamed on the delusions of the times. That's what the era was like, people say, electrified by the conquest of nature and by change: society's universal intoxication with the highly publicized construction projects that promised prosperity, "the unbroken fever of everyday life,"[25] triumphant reports, production statistics with an ever- increasing number of zeros to the right, excitement, enthusiasm, members of the Young Communist League filing out of conventions in columns singing, "We're going, friends, to distant lands . . ." How could anyone keep a clear head in the atmosphere of celebration that was continually being generated?!

If that is so, then who, after all, are we? Combat units ready to march in any direction at any command? Haven't centuries of civilization left human beings with any memory to suggest that no kind of mass hysteria, whether labeled "enthusiasm" or called by its own name, has ever led to any good? That well-being requires intelligent, cautious, and long-term creative effort, not a headlong rush to the attack? Let's not hide the fact that this was war, one more civil war against our own fields and rivers, our own values and sacred things, that, leaping from place to place, is still going on today. And, as in any war, it is the best of everything that has perished and continues to perish in its grip.

For a long time people tried not to hand over Baikal; it was too revered and too dear on the old wooden calendar of national shrines. After the long period when ordinary individuals kept silent, public opinion revived in the 1960s, essentially because of Baikal. The initial rebuff came as a surprise to the father/captains of the economy; they were used to having all their plans received with the same staunch support as divine predestination. And suddenly some writers, who existed for the purpose of creating odes, and some scientists who were also confused about the reason for their existence, and then the common folk, stirred up by the writers and scientists, began to raise the question, Won't we destroy Baikal? And they arrived at an answer: Yes, we will. Over our dead bodies.

At that time the method of fighting any heresy continued to follow the old recipes. P. Katsuba, secretary of the Irkutsk Regional Committee of the Communist party, labeled Grigory Galazy, director of the Limnological Institute and one of the troublemakers who weren't the least bit interested in calming down, "an abettor of imperialism." On the eastern shore of Baikal A. Modogoev, secretary of the Buryat Regional Committee, picked up the refrain: Galazy, in coming out against the

Selenginsk complex, was "an enemy of the Buryat people." With "merits" like these, Galazy wouldn't have stood a chance had this happened a little earlier, and he couldn't expect any favors from those years either; if he survived, this says something about the indisputable strength of the rebuff that would not consent to the fate lying in store for Baikal.

By now only a handful of people remember that at first they'd proposed putting two plants at the Solzan site. After the first wave of protest, which came in the late 1950s and early 1960s, one of them was moved out of harm's way to the Volga. For the other one, they had to revise the design and redraw the purification structures. Without these adjustments we wouldn't have Baikal to admire today, only the force that would have succeeded in destroying it in just a few years; even with these adjustments it's painful to look at the changes that have taken place in the lake.

And there was one more opportunity to renounce the construction and start-up of the cellulose complexes. Another desperate splash of protest and appeals to listen to reason came in the mid-1960s. Articles and essays appeared one after another by writers Frants Taurin, Oleg Volkov, and Vladimir Chivilikhin in which they exposed the dishonest game being played at Baikal. They were supported by distinguished academicians from the Siberian branch of the Academy of Sciences, including Andrey Trofimuk, V. Sukachyov, Sergey Sobolev, and Mikhail Lavrentiev, as well as by academicians Pyotr Kapitsa, Aleksandr Yanshin, Boris Laskorin, and many other scientists.

Leonid Leonov[26] writes in the *Literary Gazette* [*Literaturnaia gazeta*]: "All the people will take off their hats on that dark day when the first poison gushes into this purest of chalices . . ."

Mikhail Sholokhov[27] at a party congress: "But perhaps we'll find the courage in ourselves to renounce the clear-cutting of the forests around Baikal and the construction of cellulose enterprises there? . . ."

The mood of society turned tense again, to do nothing about it would have been too much, and in the spring of 1966 the State Planning Committee created a government commission of experts with broad rights and powers, all the way up to vetoing the cellulose plants.

But . . . the Planning Committee knew who to pick to head the commission.

Much later, in 1985, the U.N. gave a special award to the Soviet Academy of Sciences "for its activities in preserving the pearl of the natural world—Lake Baikal." Academician Nikolay Zhavoronkov should have gotten credit for this award, since it was his opinion that finally triumphed in the squabbling among the Baikal scientists.

Thus in the fateful year of 1966, when they were deciding for the last time how Baikal should be utilized, the head of the expert commission was Academician Zhavoronkov, with Academician S. Volfkovich as his assistant. The commission labored indefatigably for three months and came to a unanimous conclusion: it was criminal to drag out completion of the construction of the cellulose plants on Baikal. While addressing a joint meeting of the board of directors of the State Planning Commission, the board of directors of the State Committee on Science and Technology, and the Presidium of the Academy of Sciences, Zhavoronkov set three retorts on the table in front of him. They contained water from Baikal and artificially obtained wastewater from the two plants, which he proposed that the lofty gathering sample and then decide which was which by their taste. There were no volunteers; they took Zhavoronkov's word for it. When Academician Trofimuk permitted himself to question the commission's conclusions, Zhavoronkov called his behavior "tactless" and "insulting to the members of the commission, who had worked very intensely, selflessly, and impartially . . ."

Academician Kapitsa did not agree with the commission either, predicting in his presentation that, based on the completely different chemical composition of the discharged wastewater, "even a small amount of toxic pollutants from the pulp plants can utterly destroy the favorable balance of nature and totally ruin the lake's purity."

Zhavoronkov didn't dare attack Kapitsa, but he led his response off into such foggy digressions that you could understand only one thing: everything had already been decided and it was pointless to argue. And that's how it was. Someone tried to stammer out that America, whom we were hoping to overtake in super-super cord, had already abandoned this same super cord and switched to a more durable and economical synthetic fiber. The rebuttal: once we have the product, we'll find a use for it.

"Now concerning the biological productivity of Baikal," Zhavoronkov thought to add in his closing remarks. "What about the fish, the omul? We must preserve the biological productivity, of course. We must preserve the fish. But Baikal's significance to the fishing industry is not great and has only local significance. The maximum catches of omul used to be as high as six to eight thousand tons. Now they've fallen to a third of that. At the same time Baikal's pulp plant will produce fifteen thousand tons of yeast as a byproduct for fodder that will be fifty percent protein. If this is converted to standard protein, it comes to more than thirty thousand tons. This amount is sufficient to fatten enough hogs to get six thousand tons of meat, or sixty thousand centners. This can have an even greater impact on the poultry industry."

Be silent, o wretched thought, and recognize the greatness of these minds: were it not for the light of science, Baikal would keep producing omul until the end of the world, but now it will be elevated to the level of chickens and pigs.

That was it. Now the hands of the cellulose cowboys prancing impatiently in front of Baikal were untied—start throwing your lassoes! And that same summer the first plant began to belch smoke and pour its great waste water into "the purest of chalices." Hats came off, all right, but they were tossed into the air with cries of "Hooray!"

On the monument that we can spot in the future somewhere on the lake shore near Baikalsk in honor of the conqueror/destroyers of "the pearl," Academician Zhavoronkov should be easy to recognize, but next to him is something mythical shaped almost like Serpent Gorynych[28] or some other horrible thing: this is science in the hands of the Zhavoronkovs. Here there will also certainly be room for A. Beym, director of the Institute of Ecological Toxicology at Baikalsk; he, along with his willing cohorts, spent many years trying to prove that the pulp plant brought Baikal no harm, only benefit. But the institute tried to prove this so vigorously, confusing black and white as if it were colorblind, that even the cellulose fanatics were forced to decline the services of a scholarly institution (that's right, a whole institution!) that had gone overboard; it was forced to go to work for the conservation sector.

But when the plants came to life and began cooking up their brand of trouble, which flew in the face of public opinion and common sense, they required a delicate framework of legislative instructions and provisos. In January 1969 the government adopted a highly publicized

decree called "On Measures for the Conservation and Rational Utilization of the Complex of Natural Resources in the Lake Baikal Basin."
Another trace horse was hitched on in 1971: "On Additional Measures
for Ensuring the Rational Utilization and Preservation of the Natural
Resources at Lake Baikal." They'd implanted in Baikal a cancerous
tumor in the form of chemical enterprises and then began admonishing
them, "Behave yourselves. Act benign." But the duty of safeguarding
Baikal's health was then thrust upon the Siberian branch of the Academy of Sciences, which had fought the pernicious operations. And
today they lay the blame for its poor health on that very organization.

But with these decrees they finally thought of the omul and banned
omul fishing from 1969 on. They also banned the practice of floating
timber down tributaries. At least the snail reached one of its goals.

The third government decree concerning Baikal came in 1977.
Obviously it would not have been necessary had the previous decrees
been carried out. The culprits gave the appearance of complying, made
self-strengthening movements, as in gymnastics, learned to identify
which way the "concerning Baikal" winds were blowing, and issued
secret orders to whichever department had been instructed and
charged with oversight: call off the alarm.

And then in April 1987 came the fourth exalted document, billed
as "the final decisive battle."

Several years before that I, too, had somehow managed to get
involved in the Baikal epic as it dragged on and on. And although it
resembled the plot of a detective novel from one point of view and tilting at windmills from another, and although taking part in either, I
realized, would result in nothing but a loss of time and energy, we,
however, don't do the choosing but end up being chosen when rein-
forcements are needed.

And besides, how could I not get involved? This was Baikal. . . . By
that time Baikal had endured more than its share of suffering: from the
cellulose enterprises, from the airborne emissions of the industries
planted as thickly up and down the Angara Valley as carrots in a garden, from clear-cutting and forest fires, from the oceans of toxic swill
carried in by the Selenga River, from chemical fertilizers washed down
from the fields, from its proximity to BAM on the north side, and from
many other causes. It didn't take any special knowledge or vision to see

that Baikal, while becoming an ever more popular theme, was turning into an ownerless body from which, behind all the talk, everyone wanted to grab something and which no one wanted to help. Environmental protection work in nature preserves and inspections to enforce conservation laws couldn't do very much; they were like using an eyedropper to add drops of clear liquid mixed with tears in the hope of purifying the sea.

We've become so good at allegories that when I saw a sign at the front entrance to the pulp plant reading "We will defend Baikal, the pearl of Siberia," I automatically interpreted it as: "Lord, forgive us, but let us in someone else's door and help us rake everything up and carry it off."

FROM "A BAIKAL DIARY"

January 24, 1986. A meeting with leaders of the Ministry for the Timber Industry at its offices. I managed to arrange this meeting with help from the editorial staff of the newspaper *Izvestia.* So many bitter "whys" had recently been directed at the ministry and so few intelligible replies had been forthcoming that a talk with the minister had become essential.

They met me down below, escorted me to the fifth floor, and led me into a spacious, ascetic-looking office. The minister and I shook hands. I couldn't help noting his youthful appearance and vigor. Mikhail Ivanovich Busygin's knowledge of our region is not based on hearsay. He worked for six years at the level of a deputy minister as the general director of the construction of the Ust-Ilimsk Timber Industry Complex and of the town itself. I'd assumed that the minister and I would talk privately, but he had invited his deputy ministers. In came G. F. Pronin, deputy minister for the cellulose and paper industry; N. S. Savchenko, head of timber purchasing; and my fellow countryman K. M. Prodayvoda, former secretary of the Buryat Regional Committee of the Communist party.

The first question inevitably arose by itself:

"Mikhail Ivanovich, how do you react to the recent newspaper articles on Baikal?" (Practically all the major Moscow papers—*Pravda, Izves-*

tia, Komsomolskaya Pravda, Soviet Russia—had raised another ruckus about the fate that had befallen "the sacred sea.")

"Positively," the minister replies, shrugging his shoulders. "Violations sometimes occur in our line of work, too. We punish those who are guilty."

"But that doesn't help Baikal."

"What should we do? Take them to court?"

"That wouldn't help Baikal either."

"By and large we follow the decrees of the party and the government. Here they are." The minister opened a compilation of legislative decisions on Baikal. "We do abide by them. If new laws are enacted, we'll abide by them, too."

"Do you really abide by all of them?

"Do you know how many times the PDK [*predel'no-dopustimye kontsentratsii*] [the allowable maximum concentration (Rasputin)] of industrial pollutants has changed at the Baikalsk plant? Six times. And always in the direction of making them tougher. As soon as we reach the target figures, they give us new ones. As soon as we achieve those, we have to catch up again."

Here the minister was being crafty: the PDKs had changed not in the direction of becoming tougher but to accommodate the purification capabilities of the plant, and the target figures were ordered by the ministry itself.

"Violations occur at the plant every day," I reminded him.

"Where did you get that information?"

"From data compiled by the Baikal Basin inspection team and the Hydrometry Service.

"We have different data."

The truth must be told: How many times during that discussion were we unable to understand each other precisely because the evidence we were using, which should have come from the same unbiased oversight agencies concerned with the fate of Baikal, turned out to be not only different but sometimes completely contradictory? The minister assured me that the base level of pollution from the Baikalsk Pulp and Paper Complex did not exceed the allowable maximum concentration and had not increased in recent years; I, however, recalling the baby-macho figure of a projected "spot" of 0.7 square kilometers, knew of an actual pollution zone that covered dozens of square kilometers. With poisoning substances penetrating far into the water's depths. Emissions into the atmosphere covered an area of two thousand square kilometers. The forests are drying out; poisons fall on the soil that are later washed back into the lake. But the ministry believes that the plant has nothing to do with this. The forests are withering, they claim, as a result of several years of drought in the area east of Baikal and of violations of hydrological standards, and they cite the conclusion of specialists in applied geophysics. Their explanation is a strange one. The fir trees and Siberian pines felt splendid for hundreds of years when all sorts of violations occurred, and now they've suddenly gotten sick. And I couldn't refrain from asking the minister if he believes that the geophysicists' "discovery" is accurate. Yes, he does.

Believing is to his advantage.

And another thing about this "discovery." It's common knowledge that the purification technology at the Baikalsk Pulp and Paper Complex basically counts on the harmful organic substances dissolving and dispersing by themselves. Not even close to completely, of course, for complete dissolution and dispersal are impossible. The so-called conservative organic matter and insoluble mineral contaminants go into Baikal. During its twenty years of operation the plant has released about one million or, according to different calculations, more than one million tons of mineral substances whose composition is absolutely foreign to the lake's chemistry, the very ones that Academician Kapitsa warned about. The polluters found an ingenious way out of the "mineral" predicament. Since Baikal's own water is actually low in minerals, they declared it harmful. And the plant's output they deemed a useful flavoring. I remember first hearing this several years ago at the center for scientific research that the ministry uses, the Institute of Ecological Toxicology attached to the Baikalsk plant. Nothing could surprise me after that. And yet to be on the safe side I asked Prodayvoda:

"Konstantin Matveevich, do you recall if the local residents drink Baikal's water?"

"Of course they do," he answers in surprise. "What else are they going to drink?"

"But Academician Zhavoronkov and you here at the ministry believe that people shouldn't drink it. That it's harmful."

"Generally speaking, that's right," Prodayvoda catches himself. "This leads to endocrine diseases. It doesn't have enough iodine.

"You certainly aren't going to drink distilled water," the minister joins in.

"But perhaps distilled drugstore water and natural water whose properties come close to distilled water aren't the same thing?" I defend myself, recalling at the same time that Baikal water has always been renowned and highly valued precisely because it was considered almost ideally fresh, with a low content of suspended matter, silicon, iron, and iodine and a large amount of oxygen.

We continue to speak different languages. The ministry believes that the diluted wastewater from the plants has no harmful effect on the organisms living in Baikal and refers to "the many years of research by scientific bodies," having in mind by "scientific bodies" none other than the institute at Baikalsk under its control. I countered with observations that also, of course, were not my own, pointing out that during the years since the plants had begun operating, the concentration of harmful substances in more than half the area of Baikal had become dangerous to its inhabitants and that the number of unique species of algae in the southern part of the lake was decreasing. The ministry assures me that the area where the wastes are dumped is a zone of ecological well-being. But I had come to the ministry armed with the fact that amid this "well-being" the *Epischura* is perishing.

"The authorities in Irkutsk are now proposing to redesign the Baikalsk plant and make it into a different, harmless industry that might remain under your jurisdiction. Along with a series of other measures, couldn't this become the solution to the Baikal problem? What do you think?"

An awkward silence sets in for a moment, and then the minister begins to explain:

"This is out of our hands. If they tell us to make stools, we'll start making stools. Any change even in our quota assignments, let alone a decision about whether the plant will continue to exist or not, depends on the State Planning Commission."

"What condition do you think Baikal will be in by the year 2000?"

Pronin replies with certainty:

"Baikal won't suffer."

"Don't you feel that the practice of taking as much as possible from nature without worrying about the needs of the human race tomorrow undermines not only the future economy but also the morals of society?"

The minister has a hard time answering questions of this kind.

"We abide by the decrees," he says evasively.

"Do you have occasion to go to Baikal very often?"

"Not often, but I go there . . ."

We say goodbye almost warmly.

January 25, 1986. The Moscow apartment of Academician Boris Nikolaevich Laskorin. Boris Nikolaevich has also invited Vasily Fyodorovich Yevstratov, a corresponding member of the Academy of Sciences and an expert tire man, to talk with me. Boris Nikolaevich himself has served on three state commissions on Baikal and knows all the ins and outs of the Baikal story from start to finish. He says:

"We made not one, not two, but a whole series of mistakes in building the Baikalsk Pulp and Paper Complex. The main mistake was in scientific prognostication. Cord production should have developed along the lines of highly durable synthetic fibers and metal cord. We're incurring huge losses by using tires made with cellulose rather than with modern cord. Our second mistake was in choosing the plant site. Baikal's water was not essential for an enterprise of this sort, and the local timber was not suitable for obtaining supercellulose. Add to this the seismicity of the region, which could make its presence felt at any moment. The third mistake was in justifying the technological plan. There couldn't have been any illusions about the quality of purification . . ."

"Baikal's water wasn't necessary and the timber was unsuitable? Baikal cellulose acts as a kind of brake on the production of reliable tires on a world level? Is that right?"

"That's exactly right."

Vasily Fyodorovich Yevstratov, who worked in an institute for the tire industry for thirty years, adds:

"I remember that Sobolev, the deputy minister for the petrochemical industry, tried to turn it down from the very start: 'We don't need Baikal cellulose.' Its physical and mechanical properties aren't two or three times inferior to synthetic fibers; they're inferior by several orders of magnitude. Do you understand the difference?"

"But back then, in the 1960s, wasn't high-speed aviation the plant's trump card?"

"Not one gram of the Baikal plant's output was applied in that field. If we'd used it for aircraft, we would hardly have gotten off the ground."

August 19, 1986. Baikalsk. I arrived yesterday afternoon and walked along the streets: the town is clean but graceless, linked not to Baikal but to the plant. The shrivelled tops of birch trees stick up among the houses; the pine trees are withered, too. The lines in the streets have been freshly painted, the benches also have a new coat of paint, and the buses carry slogans with appeals to preserve and protect Baikal. You can have 'em all. When I arrived at the hotel the maids were laying down rugs; in the restaurant we were served without brutal treatment. There's a smell from the plant, but only a faint one: they've probably slowed production for today's event.

This morning we got up early and headed for the train station to meet the state commission that is preparing a draft of a new decree on Baikal and that by some incomprehensible means includes me. The head of the commission is Nikolay Talyzin, chairman of the State Planning Commission. They're arriving from Ulan-Ude; they had to spend yesterday examining the Selenginsk Pulp and Cardboard Complex.

As soon as the train pulled up and the commission got off, Talyzin, scarcely taking time to greet us, began saying how much he disliked the Selenginsk plant. Dirt, old equipment, and the working conditions. . . . he winced. Now, in contrast, he was about to see something ideal. I told him so when we were introduced. Academicians Yanshin and Laskorin apparently hadn't come. I was surprised that, to compensate, Zhavoronkov turned out to be on the commission; somebody needed his services again.

We drove to the plant. The rosy-faced young plant director stood beside a model and showed us a diagram of the production process. From the way the model was made, from the way the director described everything, and from the way his face shone with excitement and good health it seemed as if the gates of Paradise had swung open before us and the geometric figures linked together were happy havens for the celebration of human virtue.

We walked around the various sections. Spacious, clean, airy. We went over to the water intake, where Baikal's water begins to roll, boiling and thundering. Then we moved on to where it is discharged back into Baikal after doing the little job that appears to be its fate and then being purified. Near a plain-looking booth we performed the ritual that began twenty years earlier: visitors take a drink of the spent water and smack their lips in satisfaction. Zhavoronkov went first and drained almost a full glass in one gulp; for him this was a divine drink. Talyzin was given a glass. He hesitantly took a sip and, though trying to restrain himself with so many people watching, automatically made a face. The huge crowd then walked down across the trampled and destroyed shore to Baikal itself and stood there a few minutes, some admiring it, others horrified, still others indifferent. Zhavoronkov, who clung to Talyzin, went on and on about the advantages of wastewater over Baikal's water. Talyzin brushed him off with displeasure: "Next you'll try to tell me that we should start selling this fine stuff abroad."[29]

He clearly liked both the plant and the institute. At the institute he tried to make a point by asking what share of Baikal's general pollution came from the plant. Less than 1 percent, they told him with certainty. As I was taking notes, I became confused: how could they calculate this percentage? I went over to Ryurik Salyaev, director of the Academy of Science's Institute of Botany and Plant Physiology. He just smiled: when you want something badly enough, anything is possible.

If it's less than 1 percent, the chairman of the commission persisted, does it make any sense to spend almost two billion rubles on redesigning the plant? Wouldn't it be better to spend the money on something that would do Baikal more good? For example, on the Selenga River, which carries not 1 but 50 percent of the pollution into Baikal?

One of the journalists held up a microphone; Talyzin demanded that there be no recordings, no broadcasts, no information disseminated without his permission.

It was becoming clear that they didn't want to part with the plant. If Baikal were to be saved, they would have to clean up the Selenga, and get rid of the plant there, and do a lot of other things. Beym's team from the Institute of Ecological Manipulation had tracked down that 1 percent, once again, by dint of purely mechanical calculations.

I prepared myself to face the fact that tomorrow, when we'll have to discuss the draft, they'll want to leave the Baikalsk plant as it is.

August 20, 1986. Irkutsk. This morning, on the way to the meeting, I ran into Talyzin and V. I. Sitnikov, secretary of our regional party committee, in the hallway of the committee's headquarters. Talyzin suddenly said, for my benefit:

"We will, we will get rid of the plant. Not right away, but we will."

Not right away—that means not until the Thirteenth Five-Year Plan.[30] Not until the day before the fast begins. But after yesterday's ill forebodings even this seemed like a victory to me. When I was given the floor, I could think of nothing better than to make the same old appeal on behalf of the intelligentsia to move up the date for redesigning the plant. "Perhaps we'll find the strength in ourselves . . ." I, too, said something of this sort. Talyzin evasively replied that they would have to think about it.

But they were really thinking, What's there to think about?! We've still got the Thirteenth Five-Year Plan.

December 23, 1988. Moscow. A meeting of the interdepartmental commission at the offices of the State Committee on Hydrometeorology. This commission was created immediately after the adoption of the government decree on Baikal, to monitor compliance.

The three previous decrees had turned out to be nothing but threatening gestures; this fourth one was prepared to launch an all-out attack on the polluters of Baikal. They numbered about one hundred fifty. The intent was to restructure their work by the end of the Thirteenth Five-Year Plan in such a way that, to use a folk expression, they would stop fouling their own nest. The main measures included switching the industries along the Angara Valley to gas and all the cities and towns on Baikal to electric heat; abolishing the Baikalsk pulp plant by the year 1993 and transferring the manufacture of cellulose to Ust-Ilimsk; putting in a closed circuit of water utilization at the Selenginsk plant . . . and so forth. And now the interdepartmental commission under the leadership of Yury Izrael, chairman of the State Committee on Hydrometeorology, is charged with supervising, prodding, adding amendments, should they be required, coordinating, interceding with suggestions . . .

This is not the first time it has met. Other meetings were held earlier in Irkutsk, Baikalsk, and Moscow. In the beginning ministers would show up, then the ministers would alternate with deputy ministers, and today not one minister is present. There aren't even a lot of commission members. Everyone is in a New Year's mood. About two years have passed since the decree went into effect, but here it's always the same wavering back and forth, back and forth, back and forth, waiting to see if the situation will change so that, God forbid, they won't have to overexert themselves.

That's what happens this time, too. They discuss redesigning the Baikalsk plant. To this day there is no final plan, and Ust-Ilimsk is rebelling against cellulose. The amount of methylhydrosulfide that the production of cellulose releases as a gas will be sixty to eighty times greater there than the maximum allowable concentration. The discussion heats up: Is or isn't methylhydrosulfide harmful to human health? The representatives of the Ministry for the Timber Industry insist that it's not the least bit harmful; Mikhail Grachyov, the new director of the Limnological Institute, backs them up. The nation's chief health officer, A. I. Kondrusev, expresses amazement: "What are you talking about?! Why, methylhydrosulfide is a high-level health hazard!"

Izrael responds wearily: "Dioxin instantly puts your methylhydrosulfide in one hundred tenth place. Now that's something to be afraid of!"

They discuss switching the Angara Valley industries to gas. The representative of the Ministry for the Gas Industry gets up and declares that the dates for gasification are unrealistic. Geologists haven't confirmed the number of gas fields. The geologists reply that there aren't any major gas fields . . .

. . . I go out into the damp, slushy street with an old and good friend of mine, a journalist who writes extensively and with pain about Baikal and the surrounding forests. Our mood is glum. We talk about diseases.

I recall taking a long walk with a colleague of mine, who had come for a visit. We followed the old Baikal Shoreline Railroad for quite some distance along the edge of our sea, one of the most beautiful and striking spots at the southern tip of Baikal. It was August, the golden month, the best time of year at Baikal, when the water warms up and the hills are a riot of multicolor, when even the rocks seem to blossom, blazing with different hues; when brilliant sunlight delineates the newly fallen snow on the distant, bare peaks of the Sayan Mountains, which appear quite close, seen through air so transparent it magnifies them; when Baikal has already built up its water supply with glacial runoff, holding it in reserve, and lies sated and tired, gathering strength for the autumn gales; when fish play in lavish abundance near the shore, accompanied by the cries of seagulls, and when all along the railroad tracks you run across one kind of berry after another—now raspberries, now red and black currants, now honeysuckle. . . . And what's more, it turned out to be an uncommonly fine day: sunny, windless, and warm, the air reverberating, Baikal clear and frozen still; stones sparkling and shimmering far out in the water; and the smell of warmed air, bitter from the various maturing grasses, coming down the hill and reaching the tracks, alternating with the cool, sharp breath wafting carelessly from the sea.

By this time my colleague had been overwhelmed for nearly two hours by the lush, wild life pouring down on him from all sides and creating a lavish summer celebration the likes of which he had not only never seen until now but had also never even imagined. I repeat that all this life was in full bloom and at its peak. Add to this scene mountain rivers running noisily down to Baikal, to which we descended time after time to taste their waters, rinse our faces, and see with what mystery and self-sacrifice they flowed into the common maternal water and abated in oblivion. Also add the frequent tunnels, tidy and cool, with haystacks lining the thread of track inside them and cliffs towering solemnly and sternly above them.

Everything designed for gathering impressions became overloaded very rapidly in my colleague, and, in no shape to be further amazed and delighted, he fell silent. I kept on talking. I told him how I'd been fooled by the water the first time I visited Baikal when I was a student and tried to reach out of the boat and pick up a pebble, which, when we took a sounding, turned out to be more than four meters away. My colleague accepted this incident apathetically. Somewhat hurt, I informed him that you can see more than forty meters through the water in Baikal—I seem to have stretched the truth—but he didn't react to this either, as if such things are fairly common in the Moscow River, which he regularly drives past in his car. Only then did I guess what was wrong with him: tell him that we can read the date on a two-kopeck coin at a depth of two to three hundred meters and, having passed the point of amazement, he will no longer be amazed. He was filled, as they say, to the brim.

I remember that what dealt the final blow was a nerpa. They rarely swim right up to shore in these parts, but here was one luxuriating in the water quite close by, as if on command, and when I noticed it and pointed it out, a loud, wild cry burst from my colleague, and he suddenly began to whistle and beckon to the seal as if it were a dog. It immediately went underwater, of course, and my colleague, totally amazed at the seal and at himself, lapsed into silence again, this time for a good long while.

I recall myself standing on Baikal's ice on a clear, moonlit, warm and wide-open night. This was in March, when the days are rapidly growing longer, the air is becoming dense with smells, and twilight approaches from Baikal in the evenings in a high, transparent, ever thickening blue. I left the shore at dusk, planning to return in half an hour, and headed for the middle of the sea. A gentle breeze was blowing faintly at my back, nudging me along, and the snow, which lay in a threadbare layer near the shore, kept diminishing; it shone white in low ridged patches that drew my feet, first to this patch, then to that one and that one, and sprang back underfoot with a light, pleasant rustling. I wasn't afraid of getting lost: the lights on the shore were visible for a long way. The pure light-blue sky grew flushed and spread out above me; a full moon hung to my right. But on the windswept clearings of ice the moon glimmered with a compressed light underneath me, too, and star sparks smoldered.

Long shafts of thunder came running at me under the ice, exploding and rumbling directly beneath my feet, but I quickly got used to them and stopped being afraid. I crossed a road leading from one shore to another, which was staked out with fir trees standing gloomily and awkwardly in formation under the bright sky like bundled-up figures. Baikal spread out wider and wider before me, the mountains receded, and the breeze continued to touch my back. I walked and walked.

When I was a child this was called the *uvodina* or *zamanka*.

"Don't go far from the village," we were instructed. "The *uvodina* will lure you away and pull the wool over your eyes, and you'll be done for."

"What does it look like, this *uvodina*?" we would ask.

"Now that's something nobody can tell you. No one who saw it ever came back." Well, you sure wouldn't forget yourself and take off after Baba Yaga, so it must be some unseen beauty with honeyed words.

Out of enervation I didn't feel anything or seem to be thinking about anything. It was as if I had accidentally entered some kind of enchanted kingdom of forces different from those we know, of different sounds and times that make up a different life. A solid mirror of bare ice stretched ahead and behind; it sloped like the sky and glowed just like the sky with all its lights, but they were bent and shaped like icicles. It was radiant above and radiant below, and a light blue radiance lay on the ice; it wasn't deathly but streamed and breathed and moved like a luminous circle, like a gigantic shimmering kaleidoscope. The moon came down so low that I could see its ripeness. And a hissing, swishing, whooshing fell in waves from above and flowed out all across the smooth surface. Baikal grumbled with a muffled sweetness, somewhere little ice bells tinkled in a strumming trickle, somewhere something flowed and subsided with a sigh.

There was nothing that could have moved or made noise, but everything around me was moving and audible.

It was well past midnight when I returned, and I stood before the shore for a long time, looking back at Baikal swimming in radiance, until it seemed as if the sky that had accumulated below was trying to tear it loose—that's where the repeated crackling came from—and lift it into the air.

And I stood there a while longer after going ashore and continued to look and listen. And I kept waiting for something, for some kind of apotheosis, as people used to say in the past. I waited a long time—and it never came.

"No sign shall be given to this generation" [Matt. 12:38–39 and Luke 11:29–30].

1989

4

❖❖❖

Irkutsk

One's sense of homeland is an amazing and inexpressible thing. What pure joy, what sweet pangs of homesickness it bestows when visiting us now in times of separation, now in a joyful hour of deep emotion and response! And in that hour the person who does not hear very much or see very far in ordinary everyday life acquires, by some magical means, maximum powers of hearing and vision, which allow him to descend into the most distant hidden recesses, into the remote depths of the history of his native land.

People cannot stand firmly or live confidently without this feeling, without a sense of closeness to the acts and destinies of their ancestors, without an inner comprehension of their responsibility for the place granted them in the vast, general continuum that allows them to be what they are. Our native mother earth, a source of strength in the *byliny*, is an exceptionally important source of healing these days not just for the elite, for the *bogatyr'*,[1] but for all of us; it contains that same magic water of life that brings people back to their own image, spirit, and purpose, to their true mission. And when visiting foreign lands, no matter how much we admire their manmade and nonmanmade beauty, no matter how much amazement their degree of development and their historical memory evoke, we always remain in our homeland at heart; we measure everything only against our native land, fit in only there, and base our reading of everything only on it. And those who have lost this sense of gravity on earth, who know merely the one life they have without any unruptured link connecting past, present, and future (that is, a link with the eternal), have lost immense joy and torment, the pain and happiness of their deepest existence.

"Absenteeism! What a horrible word!" exclaimed one of Siberia's best minds and most faithful ardent supporters, writer and ethnographer Nikolay Yadrintsev, in the nineteenth century. He continues:

Separation from one's homeland! [Absenteeism is just that—separation from one's homeland. (Rasputin)] What an unnatural feeling! Not without reason does this absenteeism arouse vexation and cause us pain at heart; not without reason have we who are devoted to the interests of our region felt its harmful consequences for a long time. So many of our land's best, educated resources have vanished on its account. So many flowers of thought and feeling have borne fruit in other fields when their own field lay empty and its earth did not produce the desired shoots.

"So many of our land's best, educated resources have vanished on its account." Any land, any country has the right to make this bitter acknowledgment concerning the sons and daughters who have abandoned their homeland and disappeared without a trace, leaving no noticeable mark on any other land.

. . . There are towns that date back many hundreds and even thousands of years. They stand important and imposing, protecting their antiquity and valor with all their might, with help from their best citizens. And there are towns famous for their modern-day glory that have existed for only a few decades but that strive, in listing their accomplishments on festive occasions, to move into the forefront on the basis of their industrial might and of the macho anniversary celebrations that occur at mere five-year intervals. Irkutsk, my hometown, is middle-aged according to these standards: three and a quarter centuries have passed since Yakov Pokhabov, a boyar's son from Yeniseysk, built "His Majesty a new fort across from the Irkut River on the Verkholensk side" on the Angara River in 1661. And as I conceive it, Irkutsk, although it has suffered a good deal in most recent times from quick and clumsy plastic surgery, from the fervent, thoughtless force connected with demolition and rebuilding, Irkutsk has nonetheless managed to preserve its exterior for the time being, unlike Omsk, another Siberian town, which has lost its old features completely, or Novosibirsk, which never had any. In addition, Irkutsk has even been lucky enough to keep its name, although I'm told there were proposals to change that, too, to name it not after the river that has the habit of arranging floods for the lower part of town, but to give it some self-expressive name or one that would burn with its own light. But that's all in the past, and now Irkutsk, made wiser by history and life, stands calm and sage, knowing its strength and its worth; it is fairly renowned for both its new and former glory, fairly modest, and fairly cultured, managing to preserve its culture even in our day. Traditionally hospitable, having largely neglected to take care of itself but well aware that yes, it's been negligent, Irkutsk stands endowed with the long and exacting memory of its stone and wood, gazing with love and a good deal of wonder at the activities of its present-day citizens, who form a population of six hundred thousand, protecting them in parental fashion from intense heat and cold, giving them life, shelter, education, work, a homeland, and eternity.

There is a special hour in which Irkutsk easily responds to your feelings for it. This hour comes during the early part of a summer dawn, before the sun rises, then kindles and washes away, like a hot wave, the smells emanating from the nocturnal depths that linger all night, until pedestrians hurrying by disperse them, and before the rumble of traffic destroys the rare, brief stillness. At this hour your best bet is to head for old Irkutsk, for one of those nooks where a single community of wooden houses has been preserved not so much in a state of dilapidation and ruin as, at least for the time being, for service and for beauty. And you have only to enter their formation, to take the first steps down a narrow street warm with the warmth of its own life, before you very quickly lose your sense of time and end up in a wonderful, fairy-tale world, the one from the famous tale in which a magical power casts a spell and puts everyone to sleep for a hundred years, making everything all around inviolable. And you no longer hear the measured, drowsy female voice announcing train arrivals and departures from beyond the Angara, you don't see the new stone buildings that occasionally spring up before your eyes like huge untidy patches, you don't notice the signs of today—you are there, in that world of more than one hundred years' standing.

And it is just that—only slightly more than one hundred years old. What was perhaps the cruelest of all the fires in Irkutsk's history raged through the town in the summer of 1879, destroying a large part of it. "By the morning of June 25, seventy-five blocks in the best and most comfortable part of town were a burnt desert covered with the scorched, blackened shells of stone houses, chimneys, and stoves, with acrid, asphyxiating smoke drifting overhead" (from the testimony of the chronicler N. S. Romanov). But if, after this, the authorities decided to build only with stone on the central streets, wooden walls went up again in the neighborhoods where wood had been before. The residents of Irkutsk never got used to stone. Irkutsk burned many times, and each time it rose again from the ashes more affluent, beautiful, and spacious than before, and again and again the townspeople put up walls, most often according to their own rough drawings and blueprints, added roofs, fitted the windows with glass, moved into their new homes, and began to ornament them.

No, to build something not merely warm and comfortable to live in but also a lovely sight for everyone's delight, like a picture, like a magic tower in which a magic life might begin—that's what they considered important and, as we say now, prestigious. The spirit of rivalry in beauty and innovation never abandoned Siberians and used to spur them on to many remarkable creations. If anyone throughout all of vast Russia ever equalled Siberians in the art of wooden ornamentation, it could only have been the peasants from their ancestral homeland, from the Arkhangelsk, Vologda, and Novgorod regions and from Ustyug the Great, from which the first settlers of Siberia brought their craft. They brought it with them, developed it to a point of astonishing perfection and endless, whimsical imagination overlaid with the new expanses and the new life, and cultivated it here, there, and everywhere—in town and country, among rich and poor, among plowmen, workmen, and hunters. Only someone totally poverty-stricken in pocketbook or spirit, after putting up a dwelling, did not ornament it, did not cover it with designs, paint it, or work magic on it, and that alone remained a stamp of poverty and hopelessness for the rest of his life. A cottage like that, as we can plainly see now, aged and collapsed before the others, burying its windows in the ground; we feel sad and uncomfortable looking at the poor thing when the houses standing next to it are still sound, cheerful, and showing off, embellished with gingerbread trim. Created to delight people, they continue to bring us joy to this day despite their advanced age. Even the most insignificant house with the plainest decoration, a good deal of which has already been lost, still preserves its attractiveness and dignity along with the noble soul of the master craftsman, which remains in it forever.

Today we treat the soul of the master craftsman quite casually and without pity, now dipping it into a fire-spitting ladle of molten steel, now walling it up in the body of a huge dam, often confusing it with elementary human conscientiousness. The soul, even in its most primitive interpretation and work-related application, is still what arises from the ordinariness and common characteristics of a craft, what soars above them like a special divine love for human beings and for everything beautiful that lives in them and can live in them, what fills the great voids between dream and reality and makes reality meaningful through goodness and beauty. The soul does not serve—it reigns; sometimes it takes a heavy toll by forcing individuals out of the ranks of ordinary folk who live by bread alone and don't want to know others, but for that reason it also forces them out of the ranks of ordinary mortals buried without a trace beneath heavy layers of time.

And what is it if not the soul of the master craftsman who performed magic on the house you stopped beside in astonishment that touched you when you were in a state of pride and stirred you up, that reproached your feeble soul, which knew no flights of celebration, or that found rapture and response in your kindred, sensitive soul, which had begun to ache and yearn for just such a glorious pursuit?

Craftsmen spent long weeks and months sawing, rounding, carving, and adjusting their lacy embellishments. They began using stencils only later, when splendid, profitable houses went up and they toiled in artels, but acknowledged artists with any self-respect created directly from wood, knowing no restrictive limits. Sometimes imagination lured them into such labyrinths and worlds of fantasy that there seemed no way to avoid destroying feeling and proportion and ruining their design, but by some miracle they would find a way out and, drawing on unknown, occasionally pagan recesses in themselves, would produce the desired firebird, whose magical plumage blazed on pediments, cornices, door jambs, and window frames, on corbels and pilasters, on every tiny space: look, people, and rejoice.

"I've been in many cities and in the capitals of various countries and can say that not a single corner of the world has the same kind of wooden architecture, the same kind of amazing carved trim, that Irkutsk does." This is what the artist Ilya Glazunov,[2] a well-known expert on and defender of Russia's distant past, says of our town, having in mind, above all, the baroque fretwork that sets Irkutsk apart from all other towns, bar none.

Even Tomsk has no baroque or "plain" trim [*"gladkaia" rez'ba*], although thanks to its relative proximity to the chief capital [i.e., Moscow], Tomsk for a long time posed a challenge to Irkutsk's fame as the best and most enlightened of all Siberian towns; before the Revolution it aspired with some success to being the capital of Siberia. And although Chekhov, on his way to Sakhalin Island, referred to Tomsk as "the most boring town" and said that "Irkutsk is a superb town. Thoroughly refined," we must assume that regarding Tomsk this was not quite true even then. Concerning the distant past that interests us now and, most important, the care we give it, any comparison will clearly not favor Irkutsk, especially in connection with wooden structures. Irkutsk is merely wearing out its past and is famous for it only insofar as it has not yet managed to lose the value and appearance of antiquity everywhere; Tomsk, however, is preserving its past and has been downright cherishing it of late, using the resources of an industrial restoration workshop to renovate every house worthy of attention.

Wood is short-lived, and the very oldest buildings in Irkutsk, except for one, are not made of wood. The wooden private homes of the eighteenth century did not remain intact either. Residents of Irkutsk still recall the fight for "the hunchbacked house" [*"gorbatyi dom"*], a specimen of eighteenth-century construction that stood on Fifth Army Street, a fight that did not end in favor of society when the authorities sneakily demolished the house in the middle of the night. The same fate also befell many other examples of our ancestors' wooden architecture. The restored homes of the Decembrists Sergey Volkonsky and Sergey Trubetskoy are a miniscule part of what could have been done and of the losses we are in no position to replace.

Architecture is also the chronicle of the world: it speaks when songs and legends are silent and when nothing says a word about a people who have perished. Let it appear in the midst of our towns, even as fragments, in the same condition as when the people whose day is done were alive, so that when we see it thoughts of their bygone life will dawn on us, will plunge us into their way of living, their habits, and their level of understanding, and will arouse in us a gratitude for their existence, which formed a stage in our own evolution. (Nikolay Gogol)[3]

Wood has a rare ability to extend our memory to depths and events that we could not witness ourselves. Or better put, it has the ability to hand down to us the memory of our ancestors. Stone is colder and more immobile; wood is pliant and responsive to feeling. In parts of the wooden quarter somewhere around the former Red Army Streets [*Krasnoarmeiskie ulitsy*], which used to be called Soldiers' Streets [*Soldatskie ulitsy*], it's not at all hard to visualize old Irkutsk, during, say, the 1730s and 1740s, when the town grew and spread beyond the walls of its original fort.

Russia's lively trade with China passed through Irkutsk, which by that time had become the chief administrative center for a huge province and the main trans-shipment and distribution point for goods in all of eastern and northern Siberia. The fort, surrounded by reinforced walls, remained the seat of administrative power and nothing more. All the basic life of the town had long since crossed over to the trading district just outside its walls, where there were merchants' shops, and open-air markets, and taverns, which were blooming like luxuriant flowers by then, and various services and artisans' workshops, and where about a thousand cottages (in the 1730s) belonging to the local inhabitants "meandered," erected without any kind of building plan, placed wherever and however the owners felt like putting them, so that the streets formed strange, winding swirls that truly were reminiscent of meandering. After spreading beyond the fort, the town, in its turn, was fenced in by a palisade, a wooden wall extending from the Angara River to Ushakovka Creek at the site of present-day Karl Marx Street. As was customary in olden times, *chevaux-de-frise* stood outside the palisade beside the moat, while beyond that a third city zone, the Soldiers' Colony [*Soldatskaia sloboda*], sprang up. This is where the network of streets called Soldiers' Streets came from, which were later renamed Red Army Streets so that the former city guards would receive some attention from the Revolution, too.

Other cottages stood there then, of course, and the layout was different. Everything was different, but you don't have to close your eyes to imagine the Irkutsk of that time with such reality and closeness that you can almost see a crooked, dirty, winding little street and the stately tread of a bearded, red-eyed merchant heading somewhere in the direction of the onion domes of the Church of Our Savior [*Spasskaia tserkov'*] and Epiphany Cathedral [*Bogoiavlenskii sobor*], which reigned over the town, grunting in annoyance as he passes some kids romping in the mud; you hear the voices of women from behind tall fences as they idly squabble with each other out of boredom; you hear the neighing of horses and the creaking of a string of carts as it rolls through the Overseas Gate [*Zamorskie vorota*], heading for Baikal. It's still a good thirty years until the construction of the Moscow High Road [*Moskovskaia stolbovaia doroga*], which breathed new life into Irkutsk, and more than a century until the appearance of the third and main pillar, which, after furs and trade, became one of the fundamental reasons why the town thrived: gold fever. Irkutsk was still sleepy, dark, and dirty back then; its life consisted mainly of the clergy and the merchants battling with government officials, fighting their injustice and extortion, which even for those times resembled highway robbery. But you must remember that this outlying region was extremely remote, from which "God is a long way up and the czar a long way off" [*do Boga vysoko, do tsaria daleko*]. The voivodes acted according to this proverb, as did the vice governors and later the governors-general, along with all the numerous administrators surrounding them. Not for nothing did Rakitin, the voivode of Irkutsk during Peter the Great's time and a man who was not squeamish about robbery, mount the scaffold at practically the same time as Prince Gagarin, the first governor of Siberia; a little later the same fate also befell Irkutsk's first vice governor, Zholobov,[4] who "tortured the guiltless and burned them with fire." Strong measures, however, didn't do much good.

After that, all the authorities with few exceptions, no matter what their titles, profited from the instructions given to the voivodes in the earliest period, which read, "Act according to the local conditions and your own scrutiny in a seemly fashion and as God directs." One of them, Vice Governor Pleshcheev, found it "seemly" to have cannons fired every time he went out as a way of annoying the bishop, who was hailed by the pealing of church bells; another, Governor Nemtsov, "God directed" to invite guests out of town and to sic on them the famous bandit Gondyukhin, a man not too shy to strip the noble society stark naked, to the governor's great amusement; a third, an investigator named Krylov,[5] having gone to Irkutsk to put a stop to lawlessness, robbed the local merchants of more than one hundred fifty thousand rubles "according to his own scrutiny," placed Vice Governor Vulf himself under arrest for something he didn't take a fancy to, and rode around town inspiring terrible fear in the inhabitants and, again "according to his own scrutiny," pointing at merchants' daughters and lower-middle-class women who pleased him and who then had to be delivered to Krylov's house without delay. In the words of one chronicler, those were "disastrous" times [*"gibel'nye" vremena*]. It's not surprising that the residents of Irkutsk, recalling the happy and what they considered fortunate rule in the late seventeenth century of Poltev's young son (Semyon Poltev had been appointed voivode but passed away before reaching Irkutsk and the Cossacks then named his son, Nikolay, voivode), tried to use the same procedure again forty years later, tired as they were of Zholobov's petty tyranny and extortion, when Sytin, arriving to replace the hated vice governor, promptly died "from afflictions" [*"ot ogorchenii"*] caused by Zholobov. Sytin's son was five years old; it's impossible to create lawlessness at that age even in the role of ruler, although it's also impossible to fight it, but the town considered that a great blessing, too. Their plan, however, fell through, and Zholobov, who remained in place for the time being, began meting out punishment with renewed vigor, having those who'd contemplated replacing him "flogged" [*stavia "na pravezh"*] (using whips, sticks, and instruments of torture) on a daily basis.

"Everything they say in Petersburg about the state of affairs here is not only the truth, but also—and this rarely happens—the uninflated truth," Count Mikhail Speransky reported to the capital later, after he went to Irkutsk with enormous powers.[6]

The history of Irkutsk knows both tragic and funny, amusing stories that are tempting and useful to leaf through in the chronicles and also in memory as you wander among the old wooden streets, which easily resurrect for the inquisitive mind the harsh life of bygone days.

Here is a good place to recall that straightening up the town's haphazard layout was zealously undertaken in the early nineteenth century during the reign of Governor-General Pestel,[7] who contrived to rule

187

our vast land from Petersburg, by his deputy, Vice Governor Treskin,[8] who became renowned for his desperate struggle with Irkutsk's wealthy merchants. Treskin, not afraid of complaints, which Pestel intercepted in the capital, had few doubts about anything, especially when it came to straightening streets. On his instructions a work team was recruited from among the prisoners in the local jail, headed by one Gushcha, a group referred to in the chronicles of our town as "Gushcha's crew" ["*gushchinskaia komanda*"]. Here is the testimony writer Ivan Kalashnikov gives when recounting this episode in *The Notes of an Irkutsk Resident*:[9]

No one can deny that decorum is a good thing, but the houses that did not conform to the building plan were treated in all too cavalier a manner. Getting the homeowners' consent to make changes was considered an unnecessary step. Gushcha's crew would show up—and a house would just vanish into thin air. If the whole house did not violate the plan and only one particularly bold part jutted out, they would unceremoniously saw off enough of the house to make it flush with the street, and then let the owner fix it as best he could.

After becoming skilled at street reconstruction and developing a taste for it, Treskin then set about straightening the estuary of the Irkut River, declaring that it had "an irregular current," but the Irkut, unlike Irkutsk, would not submit to Treskin and, despite all the governor's efforts, kept its own current.

What can you say?! Rulers varied; Irkutsk was made to suffer greatly, more than any other town in Siberia or the land secured around it, from power wielded by all kinds of favorites, from their arbitrariness, bribery, and corruption, and yet it continued to grow and become more attractive and affluent, as if existing according to its own laws, knowing how to protect and ennoble itself and how to bear the losses it endured throughout its entire history with dignity.

The town's first stone structure, unfortunately, has not survived until our day. This was the voivode's chancellery, or government office, erected in 1704 within the confines of the fort laid out along the banks of the Angara, the building where power was exercised. The chancellery

had to be taken down in the nineteenth century when they began reinforcing the riverbank to preserve the site of the cradle of Irkutsk. To
compensate, and to our wonder and good fortune, Epiphany Cathedral
and the Church of Our Savior have remained intact, after standing
their ground in a most mysterious, miraculous way during the cruel
eras of breakage and demolition. These are architecturally the very oldest and most interesting buildings in all of Eastern Siberia.

They are interesting, though, precisely because they are extremely
old. They are so dear to the hearts of Irkutsk residents precisely
because, through a prophetic and imperishable memory accessible to
everyone, they bring down to us the era, spirit, and art of our ancestors, which find living, concrete expression in these walls and which
attest to humankind's aspiration toward and faith in its eternity more
truly than any philosophy. People remain alive as long as the works of
their hands and spirits last. It would be good for those planning to
serve out their earthly lot soon to remember this as they nonetheless
foolishly leave behind memorials to their meagerness, unscrupulous-
ness, and communal vanity made of highly durable material, of words
and stone. Time, as we know, with its inability to bear false witness,
can remember not only with gratitude but also with vindictiveness.

The Church of Our Savior is primordially dear to us above all
because it is the sole structure left of Fort Irkutsk and was erected only
fifty years after the town's birth. We now use it to determine the fort's
boundaries (it was built into the fortress wall, facing present-day Kirov
Square) and can visualize the cathedral's square (at the site of the Eternal Flame), where czars' and voivodes' decrees were proclaimed, where
executions were carried out, and where the townspeople gathered on
holidays as well as on the days of Russia's great and tragic events. The
church's foundation was laid in 1706 and the building was completed
four years later. You don't have to be an expert to see the pre-Petrine,
old Russian architecture that characterizes both its basic contours and
its outer appearance. At that time Petersburg was rising in a new architectural style that borrowed heavily from others, Moscow changed its
town-planning signature, but Irkutsk, far-off Irkutsk erected its first
stone creations in the old manner, in the native, ethnic spirit that
soared so marvelously after the Tatar invasions. But changes that
favored the new style were already apparent in Epiphany Cathedral,

whose foundation was laid just eight years after the Church of Our Savior; it's easy to pick out features of early baroque in the decor of its facades, which, in contrast to the Church of Our Savior, are completely covered with splendid ornamentation. Changes are visible, but the entire cathedral as an ensemble, as a single whole, is that whimsical combination of old and new styles that resulted when the master builder, we may assume, knowing full well how things were usually built, took pleasure in straying toward what was pleasant for him to build and what corresponded more closely to his taste. Epiphany Cathedral, once again in contrast to the Church of Our Savior, acquired a bell tower and a side chapel immediately, at the time it was built; the hip roof on the bell tower is, of course, an element of old Russian wooden architecture that you very rarely find on stone buildings, especially west of the Urals. And the roots and fantasy that underlie the little figures on the ceramic inlays, the "tiles" ["*izraztsy*"] that decorate the cathedral and that unexpectedly appeared on their own, luckily discovered during the church's renovation, go far back into the most distant of distances: all those circles, petals, and known and unknown birds and animals frozen on the walls are straight out of age-old legends and tales.

Generally speaking, when we talk about the shift in architectural styles we must bear in mind that in our part of the world in particular, because of our remoteness and because of the influence of local motifs, it had no fixed boundaries or firm laws, and the interpenetration, interconnection, and interharmony of different trends can be observed for quite some time both in wooden and in stone architecture. Znamensky Church, which was raised considerably later than Epiphany Cathedral (in 1762), also combines elements of old Russian and baroque decor. The Church of the Exaltation of the Holy Cross [*Krestovozdvizhenskaia tserkov'*], with its marvelous and utterly exceptional "fretwork" ["*uzoroch'e*"] and whimsical use of exotica from eastern ornamentation apparently taken from Buddhist temples, can be traced back to Siberian baroque. The laws adopted in the centers of town planning, after covering thousands of versts to reach Irkutsk and catching a whiff of local air, nearly always slipped out of their regulation molds onto the sinful Siberian ground; that's why buildings built purely in one style or another are very rare here.

The Church of the Exaltation of the Holy Cross (south façade)

"The antiquity of Irkutsk is venerable," wrote Aleksey Martos, one of the most highly educated men of his time and son of the sculptor who created the monument to Minin and Pozharsky in Moscow's Red Square, after visiting our town in 1824. "It can be likened to that period in a person's life when, having secured the happiness of his descendants, he can demand respect and attention from his progeny."

People of the past, even travelers, knew how to express their opinions with surprising sureness and at great length, but they viewed the face of a transformed land and the works of human hands not from a utilitarian or here-and-now perspective but from the position of a nation thinking about its own prosperity.

And when listing the buildings from the distant past in Irkutsk that he found particularly striking, Martos names Epiphany Cathedral and the Church of Our Savior first.

Over time these buildings, our first churches, underwent substantial changes that were completely natural considering their long and difficult fate but were not, however, always appropriate. In the latter half of the eighteenth century a bell tower was added to the Church of

Our Savior (in 1762) and a side chapel (in 1778) and scenes were painted on its facades, but if the church proper accepted the bell tower as something fitting and essential for its ensemble and merely late in arriving, the two-story stone side chapel built onto one end made it heavier on the north side, thereby destroying its symmetry and distorting the light appearance of the church, which seemed suspended, soaring above the Angara as it dispensed blessings and called parishioners to account.

Epiphany Cathedral was especially unlucky. The celebrated hip roof on its bell tower lasted only until 1742, when Irkutsk experienced a strong earthquake, after which the fallen roof was never replaced. Another earthquake struck in 1861, and again, instead of restoring the building to its original appearance, they took the damaged refectory apart down to its foundation, putting up crude walls that had nothing in common with the building's architecture, and bricked over the tiles at the same time without taking their antiquity into account. Different times had arrived, precursors of even more troubled times, and a different attitude toward the distant past arose, one that turned its back on the sensitivity and reverent attention to it that had always been present in the Russian people until then.

Now Irkutsk can pride itself on having fully restored the Church of Our Savior and Epiphany Cathedral after allowing them to fall into neglect and almost into nonexistence; that's why we can speak of their rebirth as a miracle comparable only to the miracle of rising from the ashes. And today when you walk down to the banks of the Angara, to the spot "from which Irkutsk began," and see the Church of Our Savior's shining gold onion dome and the murals on its north and east facades, when you see the tent-shaped crown on top of Epiphany Cathedral's bell tower rising in its former aspect, the way it looked two and a half centuries ago, and the inlaid tiles playing joyfully and festively as if reflecting the mysterious life of the Angara's water, then your soul feels the pure, expansive rising of a sense of the ultimate justice of all things, along with a sense of adoptedness attained through long years of wandering.

In the beginning artels were hired from the outside to construct the first stone buildings, especially the religious ones; cooperative groups of artisans came from the Urals and even from Russia (until very recently Siberians called the land west of the Urals Russia, or "Raseya"). But this didn't last long. By the middle of the eighteenth century a good third of Irkutsk had already become the home of artisans working in wood, stone, and precious metals. By the end of the century the fame of its master craftsmen had spread throughout Siberia and now other towns went with hat in hand to Irkutsk's masons and painters for help in putting up their churches and to its smelters, who cast bells known for their high notes and their high artistic qualities. The chronicles have preserved the name of Aleksey Unzhakov (probably a Buryat?), who, on September 24, 1797, cast the Big 761-Pood Bell,[10] outstanding among the memories of Irkutsk's old-time residents, which practically the whole town hauled to the cathedral using ropes and a special sleigh made out of thick beams, while all the churches rang their bells. Curiously, fewer than one hundred years later, when Irkutsk needed a bell for a cathedral (now we can only point out the site where this cathedral stood—on present-day Kirov Square), once again an artisan had to be hired from the outside, all the way from Yaroslavl, to cast it. To compensate, a different problem faced the bishops concerning construction of the iconostasis in the new cathedral: Which of Irkutsk's numerous master craftsmen should they choose so as not to offend the others? After long reflection and consultation they asked a fairly young man named N. Popov, who, everyone generally agreed, did an excellent job.

In a book published several years ago by Academician Aleksey Okladnikov and Ruslan Vasilievsky titled *Travels in Alaska and the Aleutian Islands*,[11] which describes the activities of a joint Soviet-American archaeological expedition in those regions, I was pleased to find a complimentary reference to the old masters of Irkutsk. In a Russian church in the Alaskan village of Nikolski the authors' attention was drawn to an icon of Saint Nicholas the Miracle Worker, "clad in a silver mounting, a superb specimen of baroque style. And, most important, the mounting was dated 1794, the heyday of the Russian-American Company, in which the merchants of Irkutsk, including Grigory Shelikhov[12] himself, played a leading role. Just such mountings were made in old Irkutsk by the highly skilled local silversmiths. The articles they created out of silver were famous far beyond the city itself."

And, needless to say, not only church-related arts and crafts were well developed in Irkutsk.

Silver icon mounting by Irkutsk silversmiths (eighteenth century)

When you check photos of the Irkutsk cathedral that didn't survive until our day against photographs of the Church of Christ the Savior [*khram Khrista Spasitelia*] in Moscow, it's now easy to see that the cathedral in Irkutsk was erected in the image and likeness of the Moscow church, whose architect was the renowned Konstantin Ton.[13] Construction of the Church of Christ the Savior continued from the 1830s through the 1880s, a time when the Russian national spirit revived and flowered in art as well as in social thought, a time of cruel disappointment in the existing way of life and of profound hope in the special role and "Messianism" of Russia, a time of reassuring freedom and reform, especially at the end of the period. This era also gave rise to the "Russian" style of architecture, one of whose founders was Ton, who harkened back to the sources of pre-Petrine architecture, adding new experience and a new base.

Professor S. V. Shostakovich, an old-time resident of Irkutsk and an enthusiastic supporter of his town, wrote in the local newspaper in the late 1860s:

Even now some people still think that this "new cathedral," which they claim has no special artistic value, should not have been preserved. But this is a profound delusion. Along with the Church of Our Savior, the old Epiphany Cathedral, the Polish Catholic Church, the private family chapel, and several other old buildings, it joins in splendidly with that remarkable architectural ensemble, forming an integral part of it. Here, on the steep banks of the Angara, which afford an astonishing view of the broad river valley, an amazing corner of the old Siberian capital has been preserved, despite Irkutsk's fires, creating a kind of Irkutsk citadel.

The Russian people (and this is not some idle invention of mine) follow with keen attention the fate of those who were guilty in their time, even if they merely carried out orders, of destroying buildings from the distant past, consigning them to oblivion, and are ready to view any trouble in those individuals' lives as rightful retribution. Even when they understandably exaggerate such deeds and want to pretend something happened when it actually didn't, it's still worth recalling this exacting expectation, instinctively and uncontrollably alive; people want to believe that impunity does not exist.

Irkutsk was long regarded as a commercial town. We've gotten used to seeing only one meaning in this notion—a ponderous and sluggish social and moral existence—and we forget or don't know about the merchants' activities in building the cultural and learned institutions of their native land. These activities basically boiled down to cash contributions, but this wasn't such a bad thing; everyone does what he can. You can't expect the Messrs. Sibiryakov and Kuznetsov to be Potanins and Yadrintsevs (Aleksandr Sibiryakov, incidentally, was both a writer and a scholar), but the fact that they helped the Potanins and Yadrintsevs merits an unbiased place in our memory, too. Siberia's merchants as a whole deserve serious research that would do them justice in matters of personal enrichment as well as in the ways they benefited their vast, distant outlying region, which God had forgotten about in all respects. Needless to say, Siberia harbored quite a few types who resembled characters in an Ostrovsky play; fabulous wealth was impossible, of course, without the crude and dishonest practices involved in the art of acquiring it—no one is about to single out and idealize the Siberian merchant, to seek a special pedestal just for him. "Dominating both the representative assembly and the town council, the rich and powerful merchants of Irkutsk ran the show in all public and municipal matters in the late eighteenth and early nineteenth centuries, and they ran it exclusively in their own interests," writes Vladimir Sukachyov, a long-time mayor of the town who himself belonged to this group, in a book called *Irkutsk*.[14] "Things reached the point," he notes with indignation, "that the right to sell meat in Irkutsk in 1810 was granted to only three merchants: Lanin, Popov, and Kuznetsov."

But just as Siberians differed psychologically from the inhabitants of Russia proper, so, too, did Siberian merchants differ from their counterparts west of the Urals, if only by virtue of local conditions. In the late eighteenth century two Irkutsk merchants, Shelikhov (whom Derzhavin called "the Russian Columbus") and Baranov[15] became the discoverers and founders of Russian America, achieving not only commercial but also political supremacy over Alaska and the Aleutian Islands. The headquarters of the Russian-American Company's governing board were located in Irkutsk from start to finish. The expeditions led by Irkutsk's Count Muravyov,[16] the governor-general of Eastern Siberia, during the 1850s, which resulted in Russian annexation of the Amur Valley, were financed mainly by the local owners of gold mines. The numerous scientific expeditions of the past that explored the Far North and East, Mongolia, China, and Japan likewise could not have managed without the help of Irkutsk's rich men: it was from there, from Irkutsk, that the Siberian (later the East Siberian) Branch of the Russian Geographical Society operated energetically beginning in 1851; essentially all its investigations of the vast and little-studied eastern regions originated there.

We might also recall that the Irkutsk merchants, who showed almost constant hostility toward the official government apparatus, associated both with Decembrists and with Polish exiles, carried on friendships with them openly, and turned their children over to them for instruction, considering this an honor not for those who had fallen into disgrace but for themselves. Many of the men we label moneybags had received a broad, well-rounded education; they subscribed to the best journals and ordered the best books from Moscow and Petersburg not just for themselves but also to build up public libraries. Generation after generation of Sibiryakovs kept a chronicle about Irkutsk; V. N. Basnin was famous around town, apart from his wealth, for his collections of books and engravings, for the musical evenings to which he invited performing artists from the capital cities, and for a greenhouse full of unusual flowers and fruits; admission to Sukachyov's picture gallery, which later formed the basis of the Irkutsk Art Museum, was free for schoolchildren, while the fees collected from adults went to benefit the town's public education system. All this could be called simply the whims of rich men wallowing in wealth and showing off in front of each other if so much benefit hadn't resulted and if they hadn't created the special, unprovincial environment that set Irkutsk apart from a great many Siberian towns. Its exceptional level of culture and refinement was universally recognized, which is why bad to mediocre theater troupes didn't dare stop in Irkutsk when on tour, fearing the local audiences; the freethinking attitude of the townspeople startled and frightened the high officials who showed up to make inspections and amazed the illustrious individuals who passed through and left numerous descriptions of it. All this, of course, grew mainly out of Irkutsk's status as a place of exile, and the exiles there did much more than sit out their terms at home: they worked in schools and colleges, for scientific and technical societies, in the governor-general's office, and for newspapers, thus gaining opportunities to influence public opinion and public taste. The Decembrist Dmitry Zavalishin once declared outright war on Muravyov-Amursky, denouncing him for the injustices being committed in the Amur Valley and in the region east of Lake Baikal. Mikhail Korsakov, Muravyov-Amursky's successor, was forced to send the Decembrist from one place of exile to another, from Transbaikalia to Kazan. The first printed publications, the newspapers the *Irkutsk Gazette* [*Irkutskie viedomosti*] and the *Amur*, were the work of the famous Mikhail Petrashevsky[17] and his like-minded compatriots Fyodor Lvov, Mikhail Zagoskin, and Serafim Shashkov. Ivan Popov, a political exile, served for many years as editor of the *Eastern Review* [*Vostochnoe obozrienie*], a newspaper published in Irkutsk, and of the journal the *Siberian Miscellany* [*Sibirskii sbornik*], both of which Yadrintsev had founded and published before that in Petersburg. In his book *The Past and My Experiences*,[18] Popov recalls:

I've already said that Governor-General A. D. Goremykin reproached Gromov because he employed only state criminals, but Gromov [from a family of well-known Siberian merchants (Rasputin)] replied that the views of these political types were no concern of his: the exiles were splendid workers and honest people, and he couldn't part with them because his business would suffer. And his business was immense: supplying furs to all of Russia and abroad and conducting trade in Yakutsk Province. The Gromovs' central office, like the editorial offices of the *Eastern Review* and the Irkutsk Museum of the Geographical Society, were a kind of secret address where you could get all kinds of information about "political types."

Concerning the merchants of Irkutsk, they combined serving God and Mammon quite well, better than anywhere else: often rolling in money, Siberian industrialists could afford to fork over fat sums for the good of their native land as well as for their hometowns without any particular detriment to their pocketbooks. The majority—and this is no exaggeration—an actual majority of the churches, hospitals, asylums, trade schools and schools for general education, including those for orphans, prisoners' children, and immigrants, as well as the majority of the secondary schools and libraries that operated in Irkutsk in former times, were built and maintained by private donations. "If you compare all these institutions and all this capital with the number of people living in Irkutsk, you'll have to admit that in terms of charitable facilities Irkutsk stands practically in first place among Russian cities," writes Sukachyov, referring to the 1880s and 1890s. If Petersburg at that time had one grade-school pupil for every eighty residents and Moscow one for every seventy-five, Irkutsk had one pupil for every twenty-nine residents. The difference, as you can see, is considerable.

Although Irkutsk was the most distant of all the outlying provincial centers for a long time, it nonetheless occupied such a convenient and advantageous spot from the very beginning that not much could avoid it, including water, land, and air routes, trade and industrial fevers, political and reform activities, revolutionary storms and palace coups. No matter where something happened, the echo reverberated in Irkutsk, to which or through which the participants were sent to serve terms of hard labor and exile. It was verily an involuntary Mecca: of those whose names remained part of Russian history for good, whom didn't Irkutsk see during its lifetime? These included the unfortunate *strel'-tsy*[19] at the beginning of Peter the Great's reign; and Peter's favorite, Gannibal,[20] driven out by another favorite, Menshikov,[21] who shortly thereafter followed him to Siberia, too; and the young daughter of Volynsky,[22] who was executed during Empress Anna Ioannovna's rule (the girl, also named Anna, was kept secretly at Znamensky Convent and later elevated to a high position in the court of Empress Elizabeth); and numerous adventurers of various stripes who felt the firmness of authority and the state. The notorious fate of the famous anarchist Bakunin (who was related, incidentally, to Muravyov-Amursky) did not let him bypass Irkutsk. Neither did Radishchev, or Chernyshevsky,[23] who called on German Lopatin, one of the Russian translators of *Das Kapital*, and the populist Ippolit Myshkin to free him from exile in Vilyuysk and send him to Irkutsk, or the *petrashevtsy*, headed by the leader of the secret society himself, or the revolutionary democrats Mikhail Mikhaylov and Nikolay Serno-Solovievich. Decembrists and Polish exiles exerted enormous influence on the social and moral development of our town, as if they, considered criminals, had not been handed over to be educated and improved, but rather local society had been turned over to them, which culminated in Decembrists teaching in the home of the governor-general himself. Among the Polish exiles, Ivan Chersky, Aleksander Czekanowski, and Benedykt Dybowski added, as people used to say, a certain luster to the scientific activities of the Geographical Society; their names remain forever on the map of Baikal and the Sayan Mountain region, which they spent a good number of years studying.

On this subject Sergey Maksimov, author of an important work called *Siberia and Penal Servitude*,[24] remarks:

Through the help and participation of the foreigners among the Siberians, it was above all precisely here, in Irkutsk, where that mighty force called public opinion was born, began to grow, and became strong, a force that hadn't existed until then and that had no place in Siberia, a land whose rulers governed with an amazing amount of arbitrariness.

Here's a fact that shows the strength of public opinion in Irkutsk at the end of the nineteenth century. The following incident occurred in 1883. Governor-General Anuchin paid a call on K. G. Neustroev, a teacher charged with spreading revolutionary propaganda, who was incarcerated in the local prison. While visiting him in his cell, the governor-general, stung by something, began to insult the teacher. The latter wouldn't stand for this and slapped him in the face, for which, in addition to the previous charges, he was sentenced to death. The execution took place in spite of public protests, but the town was not willing to forgive Anuchin for such cruel and unjust punishment. The townspeople literally wouldn't let the governor-general, an all-powerful high official, the most important man in the region, pass through the streets on foot or by vehicle, calling him a murderer to his face and writing his name beside that word on fences and houses, so that Anuchin finally had to submit his resignation and leave Irkutsk.

This was a far cry from the town and the inhabitants that, one hundred years earlier, when Investigator Krylov arrived in Irkutsk, was willing to put up with all sorts of extortion, mockery, and petty tyranny. By now the town had acquired a sense of honor and dignity that would not allow Anuchin to do anything he pleased.

During the largest wave of mass banishment, which occurred just before the Revolution, almost half the leaders of the October events paid a visit to our region and to Irkutsk. Their names, with the sole exception, it seems, of Trotsky, remain to this day in the names of our streets. In general, judging by street names, you'd think the French Revolution also took place in Irkutsk and that the worldwide revolutionary movement arose there. The art museum can't secure for itself the name of its founder, but Marat continues to "sound forth" not only as one of the best streets but also as a huge suburb.

It is worth recalling that such progressive statesmen for their time as Mikhail Speransky and Nikolay Muravyov-Amursky, who left behind good reputations and fond memories of themselves in Russia's history, served as governors-general in Irkutsk.

Jaroslav Hašek[25] worked there in the political section of the Fifth Army in 1920.

Irkutsk contains the graves of Grigory Shelikhov, of the Decembrists Pyotr Mukhanov, Nikolay Panov, and Iosif Podzhio, of Yekaterina Trubetskaya[26] and her children, and of two native sons and eminent figures in prerevolutionary Russian thought, Afanasy Shchapov, a historian, writer, and ethnographer, and Mikhail Zagoskin, a social and political commentator. Admiral Kolchak,[27] as we know, has no grave, but he, too, spent his final days in Irkutsk.

Irkutsk does indeed have something to remember and will have plenty of its own history and distant past to hand down to its descendants if we who have now come to replace the many generations that created its noble reputation treat the past judiciously and resolutely, for the sake of how others will remember us, and if we preserve what still remains. No matter how much we honor and glorify our own era and society, we mustn't forget that they would have been impossible without the past, without those who, through their labors and selfless devotion, through struggle and martyrdom, established us in life and gave us a homeland that we have every right to be proud of. What our predecessors experienced cannot be dark and gloomy—it's the future that's gloomy when the past has been shoved aside and the present, lacking a firm foundation, requires support.

1987–91

5
✤✤✤

The Gorno-Altay Region

A VIEW

The grandeur of the human race lies in the increase of its beneficial capacities, in the great strength and brilliance of its inner workings. The grandeur of the earth is its outer contours, its "God-madeness," and the splendor in its unique, large-scale movements. The Most High must have planned humankind even before the creation of the world, so there would be someone to enjoy and admire his work. The human race must have been started for this reason, out of which its sensual perception and morality should have grown.

But what can you do?! We've turned out to be a poor, inadequate audience. What nature has to offer finds in us only a faint response. And not out of arrogance, not out of plebeian inclinations—that's another matter, though they, too, appeared as the result of a general lack of development and a foreshortening of feelings that cannot sufficiently fathom or penetrate the depths of beauty and grandeur. Even Nikolay Karamzin, one of Russia's most remarkable penetrators, demanded, "Give us feelings, not theory." But his demand came too late. And feelings have sunk further and become even more material-ized since his day.

When I saw Mount Belukha for the first time in all its free, power-ful, severe sculpturing, I experienced only confusion, nothing more. I saw the whole mountain—it was a rare piece of luck that Belukha revealed the outcropping for which it is named—and I couldn't put a label on what I saw. Words, feelings, stirrings of the soul were not enough. They all backed away and froze voicelessly before this sover-eign illumination, which rose up with such strength and wholeness that it was impossible to scrape off a single pebble or fleck of light that could be described in words. It must have been a similar confusion, experienced over and over, that formed the Altay people's superstition that you should never look at Belukha.

That same day I'd visited the regional museum in the town of Verkh-Uymon and read the words of Yegor Meyer,[1] an artist who had accompanied Pyotr Chikhachyov[2] on his expedition to the Gorno-Altay region in 1842. I felt a certain proud relief on discovering that even then, a hundred and fifty years ago, when human beings were far closer to nature than they are now, they were just as powerless to depict it. Meyer writes:

Breathing with difficulty, I climbed to the summit and began trembling with delight. Ice caps sparkled in the distance like an ocean frozen during a storm, and the Katun Columns rose among them like a jagged giant, disappearing in the pale light-blue tint of the sky. Mist wound through the ravines like snakes. But where are the words, where are the colors to convey this scene?! There's no point in racking your brain or searching through your paints for the right shades! . . . I looked at all this and then at myself—what, then, am I? An insignificant grain of sand in this enormous labyrinth! . . . I grabbed my sketch pad, but my hand was shaking: I seemed to be looking at the living God, with all his strength and beauty, and I began to feel ashamed that I, a poor mortal, had even dreamt of conveying his image!

Right before and during the Russian Revolution there lived and worked in Siberia a remarkable writer named Aleksandr Novosyolov,[3] to whom I couldn't help turning while writing this essay and others, once I'd put my hand to the Altay plow and there was no going back. He was a master of words, not simply as a designation of his profession but in his use of them, yet he, too, forgot about his wonderful gift while in the Altay Mountains and held his tongue:

I felt like praying to this grandeur, to this genuine beauty—such was my frame of mind. Yes, to pray was exactly what I wanted to do. Humankind has neither the colors nor the words to convey the grandeur of nature. The very best description would be nothing but lifeless words.

When people were in desperate straits in the old days, they always had prayer. We, with our self-styled self-confidence in our own grandeur, must do without it and look for different paths: we can either add fire to our language or close our eyes. The latter, of course, is easier. How many, many times during my trips to the Altay region did I, bewitched by nature's magic all around me, feverishly hunt for anything in me capable of even faintly responding to its essence, and I froze in helplessness every time. My tongue was my cross. Heavy, and more than I could bear.

And I never did manage to carry it up into the Altay Mountains in order to describe them. And I still don't know anyone who could. For the creative artist the Altay Mountains remain a dream: miraculous and supernatural, woven out of predictions, premonitions, and portents, out of alluring promises and enticements. For the creative artist they remain a dream, but for each of us they may well be the last recollection, on the eve of massive transformation, of a land that allows us, if we work at it properly, to glimpse paradise on earth.

ENDLESS TRIBUTE

We figured we would fly out in the morning, but we weren't airborne until after three o'clock. The governing board of the hydroelectric power plants then under construction had rented a helicopter for us, and Yury Ivanovich Tashpokov, the director of those power plants, rode along with us. A likeable, middle-aged native of the Altay region, he is, like all Altaians, a man of few words who looks and listens attentively but stubbornly sticks to a decision once it has been made. Before being appointed to his present post, he had traveled the world a good deal, and in every place he visited as a professional builder of hydroelectric power stations, rivers began to turn turbines. No wonder Yury Ivanovich has no doubts that this is actually the chief job of rivers, including his own Katun, which until now has done no work but has just kept flowing idly along.

That summer passions were raging more furiously over the fate of the Katun than the water in its ravines and unfinished dams. Citizens' groups had become active in Moscow, Leningrad, Novosibirsk, Barnaul, and Biysk, contending that hydroelectric plants should not be

The Katun River

built on the Katun, that they would do irreparable harm to the river
and the region. Not that this required any special proof: wherever dams
are put up and reservoirs swell, a river ceases to be a river and becomes
a disfigured beast of burden with the life squeezed out of it. After that,
the river contains no fish, no water, no beauty. Energy will begin to
draw industry, industry will demand new energy, then more industry
will move in, and so on until the Katun, its banks, and the land far
around will simply vanish into thin air. You don't have to be an oracle
or an expert to predict such a fate: our country's approach to hydroelectric plants shows that we don't build them any other way.[4] Those
who see an ally for the dam builders in Nikolay Rerikh,[5] who referred
to the Altay's "thundering rivers calling out for electrification," forget
that Rerikh was not acquainted with our construction practices; had he
known about them, he would certainly have warned us, in the name of
the future of the land in which he placed special hopes for humankind,
to listen carefully to that call for electrification. What seemed an
unqualified blessing sixty some years ago, at the time of the Rerikh
family's trek through the Altay area, when the cost—like any cost that

went beyond your pocketbook—could prevent the achievement of this blessing, has now been modified: expensive efforts that make a profit for the Ministry of Energy have become its goal, and it agrees to advance its armies only where it can conduct military operations on a broad front with a completely free hand, seizing position after position without taking a region's needs into account. Likening dam construction to military operations, to warfare, does not stem from a passion for strong comparisons; this image has been used for a long time, and rightly so. Wherever an armada of dam builders passes through, nature is left incurably ravaged.

The whole time that Yevgeny Gushchin,[6] a writer from Barnaul, and I were in Gorno-Altaysk, the second secretary of the Communist party's regional committee, Valery Ivanovich Chaptynov, came to see us every evening. We would argue late into the night about one thing only: What will power plants on the Katun do for the Gorno-Altay region? Valery Ivanovich asserted that the area needs to develop, that it is already lagging behind economically, in housing construction, and in social services, that everyone else is moving forward while they have long been marking time, and that progress is impossible without their own electrical energy industry. We replied that it would be a great sin to turn the Gorno-Altay region into an ordinary industrial zone, that it serves and befriends us in a different way: by preserving its beauty and purity, which will be worth a lot of money even tomorrow, and the day after tomorrow—life itself. People will give anything and say thank you for a whiff of Altay air, for a look at its natural fairy-tale beauty, for the sound of the wind in a stand of Siberian pine and the peal of mountain streams, for just a single stay amid all this if it has not been squeezed out by the wheels of industrialization. In our counterarguments we even brought up scenery therapy; now there is actually a science devoted to treating patients by using landscape in its natural state. Some countries live entirely by their natural endowments. Grain gives more than bread alone. Cattle breeding is highly developed in the Gorno-Altay region, its earth holds precious and semiprecious stones, and its mountains and taiga give birth to so many riches of every kind that you couldn't begin to collect them all. But instead of continually gathering nuts, they're cutting down the Siberian pine once and for all—and destroying birds, animals, and the rootplants of the taiga as well as undermining age-old hunting and fishing grounds. Why does our country normally view a region's well-being solely in terms of large-scale industrial construction and measure it only with indicators of gross output? Isn't it true that such a large nation needs many different types of construction, intelligent and economical, that take the special features of each area into account? If nature itself intends the Altay region to have Siberian deer and pine, bee gardens and buckthorn berries, cheeses and orchards, herds of horses and flocks of sheep, then why exterminate them there and cultivate them later in some other place? The Gorno-Altay region has been lucky: until now it has miraculously preserved its original physiognomy. Don't hand it over to be completely altered and pulverized, especially since no one is pressuring you; all the fuss about not missing out on constructing hydroelectric plants is above all your own local doing.

This was how Yevgeny Gushchin and I countered Valery Ivanovich Chaptynov, an Altaian by birth, a party worker by profession, and a refined, considerate man by nature who is not indifferent to his native land and who sincerely wishes it well. But somewhere he got the idea that its well-being should now be calculated in figures. Valery Ivanovich fully realized that a great deal hinges on the choice the Gorno-Altay region makes. At present, big industry has spread no farther than Biysk. But with the first hydroelectric plant it will make a dash deep into the mountains, into the domain of small farms and the taiga. And this won't be painless either for the taiga or for the people who live there. They'll have to get out of the way. Hoping to see small farmers better off in ten or fifteen years than they are now, I don't even want to contemplate what else they'll have to do.

Chaptynov attentively heard us out, displaying a nonstandard quality for a party worker in his very ability to listen and to try to understand the viewpoint of nonspecialists without brushing them aside. He agreed with some things, but his dial had already been set to "build" and, like the needle of an instrument that indicates the necessary direction even while oscillating, he stood his ground. He was candid: "If they build a hydroelectric plant, the district will get to keep their housing-construction factories. We need them badly. We'll never get any otherwise."

We matched his frankness with our own: "But don't you know that people will say you sold the Katun for a pre-fab housing complex?"

He knew this and asked in turn: "And don't you know that we have shepherds in remote nomads' camps who sit around kerosene lamps the way they did a hundred years ago?"

"All the more reason," we replied, "for building windmills and small dams on tributaries like the one at Chemal, which are ecologically harmless, in proximity to the consumer, and inexpensive. You can be sure that even with a whole series of power plants, your shepherds in remote camps will still be stuck with kerosene lamps. Strings of power plants aren't erected for shepherds."

Usually calm and reserved, Valery Ivanovich began to get angry: "There won't be a series of power plants—we ourselves are opposed to the idea. We're talking about one plant with a counterregulator. We've got an agreement for only one."

"But," we pressed him, "can you really make a nine-headed dragon agree to carry off just one victim as a form of tribute and then head home? The ministry looks after its own interests. It won't leave until it completely satisfies its appetite. Once it consolidates its position, the advantageous principle of deploying one labor front in a single territory, without any bothersome, long-distance redeployments, will come into play."

What choice did we have?! To avoid looking like creatures from the moon who knew nothing of earthly interests, we fired away with learned words of this type, using the most up-to-date jargon. And yet every now and then we got the impression that Valery Ivanovich was the one who'd recently dropped down from the moon and was just barely beginning to adjust to the way we do things here. For example, he assured us that under no circumstances would they ever go so far as to allow a whole string of power plants, that this decision was in their hands, which made us peer at him even more closely. And it became somehow awkward to remind him that in our country they don't consult local folk, that if someone starts insisting on being consulted, he is conveniently transferred to some place in Kosh-Agach, a not-terribly-pleasant region in the Altay that, because of its rocky, deserted terrain, is called, incidentally, the reverse side of the moon.

Yury Ivanovich Tashpokov, the director of the hydroelectric project, reacted to the passions raging around the Katun with the solid wall of calm borne of experience: if there's a director, then there will also be power plants. The site has been designated, the motor pool has arrived and is already in operation, the company town is going up, they've built little houses for the bosses that are pretty as a picture, there's a day-care center with a swimming pool (the envy of Gorno-Altaysk), millions and millions of rubles have been spent—who would ever back out after all this? So what if there is no ecological justification, no decision authorizing construction? There will be. For power-plant builders this is only natural: start before a decision has been made and in this manner influence the decision. The public will raise a fuss for a while and then simmer down. The builders will prevail the same way they always do: What's wrong with you? Are you in favor of restoring the old barbarian, patriarchal way of life? Are you against the well-being of the Altay people? We'd like to know whose song you are singing, whose boots you are licking. You want beauty, you want pristine surroundings, but can your beauty feed anyone or strengthen the mightiness of our nation? Or haven't you thought about this? That's why we're doing the thinking for you and for ourselves and taking responsibility for the whole country. Sentimentality is not our department.

And so it continues to this day: *kto kogo?* Who will get the upper hand? A number of meetings have been held at the highest levels, a number of debates have made people hopping mad—and the Katun is still waiting for its fate to be decided once and for all.

THE MISTRESS OF THE HOUSE

It was after three o'clock on a long July day when we rose above Gorno-Altaysk in an Mi-8 helicopter rented by the directorate of the hydroelectric project and set a southward course, following the Katun. Down below, the ancient land of the Oyrats[7] began to sway and swim as if cinched together by the Katun; the city we'd left behind had been known until quite recently by the cattle-driving word Ulala.[8] As soon as we were airborne, Lake Aya flashed out and unfolded on our right like a round precious chalice; in its center stood a high stone altar guarded by trees, and we could see figures swimming toward it as if they were crawling up to the feet of some archbishop or metropolitan, begging for mercy. Three days earlier Yeygeny Gushchin, who spent his childhood at Aya, which he considers home, and I had also washed off the road dust there, and I was quite surprised to find such warm, soft, silky water in a mountain lake. Laughing and looking around, Gushchin had pointed at the dense crowd of people swarming listlessly on the shore as if a storm had brought them up from the bottom: that'll heat it up. He clearly remembered the lake differently, as clean and full of fish. Rumor has it that at one time the collective farm to which the lake belonged, prompted by poverty and folly, gave it to a chemical works in Biysk in exchange for a registered bull. And of course the bull promptly passed away during its brief labors, while Aya remained the property of the chemists forever. Even if this is only a fable (the local folk insist that it's the honest truth), it still contains a moral.

Katun'—*katyn* in the Altaian language—means wife, mistress of the house. Like a woman in charge of a household, it gathers up and sustains all surrounding life. A natural reservoir flows into it, forests and grasses crowd up close, birds and animals hold it in memory from birth to death, and the mountains, of whom it keeps endless count, alternately press against it and retreat, making room for fertility, as if on command. Ancient human beings spotted and singled out the Katun in such depths of time that your head starts to spin after one look in that direction. Before Aleksey Okladnikov's excavations along the Ulalinka River,[9] archaeologists had cautiously and somewhat generously estimated that human activity in Siberia began up to twenty-five thousand years ago; the Ulalinka site increased that date by at least tenfold. The scientific world should have gasped, and certainly did gasp, at our antiquity, and only those of us who live in Siberia didn't hear it. Comparatively recently, a mere three thousand years ago, an Asian Scythia—affluent and cultivated, with a well-developed class structure—flourished in the Altay region and for the time being is considered older than the Scythian civilization on the Black Sea. Rerikh, a serious student of the vissicitudes of the human race, said, "The Altay region is one of the most important spots for studying the migration of ethnic groups. . . . In respect to history as well as prehistory, the Altay remains an unopened treasure house." Now we are starting to open that treasure house, but if we partition the Katun with dams, no one knows what we will permanently submerge and destroy.

And the Katun keeps on running its course just the way it did thousands of years ago; before its white, milky waters have finished playing on one set of rocks, they are pounding against the next. But the river is white not because of its boiling rapids but because it originates in the ice cap on the south slope of Mount Belukha, where we were now headed. Only toward the end of summer does the Katun become clear, but even then not to the point of transparency. July was now approaching August, and it hadn't changed a bit. The murky current seemed to have an off-white cast, resembling not simply milk but scalded milk.

The day turned out to be sunny, warm but not hot, and ringingly clear, so clear that your eye seemingly had only to fall on something and whatever it fell on would begin to resound. Gazing all around from above, you could see as far and as clearly as if you weren't actually doing the looking, but rather the sky's vision were streaming through you: bald mountains crumbling in the distance (only after an hour would I realize that those weren't mountains but just an amusement, a warm-up exercise for the real mountains), haystacks in small hollows, ribbons of pine and birch along the Katun, the even, taut line of the Chuysky Highway along the right bank, and the stirred-up, quartz-shiny Katun coursing along, casting a spell with its color, faceting, boiling, passion, and power. Now it's pounding against some rocks and forming rapids near Manzherok, the settlement glorified in the hikers' song;[10] now it's resting up as it goes in circles, now it's calm, and now it's attacking boulders again in a shaggy, fibrous tangle. And island after island . . . low, alluvial islands, rocky islands with splintered cliffs, bare islands and islands overgrown with woods, solid islands and islands with small lakes tucked here and there, with sandy beaches and perpendicular walls, with whimsical stone figures and cozy resting places surrounded by new greenery. All this flows along with the Katun; everything sounds forth in multivoiced harmony, calling us to itself, welcoming us, dwelling brightly and festively in the holiday of summer. Everything drifts and dashes to the music of sight and sound, reaching the point of torture.

Don't believe the nonbelievers: they are evil because they do not see.

Not far from Ust-Sema, where the Chuysky Highway turns off to the right, away from the Katun, the mountains are blanketed with forest. The ascents rising from the riverbank on both sides are broad and resolute. Up in the air, above this majestic flourish, you don't believe in the mightiness of humankind. I lift my eyes to look at the director of the hydroelectric project, who is sitting in front, but he, too, is glued to the window in fascination, and I can't bring myself to ask him. . . . Or rather I don't even know what to ask; the impulse to ask was simply involuntary.

Even after the highway turns off in a different direction, the Katun is still quite densely populated. On the right (that is, on the left bank), beyond the town of Cheposh, lies a broad semicircular valley overgrown with woods and girdled by a clear strip at the foot of the mountains. Ah, yes, we must remember that the first power station—not the first to be built but the first in the series shown on the Hydroelectric Projects Office's map—is supposed to be at Cheposh; consequently, this is the area the reservoir might flood. Only the day before did I read the legend about the origin of the name *Cheposh*. It seems a man went walking one morning and quenched his thirst at a little spring on this spot. When he returned that evening, he couldn't find the water. Disappointed, he exclaimed, "*Chyoyok-bosh!*", meaning, "Aw, it's dried up!" Reality is mirroring legend to a surprising extent, as if making sure that a fanciful sequel will follow.

Even from our height we couldn't see the little village of Anos hidden behind the woods, the place where the Altaian artist Grigory Gurkin[11] lived and worked. An hour hadn't passed before the pilots, approaching Belukha from the left, heading east, pointed out something else: "Right over there, beyond those cliffs, is the Yungur River, and beyond that is Gurkin's 'lake of the mountain spirits.'"

. . . Below us lay orchards that seemed cloaked in smoky shade, distinctly different from the dark green of the local forests . . .

We dipped down over Chemal, which has a sanatorium and a small hydroelectric plant that serves it and the town. The dam looked tiny; it was releasing pure, light-blue water from a tributary, which brightened up the Katun as it rose gently to the surface. The dam was built during the 1930s, when Yekaterina Kalinina,[12] wife of "the all-union chief,"[13] was exiled there. Under the pretext of seeking medical treatment for his lungs in a mountain climate, Mikhail Ivanovich himself made two trips there, in 1931 and 1934. More than once he must have stood on that platform above the precipice to the left, with the white strip of a beaten path leading up to it, and admired the Katun. It is indeed a feast for the eyes: at this point the Katun swings sharply toward Chemal and, after receiving the tributary, is hemmed in along its right bank by cliffs; its left, alluvial bank lies low and open to the eye from all sides, allowing the gaze something rare along the Katun: to stretch out and spot a sandy beach and bushes and woods before running into mountains again. Farther down you see a gorge and water capped with lather.

Here, just before the bend in the Katun, planners spotted something, too: a site for a new dam, which they designed to be forty meters high. But no, they've chosen to put the Katun hydroelectric power plant farther upriver (we hadn't come to it yet), while Chemal will have a counterregulator—which is the same thing by a different name and not even a power plant but an additional weight. We flew on. Ribbons of pine forest framed the Katun corridor here and there and large wooded areas spread from right to left and left to right, as did the mountains, now tightening up, now opening out, but most often revealing single openings along the valleys of the inflowing rivers; the pace of the water would alternately abate and increase, humpbacking the rocks. There were fewer and fewer figures of sunbathers spread out like scissors along the straight stretches, and the settlements likewise kept getting smaller and farther apart.

But there's Yelanda. About two kilometers upriver from this village the construction site is being prepared for the first hydroelectric power plant on the Katun, one of the six with which they plan to partition the river. We lost altitude and hovered briefly over the section where the dam will be. A visual estimate put the width there at about fifty to sixty meters; it turned out to be more than twice as wide. A narrow road at the base of a cliff on the left, a screen-covered hole in the cliff that leads to an underground tunnel, and a low burial mound with metal rods sticking out of it on the opposite bank—the dam will go up along this line. The high-voltage current of human passions has probably been traveling along it for several years already. A lone pine tree stood dry and withered on the bank by the tunnel's entrance; workers will throw odds and ends of wire on it . . .

We had driven along that bank the day before. We'd glanced into the tunnel and stood near the pine tree for a while, peering at the Katun with strained attention. The scene begged us to push the buttons of feeling, to find, say, that the Katun, foreseeing its fate, shuddered at this spot, stumbled, and then straightened out its current only slowly. But no, it stumbles in many places; that's the sort of river it is. It hears the rumble of explosions as they build a new road, but even that shouldn't scare it: this isn't the first time explosions have thundered here, and they weren't any softer sixty years ago when the Chuysky Highway was brought over to this side as the shortest route. The shortest way turned out to be impassable, so they abandoned it. On that bank there now stands a monument to Vyacheslav Shishkov,[14] a writer who spent many years here during the surveying and construction of the highway and who sang loud hosannas to the beauty of the Katun and the Chuya Rivers. After several years this monument became as much a part of the Katun as the islands, the wild rocks, the trees, and the road laid earlier, as if it had been there forever. The earth should know its organizers and poets; then it will also know its own worth.

No, even explosions aren't likely to scare the Katun. Born freely and living freely, it can't understand that they are carving out this road not as a convenient approach to the river but to pierce it, once, twice, who knows how many times . . .

Valery Ivanovich Chaptynov drove us to the bottom of the future reservoir. The woods were indeed sparse there and the land rocky. The grass, barely rising above ground that dry summer, faded instantly in the sun. The dam would flood an area extending seventy kilometers from the backwater, a drop in the bucket compared to the lands that have vanished underwater because of the hydroelectric plants at Bratsk and Ust-Ilimsk.[15] One village, Kuyus, is doomed to destruction. We drove all the way over to it, opened the heavy metal gates at the entrance (the village pasture was still fenced off from the fields), and, raising dust behind us, tooled up and down the streets awhile, then left. The village is unsightly, with a disorderly array of shoddy log cottages. I had to agree with Valery Ivanovich that not many tears would be shed over it. The local residents, of course, take a different view, and their tears aren't ours, the tears of passing tourists, but in cases like this we probably ought to act out of common sense. And if we act out of common sense, it's not a matter of rocky soil, or the loss of forests and good farm land, or the naked-standing little steppe village of Kuyus—a lot more of a lot greater value went to hell with the other manmade seas! No, this is something entirely different. Once burnt, twice shy: it's time we learned from past experience. A lot more has been lost, but shouldn't we put a stop to these losses if we can get along without them?! The main losses on the Katun won't result from successful measuring and calculating or constitute an injury to the whole from altering a part; we could somehow resign ourselves to losing a single part. It's just that, like tampering with a great master's violin, nothing, not even a tiny piece, can be removed from this uncommonly well-made natural instrument without ruining the whole apparatus. For the businesslike people directing the dance, this is empty prettiness, nothing more, and they'll make do on the dance floor with recorded music, but that doesn't mean we'll start dancing to their tune forever.

The pilots called me into the cockpit, from where we could see down, forward, and to the sides. I saw a line of pine trees along Edigan Creek as straight as if someone had planted them, a line of horses carrying a party of tourists, who looked like baggage, a patchwork of cultivated fields near Kuyus that resembled ancient hieroglyphs, the bright tents of an archaeological expedition working at excavation sites along the bottom of the future sea, the sheer rock face of the old Chuysky Highway. Beyond that lay an absence of roads, a frontier, and another region where, after a short distance, I could see fertility, gardens, and inhabited areas again.

And in the future will we be able to list the tributaries and channels, the floods and rapids of the Katun, everything with which the river makes noise and flows from place to place the way a tree, putting out branches, breathes through its trunk and crown? Will we be able to check its colors and signs, the rocky overhangs and the shallows along its banks, and to look for comparisons the way we used to? Will we be able to list the animals that come out and follow paths to watering holes or measure the feelings that respond sometimes rapturously, sometimes prayerfully, to a sense of kinship, as if the Katun brought you to life, assembling you bit by bit from here and there, and then at some point gathered something into your soul, even though you were actually born in a different locale? . . . But Homeland is not merely one's place of birth; it is also a place of parentage and ancestry. The first time I found myself at the Katun fifteen years earlier, my memory stretched as far back as if I'd actually been a nomad there during distant antiquity and then had left to wander around a neighboring area and forgotten about it. This is probably how Russians feel when visiting any part of their ancient land. Even more so for those of us in Siberia, where the whole land from one end to the other lay under a single huge bowl—nomadic freedom—and where it is a grievous sin not to recognize migration routes.

We continued to thrust deep into rocky country, staying above the narrow white spread of the Katun. The Katun continued to run its course, and its banks, time and again transforming themselves, playing, pulling the scanty low-lying areas back and forth away from each other, continued to flow toward us. Nothing is more thrilling, fascinating, and heart-stopping than river banks, especially those along mountain rivers, where everything is pure, sonorous, quick, and free. But what's the use of my being moved and delighted, of my ooing and ahing? You have to be there yourself, to take that air into your lungs, to let the beauty of that remote hinterland imbue you with courage and tenderness. Everything lives its own life there, everything shines, glows, rings, runs, or hangs in the air according to its own laws and needs, everything exists without death and decay, infinity hovers over all: How can you help being drawn across all obstacles and distances, the way people in days of old were drawn to holy Mount Athos, to strengthen your soul?!

The deeper we penetrated, the higher, mightier, and more jagged rose the mountains, the more confident became their flourishes, the thicker the forest. If any *chern'*—taiga of fir and pine that admits no light—remained anywhere in the Altay region, it had to be there.

And the mountains rose even higher. The Katun ran in a deep crevice. A series of jagged peaks began to screen off the heavy fallen boulders that propped each other up. The peaks were positioned like soldiers of different sizes, an army that kept rising higher and higher. What direction did this host face, and what territory was it defending? This was no longer land in the usual sense of terra firma but a graduated rise to the sky, a monolithic and inescapable ascent that everything had been preparing to climb or descend with the stride of a *bogatyr'* since the beginning of time.

But meanwhile cranes were flying over the Katun. We managed to count them—two flocks of seven—and then said goodbye to them and to the Katun before turning off to the left, straightening our route to its headwaters. It's closer to Mount Belukha if you follow the Ak-Kem River.

THE PROPRIETRESS

If the Katun is the bustling mistress of the house, the nourisher/nurturer, then Belukha is the reigning proprietress, the sovereign who makes vast domains bow down to her, extending her will to everything all around.

. . . We had been flying over the Ak-Kem for less than five minutes when Belukha appeared up ahead. It didn't rise smoothly from behind neighboring peaks but seemed to throw off a wrap and show its height and depth all at once, standing behind the holy gates of the iconostasis like a gleaming icon.

Ah, yes, its height. The gauge said 1,600 meters, and Belukha is 4,500 meters high. After hovering above the cliffs, we began our climb. Nothing can compare with the wooded tilt of those white-capped mountains, with that whole mighty and motionless above-ground archipelago. When faced with this sort of architecture, our language has nothing in reserve; what we call *grandeur, power,* and *height* get these names only when flowing from that point. But there's the outflow, and over there it's all slopes and humps—the summit is higher.

Lake Ak-Kem, an oblong body of glacial runoff and the source of the river, lay to the left; beside it the little houses of a meteorological station and the tents of a camp for international mountain climbers formed a distinct picture. The helicopter seemed drawn in by Belukha's breath; those great statues, those leaps into the sky that together make up a single metropolis larger than the eye can encompass, cannot be lifeless. Here there is no nature as we are accustomed to seeing and understanding it; nature begins farther below. Here, above nature, everything is cut from the same cloth and carried many hundreds and thousands of versts; here is the birth of wind, water, earth, and, it seems, even time; here are the beginnings of pure breath and pure birth as they emerge from eternity, a sublunar kingdom that the sun was forced to give up, a cosmic mural . . .

It was hard to talk and breathe—there wasn't enough oxygen. But it was also hard to see—there wasn't enough vision. You couldn't take your eyes off that truly unearthly picture, which was beyond the eyes' strength, beyond the forces that usually guide them; and it still remains unrecordable. An cosmonaut probably experiences the same pity and despair when looking at the Earth from orbit: everything is visible but cold and beyond the ken of his alien, cyclopean gaze. And all this turns out to be—nothing.

We were struggling toward Belukha from the northeast corner. But it seemed as if we were backing up with all our might while being drawn in. I saw, from almost the same level as the summit, its camel's saddle with the two humps. From our side I saw a rock face beyond the vertical, as mountain climbers say—a slope with a negative incline—with a heavy awning of snow on top, the sharp outlines of fractured rock, black and white patches of slopes and corrugations alternating on a white background. This is probably how a bug that has climbed up a tree studies a human face, and what for us represents beauty and a perfection that is aesthetic and instrumentally cognitive, the bug perceives as gaps, breaks, and bumps.

Belukha displayed itself slowly and majestically. We circled it from the east and then continued on down its spine, where it fell away at a gradual, persistent slant. Heaven only knows how a lake could be suspended on that slope, with yet another one beyond it. . . . It took me a while to guess that those were glaciers, and then suddenly I saw the source of the Katun.

Vasily Sapozhnikov,[16] a professor at Tomsk University who devoted his entire life to studying the Altay region and who was the first to climb into Belukha's saddle, describes the origin of the Katun this way:

The Katun begins in two places under the Gebler Glacier. The right-hand stream, somewhat larger than its companion, flows out from under the ice about twenty sazhens [about 135 feet] from the end of the glacier and runs rapidly between a wall of ice on one side and heaps of rock in the last moraine on the other. According to various accounts, there used to be a big grotto where this stream leaves the glacier, but now it has caved in and shrunk, leaving only a small dark crevice of irregular shape. The lefthand stream also begins under the end of the glacier but closer to the left side. Both streams wind noisily through their stony channels until they come together . . .

How can we resist going along with the scientist and his companions (on their expedition of 1895) and climbing the plateau of ice that feeds the Katun?

The ice that hangs out over the horizontal crack from which the Katun emerges is 8–10 sazhens [about 50–60 feet] thick, and it is difficult and dangerous to climb directly onto the glacier because of the possibility of an avalanche. It's easier to make use of the moraine, although this, too, presents some inconveniences. Immense angular rocks are strewn about in total disarray; many lie in unstable positions and give way underfoot, revealing deep crevices. After walking across the moraine for several sazhens, you can turn right and step up onto the glacier by following one of the ridges of ice between the cracks that run all along the edge of the glacier but pose no danger whatsoever because they are easy to spot. As you move away from the edge, the big cracks practically disappear, and the glacier presents a smooth surface eroded by shallow rivulets and covered with rocks. Large rocks form low, icy tables; small ones have eaten deep holes in the transparent ice, while heaps of detritus tower above them in the shape of regular cones. Closer to the high middle moraine the glacier is again broken up by deep cracks that form a solid line of dark crevasses right in front of the rocks themselves; streams of water running across the ice plunge into them noisily. Sometimes a partially thawed rock breaks loose from one of the moraine's ridges and hits the water at the bottom of the crevasses with a muffled sound.

That's where the Katun originates; that's why its water is white. And right nearby, just two steps from the solid ice, undersized spreading firs, dwarf arctic birches, willowweed, and sweet vetch appear among the rocks, with willow trees beginning a bit lower. The cloudy Katun twists and winds, leaving old river beds in the loose, alluvial soil and finding new ones, and then branches out into channels. But by the time it receives the offshoot from the other glacier, which empties into it on the right, the Katun is already flowing through forests and high grasses as tall as a person, continually collecting water; it then turns westward with a powerful current in order to go around the snow-covered mountains by a convenient route, making an enormous loop.

None of this, of course, was visible from the air. All I could see was a gigantic white beast with dark spots and stripes that had lain down on the slope of a gigantic mountain, spreading out its long fluffy tail, and raised its two heads, peering into the devil's abyss on the other side. But Belukha is overwhelming even from the air. And you don't have the feeling that you're looking down; even while lowering your eyes, you seem to be standing at its base. You can climb it, as a great many people do nowadays, and feel no sense of victory. No matter where you are, it remains superior by exactly as much as its actual height. But Belukha affects you even more by what you can't see, by some kind of palpable sovereignty. Altaians have experienced a sacred trepidation before it from time immemorial, and for good reason. Human beings were considered unworthy of looking at the mountain, which was like looking at a deity, and if anyone went near it, you couldn't drag him away with a lasso. Even in our enlightened times, scientific and amateur expeditions to Belukha have not been able to find guides among the local residents: money is fine, but steering clear of "the proprietress" is even better. She is the one who sends down winds and fog; she has the power to decide when the snow will melt and the grasses turn green, in what direction and quantity the animals will head, and whether or not the summer will be bountiful. She dispatched her favorite, the Katun, to go around to all the mountain ranges, suggesting that they be called the Katun's, and, while making the rounds, the Katun picked up so much strength that no one could match it. And it was Belukha who, by some magical tug, separated one and the same river and made it run in different directions, forming two: the Koksu, which flows into the Ob, and the Berel, which empties into the Irtysh. Even an experienced eye can't tell where the kink in the land is and how two mighty river systems begin from a swampy bulge.

Numb with delight, we flew around Belukha and began to descend—over the outstretchedness of Lake Kucherlinskoe, over the Kucherla River, which rushes out of the lake toward the Katun like an uncombed hank of white hair, over the quieting tempestuousness of the land. Lake Talmenye, or Taymenye, flashed on our left; it is named after a species of fish that I hear is not in short supply even now. I strained to spot Rabbit Creek [*rechka Zaichikha*]; somewhere along it stands Rabbit Village [*derevnia Zaichika*], which was completely abandoned by its inhabitants during collectivization,[17] when they went in search of Belovodye. But I never did spot it.

Everything happens fast in a flying machine; soon we were over the Katun again. Now we turned left, against the current. The mountains parted; the valley kept widening out. And the Katun itself kept growing calmer and calmer until it dispersed of its own will into numerous branches overgrown with willows and woods. Here was a completely different world. There were villages on the left, villages on the right, plowed fields, water meadows, pine forests, and sandy banks, like somewhere far, far away on the plains of Siberia.

This was the Uymon Valley, the northern corner of the legendary Belovodye.

BELOVODYE

Here begins one of the most colorful pages in the Russian colonization of Siberia, pages that are almost completely forgotten today and that, along with the cryptic writings and symbols recorded not through reason but through impulse, formed the basis of the old scripts that interpreted the old religious rules. Just as a person experiencing the anxiety that comes before illumination blindly and impatiently urges himself toward a flash of understanding, so, too, do these symbols, which, jumbled together with the continuous development of the storyline, created over the course of two centuries the sad and beautiful tale of Belovodye.

Many, far too many, people who don't even know what it is automatically shudder at the mere sound of this word, as if reacting to a mystical call reminding them of an unfulfilled behest: Go some place, I don't know where, and get something, I don't know what.

We're all aware that there are different kinds of dreams. Personal dreams concern the happiness an individual desires, not a large amount but enough for one. Dreams for a community arise in the name of order and prosperity for a group. Dreams for society underlie the planning and construction of systems designed to entice and unite an entire people. And they all look to the future, to progressing toward a result that has never been achieved before and to which human beings, because they were spiritually stunted, could not even come close to attaining before.

But apparently there were dreams directed backward, not forward, toward the time when no government authority oppressed anyone and people could celebrate life freely, without tripping over some restrictive law at every step, when lands were not worn out or forests mown down, and when consensus and faith kept people more steadfast and honest than laws did. When the lands in Russia were gathered together under one power and a system of taxation was introduced, these people fled to the Wild Field, to the lower reaches of the Volga and Don Rivers, where they established their own customs and means of livelihood and lived in bands inspired by the traces of nomadic blood in their veins. Later on, when, thanks to them, Siberia was discovered, they rushed past the Rock and paced off an immense landmass in its entirety from west to east in little more than half a century. They hastened to find more and more vast new lands not only for the sake of riches but also for the sake of liberty, no matter how short and temporary, as long as they found it. They couldn't keep those lands and tillable soils a secret, so they would be forced to hand them over to the authorities they were unable to live under and move on. They reached the Pacific Ocean, but even the ocean didn't stop them; they began looking for a place to set foot in its domain, too.

By this time the Russian Orthodox Church had split into two factions [during the 1660s]. No one could have planned it better: Patriarch Nikon[18] gave Russians a fine opportunity, on the heels of this physical upsurge, to demonstrate the power of the spiritual upsurge that had risen to defend the church's former rites and liturgical texts with a zeal that could only occur in an uncommon nation. Had the government authorities sided with Archpriest Avvakum rather than with Nikon and begun to persecute Nikon's followers, the New Believers would probably also have displayed no less steadfastness and willingness to burn themselves alive than their opponents did. The young

nation sprouted a new organ that, like a tumor, had to make its presence known, whether on one side or the other. Within the tumor appeared cartilage, which hardened into bone—and here's a set of character traits for you: stubbornness to the point of perishing, faith to the point of fossilization, liberty to the point of enslavement—all to appease the will.

It was the Old Believers who suffered persecution. Centuries of the authority of their texts stood behind them,[19] making their confidence all the firmer and their break with the church all the stronger. They were sent as far away as possible, but they strove to escape their supervised exile by fleeing even deeper into the hinterland. The deeper the better. "We do not have a real city, but we shall seek one in the future."[20]

Russian colonization quickly reached the depths of Siberia during the seventeenth century by following river routes and began to branch out only later. During the eighteenth century the colonists were not so much hunters and trappers as peasants seeking a comfortable, settled way of life. The southern foothills rich in fruitful land were especially attractive. But the government had added a line of Cossack sentries with forts, outposts, redouts, and signal fires to keep them out. Mount Piket in the village of Srostki, Vasily Shukshin's hometown, is the site of one of these posts.

But "keeping them out" came later, in the second half of the eighteenth century. Before that there was nothing to keep them out of. The line of sentries formed a boundary south of which roamed the Altaian tribes who formed part of Dzungaria.[21] The Russian and Dzungarian authorities quarreled constantly over lands, payers of tribute, and incursions by each other's subjects, who would regularly cross the line from one side or the other. Both parties, we must assume, understood perfectly well that this boundary was temporary and that they couldn't avoid lowering it, or rather raising it, into the mountains, while nomadic tribes would always move to new places in the czar's territory, all the more so since some of them had already left for Siberia.

It sounds strange to us now, when we can't imagine Siberia as anything but a single geographic entity, that at one time the Altay region, or Khakasia, lay beyond Siberia and did not become part of it until later. But in those days the government tampered with place names: only what belonged to Russia was considered Siberia, and whatever did not belong to it was not Siberia but a beast of a different stripe.

And now, in order to clarify even slightly the confusing and sticky history of annexation and of how Russia established control over the Altaian tribes, we must go back in time for a little while, to the seventeenth century.

Tomsk was founded in 1604 and the fortified town of Kuznetsk, farther south on the Tom River, in 1618. In this manner the Russians stood with one foot in front of the Sayan-Altay Plateau, poised at first in a cramped, uncomfortable position; they did not put down the other foot until they built Fort Ust-Kamenogorsk in the Altay's ore-bearing region one hundred some years later. But it goes without saying that no matter how shaky they found it at first to stand on one leg, they didn't waste any time in annexing the northern territory of the Altaian peoples. The Teleuts along the Ob River had adopted Russian citizenship as far back as 1605, and the authorities immediately began demanding tribute from everyone around Kuznetsk as well. The Cossacks would make a sortie, collect tribute, and report that they had annexed the area, but the following year they would have to annex it all over again. And this went on for several decades. In 1633 a boyar's son named Pyotr Sabansky penetrated the domain of the Teles tribe, reaching Lake Teletskoe, and laid them under tribute, but when he went back again in 1642, the Teles people had completely forgotten whose subjects they were. Yet even during his second expedition Sabansky failed to put up a fort on the lake—he merely chose a spot for one on the Biya River—and everything started all over from the beginning.

But the Altaian tribes living in the northern part of their land were in an even less enviable position: more often than not they had to pay twice, handing over tribute both to the Russian czar and to the *kontaysh* of Dzungaria. This highway robbery dragged on for quite some time, more than one hundred years. The lands definitely belonged to Russia by then and the boundary line had been moved farther south, but whether out of ethnic kinship or out of habit, the Dzungars continued to regard the Russian Oyrats as their subjects and to assess their own tax, called *alman*. If the Russian system of tribute extorted one sable per person, the collectors of *alman* squeezed out five. And just try crossing either the czar or the khan.

Dzungaria tried more than once to claim lands ceded to Siberia, including territory along the Yenisey, Ob, Irtysh, and Tom Rivers, even during the reign of Peter the Great. This forced the Russian government to fortify its southern line of sentries. By the middle of the eighteenth century the line had edged down into the Altay region, into the Bukhtarma Valley, in two strips, forming the Irtysh zone (from Omsk to Ust-Kamenogorsk) and the Kolyvan-Voskresensk zone (from Kuznetsk to the Demidov mining works). The latter also included Fort Biysk, which had been erected in 1710 at the spot where the Biya and Katun rivers flow into the Ob.

The fate of even the mightiest empires is unpredictable, let alone that of such loose formations as the khanate of Dzungaria. Still strong during Peter the Great's time, it had begun to come apart at the seams by midcentury because of internal feudal strife. China took advantage of this and destroyed Dzungaria in 1755–56. The domain of the *kontaysh*, so recently a threat to Russian Siberia, fell prey to robbery, pestilence, famine, smallpox, and panic. Historian Serafim Shashkov[22] writes: "Everything that had legs and could move rushed to Siberia."

High up on the Syomin Pass stands a monument to the Gorno-Altay region's voluntary union with Russia. Immediately following Dzungaria's defeat, twelve Altaian *zaysany* (princes) turned to the Russian czar, asking to be taken under his authority. Thus in 1756 the Russian boundaries in the Altay region were lowered far to the south.

The boundaries were lowered, but the line of Cossack sentries remained in place, partly at first because the Russians didn't trust the *zaysany*, whose tribes even tried to migrate to the Volga, and partly, later on, to safeguard their independence. Tales of the czarist government's cruelty toward the indigenous peoples of Siberia are greatly exaggerated or simply don't correspond to reality. Oppression and extortion did occur, of course, but the administrators and tradesmen who engaged in such practices were violating the law, not observing it. The law, as a rule, was merciful to non-Russians.

An area of 110,000 square versts [about 50,000 square miles] on the righthand side of the Kolyvan-Voskresensk line, that is, practically within the former borders, was set aside for "the Kalmyk nomadic encampments" (in olden times Altaians were called Kalmyks, probably because of certain similarities). Their Russian brethren were kept out. The Cossack sentry posts came in handy for this purpose, too. They made an exception for missionaries, who were trying to convert the Altaians to Christianity; traders claimed the same right for themselves, establishing small settlements of merchants on the other side of the line. And it goes without saying that Russian peasants immediately began testing the line's strength, too.

This began in the southernmost corner, which Akinfy Demidov[23] had chosen as the site of his renowned Kolyvan factories and mines, which later became the property of His Majesty's Imperial Cabinet. As was customary in former times, the closest villages were attached to the mining works and more settlers moved in, but the lands were declared to be the cabinet's. Ending up on those lands brought little joy: you were neither a plowman nor a worker, and you were made to grow crops and forced to work in the mines. It was just like the serfdom they'd fled, with the same kind of enslavement. The factory peasants had no desire to accept such conditions; Siberian peasants, as opposed to their counterparts from European Russia, were quite obstinate. Moreover, among those attached to the mining enterprises were banished Old Believers, who found any kind of pressure absolutely intolerable.

An 1858 issue of the *Tomsk Province Gazette* [*Tomskie gubernskie viedomosti*] (the Altay area along with the Bukhtarma Valley used to be part of Tomsk Province) describes the beginning of the amazing colonization of the Altay region this way:

First of all, about ninety years ago [i.e., ninety years before 1858 (Rasputin)] four men of pious disposition took up residence near the Ulba River [a mountain tributary of the Irtysh (Rasputin)]; but soon one of them got caught and the others fled into the wild ravines of the Bukhtarma Valley. From there they began to visit settlements, especially those where the residents were inclined toward the Old Belief. These communities treated them with respect because of their devoutness and supplied them with food and other provisions. Many residents were swayed by them and moved with their wives and children to wild, uncharted territory to join them. Within a short period of time a sizable number of new residents, primarily peasants, had gathered there, in those inaccessible areas surrounded by high mountains: the colonists built huts on the banks of the Bukhtarma, Belaya, Yazovaya, and other rivers and took up cattle breeding and farming. They lived peaceably, strictly observing the rules of the Old Belief, and they prospered. Although the government took measures against these fugitives, the inaccessibility of the land protected them well.

This is just one account of the "stonemasons" [*kamenshchiki*] (as those who fled into the mountains were called); you can find many such stories throughout the Altay region. In 1743, even earlier than ninety years before 1858 and before the annexation of the tribal territory in the south, the government issued a special decree prohibiting incursions into the lands beyond the boundary line—which means there were plenty of people doing just that. Some left forever, in such a manner that no trace of them remained; others secretly put up hunting shacks on Kalmyk and Kirgiz (Kazakh) land, had fun skirmishing with the natives they encountered, and stole horses from one another.

Nikolay Yadrintsev, in an article titled "Old Believer Communal Societies on the Chinese Border,"[24] cites a case in which a community of "stonemasons," attempting to escape persecution by the czarist authorities, tried to put themselves under the dominion of China. But China, for some reason, would not accept them. I must point out that this case is an extreme exception, that they usually didn't go so far as to spit on their country and break all ties for good. People did flee across the boundaries of their native land but not to change citizenship; they were hoping to do without any citizenship whatsoever. Within their own boundaries, even in the most remote, well-hidden spots, things were gradually heading in the direction of another round-up. For that reason, around 1790 a deputation of "stonemasons" representing several dozen secretly existing villages gave themselves up and requested, through local authorities, that Her Majesty Catherine the Great pardon them and make them wards of the state. Through an imperial rescript the empress brought them under her authority in 1791 and made them, like non-Russians, subject to paying tribute. And for almost one hundred years Russians living along the Bukhtarma and Katun rivers in the Uymon Valley paid tribute and enjoyed the privileges of small minority groups right along with the indigenous Altaians. The most notable privilege was exemption from military service.[25]

They managed. And they managed pretty well. But they never got used to this arrangement and never became resigned to it. Those who had gone in search of Belovodye even once, who had heard about it from their fathers and grandfathers, could not be satisfied with any amount of good fortune. It was like an itch. Decades of living freely had made this group of Russians edgy, cunning, restless, and bold to the point of desperation. Afanasy Shchapov attributes these traits to the influence of the mountains:

The free air coming down from the mountains, the wildness of nature in the rocky, terrifying desert, filled only with the roar of wild animals and the rumble and murmur of rivers and streams, the barren view of vast piles of rocks leaning against each other and threatening to break loose, the lifeless monotony of the undulating, rocky mountain ridges, crests, and snowy peaks, the untrammeled expanses and wilderness running between the cliffs and through the copses and mountain forests, the wild caves—all this had a daily effect on the healthy, vigorous natures of the mountain-dwelling stonemasons, and the wildness of everything naturally made them wild . . .

Be that as it may, no one living in the Bukhtarma or the Uymon Valleys could resign himself to being anyone's subject. Whoever found a nugget of gold suspected that if he just dug a little deeper, he would find many more. Whoever discovered what was practically the Promised Land, with extraordinary fertility (to which Yadrintsev alludes: "Harvest yields of tenfold are average in these parts, but some farmers get twenty- and thirtyfold yields"), with grasses taller than a person, with plants whose sap was sweet and whose roots and tops had healing powers, with a wealth of animals and forest birds . . . No, whoever discovered this couldn't help torturing himself wondering whether he had overlooked some place even more beautiful and fruitful. The very sight of a police superintendent or village constable, who reminded them of their yoke, light though it was, the mere proximity of their apostate neighbors, a mere piece of paper from the local *volost'*,[26] which made them feel like wild sheep forced into a pen before shearing, compelled those people to look longingly at the mountains and become intoxicated with the memories of past quests.

Belovodye! It was like a summons from those who had left and never returned, like the groan of an exhausted woman, like a dim flash, like form and light, like a blow, like a reproach, like a jolt, like a calculation that can never get past the magic number.

Novels have been written about Belovodye. But there is also much factual testimony, many memoirs and documentary accounts, about how people set off alone and in groups, in families and whole settlements, wandered God knows where for months and years, and then went back ragged, impoverished, and ruined, their ranks reduced, leaving the paths of wild animals dotted with their graves. They went back cursing those who had stirred them up and enticed them with beautiful promises; they settled down to farming again, to plowed fields and beehives, insisting that paradise was where bees lived. But the more days they counted since their return, the firmer, stronger, and more vocal became their certainty that Belovodye simply hadn't revealed itself. It existed, all right. It simply hadn't made its whereabouts known. And if they just picked out the most faithful adherents to the true faith, the purest and most reliable souls, it was bound to reveal itself.

Where endless forests come to an end and rocky mountains rise high and higher, where mountain rivers and streams rage violently, leaping from rock to rock with white foam, where a desert unknown to anyone stretches to the horizon, there, somewhere in the impenetrable wilds beyond the Chinese border, lies the mysterious land called Belovodye. No one knows this place, no tax assessor ever rides that far, yet somehow some Russians managed to reach it on foot and are living there in freedom. They have a lot of land and many advantages, with no oppressive burdens and none of the sorrows of the harsh peasant way of life. There are churches there, and the pealing bells rouse the desert with their sound. No one knows Belovodye except the schismatics and the Russian peasants who fought their way in.

This is Yadrintsev again, who admitted that "my eyes are constantly turned toward the blue peaks of the Altay Mountains, where I left my heart."

But the quest for Belovodye was not completely and utterly fruitless. Above all, it populated the fertile mountain valleys, including the Uymon. While apparently pursuing a legend, a mirage, a myth, Russian peasants kept moving their settlements and arable lands closer and closer to the Chinese border and then actually crossed the border. At one time the upper reaches of the Bukhtarma and the Irtysh Rivers belonged to China, but even before they were ceded to Russia by treaty they were made Russian by peasants. The settlers conducted their own diplomacy, which statesmen had merely to formalize, and they achieved this, without asking permission, not in the deep, dark past but as recently as the nineteenth century. Those tireless frontiersmen, seekers, dreamers, and intriguers did not leave us their names. Or rather their names are buried forever in archival material about fugitives and people without passports, and they received no gratitude either in their own lifetime or afterward. The gains they made, from which we benefit, brought them no glory, and the last hills to rise above them have long since become level with the ground, in contrast to the most ancient burial mounds of primitive Siberians scattered around the Altay region. All they left us was a beautiful tale that can still be heard, that has not faded or cooled, that still stirs the blood with its distant, incessant call.

Any human being who lived in those mountains, surrounded by pure, powerful nature, who performed healthful labors in a fertilizing environment, also had to be made of different stuff. Everyone who has been there writes about this with amazement. Yadrintsev observes that "the inhabitants are big and strapping, with athletic builds. One hunter living near the Bukhtarma River is famous for his resemblence to a *bogatyr'*." In another place he writes, "The people in these communities were noted for their tall, strapping physiques, robust health, and exceptional strength. In the Altay region we saw a young woman with shoulders one arshin [28 inches] wide who could lift twelve poods" [almost 450 pounds]. He also states that "it was hard not to look at this strong and mighty populace with admiration, and then we would involuntarily shift our gaze to the mighty natural features that surrounded them." Shchapov writes, "The mountains, with their rocky defenses, automatically filled them with fearlessness, boldness, and courage." Pyotr Golovachyov,[27] an ethnographer, notes, "The health and musculature of one of them—Ivan, a guide—are enviable: you could undoubtedly get at least two, if not three, average Altaians out of this tall, solid, hefty guy. Only a mountain climate and a free life that knows no hopeless, oppressive want can create such fine fellows." When Shchapov discusses the influences of the mountains on human character, he clearly overstates the banditry of the Altaian "stonemasons" in order to bolster his stereotype, but they could never have penetrated those rock walls and beyond to such depths or gained a firm hold with meek dispositions and prayer alone. And of course no one can deny that the mountains imparted their boldness to the people who lived in them, just as it did to everything else that grew and walked there.

Boldness can be imparted, but what about heroic proportions and athletic builds? Where did they come from? Why, from those very same health-giving powers inherent in nature and in the mountain dwellers' activities. The pursuit of wild animals, long journeys on foot to stock up on supplies and have a look around, luxuriant beehives with amber honey, life in an alpine region where everything was pure, fresh, curative, and primordial, abstinence instilled by the strict letter of the Old Belief, spiritual uprightness influencing physical uprightness—all this had an effect on the growth of bone and the length of life. Altaians did indeed live a long time; they kept their strength until extreme old age and had rosy cheeks even on their deathbeds. Women pranced around on horseback like Amazons and gave birth to lots of children, and not little worms that ripened into the likeness of a human being only afterward and with difficulty, mirroring centuries of evolution, but small round loaves that their mothers would put in the saddle even before they could walk, taking them along when they dashed off to the beehives.

In an article titled "In the Altay Mountains,"[28] Golovachyov describes an incident in which an avalanche in the mountains in the middle of summer cut off the descent of four travelers, three Altaians and a Russian peasant who was an Old Believer. When they ran out of food, the Altaians slaughtered a horse. The Old Believer went hungry for several days, refusing to take any horsemeat because his faith considered it "unclean food" ["*poganaia eda*"]. But he finally gave in. The travelers were rescued and returned to their homes. The elders in the Old Believer's village were indignant with their fellow parishioner, believing that he should have died rather than defile himself with horsemeat. This story had a happy ending—they "purified" ["*ochistili*"] the guilty man with communal prayer—but sometimes communities did not forgive offenders and expelled them.

The Old Believers did not drink alcohol, smoke tobacco, or burden their souls with doubts. They drank tea brewed only from herbs and roots. The dark leaves from last year's bergenia along with red and golden roots made their tea concentrated and potent and ten times stronger than normal. The Altaian schismatics stood by their rules like rocks. When the official church began to regard them with more tolerance and when discipline among the Kerzhaks[29] began to slacken, they formed a new schism, a schism within a schism, and successfully defended their stronghold of fanaticism. This happened a number of times; thus more new interpretations kept appearing that were irreconcilable with the defilement caused by contact with those of other faiths and that brought them to the brink of a complete ascetic withdrawal from the world.

Novosyolov, well acquainted with the Altaian brand of the Old Belief, describes in one of his essays a visit to a convent belonging to a White Sea sect that had declared not only meat but milk, too, a sinful food. The nuns made do entirely with garden produce. He also observed how one Old Believer of that sect, on returning from a trip to another town where the people mingled easily with adherents to other faiths, imposed penance on himself: he saved his soul only by bowing down and touching the floor with his forehead one thousand times a day.

In Uymon the Old Belief has not completely died out even now. It remains intact, naturally, among the old folks, who in this day and age still keep separate dishes in their homes, "clean" ["*chistaia*"] and "secular" ["*mirskaia*" posuda], for themselves and for guests. They don't acknowledge radio or television, and with respect to television they certainly aren't far from the truth in believing that the devil is the guiding force behind it. Even the cemetery in Verkh-Uymon is divided into two parts, for the "good" ["*dobrye*"] and the "secular" ["*mirskie*"]. There are homes that refuse electricity and old folks who refuse pensions. Last fall I witnessed an extraordinary incident in that same town involving one such old woman, and quite by accident because no one there saw anything unusual in it. She was pickling a vat of cucumbers. After she'd put nine pails worth of cucumbers into the vat, laying them side by side, one against another, the last one suddenly slipped out of her hands while she was washing it and landed in the slop bucket. A drop of liquid splashed out of the bucket into the vat. And without giving it a second thought, the old woman sent all nine pails of cucumbers to the dump.

In our bright and shining times we could laugh at such extremism, such throwbacks to the past, and find them amusing, but . . . our souls won't let us laugh. These customs and strict ways did not arise out of ignorance and stupidity alone. Everything that exists in the common people, even in a portion of them, exists in us, too; we are the repositories of all their synods and schisms. As a tree builds up annual growth rings, it adds not simply a record of time passing but the character of the times as well; in a Russian, every scar and every stroke of the Russian people's fate repeats itself like an echo and a reflection. Inside us sit a stern schismatic and an ordinary believer and a new believer, each with his own prayers and truth. Which of them you agree with and which you don't is up to you. Or don't agree with any of them and find your own truth, but even in this case the sincere delusions and sincere motivations of the common people helped you arrive at it. And just picture how many threads stretch into the past: from your father and mother to their fathers and mothers, then double that number and double it again each time you go back to their fathers and mothers. No, nothing goes around us; we live side by side with the sum total of it all.

And how can we not take off our hats to the endurance and fortitude of this people? How can we not give them their due? We've gotten used to thinking that human beings are weak. No, human beings are strong, as the Old Belief has shown, displaying a staunchness of faith and mores that most likely appeared nowhere else in the world ever again. "Those people are as stubborn as mules!" others said of them and they even said of themselves. Resistance, elitism, and pride became their nature, sacrifice didn't scare them one bit, and the willingness to sacrifice lay just as close to the surface in the character of the Old Believers as the willingness to retreat lies in ours.

Next to Verkh-Uymon lies the village of Tikhonkoe. It's a small place near the bald hill, friendly and tame, of a burial mound. According to legend (here's what's galling: maybe a hundred and fifty years at most have gone by, yet already we have to fall back on legend), the longtime residents, when harassed because of their faith, dug a common grave, dressed in white, said one last prayer, and descended all together into the pit. From there they knocked down the supports that were holding back the earth.

In 1926 the Rerikhs spent several weeks in Verkh-Uymon, and the local folk made such a strong impression on Yelena Ivanovna that she talked about them to the end of her days. Nikolay Konstantinovich himself saw in the Gorno-Altay region, particularly in the environs of Belukha, a place naturally and spiritually sacred that influences the whole planet, and he spoke of this so convincingly that he has inspired pilgrimages to the Uymon Valley even in our time.

When you're there, you automatically look for some proof that the legendary glory of this land has paid a call on the present. And you do find something, for something does remain, though only in the form of echoes. The people are robust, not having lost their taste for work or the strength in their arms. Now Verkh-Uymon has a state farm, and before that it had a collective farm,[30] but whether working on the collective farm or the state farm, the people have never once let snow fall on standing crops or neglected to milk their cows. And the very best workers come from Old Believer families. Moral standards, of course, aren't what they used to be. Moral standards have declined there just as they have everywhere else, but not so noticeably. In the cemetery, which is badly neglected and overrun with wild-looking grass, you are struck by one of the most recent burial sites, the common grave of two sisters, dairy workers, who were dispatched to the next world together by the husband of one of them after vodka had turned him into a brute. It stung everyone to the quick that he was a local.

But I observed attractive features, too. People do not simply regard the Old Believers without mockery or malicious joy at their misfortunes; they view them with understanding and, in recent years, almost with pride, claiming them and the whole phenomenon as their own. And today's sense of justice, springing from this same root, has the intelligence not to cast lethal stones at its own past. The largest and most beautiful house in Verkh-Uymon is the regional museum. It contains just as much of the old days as of socialist transformations, and it displays the distant past without the explanatory lying that is still the practice almost everywhere among all our various Palestines and Altays.

In the land of Belovodye, I, too, paid homage to the quest that lives on in human memory. And you might say I found no trace of it: the old folks kept quiet, while the young ones smiled ironically. But with a glance in that direction, toward the mountains. A quick involuntary glance that seemed to wonder, Who's asking about that tale this time?

While in Gorno-Altaysk, following my trip to Uymon, I made the acquaintance of Edmund Vilgelmovich Fol, the director of a local cheese factory (and oh, what cheeses they make in the Gorno-Altay region!). He is of German descent, lively and energetic, his age deeply hidden beneath agility and physical fitness. And he turned out to be one of those nuts who can't sleep until they've hiked along every river and across every mountain in the Altay area. We talked first about the mountains and then about cheese, but when we were saying goodbye, Edmund Vilgelmovich couldn't restrain himself any longer: "Wouldn't you like to join us next summer? There's a 'Big Foot' in the upper reaches of the Chulyshman River. It's absolutely true. We plan to meet him."

And I pictured that persistent seeker of Belovodye as he wandered tirelessly without a home, shunning society like a wild beast, covered with animal skins, his eyes weary . . .

THE LAKE OF THE MOUNTAIN SPIRITS

When you think of Lake Baikal, when you look for comparisons, Lake Teletskoe immediately springs to mind. They are not equals—nothing in the world can equal Baikal—but Teletskoe is like a younger brother, like a splash made by the same hand, a seed from the same clan.

Altyn-kol'—that's what the name sounds like in the Altaian language: Golden Lake. But the word *Teletskoe* comes from the Telesy, the same nomadic people whom the boyar's son Pyotr Sabansky subjugated twice during the seventeenth century and who camped on its shores. Now the various Altaian tribes have intermingled and become as alike as two peas in a pod, but in the past they tenaciously held on to their territory and their differences, and the Telesy were a strong and populous tribe.

Why Golden Lake? One legend has it that a shepherd found a nugget of gold during a lean and difficult year and tried to trade it for food. But he couldn't; such poverty prevailed that gold was viewed as an ordinary stone incapable of satisfying hunger. Out of despair the shepherd threw the nugget into the waters of that lake, which has been called Golden Lake ever since.

This legend is so straightforward that you can safely take it for fact. A professional hunter from Iogach told me another story (and I believe him), about how just two years before, when he was returning to his winter camp after a daylong trek, he got lost, became exhausted, and, to top things off, tumbled down a precipice along with his skis. Fortunately the skis weren't damaged. There was no point in even considering climbing back up the way he'd come down, for a wall rose in front of him. So the hunter headed down the slope and came out at a half-rotten winter cabin, blackened with time. Sticking up out of some rocks not far away was a key encrusted with ice. After looking around, my storyteller touched the door and, just like in a fairy tale, it opened and fell away. It was dark inside, with a sharp odor of flesh. The hunter peered into the blackness for a long time, barely making out a stove, a bench, a little table, a bunk. Something was visible on the bunk. He took another step and recoiled. Before him, partially covered with shreds of clothing and partially exposed, lay the remains of a human being. Only later, after he'd caught his breath out in the fresh air and gone back in, did he discover one more thing that made his heart stop. On the bench at the head of the bed stood a jar into which someone had poured gold dust. The hunter figured that the lone prospector, gravely ill, had foreseen his end and had intentionally set out the fruits of his labors, which destroyed him. I also believed the hunter when he said he fled in fright without touching anything; if I'd been in his place, I would have done the same thing. It was nearly night when he found his hunting shack [okhotizbushka], as winter camps [zimov'ia] are now called, and he told his partner everything that had happened to him. The two of them spent several days talking over what to do, and they decided to leave the prospector and his jar in peace. They had enough worries already. They would forget about it, as if nothing had happened. The story's ending was what convinced me more than anything that it was true. "And you know what?" The hunter's amazement hadn't cooled a bit in two years' time. "A lot of sable suddenly showed up. There hadn't been any—we'd tramped around for two weeks with no luck—but after that they just showed up. We made a good haul."

For those who smile at this story in disbelief, I will add, So what if the hunter made it up? Could such a thing have happened? Yes, it could. The foothills around Teletskoe are rich in gold and a good deal of prospecting went on there.

But author Vladimir Chivilikhin is probably right in believing that Teletskoe is called *golden* not because of gold ore but because of its beauty, the way the word *red* in Russian also means *beautiful* [*krasnyi*]. And because of the value of what is now the most important resource on earth—water—for its waters, carried down from the mountains by rivers, creeks, brooks, and waterfalls, are pure and plentiful.

If you sail across the lake from beginning to end and look at the water and shoreline carefully—not like a tourist, a golden-eyed rooster flapping its wings alongside some speckled trout—you'll get the impression that Teletskoe has escaped destruction from the environmental disasters that have predominated in recent decades. No pulp plants stand beside it, no fields treated with chemicals lie nearby, no railroad approaches it from any direction, and practically the entire righthand shore was turned into a nature preserve long ago. You'll think that, unlike Baikal, Lake Teletskoe itself took pains to ensure its own preservation. It is inaccessible everywhere except for one spot, where it left a wide valley at the source of the Biya River; it offers nothing else to encourage the establishment of industry, which loves lording it over everything in wide-open spaces. Teletskoe slipped up in only one place, but there is every sign that the lake will pay a heavy price for this blunder. About twenty years ago the Gorno-Altay Experimental Conglomerate for the Comprehensive Utilization of the Siberian Pine Taiga settled at the source of the Biya like a spaceship from another planet. What a name—simply music to the ears! In truth it is an ordinary logging enterprise that tries to hide its true face behind small, cunning side operations while carrying on the long-standing destruction of the pine forest around Teletskoe. Those who recall Chivilikhin's essays on the celebrated Kedrograd, which truly was conceived and began life as an experimental, comprehensive venture, can bow their heads before yet another grave filled with good intentions.

When compared with Baikal, Teletskoe actually does resemble a younger brother. It has almost everything Baikal does, but on a smaller scale. It contains less water, is less transparent, and has much less life. There are fewer colors and tints, rivers and streams, currents and winds. It is shallower and narrower, and, not counting the chunks of rock that have broken loose from the cliffs, it has no islands whatsoever. And there are no nerpas. If Baikal is an oratorio, Lake Teletskoe is a ballad. It was constructed with two beginnings and created in two parts: the first proclaims power, while the second displays grace. The first section, a long corridor fifty kilometers from south to north, is deep and austere; then comes a bend, like a leg bending at the knee, and a peaceful turn to the west. The southern corridor is solid cliffs whose eastern side has widely spaced terraces and narrow peepholes that let you see back along the inflowing streams; the northern knee-like part resembles a broad river, and finally turns into a river, the Biya. You can't take your eyes off the shoreline in either place.

But Teletskoe and Baikal have the same architect. They lie at the same elevation, and each is fed by one main river with many tributaries (the Selenga at Baikal and the Chulyshman at Teletskoe) and drained, like every lake, by one river (the Angara and the Biya). The Biya looks like it was planned first and created earlier, at the knee joint, where there are huge underwater cliffs resembling those at the source of the Angara. But then the creator changed his mind and added more water. That's why no cliff broke the surface, as happened at Baikal, to give Teletskoe its own Shaman Rock.

One thing Teletskoe has in abundance is cliffs: it lies entirely within a framework of rock. And it has preserved its old, pre-Russian names better than Baikal. You sail along, look at a map, ask questions, recall something, and the old names ring out like virgin music derived from a combination of wind, water, sun, and rock: Yay-lyu, Kor-bu, Be-le, Ky-ga, Kam-ga. And if you forego the cruise ship full of tourists, where some queen of the stage is bellowing away, filling the mountains with racket, and if you wait until the rockfall caused by her voice subsides and try to forget the scare it just gave you, little by little pure sounds will spring up and form a pure song, your eyes will behold festive scenes, and you will become lost in other times and peoples . . .

There are fewer and fewer places where you can distract yourself amid nature from the tragedy of the Earth. There are more and more wounds and defeats caused by the bloodless war, undeclared and unacknowledged, that will last until the end of life. And once you decide to skip the cruise ship and have forgotten about it, once you immerse yourself in a cloister and plunge into a font that has escaped destruction, you don't feel joy, or happiness, or peace and a sense of good fortune. But your soul, a wrinkled and pathetic reject rendered voiceless by fear and suffering, crawls out and timidly perches on the very edge of you, as if on the rim of a precipice, and quietly looks and listens without moving. No, it doesn't look and listen but bathes in everything before it, washing away suffering and oblivion. And if you don't scare it off with coarse memories or words, then it will start singing away obliviously somewhere between joy and sorrow, lighting up something lost or forgotten with its piercing strumming and streaming. And if you feel it and listen to it until you freeze in place and fall into a faint, don't take this as something harmful. If our various Palestines and Altays were alive, our souls would be alive, too.

Then, as though peering through a magic spell or a swoon, you'll see an ancient sight: a mighty stream, white with foam and boiling rapidly, rounds a tight bend, falls from an enormous height, and smashes apart on the rocks below, rolling across them in a subsiding runoff. And you'll discover yourself, like an eternal pilgrim, sitting on a boulder near the waterfall, wet with spray, not taking your eyes off the slow, quiet course of the river as it flows toward you in two streams through its moss-covered embankment. And suddenly thunder roars, a ridge rises up, and two furious waves, split by a rock wall, fall from the ridge, hit a terrace halfway down, and keep crashing downward, looking like two manes. But some of the water splashes off the terrace and the rock wall above and some is squeezed out of the rocks and grasses, forming drops and little rivulets, all of which trickle down separately, their voices chasing each other. They also hit bottom and dissolve into spray, then suddenly remember what they're doing, come together, and go off into the general channel.

And you will ask in wonder with a childlike need to rejoice and marvel, Doesn't this ever come to an end? Was there actually this much water and height a hundred and a thousand years ago? And did the waterfall utter its name just as clearly amid the heavy roar and undertones—Korbu! Kor-bu!—the way a hammer rapping on an anvil announces its task?

And everywhere, whether you go down into the southern part, as we did, or up north (although according to the water's movement it's the other way around: you go down north; that's why the side with the nature preserve, where we saw Korbu, is considered the right side), everywhere you look you see shaggy, frothy manes, tidy, thin little ponytails, and the short curtains of waterfalls. There are more of them in the spring and fewer toward autumn. You spot them in the middle of forested slopes before they vanish in the calm current. You see them falling from overhangs above the lake, winding picturesquely high overhead and far away like frozen marble, carving out ravines and turning aside to roll down into the lake after meandering all over the place, flowing across the gravel bottom in a murmuring stream as if nothing had happened.

And cliffs, cliffs, and more cliffs! They hem in the lake to the point of constriction. The side where the nature preserve is located also has a gentle incline, a shelf about three kilometers long, with room to put a cottage, dig a garden, beat a path—pure charity, it's true, but this anomalous terrain feature called Bele is a real gift all the same. The left side shows no compassion; it's a solid mass of huge, somber cliffs indented by ravines and breaks and pocked by landslides. As soon as any water manages to collect itself into a flowing stream, it is forced to fall. The cliffs either come right down to the lake in a sheer rockface or descend in steps made of fallen stones. The rocks are covered with brown and yellow lichen, and there's a lot of bergenia. You'll be struck over and over by how little a tree needs to take hold: larch and birch and Siberian pine cling to what looks like bare rock, with wild rosemary bushes, black and red currants, thin tubes of wild onion, and bunches of rhubarb growing beside them. There are no openings anywhere; your gaze hits nothing but a wall. But down by the water, at the shoreline, you find tiny coves, and grottos, and remarkable stone figures chiseled by the waves, and little gates, and small overhangs, and sand trying to deposit itself and make a tiny beach . . .

But when the sun peeps out, there is no unfriendliness on either shore. Everything softens and blossoms and begins to speak and sing, and everything unites in an indivisible scene of enchantment.

We spent the night at Koldor. This is a shallow bay in the Biya part of Teletskoe not far from the bend. It has a ranger station at the mouth of a stream, along with the forest ranger's house, but the house is positioned so that you can't see it even when you're looking right at it, as if it has grown into the shore. You can, however, easily make out two neat buildings with attics, neither cottages nor houses but storybook structures whose wood gleams like semiprecious stone in rain or shine. And a little bathhouse nearby. This is the logging conglomerate's guest facility. Many celebrities of obvious and hidden merit have stayed there, and all were pleased. Inside it smells like pitch, but if you go outside and walk down the wide steps from the wooden platform to the pebbly beach, if you take in at a glance all the beauty laid out in readiness before you and inhale deeply and eagerly, absorbing the smells of water, taiga, and rock, if you listen to the gentle waves combing the shore, you'll forget about everything except that there still are some heavenly spots left on earth. And when you sweat in the bathhouse and plunge into the lake two or three times in your birthday suit, washing away your last anxieties and doubts, and then try some soup made with whitefish from Teletskoe and flavored with burbot liver, and when finally, toward the end of the meal, faint from fullness and satisfaction, you wash it all down with taiga tea made from roots and herbs, you are ready to believe that everything is just splendid! To hell with the logging conglomerate! They probably won't chop down every last Siberian pine. Some will remain. And you'll fall asleep with this thought, lulled by the waves, the wind, and pleasant memories of pleasant people.

In the morning Yevgeny Titov, one of the first inhabitants of Kedrograd [literally, "Pine City"], dropped by to see us on his way to the pine-forest preserve. Here, in the taiga around Teletskoe, is where Kedrograd was set up in 1960. At that time its fame spread throughout the whole country (thanks in large part to Chivilikhin's essays).[31] It was an immense operation covering immense territory whose last intention was to fell trees and whose first order of business was to make use of the stands of Siberian pine by gathering their wealth, which the taiga replenished annually: pine nuts, oil and oleoresin, furs, antlers from young Siberian stags, herbs and roots, meat and fowl, berries, buds [used for medicinal purposes], and honey. About a thousand people were working in Kedrograd five years after its founding, and not casual workers drawn by rubles but employees motivated by care and concern for the forest. The operation became profitable and confidently began to expand and to increase its harvests from the taiga without felling more trees. People talked about Kedrograd, praised it, gave it awards, copied the experiment, and began to create other enterprises modeled after it. But . . .

In such cases everything usually ends with a *but*. Kedrograd stuck in the craw of the timber industry's local administrators and of its boss at the time, V. Vashkevich. And it rankled the ministry at the national level, too. They firmly believed that forests are good for only one thing—cubic meters of timber—and they began to channel popular enthusiasm in that direction. Pine City was fated to become Decline City: they began to clear-cut stands of pine, and the so-called secondary products (nuts, meat, furs, berries) dwindled to a drop in the bucket. They corrected the "mistake" made by the graduates of the Leningrad Forestry Academy, who, in creating Kedrograd, had recalled the old ways in which the common folk made use of the forest, and everything slipped back into the usual tree-felling rut once again.

And we're talking about the Siberian pine, the czar of the taiga, its Adonis, its nourisher and preserver, which makes up less than just 3 percent of the total area of our forests! Yet even the pine trees are being felled without mercy despite scientific substantiation of their benefit, despite warnings and cries for help. A hundred years ago more than one hundred thousand poods [about 1,800 tons] of pine nuts were shipped by steamboat out of Biysk and Barnaul alone; now the logging conglomerate stockpiles about forty to fifty tons per year and considers that a lot.

During the twenty years that have passed since the demise of Kedrograd, fate has scattered its citizens and founders in various directions. The summer I visited the Altay region, Vitaly Parfyonov, former chief engineer at Kedrograd and now a consultant with the Russian Republic's Council of Ministers on matters of environmental protection, went to Iogach, where a conglomerate is located, to attend a conference on the theory and practice of utilizing Siberian pine forests. Parfyonov once fought to the bitter end for the sensible, beneficial, and preservationist idea of Kedrograd, but now such conferences on theory and practice have resulted in the clear-cutting of fifty thousand hectares of pine forest in the Gorno-Altay region during the past twenty years and three times as many in the Tomsk District. The deciduous part of the taiga surrounding Teletskoe has been completely cut down at the middle elevations. And these conferences produced scientists who have grown old and wise trying to prove that using up the Siberian pine can only benefit it. It's no exaggeration to say that putting science in their hands is like giving them an axe—and blessing the axe. The same flail was used by the regrettably notorious Institute of Ecological Toxicology at Baikal to acquire and obligingly present the fruits of scholarship to the ministry. But they overdid it: even the ministry was forced to turn down its services.

Yevgeny Titov is now a research associate with the Central Institute for Forest Genetics and Selection at Voronezh. But he spends every summer in the Altay area. His institute owns several forest preserves in the Teletskoe taiga that are devoted to the selection of the Siberian pine; there scientists carry on the great and reassuring work of creating arboretums and increase yields with the aid of grafting. Titov was heading for one of those nurseries when he dropped by to see us. He believes that preserves are just about the only way to save and develop Siberian pine forests. And he is trying to interest the logging conglomerate in these endeavors, to get them to include this sort of work in their plans and thus start taming the wild beast that the conglomerate is at the moment, hoping to turn it into a beneficial creature.

We sat around the massive banquet table set up out in the open air next to the little bathhouse for a long time, talking on and on as we lingered over tea. Our group included one of the facility's official hosts, Vladimir Karpinsky, chief forestry officer for the conglomerate and a fellow of gigantic proportions, and Aleksey Solichyov, who has the same strapping build (no, Altaians don't take a back seat in this regard) and who heads the research division of the Kirov Institute of Fur-Breeding and Game. One knew everything about the conglomerate and the taiga, while the other knew all about animals. Supporting the views of Yevgeny Titov, that caretaker of the Siberian pine, and present only in spirit, as they say in such cases, was Genrikh Sobansky, a holder of a candidate's degree[32] specializing in the biological sciences who lives in Iogach and whose article on the Altaian Siberian pine had just appeared in the journal *Siberian Lights*.[33] I regret not having the chance to meet Sobansky and finding out how this name stretched all the way from the boyar's son, the first Russian to reach Lake Teletskoe, down to him. In his article Sobansky cries out with great pain in his heart, "Help! They're pillaging the Teletskoe taiga and destroying the lake without factories, chemicals, or cellulose!"

Karpinsky was restless; he had to bring another group of visitors to Koldor to use the bathhouse that day and we had stayed too long. Solichyov, chuckling, dragged out of him that some high-level trade officials were scheduled to take steam baths after us. I dare say you'd worry, too. The conversation started out calmly, but the fate of Kedrograd and the practices of the logging conglomerate, which we couldn't get away from, automatically made it prickly. Titov couldn't help recalling that Kedrograd had harvested three times as many pine nuts as the conglomerate, whereas the conglomerate, to compensate, had doubled its wood-pulp production—and was losing money! Systematically losing money, that's what it boiled down to! In the best years the secondary products accounted for only 5 percent of the quota or less. What kind of comprehensive operation was that?

Karpinsky made his excuses lethargically; he knew all this already. But things had gotten so out of hand, and not overnight, that he couldn't turn them around by himself. When designating felling sites, he at least tried to save the best tracts of Siberian pine; other operations didn't even do that.

"Where are the best tracts?" two or three people pressed him at once. "What happened to the Pyzhinsk Taiga, the richest in the Altay?" Solichyov mentioned a certain Kapitolina Kashcheeva, who used to trap more than two hundred sable a season by herself, whereas now all the hunters put together could barely bring in that many.

"There are fewer animals and birds, the pikas have almost completely disappeared, and so have the quail. Besides, isn't it wrong for a forestry officer to belong to a logging conglomerate? You ought to be making government inspections and blowing the whistle, not standing at attention and saluting." Karpinsky became indignant.

"No one stands and salutes. Whatever its faults, we still have a diversified conglomerate. Why, we've even added beehives. At Baygol there aren't any secondary products at all, just a naked lumber mill, but that's also called a conglomerate. Why do you always pick on us?"

"Or look at what Kedrograd has degenerated into. A section of the Karakosh Mill's holdings is located right where Kedrograd used to be, as if they're trying to take revenge. Three logging operations working three shifts are mowing down the taiga, nearly three hundred thousand cubic meters a year."

"Starting this year we aren't clear-cutting anymore," Karpinsky replied.

"You've cleaned out all the timber and hauled it away, that's why. And the local authorities! What kind of authorities are they?! The region gets paid for the number of trees felled, so even if you strip the forest down to the rocks and cart off absolutely everything from root to crown, they won't even let out a peep."

I recalled Chivilikhin's final words on the subject of Kedrograd, when its fate had essentially been decided and he wrote in despair: "The last bountiful tract of Siberian pine, the Pyzhinsk Taiga, with which the reader is familiar, still stands in the Gorno-Altay today, but the logging operations have had their eye on it, too, for a long time, sharpening their axes in anticipation." And I asked to see the Pyzhinsk Taiga. Two days later Yevgeny Gushchin and I climbed up to the Oboy Pass, from which we could see its enormous sweep. And the whole right side lay plundered and devastated, as if the Tungusk Meteorite[34] had landed there. As we were hiking down to the clear-cut zones, we came across a sign nailed to one of the surviving pine trees. Its inscription read: "Welcome to a restful outing in the woods. While enjoying the woods, do not break off or cut down any bushes or trees: protect the birds and animals and do not destroy their nesting places."

Well, how do you like that?! Here is the beneficent twist that our attitude toward nature rests on: the robber, after finishing off the house's occupants large and small, pats a lifeless victim on the head before departing and instructs him in the rules of good form.

. . . Lake Teletskoe appears to have blocked itself on all sides with cliffs that make it completely inaccessible. But beyond the cliffs lie the taiga and the rivers that collect and bring it moisture. The fortress walls tower as impregnable and untouched as ever, but Golden Lake is already beginning to experience cold and hunger. And it is only outsiders who imagine that the water thundering, running, flowing, and trickling down from all sides is in no danger of drying up, which has never happened before; long-time residents observe that no, the water keeps decreasing, and many streams barely live up to their names.

SMIRNOV'S POST

There is an article by Yadrintsev of one hundred years' standing titled "The Wanderer at Golden Lake"[35] in which the author describes an encounter with a migrant from distant Voronezh Province. There was this migrant, a pathetic, submissive little peasant by appearance, who had a young son, and they wandered along prospectors' roads, perhaps looking for Belovodye, until they came to Lake Teletskoe, where misfortune befell them: out of carelessness, they lost their passport and all their cash. This did not bode well for the poor peasant, who faced a legal investigation and expulsion, possibly all the way back to Raseya. But he liked Teletskoe so much that he didn't want to leave and kept pleading with the authorities, repeating, "Let me work, let me work!" "To work was his faith," Yadrintsev concludes and raises his voice: "In hazy reveries I no longer saw a wretched little peasant but a Titan—the Russian people—stubbornly fighting his way through woods and pine forests to enchanted Lake Teletskoe. Mother Wilderness! When, oh when will you give this hard worker refuge?!"

To this we might add that nowadays that "hard worker" is transforming the Teletskoe taiga from a wilderness without human inhabitants into a wilderness without life. But no, it's not the hard worker who's at fault. It's the *durolom*, as the common folk have long called the kind of laborer who doesn't use his eyes or his brains.

N. P. and D. Z. Smirnov in their orchard

. . . I had heard a lot about Nikolay Pavlovich Smirnov. I'd read what Vladimir Chivilikhin and Gleb Goryshin[36] have written about him, and during our travels I'd questioned Yevgeny Gushchin, who used to work as a forest ranger's assistant in the nature preserve at Teletskoe and knew practically every other person around there. But he wasn't acquainted with Smirnov. I have no desire to follow in other people's footsteps and discoveries, to visit the places everyone goes to, marvels at, and writes about, but running counter to his fame in print was Smirnov's reputation among the lake's local residents as a strange character not at all like them. For example, when people gathered at his house to celebrate his seventieth birthday, he didn't give them enough to drink even on that worthy an occasion; he merely teased their palates. Or there was the time a gamekeeper's dogs killed a doe and Smirnov, kowtowing to the law, made the hunter go to the nature preserve's headquarters and report it. But he got a dose of his own medicine shortly thereafter when the same thing happened to him— and he went in and reported on himself. Local gossip, as usually happens, kept picking up on whatever did not fit the general pattern, thus showing its true face. The latest piece of news provided more damning proof that he was different—Smirnov was building himself a mausoleum. For an ordinary mortal this was completely out of line.

In the southern extremity of Teletskoe, at the very beginning of the righthand shore, there is a noisy stream called the Chiri. It looks like every other mountain stream, a rapid, restless waterway that might, as has often happened, change its mind without rhyme or reason about which channel to follow when flowing into the lake. Several decades ago it was selected as the site for the area's hydrological station, the place for making continual observations and taking the measurements needed to draw scientific maps of Teletskoe. On the other side, across from the Chiri in a diagonal direction, the Chulyshman empties into the lake and another stream, the Kyga, flows in farther south. Sharing a deep indentation in the shoreline, the Chiri and the Kyga form something like a pocket, a cozy flooding together that looks as if the lake has come out to meet them.

It was already close to evening when our boat began to approach the Chiri. A thunderstorm had been trailing us for over an hour, giving us periodic scares, but then it appeared to be drawn up the Chulyshman, for suddenly everything grew quiet and light. An open slope, exposed to the warm afternoon sun, added more light. And now sunshine streamed across it through the torn stormclouds and we caught sight of a long ledge stretching along the slope like a ski jump, with a low abrupt wall of chiseled rock and even rows of trees. I can sooner tell a regular pine from a Siberian pine, and at a greater distance, than an apple tree from a nut tree, which my eyes are not accustomed to. But I had no trouble recognizing that those trees were neither local species nor volunteers. That meant we had instantly spotted the main result of Smirnov's handiwork: his famous orchard. To the left the ledge turned into a multitude of tiers planted with mounds of something green, while up above lay a family cemetery, like the seat of ultimate learning. Below it three figures—large, small, and medium—stood out against the background, leaning on spades and gazing at our cutter. When it became clear that the cutter was docking, the large figure began to descend.

We climbed out onto the shore and started looking around without straying too far. Ten paces from the water a patch of woods containing pine, Siberian pine, and bushes began abruptly; a smooth rock-paved trail, knowing not only feet but hands as well, led through it. There was a clearly visible sign stating the name and purpose of the post, with a framed, decorative mosaic of colored stones beside it. Farther on some driftwood had been neatly spread out to dry. An invisible stream burbled behind the bushes; the hot sun, alternately hiding and appearing, beat down in burning waves, while coolness wafted from a nearby cliff on the right in response.

He floated up to us without making a sound, standing in his boat and poling with an oar. A tall, bareheaded old man with a short moustache and glasses stepped from the boat onto the rocky shore; he was wearing a black workman's apron and rubber boots. As he got out, he promptly told us, as if we were already acquainted, that he wasn't light on his feet any more; in a few days he would be eighty-five. We gasped awkwardly; the oldest in our party was only fifty, and anything over seventy seemed unreal to us, like the life spans in the Old Testament, as well as overwhelmingly oppressive. Beneath the white stubble on his face Smirnov's cheeks were ruddy, and his eyes behind the untinted glasses were clear and sparkling and an unfaded light blue. He stood tall and straight, even though he'd picked up a walking stick from the bottom of the boat; but he didn't so much lean on it as tap with it when he walked, as if testing to determine where there was ground and where there was rock, where to speed up and where to slow down.

He wasn't the least bit surprised at having visitors. He was used to them. He led us down the trail into the woods, which grew out of the rocks and soon ended, and a farmstead came into view: we saw a house next to a long building that looked sort of like a greenhouse or something similar with a roof over it, along with stables, pens, and a barn.

The long building, as it turned out, had actually been intended as a greenhouse, but there was too little sunlight in the woods and it had ended up resembling a corridor with an entryway, which could be lived in during the summer. That's where we found places to sit, some of us at the table, others on stools to the side, as we questioned Nikolay Pavlovich, listened to him, and marveled more and more at his life, in which he had single-handedly accomplished enough to compensate for the human uselessness and emptiness of ten.

He had seventeen children, three of them no longer living. His wife, an Altaian from a village on the Chulyshman, had given birth seventeen times. He'd started out in the capital cities, living first in Petersburg and then studying at a workers' school[37] in Moscow, where he shared a dormitory room with Pavel Suslov, the older brother of Mikhail Suslov,[38] the all-powerful member of the Politburo. His roommate's younger brother would often drop in on them. When the nature preserve was closed in 1967 and loggers set to work on the right shore, Nikolay Pavlovich couldn't stand it and wrote to Suslov, reminding him who he was, inquiring about his brother, but most important, asking that the preserve be reestablished. Suslov wrote back (Nikolay Pavlovich showed us the letter), saying that he remembered him, that his brother Pavel had been killed at the front during World War II, and that he promised to look into the matter of the preserve. The following year the preserve was restored. If that hadn't happened when it did, there wouldn't be any Siberian pine or deer there now. But today there are more than enough wolves and bears; the population needs to be thinned or pretty soon they'll take over. They've already killed two out of every five sheep. Not long before our arrival a doe had come down to calve (animals always go to people when there's danger) and right in front of Nikolay Pavlovich's granddaughter, who was visiting at the time, a bear devoured the fawn. The doe came back the next day. It stood and looked at them as if to ask, Why didn't you protect us, good people?

Placing his big, strong work-hardened hands on the table, he talked about himself, his face alternately clouding over and lighting up (he didn't simply smile; his whole face would blaze). He'd come here, to the Chiri, in 1926, before the hydrological station was built, and gotten a job as a mounted forest patrolman. He'd come to live out what remained of his life amid unspoiled nature; he already had one foot in the grave because of illness. He spoke willingly, with the correctly constructed sentences of an educated man. He had a keen memory, only occasionally mixing up the names of his children, but who among us wouldn't get confused with seventeen of them?! During the summer there were lots of people around and he had no time for anything except receiving guests, strangers as well as family, but during the winter, ah yes, during the winter there were just the two of them, for the children would all scatter then. He had no television and didn't need one, but he couldn't get along without newspapers and magazines. He said bitterly of his sons, "They're not teetotalers." In the next breath he praised them, saying, "They're all good with their hands and keep themselves busy."

Thunder cracked somewhere nearby; the storm, having lost us earlier, was now pursuing us again. We set off in a hurry to look at the orchard before it started to rain. He got up without any unsteadiness and stepped aside to let us pass, a strong, wiry man with young-looking skin whose face shone with an inner luminescence, like a patriarch who had adopted the simple life. Thunder pealed again, strong and pitted, practically overhead. He seemed not to have heard it and didn't turn his head to find out where the storm was coming from and whether it would last a long time, apparently accustomed to accepting everything in nature as unavoidable and remedying its excesses afterward.

We started out walking side by side, then suddenly climbed up onto a plot of ground stretching out across the slope and lined with apple and pear trees whose fruit was just barely beginning to ripen. Nikolay Pavlovich told us where each apple tree had come from—he had extensive and long-standing ties with horticulturists and selectionists—while I walked over to the edge of the plot and, looking at the high bedrock with its smooth, chiseled surface extending for about three hundred meters, tried to imagine how much earth had been hauled in and lay underfoot. The earth was now completely one with its environment, but it hadn't been there before; there'd been rock upon rock, the same as on the slope. How much strength, how much horsepower, as we say, it must have taken to bring in all this soil, cultivate it, and make this Teletskoe Garden of Eden fertile! And all manually. Month after month, meter after meter, layer after layer, year after year—in bags and boxes, by wheelbarrow and by hand, with a fair amount also shipped over by boat from the Chulyshman, where the soil is good.

Thunder cracked again and rain beat down. We had to take cover under an apple tree. Long, slanting threads of water, attached somewhere up above and tinted by the distant sun, hung down over the lake like iridescent laundry. I could have watched forever had I not been out in the wet.

We turned out to be standing under the very apple tree that a bear had appropriated for itself and whose fruit it shook down before human beings got a chance to. It liked the apples from that tree and that tree alone, singling it out from all the others. But there are enough apples for people, too. Plenty, with a lot left over. The yields are huge, but this is no cause for joy since there are no farmers' markets nearby to send the fruit to. About four tons of apples went to waste the previous year. When they suddenly thought of pressing them to make juice, they filled forty three-liter containers, but because cider will turn sour without sugar, they'd added some sugar—and the overripe mixture became hard cider. And to prevent anyone from getting drunk, Nikolay Pavlovich had poured it all out. It was a shame, of course—this wasn't just lake water—but looking at drunks was even worse. He himself has never smoked; he used to take an occasional sip of wine, but even that he didn't enjoy. Those who work to their heart's content can't understand the joys of drinking.

The sun appeared over the Chulyshman and pushed the rain aside. We got out from under "the bear's" apple tree and moved on. There were apple trees, pear trees, and walnut trees; grapes, watermelons, cherries, and plums were ripening. True, the nut trees had recently suffered from frost. But all the others—there they stood. Soon they would again produce enough to feed a whole village. The previous autumn Nikolay Pavlovich had picked thirty kilograms of tomatoes from every plant. And how many plants were there? He didn't know how many he had at the moment. I tried to count them later and came up with over three hundred. How many apple trees? He didn't know that exactly either, about sixty or seventy. His children, when they were growing up, were the ones who did the arithmetic. The important thing for him was that the plants were there. He didn't need that many, of course, but he couldn't let any space remain empty, so he kept on planting. Why should the land lie fallow? It ought to work, just like human beings, and it will be better off as a result.

The ledge with the fruit trees finally came to an end; plantings of tomatoes and grapevines lined the shelves that hung one above another with the same kind of stone walls. Everything had been loosened, weeded, pruned, and smoothed; everything down to the last grain and smallest leaf was tended with care and affection. A spade had been driven into the ground where there seemed to be nothing more to do. Up above, laid out with almost no interval so that it would be close at hand, so that as you bowed to the earth you would be facing it, too, a modest cemetery with three or four graves reared its head. At the foot of the cemetery lay something covered with sheets of metal.

We tried to keep Nikolay Pavlovich from going up there—the path was steep—but he climbed as easily as his young and middle-aged guests and stopped beside the metal sheets, which were lying across the top of a low concrete wall that encircled something. What was it? Eternal refuge. "If I die in the winter, they'll never be able to dig a grave here; it's solid rock." And so to avoid burdening the living, he'd gouged out a wide niche in the rock for his wife and himself, below their dead children and above his labors. One of us (a group of six was following Nikolay Pavlovich around) asked awkwardly, "How in the world can you live beside an open grave?" He replied simply, shyly, and with certainty, "Why, what's wrong with that? It doesn't hurt to be prepared."

We returned by way of the shoreline, where stones had been piled up in a ridge like a dike. That meant he'd even dragged them down here while clearing his orchard/garden. He was the first to catch the sound of a boat's motor coming from the large body of water and he pricked up his ears: someone was heading this way.

His youngest daughter, a tall, pretty young woman with Altaian features and the mother of the granddaughter who was visiting them at the time, had just arrived from Mayma (near Gorno-Altaysk). Nikolay Pavlovich refrained from hugging her in front of strangers, but he was overjoyed and very excited. His wife looked out of the summer house with wet eyes, became bashful, and hid; their granddaughter skipped around near her grandfather, trying to tell him something and urging him to go somewhere.

It was time to say goodbye. Nikolay Pavlovich began to fuss, holding us back as he bid farewell, but his granddaughter was pulling him away from us and he retreated, inviting us to come again, telling us not to forget, the tap of his walking stick echoing his words. But he returned to the shore once more before we left—with some dried fish for the road. And as we climbed into the cutter and cast off, he stood there against the green, wooded background—tall, straight, and not the least bit infirm, with one arm hanging down over his apron like a spade or an oar, the other resting on his staff.

1988

6
❖❖❖

Kyakhta

We arrived in Kyakhta late one evening, and the next morning, after climbing a hill from which all of Kyakhta unfolded before me as if it lay on the palm of my hand, I thought of my grandmother, Marya Gerasimovna, an illiterate, wise old country woman who never strayed from the Angara, who regarded the existence of English and French people as highly doubtful, but who strictly believed in Kyakhta. Ever since childhood I'd heard her sigh, "So what's going on here? How come old Kyakhta's twiddling its thumbs?" whenever she had trouble getting tea, which my grandma couldn't do without. She could do without a lot of things, but she couldn't survive without tea. She suffered so greatly without it, bringing up and entreating Kyakhta time after time, that her words created a lasting impression in my undeveloped little mind of Kyakhta as a city second in importance only to Moscow, influencing the fate of one and all.

And now before me lay a small provincial town, the kind formerly called downgraded [zashtatnyi] when it ceased to be an administrative center, a town whose old part was built almost entirely of wood and that spread down the slopes of three hills in plain view but faced the fourth direction—the Mongolian border—with a certain timidity. And it lay there somehow limp and unmuscular and even seemed depressed, as if it still hadn't recovered from the last decisive twist of fate. This impression, although it wouldn't change, would at least soften and become fairer and more precise later on, but at first this is exactly what I thought: Can this really be Kyakhta? Can this really be the Kyakhta whose name resounded throughout Russia a hundred years ago, that was regarded with respect in Paris, London, and New York, that was called "the Sandy Venice," whose orders everyone filled first, knowing that Kyakhta was not stingy, and that of all the towns in Siberia was the one to take over Mangazeya's reputation as a "gold-rush town" a hundred and fifty years after Mangazeya itself ceased to exist?! Did all this really happen here? From right over there, from across the border, where the Mongolian town of Altanbulag now stands, camel caravans came day and night bringing tea and linen and unloaded their wares over there, behind the walls of Merchants' Square, where a spinning mill and a knitwear factory are currently located. Merchants arriving from the depths of China went to rest over there, in that two-story stone Ambassadors' House [*Posol'skii dom*] at the site of the border checkpoint. Is it really true that only two or three churches in Russia could rival the richness of the Cathedral of the Resurrection [*Voskresenskii sobor*], which now stands stooped and lonely, that it used to have crystal columns inside, that it was built and decorated by Italian masters, whose murals were later refurbished by the Decembrist Nikolay Bestuzhev?[1] That the three dark, half-ruined two-story houses near Kyakhta Creek are the remains of a settlement of millionaires, undoubtedly the only one in the world where the fabulously wealthy, each richer than the next from wheeling and dealing, from huge turnovers of capital and goods, congregated in a colony of twenty gigantic villas? And that was only in Kyakhta—they also led a fairy-tale life in the neighboring town as well.

Even most local residents don't know that present-day Kyakhta absorbed the small colony by that name, along with the town of Troitskosavsk. Now they have merged into a single whole. The line between them is practically indiscernible. It probably lies over there, where a monument to Aleksandra Viktorovna Potanina,[2] wife of the renowned Siberian writer and scholar Grigory Potanin and assistant in his difficult labors, stands on a burial mound/embankment to the right of the road and where a stadium has been built on the site of the cemetery in which Aleksandra Viktorovna is buried. The town remained on this side of the cemetery, while the commercial colony lay on the far side, a little closer to the border. The Chinese town of Maimachin, of which nothing now remains, began literally one hundred meters from Kyakhta. Here, in Kyakhta, it is especially easy to see what changes took place in this part of the world during the twentieth century.

In vain did my grandmother pin her hopes for supporting her sinful habit during World War II and the postwar period on Kyakhta.

Kyakhta had been cut off from the tea trade and had lost all commercial significance a good deal earlier. Its decline began back in the nineteenth century, but Kyakhta had also experienced crises before that, knew how to overcome them, and remained viable right up until the Russian Revolution, even until the Mongolian Revolution of 1921.

If history is always right, then fate frequently treats its favorites cruelly. When I was in Kyakhta, the town that once provided tea for all of Russia had long since forgotten what real tea smells like and never laid eyes on anything except bad Georgian tea that reeked of bathhouse birch switches when it was steeping.

Kyakhta is the child of the commercial marriage between Russia and China. Before that, to use a folk expression, they had an affair. Under both Czar Alexis and Peter the Great all attempts to establish serious ties with Russia's proud and cautious neighbor on the far side of Siberia came to naught: the Chinese did not abide by agreements and Russian merchants were sent back across the borders of Mongolia and China. The groundwork for what Count Savva Raguzinsky's[3] special delegation managed to accomplish was essentially laid by Peter, but those gains were made only after his death. The delegation spent many months in China discussing the various points of the treaty, put up with a lot of humiliation and red tape, moved from place to place, and finally concluded an agreement in August 1727, which has gone down in history as the Bura Treaty: the parties signed it at the Bura River eight versts [slightly more than five miles] from Kyakhta. According to its terms, Russia's southern boundary was determined and Russian merchants were granted passage into the neighboring territory; the countries decided to establish two centers for bartering, one on each side of the border, which would maintain constant ties with each other.

The selection of a spot on Kyakhta Creek for the Russian center was a special condition set by Raguzinsky. Much discussion went on in later years about why the town was founded not on the deep Selenga or Chikoy Rivers but on a tiny little stream whose dimensions even in those times evoked merely a gentle smile. I must point out that Kyakhta, whose water supply now comes from the Chikoy River, still suffers a water shortage even today. But the cautious ambassador from Moscow, taking the smallest details into account, chose a stream that flowed not out of China but into China. It doesn't flow in that direction very long, but that's precisely how it flows at that point, which certainly played a part in his decision. Why there? Probably because Count Raguzinsky feared perfidy from neighbors who could poison the water during disagreements. Don't forget that this happened two and a half centuries before our time, and such things were of no small importance back then.

This was the twist of fate that chose the site for Kyakhta, and so a fort appeared on the tiny stream, which later became the town of Troitskosavsk. "Savsk" was in honor of Savva Raguzinsky. And a commercial colony sprang up beside it. The Siberian merchants of old didn't need any encouragement to open up new lands; they were prepared to go to the ends of the earth if this promised business opportunities and financial gain. Kyakhta was not one of the most heavenly spots in the world. It offered sand, enervating heat in summer, and violent winds in winter; moral standards, which weren't noted for their gentleness and nobleness at that time in Petersburg or Moscow or Irkutsk, must have been a mixture of bad and worse in Kyakhta. We can only try to imagine what the merchants hoped for besides profit when they sent their family carriages off to the lower rim of Russia. Profit was enough to satisfy those in the major cities who sent out representatives and agents to handle their affairs, but it was not enough for the families that settled there. You couldn't tamp down the sand, stop the winds, or cast a spell over the heat; that meant you had to create a life befitting your pocketbook and your honor in the sand, in the heat and wind, a life you wouldn't be utterly ashamed of before an out-of-town guest or your own daughter, who was learning refined manners and French. That's probably how it all started and then went on from there.

The commercial colony grew, not suddenly, not immediately, but also without long scrutiny, without planning where the houses would go. Its architect and builder was above all business, profitable trade. By the 1820s the two places had switched roles: the town didn't rule the colony; the colony ruled the town. It provided work for the town and the surrounding villages, acted as the town's patron, opened schools, built churches, and legislated taste. The town beside the colony became affluent, too, but as it grew affluent it lost authority and looked to the colony more and more often: What will they say in Kyakhta? Kyakhta gradually began to replace Troitskosavsk even in name.

Later Kyakhta attained the nearly impossible. It alone in all of Russia demanded and received the right to be a self-governing town. Everyone in Kyakhta and in Irkutsk understood perfectly well that the formal subordination to a governor-general meant practically nothing. As a subterfuge, Count Muravyov-Amursky, governor-general of Eastern Siberia in the middle of the nineteenth century, sent Despot-Zenovich, a relative who had ended up in Siberia for free thinking, to Kyakhta as governor of the frontier. The illustrious count had some strange kinfolk: another relative, none other than the dangerous state criminal Mikhail Bakunin, fled Siberia in an American bark while acting as the proxy of a Kyakhta merchant named Sabashnikov.

The frontier governor's duties included initial resolution of any misunderstandings that might arise between the two powers as well as leading the fight against smuggling. The town was basically governed by the Council of Senior Representatives of Merchants Trading in Kyakhta, which regulated trade, levied taxes on consignments of tea (a source of big money), and allocated this revenue for commercial and municipal needs.

Nowhere but in Kyakhta. . . . These words, embodying explanation, bewilderment, and surprise, spring to mind time and again as you become acquainted with the town's history.

Let's begin by noting that Kyakhta's place was there, in that corner of the world where the different religions, cultures, and destinies of various peoples came together, that it didn't and couldn't appear in any other spot on earth, that it was ordained to be born right there. Rising out of the depths of the exotic, it was itself an exotic thing from start to finish, though perhaps without fully realizing what that meant. But it was Russian territory and was obliged to obey Russian laws, which did not always sit comfortably with the peculiar features of its occupations and way of life.

Nowhere but in Kyakhta . . .

For example, there were no restrictions or inspections of the traffic moving back and forth between the Russian colony and the Chinese town of Maimachin: "go where you will" [*"khody kuda khoty"*]. But on the road from Troitskosavsk to the colony, from one Russian place to another barely separated by one and a half versts [a little more than a mile] stood a customs house that searched everyone from His Highness to His Lowness who passed by on horseback and on foot. Looking for logic in Russian laws has always presented considerable difficulties, but in the mid-nineteenth century it was sheer stubbornness that dictated the laws concerning Kyakhta. Trade could be conducted only on the basis of barter: you give us tea and nankeen (cotton cloth) and we'll give you furs, textiles, and hides. But this exchange of goods did not suit the Chinese, who demanded silver and gold for tea. The Chinese demanded gold, yet the Russian government absolutely forbade, on pain of penal servitude, the use of gold in commercial transactions: either unload axes and hides or close up shop. It became a question of whether Kyakhta would exist or not because neither the Chinese nor the Moscow authorities would compromise, and the customs office was under strict instructions: in order for trade to be carried on, its account books had to show what was exchanged for what down to the smallest amounts, to centimeters, grams, and kopecks, so that the value of the goods given corresponded exactly to the value of the goods received.

What choice did that leave the merchants of Kyakhta? Young and old, they all joined hands in smuggling. This became a vast scheme for defrauding institutions unfavorably disposed toward them, which all of them knew about, all of them took part in, and all of them closed their eyes to, pretending that nothing illegal was going on. In this way trading for precious metals could continue, and continue it certainly did. "Carriages were made with two bottoms, with secret compartments in the shafts, axles, wheels, horse collars, shaft bows, in short, everywhere it was possible to create space for gold and silver." This testimony comes from Dmitry Stakheev,[4] a writer and journalist engaged in commerce in Kyakhta at that time who was well acquainted with local ways. Governor Despot-Zenovich, sent to combat smuggling, very quickly figured things out and gave up on his mission, considering it a better use of time to devote himself to publishing the *Kyakhta Blade* [*Kiakhtinskii listok*], acting as a censor who protected it from censorship. Trading for precious metals continued, while the goods shown in the documents as barter remained with the merchants and, traveling back and forth between Kyakhta and Troitskosavsk, the same items would enter the account books a second, a fifth, an eighth time.

In this manner decades went by in which Kyakhta not only did not suffer but, on the contrary, thrived, with a beauty no less fetching because it was illicit and criminal. The residents built Merchants' Square in the commercial colony and another Merchants' Square in the town; to the two little wooden churches they added three big stone cathedrals, one of which—the one in the colony—displayed a splendor that was quite likely beyond the means even of the capital cities. They laid out a boulevard, installed water pipes to irrigate it, opened schools named after various individuals, and ordered books to create libraries for them. Two things had a strong effect on the travelers of those years who described their impressions of Kyakhta: the colorful gaudiness of Maimachin, where Chinese laws did not allow women to live close to the border, and the defiant affluence of the commercial colony.

Trade restrictions were lifted in 1861. This is the same year in which the Decembrist Mikhail Bestuzhev wrote a letter to his sister in Petersburg that was later published in the *Kyakhta Blade*. In his letter the younger of the Bestuzhev brothers who served terms of exile in Selenginsk[5] describes how he and his small daughters arrived in Kyakhta and the way it looked to them:

They were astonished and stunned by the novelty of it all, brimming over with questions and exclamations. Wooden sidewalks lined with rows of curbstones and lampposts had been built on both sides of the street we rode along. Night was falling, the heat subsided, we were no longer swallowing dust. Crowds of people out for a stroll, drawn outside by the evening's quiet coolness, stretched down the sidewalks in a long line. Cheerful, neat houses flashed quickly by, but the merry eyes of my Lelya managed to scan the inscriptions in large gold letters above the public buildings, and she would loudly shout, "There's an orphanage, there's a girls' school, and that's a parochial school, there's a pharmacy, the offices and press of the *Kyakhta Blade*, a public meeting hall. . . . Oh, Papa! Look! What a huge church . . . a garden . . . with music playing. And people are dancing!" After our peaceful, almost monastic life in Selenginsk they were stunned by the activity of a commercial town, by these crowds of Chinese dashing around in all directions, by these bronzed Mongols on camels.

I have only to add that after this trip Mikhail Bestuzhev, who'd planned to send his daughter to his sister so that she could study in Petersburg, preferred to leave her in Kyakhta at the school run by S. S. Sabashnikova, the mother of the future famous publishers.[6]

More than twenty years went by. Ivan Popov, whom Siberia remembers for his activities in public life and for serving as editor in Irkutsk of the *Eastern Review* and the *Siberian Miscellany*, Yadrintsev's publications, first arrived in Kyakhta as a political exile in 1885. Popov was the son-in-law of Aleksey Lushnikov, Kyakhta's most prominent patron of the arts and the most progressive public figure among the merchants; he lived in Kyakhta for several years. In his book *The Past and My Experiences* perhaps the most fully developed, interesting, and lively reminiscences concern this town. These aren't the impressions of a traveler or a visitor but the testimony of an eyewitness and participant in many events, which you read literally choking with excitement. Popov might describe Kyakhta too rapturously at times, but to wax rapturous he had to maintain a certain frame of mind and not yield to the usual custom of cleverly smoothing over and belittling everything under the sun. To prevent this from happening required, of course, a far from ordinary environment. Popov writes:

The luxurious living quarters of Kyakhta's merchants were spacious and laid out in two stories. The second story contained formal rooms for entertaining. These rooms were always furnished in good taste; in Kyakhta I never found the tasteless furnishings that I saw in the homes of merchant families in Russia. Paintings, books, musical instruments, billiard tables, sometimes a conservatory and always luxuriant houseplants, varieties I rarely found even in Russia. The estates of Kyakhta's merchants took up relatively vast amounts of space. They consisted of a main house, additional wings, a kitchen, a bathhouse, outbuildings, coachhouses, stables with dozens of stalls, cowsheds, horse and cattle yards, a flower garden where there'd often be a fountain gushing, etc. The home of a Kyakhta merchant overflowed with abundance, including hordes of workers and servants, cellars of rare wines and provisions ordered directly from the capital cities or from abroad, coachhouses full of various carriages, stables with thoroughbred trotters, horses for traveling, saddle-horses, racehorses, and workhorses, of which forty to sixty were kept for domestic use alone. For the children there were little donkeys, which also had their own carriages. The cattle yard was full of cows and all kinds of poultry. Everything they ordered was durable and of high quality. "You have to pay through the nose anyway when you fork over a silver ruble for one bottle of wine, so it's not worth ordering cheap junk"—this is how the merchants of Kyakhta reasoned. And they sent for footwear, clothing, furniture, and so on from the capitals and often ordered women's finery from Paris, from Worth[7] himself. Novotnya,[8] the famous Petersburg tailor, found it lucrative to go to Kyakhta once a year and take orders there. Once he had his clients' measurements, he would also receive orders by telephone. Performing artists were not afraid to bump along and freeze for several hundred versts during the journey from Irkutsk; they knew that their road tour would pay for itself with interest.

Let's pause and take a breath. I permitted myself to cite this long excerpt not simply to show the kind of luxury the upper crust of Kyakhta wallowed in. What else would you expect from a town sticking out like a lucky sore thumb, which you could take Kyakhta for, where there were millionaires on top of millionaires, all spurring each other on! They did, of course, blow their own horns for one another's benefit. They couldn't do otherwise: wealth demanded fanfare and demonstration. But their extravagant wealth could also have displayed itself as extravagant ugliness and bad taste, which is often just what happened; you don't have to go very far in either Russia or Siberia to find examples. But in Kyakhta an independent, educated society with relatively advanced views gradually took shape among the merchants during the nineteenth century, which we will have another opportunity to discuss later. This group, naturally, was not large, but they had influence and others listened to them and imitated them. While competing in the external demonstration of wealth, these merchants were accustomed to competing in its beneficial application as well. With all that Kyakhta contained of good and bad, of the remarkable, the exceptional, and the incomprehensible, it was still the same old Russia, but with a difference: this piece of Russia had been dragged through Siberia, which shook up some of its old qualities as they jolted along its roads and polished some of its new ones, coming to a stop where it was closer to Europe by sea than it was to its own capital. This came out one way or another in the views of Kyakhta's industrialists.

Operating a profitable business is any tradesman's first commandment. The immense, unexplored land itself required Siberian merchants to have quick wits, lively minds, and an education, which they could still get along without in the eighteenth century but not in the nineteenth. In order to compete with their own fellow countrymen and with European merchants in the nineteenth century they had to look closely at how Europeans managed their businesses, to find out what methods and equipment they had at their disposal, and to guess which markets they were aiming at. All sorts of exceptions cropped up among Siberians, of course, but exceptions appear in every age; I'm not talking about them. In addition, Kyakhta's merchants were influenced by the frontier location of the town they lived in, by the utter isolation that surpassed remoteness, which doomed them to spiritual penury and the influence of a strong neighboring culture. Individual, sporadic efforts could not provide enough resistance; to maintain order and keep their spirits up they had to develop permanent public measures and revenues. Thus the *aksidentsiia*—a local tax on consignments of tea—was introduced, which generated considerable sums of money. This, according to logic, should have made the hearts of Kyakhta's merchants swell with pride, a pride egged on by wealth, which, of course, is just what happened. The Moscow merchants are putting up a new cathedral more beautiful than the old ones, so let's not be stingy either; let's commission Botkin to make an agreement with the Italians to come here and try to outshine Moscow. Petersburg gets its clothes from Novotnya; are they any better than we are? You say Petersburg is a long way off and it's inconvenient to go there for a fitting? Never mind, Novotnya himself will come to us; he won't regret it. Princess K. ordered a dress from Worth in Paris? All right, we'll order one for Klavdia Khristoforovna, too; what's so strange about that? If my daughter has talent, why shouldn't she take sculpture lessons from Rodin? And Lushnikov's daughter, Yekaterina, actually did study with Rodin, who considered her his best pupil. People from Germany took up residence in Kyakhta and people from Kyakhta went to Switzerland, and no one was the least surprised.

"To display your wares in a good light" ["*pokazat' tovar litsom*"] had broad meaning for Kyakhta residents. First of all it meant displaying themselves, their solid social standing and European tastes coexisting with democratic natures and a preference for doing things in a big way. They might give a daughter in marriage to a French businessman and have a son marry a maid. George Kennan, an American who wrote a book widely read in Russia called *Siberia and the Exile System*,[9] visited Kyakhta and remarked on how small the earth is: there he found Europeans, and European culture, and objects from the New World on sale in one of the shops. Semyon Cherepanov,[10] whose memoirs describe Kyakhta during the 1820s and 1830s, calls the local merchants even of that time "highly educated people, a kind that did not exist among the merchants of European Russia." It can hardly be true that they "did not exist"—blatant contrasts such as these are usually unfair—but the Kyakhta side of the scales, which led him to this opinion, included the weight of local culture, which was thus not inconsequential.

"To display your wares in a good light" also meant displaying their town, which, located where it was, constituted the face of Russia. Kyakhta residents obviously decorated and equipped their town with modern amenities mainly for themselves, to create a tolerable and even attractive existence in order to lessen the feeling of remoteness, but "display" had its place, too. China's Maimachin stood right next door, and they couldn't help competing with it constantly and in everything. Kyakhta was not only not supposed to fall flat on its face, but, according to many expectations independent of the traditions and moral standards of various peoples, it was also supposed to excel. Russians as a whole were judged by how people in Kyakhta lived and worked. Almost all the travelers who crossed the border were impressed by Maimachin's cleanliness and Eastern elegance, but most of all by the succulent and unusual dinners consisting of forty to sixty dishes. Martos: "Don't make me describe every last detail of Chinese cuisine, which is incredibly complicated and completely new to a European; such a thing is scarcely possible." Kennan: "If the Chinese dine in this way every day I wonder that the race has not long since become extinct. One such dinner, eaten late in the fall, would enable a man, I should think, if he survived it, to go into a cave like a bear and hibernate until the next spring." Kennan had every right to make such a proviso: after dining once in Maimachin, he spent two weeks in bed and was sick for three months.

People in Kyakhta also liked to regale guests and frequently wore them out with tea, which was not in short supply, while the tables next to the two-and-a-half-gallon samovars were not empty either, but this wasn't the main thing that stuck in travelers' memories after Troitskosavsk and Kyakhta. Nor was it a menu that made visitors remember "the Sandy Venice." Rather, it was something relating to the manner of life and the manner of thinking, and to some extent even the manner of wealth, which had noticeable distinctive features.

But "to display your wares" also meant literally to show wares: the ability to conduct trade and the rejection of dishonest trading practices. That last point, I dare say, proved hardest of all. During the first hundred years of trade, both sides competed in the art of swindling each other, unashamed of engaging in the crudest, ugliest methods and justifying them with children's logic: "They started it." Giving preference to one or the other in this age-old art was impossible; they were both, as we say, good at it. The Chinese hid chunks of wood in bolts of material, which they would not allow anyone to unroll; our experts sewed lead into the paws of fur-bearing animals, which were sold by weight. The Chinese substituted brass for silver; the Russians passed off Mangazeya rabbits as polar fox. The Chinese rolled blocks up in pigskins, sewed them shut, and sold them as ham; the Russians shortened the arshin [a unit of linear measure equal to twenty-eight inches]. Business sank to the level of outright robbery, which led more than once to long interruptions in trade. Moral standards don't change as rapidly as we would like, but they nonetheless do change if we want them to, and Kyakhta is proof of this. Years went by, and nimble, thieving agents from the outside were replaced by merchants interested in long-term gain, which they could not maintain on a constant basis through deception. The commercial community worked out its own rules and made anyone who hoped for favorable treatment observe them. In the second half of the nineteenth century the Chinese, suspicious of everything, trusted the Kyakhta merchants completely. Deals involving huge sums were usually made orally, and this became as natural as the deception that occurred earlier. We know of only one instance during the last decades of the nineteenth century when a Kyakhta merchant almost broke his word; as soon as the other merchants found out about it, they pooled all their ready cash and saved themselves and their colleague from disgrace.

I recall being pleasantly surprised to learn that before the Revolution Irkutsk was way ahead of Petersburg and Moscow in the number of grade-school pupils per thousand residents. But Irkutsk can't compare with Kyakhta, which was light-years ahead of every other city in this regard. In the 1890s it numbered between eight and nine thousand residents, practically nothing, yet it had a municipal public high school, a secondary school specializing in science and math, a girls' school, a vocational school, four parochial schools, a boarding school for orphans, etc. And all of them were housed in beautiful buildings and generally maintained with public funds.

The Botkin,[11] Sabashnikov, Belogolovy,[12] and Pryanishnikov[13] families, who served Russia in many more ways than with their pocketbooks, all came from Kyakhta. The first publisher of Lenin's works in Russia, Maria Vodovozova,[14] was the daughter of a Kyakhta merchant named Tokmakov. Ivan Shcheglov,[15] the well-known Siberian historian, taught at the math and science school. Dorzhi Banzarov,[16] a Buryat who later became a renowned scholar, attended the Russian-Mongolian military academy. Dmitry Davydov, author of "Glorious Sea, Sacred Baikal," lived and worked in Kyakhta. The Decembrist Nikolay Bestuzhev's son, A. D. Startsev (he was brought up in the family of a Selenginsk merchant named Startsev and took his name), assembled the finest collection of Chinese manuscripts in Europe. Grigory Potanin and Nikolay Yadrintsev, Nikolay Przhevalsky and Grigory Grum-Grzhimaylo, Pyotr Kozlov and Vladimir Obruchev, all explorers of Asia, outfitted their expeditions in Kyakhta; they spent long periods of time there, gave lectures for the general public, and helped start the regional museum and a branch of the Geographical Society.

When reflecting on the fate of this little town with the big reputation, the question automatically arises: What would have happened if Kyakhta's merchants hadn't taken the direction they did, in which wealth did not lapse into arrogance and petty tyranny, didn't turn its back on the arts and sciences, and could see Russia's troubles even through a well-lined purse? The view through a well-lined purse was naturally somewhat skewed, but no one can take away the merchants' boldness, independence, and critical, half-closed eyes. They acquired erudition, familiarity with European ways, and contact with many of the foremost people of that time. On several occasions the residents of

Kyakhta, exercising no caution whatsoever, collected money and sent it to Herzen[17] to help him publish the *Bell*. Correspondence went to London through Kyakhta and issues of the paper arrived from London through China. In Kyakhta people weren't afraid to discuss them openly and pass them around. Their strong position and remoteness, their provocative egoism and independence from the authorities created a special social climate in which opinions and views could be expressed frankly, in which haughtiness was mixed with democratic instincts and stubbornness with common sense. Anything could happen there. It happened that one of Kyakhta's biggest bigwigs, N. L. Molchanov, sent a telegram to Katkov,[18] publisher of the *Moscow Gazette*, criticizing him for printing something stupid, then walked off to a rehearsal of the amateur theater group to practice his part alongside officeworkers and a teacher. And it happened that another bigwig, after talking about Herzen, bought up all the tickets to the performance of a touring company and gave them to his servants, not with any educational aim in mind but to annoy "the merchants trading in Kyakhta." Without all this Kyakhta wouldn't have been Kyakhta, but only a name on a sign. Yet even with all its multicolors and multitypes, with its rules and the accompanying exceptions to the rules, it had a distinctive face, and that face with the fat cheeks looked important and refined.

But could or couldn't Kyakhta, given another direction and another local order of things, have become a different town, benighted, sated, and sluggish, of which Mother Russia had a goodly number? Why is it that Minusinsk, unremarkable in all respects and located far from major roads, has long lived by culture, establishes splendid libraries and a museum, subscribes to the best publications, and organizes a spiritual life, while a nearby town that has more wealth and a lucky, advantageous location leads a drowsy existence, suppressing lively thought with a heavy shortness of breath? Why is this? Isn't it because in some cases the townspeople regard their sole business as "business"—capital, using any means to get rich and affirm their wealth in a material way—whereas in other cases the intelligent opinion prevails that capital cannot exist merely for the sake of capital without the threat of human beings degenerating into beasts? This logic is so simple and true that in practice it most often proves unattainable.

Times change, and moral standards change, too. But even during the greatest social upheavals human morals possess the ability to adhere to their fundamental rules and laws. Today's young cities also have their bosses and owe their appearance in the world to one or several ministries who settled in them with their "business." The connection between "the merchants trading in Kyakhta" and "the governors ruling the Angara Valley" is that the fate of the towns entrusted to them depends on them to an almost identical degree. And things are no better now than they were in the distant past: it's all a matter of luck. In Angarsk the present-day "merchants" turned out to include cultivated people who looked after its spiritual valor from the very beginning, and this mark of noble reputation, like the stamp of God, does not harm Angarsk's "business" but only enhances it. Such people did not turn up in Bratsk, and the town's resonance, romantic until quite recently, became covered with the scale of an insensitive Moloch. In every age "business" that is not held in check by the soul, that lacks the ability to look around at the beauty and artistic expressiveness of the world, will inevitably be carried out in a casket no matter what good intentions it uses to fence itself in.

Much has been written about Kyakhta; the smell of wealth and of the exotic attracted outsiders for almost two centuries. Money doesn't produce a smell; the use of money does. If human beings automatically contain original sin, then wealth is all the more guilty for being wealth. If poverty did not exist, you might not notice it, but you can't help noticing when you see signs of its opposite. Trying to expiate his sins through prayer, the rich man turns to God and gives money for churches, thus paying his dues. But this is clearly not enough to assuage his soul. Something more is required, something of an earthly nature. He can't support all the poor; no amount of profit is sufficient for that. And then, in a quest to reconcile himself with reality, which is, of course, futile, the rich man pays his dues for worldly happiness in order to attain spiritual happiness—as he understands it. He builds a hospital or a school, sets up scholarships for students, and protects and sponsors those who are not of this world—artists, poets, and actors— seeing in them some vague sign from the Most High that has not been fully revealed or carried through to the end, that is on its way to a clear depiction, which will result when the benefactors' names stand out on their handiwork. This is the psychology of feeling guilty for being rich, the psychology, when it exists, of farming out wealth. "When it exists" is crucial here. It could be absent, too, and more often than not was. This depended as much on the "ripeness" of the owner's soul as on the rules adopted in his social circle. But when it actually did "exist," why must we always suspect this guilt of bad intentions if it was put to good use?

Among the many, many comments about old Kyakhta, mostly rapturous or relating to business, concerning commerce, the impressions and essays of the above-mentioned Stakheev are noted for their sarcasm and restraint. The future editor of the *Field* [*Niva*] and the *Russian Herald* [*Russkii viestnik*], who tried his hand at writing in the early 1860s at the *Kyakhta Blade*, found little to like in Kyakhta. According to him the merchants were lazy and inactive, morals and manners were uncivilized, the merchants' meetings and elections of senior representatives were worthy of a comedy, the *aksidentsiia* levied on each consignment of tea, which ostensibly supported the improvement of trade, went for who knows what, officials were bought off, and public funds were wasted on acquiring books in Irkutsk to start a library—what did Kyakhta need a library for? Here's the crux of the matter: the last outpost was supposed to be last in everything—in morals, in views, in the organization of its business activities and way of life, and in all public strivings for refinement, which deserved nothing but the mockery of educated visitors. So they're buying books, just dying for erudition? You don't say!

Stakheev's observations probably contain a good deal of truth, for he lived in Kyakhta and based his judgments on personal experience, but it's hard to agree with him now, one hundred some years later; he should have minded his own business. The boondocks, it seems, were boondocks just so they could stay that way forever, geographical remoteness meant remoteness and utter isolation in everything, and the difference between standards in the middle of nowhere and in the capital cities was insurmountable, imposed on human development by nature itself. Siberians who received an education in Petersburg were probably capable of achieving no less in intellectual and business pursuits than Europeans if they chose fertilized soil for their activities, but at home the entire surrounding environment had a numbing effect and subordinated everything to itself.

The environment had a numbing effect, but all attempts to change the environment evoked ridicule. And this view of Siberia and of Siberia's enlighteners persisted for a long time. Siberia was granted one role: to be a trafficway for contact with other lands and to contain wealth for the satisfaction of His Imperial Majesty's current and future needs. To introduce culture, to beautify a town, to nudge the local inhabitants toward building a spiritual life were roughly equivalent to extracting a mammoth from the permafrost and waiting for a nightingale's warble. When Sibiryakov acquired Zhukovsky's library for Tomsk University, this evoked the same reaction later on within a certain elite milieu: Why should Tomsk get Zhukovsky's library, the property of the Russian people?

The merchants of Kyakhta can be accused of this, that, and the other, but not of sluggishness or lack of initiative. When tea began to enter Russia by sea through the newly opened Suez Canal in the late 1860s and early 1870s, they suffered a terrible blow. Transportation by water cost ten times less than hauling goods across all of Mother Siberia in rain and freezing cold. It was precisely then, when disaster struck, that Kyakhta's significance for Siberia came to light: the hauling of goods all the way from the Chinese border beyond the Urals, tanneries and textile mills operating only because of Kyakhta, numerous handicrafts scattered throughout the population, and the procurement of furs from the Ob River to the Kamchatka Peninsula. The merchants of Kyakhta did everything to make sure that their petition reached the czar and that their suggested remedies were regarded favorably and put into practice: the duty on a pound of tea was lowered from forty kopecks to fifteen and on flower tea from sixty kopecks to forty, and the customs house was moved to Irkutsk, allowing duty-free trade with neighboring regions. Kyakhta lost Europe as a market but kept Siberia and part of Russia. And it continued to thrive for another thirty years and to compete successfully with sea transportation until the next and even mightier blow. Kyakhta's merchants enjoyed the respect of all industrial and commercial Russia; Kyakhta's merchants belonged to the first guild, a special high rank with enormous authority. They penetrated Mongolia and China and became partners in tea companies there, opened factories in Beijing, mined gold on the Lena River and killed beaver on Kamchatka, took part in penetrating Alaska and grew cotton in Turkestan. And they even managed to use the Suez Canal, which nearly ruined them, to their advantage, transporting tea around Europe through the Arctic Ocean to the mouth of the Yenisey, where there was no import duty. They built their own tea highway to Baikal, which was considerably shorter than the post road, with way stations, drivers, and workers, and ran their own steamships on Baikal and on the Amur River, bringing them by long, dangerous routes not from any old place but from the shipyards of London.

It would probably be more accurate to call these men a new type of Russian whose activities shattered the fairy tale of gloomy Russian contemplation and likable laziness. After the Cossacks' strikingly stubborn, swift dash through Siberia to the Pacific Ocean in the first half of the seventeenth century, after the hunting/trading miracle of Mangazeya, which arouses wonder to this day, after Shelikhov's campaign to penetrate America, Kyakhta was the next "spring" action of the Russian character in the expanses of Siberia, where it demonstrated an ability not only to store up energy but also to apply it powerfully.

A new blow awaited Kyakhta at the boundary between the nineteenth and twentieth centuries. And here Stakheev is correct when he writes:

The circumstances that caused the decline of commerce in Kyakhta did not set in suddenly—they developed over the course of many years—but the trading folk didn't notice; the ruling elite likewise did not distinguish themselves with sufficient perspicacity regarding the danger in store for Kyakhta. The enemy, once it encroached on Kyakhta's interests, was stronger than any ruling body; in a fatal, unstoppable fashion it destroyed all obstacles lying in the path of its triumphant procession. That enemy was steam. And it killed Kyakhta.

That steam was the Trans-Siberian Railroad, which took on the job of transportation. The merchants of Kyakhta still tried to resist by seeking new business ventures, attempted to get a concession to help build the Trans-Mongolian Railroad, and took part in prospecting, but World War I began, and then came the Revolution and the civil war. Kyakhta was occupied by interventionist forces. It still had one more important role to play: to become the center of preparation for the Mongolian Revolution. Kyakhta's big shots, certain until quite recently that there could be no dissatisfied workers among the local populace, stared with surprise and fear at the processions marching through the streets with red flags, protesting against foreigners and the old order. And finally Kyakhta woke up one day and saw Maimachin, its trading partner in China, with whom it had lived side by side for almost two hundred years, burn to the ground.

The thought keeps nagging me that history raced forward, losing its favorites along the way. And history rarely returns to its favorites. But how I wish that Kyakhta would acquire greatness and dignity and glory once again.

Indian summer had already burned itself out and October had arrived, but such heavenly weather roamed the area east of Baikal, bringing unforced sunshine and warmth, that we had to keep checking the calendar. No one wore a jacket, the scenery in the distance was clear and distinct, the rank smell of grass that would suffer no more hung in the motionless air, and the wooden houses gave off an aura of heatedness and the distant past. We walked around Kyakhta for a day, and a second, and a third, asking questions, comparing and reflecting, sometimes rejoicing, sometimes distressed and perplexed; we climbed the low hills, first one and then the other, that rise along the sides of the town and peered at the pattern of the streets as carefully as if at least the shadow of some hidden outline might appear.

Time, moving in one mighty, general current, is subdivided for each of us and takes the form of our homeland. If it didn't bow down over our towns and settlements, lingering there, then where do the traces of irremediable stops for gifts and retribution come from? And how do you explain why a town finishes building itself with zeal and taste, then destroys itself, then loses its memory, and then begins sporadically to search for and restore the material and spiritual symbols on which an undespairing reasonableness might base itself and settle beside?

Looking at Kyakhta automatically gives rise to thoughts about the commanding weariness of Time as it finishes up its second thousand years, with its haphazard establishments and muddled orders, one canceling another. A plaque still hangs in the park at the half-ruined Holy Trinity Cathedral that reads "Protected by the State." Next to the Cathe-

Holy Trinity Cathedral (eighteenth century)

dral of the Assumption [*Uspenskii sobor*], which has been restored and made into a museum, a stadium stands on the site of the old town cemetery; some of the gravestones that were pulled out and dragged aside are kicking around right next to the bleachers, while present-day youths chase a ball over the bones of their grandmothers and grandfathers. The monuments honoring the fighters of the Revolution and the victims of the White Guards' torture chambers (fifteen hundred prominent revolutionaries brought from all over Siberia and from the Urals region were executed in Kyakhta during a two-week period at the beginning of 1920) have a cold, faceless, unfinished appearance that is a far cry from sculpture and bespeaks brief, official attention; the latest one, erected for the fortieth anniversary of victory in the Great Patriotic War, is covered with indecent graffiti. What can be more cheerless and sad than an instructive memorial created on instructions, and what can be more sacrilegious and destructive of the people's morality than an entertainment facility on a burial site?!

No, it's not as easy to overcome the pride of benighted ignorance as it is to accumulate it.

But who can explain why the ruins of former grandeur attract us? It's probably not a matter of uncovering secrets, but of something that should be closer to us than secrets: the fateful justice of action and reaction. After an amplitude of power comes an amplitude of carelessness and neglect. Or is it that the nature of the world order, which is mightier than nations and economies, holds no hope of permanence for anyone? Or is it something else? In the name of what has retribution occurred there, in that commercial colony, serving as one more confirmation of some all-powerful law that rules the whole world?

The total number of properties in Kyakhta, counting Merchants' Square, the cathedral, the firestation, the veterinary clinic, the pharmacy, the houses of the two doctors and the border commissioner, the public meeting hall, and two or three houses belonging to officeworkers, was thirty-five to forty. All the private estates were arranged along a wide street with a boulevard running down the middle and ending in a public garden. On a hill in the square in front of the garden rose a cathedral built in the 1820s by Italians who were specially sent for, while behind the cathedral lay the vast Merchants' Square. But this Merchants' Square had no shops, and no trading went on. Various goods were stored there, including large shipments of tea, and various jobs were performed, such as cleaning brick tea, pouring bohea tea into containers, sewing up (*shirit'sia*) hides containing different teas, etc. A firestation with a fire brigade stood next to Merchants' Square, which the merchants of Kyakhta maintained, although the brigade was supposed to protect all of Kyakhta from fires.

This is how Ivan Popov, whose memoirs I cited earlier, saw Kyakhta in November 1885. We visited Kyakhta in October 1985, one month shy of exactly one hundred years later.

A spinning mill and a knitwear factory are now located in Merchants' Square. The Cathedral of the Resurrection, once fantastically splendid and beautiful, whose beauty Nikolay Bestuzhev refurbished after the Italians left, suffered most of all—as if according to that same law regarding the degree of its splendor and beauty. Now the cathedral wears the scaffolding of restoration, which dragged on for fifteen years before the authorities decided to put in a museum devoted to the geographic discoveries in Central Asia. The cause is worthy, and Kyakhta is just the place for such a museum. Only when will it ever happen?! Meanwhile the cathedral, first animated, then losing interest in life, and now mummified from top to bottom, stands blindly and apathetically twenty paces from the border barrier and actually seems to be drawing closer to it, pulling away from the side where there used to be a street with a boulevard and a public garden beyond its entrance.

There's no trace of the garden or the boulevard or, we might add, the pond. They are long forgotten, overgrown with grass, taken over ages ago by a vacant lot along which the factory is starting to put up one-story residential buildings. Of the street where the millionaires lived three houses remain: one, near the border, probably belonged to an educated man named Shvetsov who knew foreign languages and European culture and who kept a governess in that house for his children, something not normally done in Kyakhta; the second house, on the opposite end, has lost its owner in human memory as well as in fact; and the third house, in the middle of the street—and here somebody or someone's preservation instincts restrained the hand of destruction when the nonproletarian estates were taken apart for firewood or carted across the border—that house belonged to Aleksey Lushnikov.

Fate did not begrudge the merchants of Kyakhta sweeping gestures even in death: A. V. Shvetsov is buried in Switzerland, while Lushnikov rests in peace at his dacha in Ust-Kiran, thirty versts [about twenty miles] from Kyakhta. At one time the merchants built the dome of Holy Trinity Cathedral, the town's main church, in the form of a globe, as a reminder of the potential sphere of activity for trade. But the dome/globe went up in flames about thirty years ago, while the graves of Kyakhta's merchants are actually scattered throughout the whole wide world.

Lushnikov's house, currently no. 15, rarely lacked visitors. The Bestuzhev brothers, Nikolay and Mikhail, used to stay there, and that is where they would bring Ivan Gorbachevsky,[19] their comrade in hard labor and exile, from Selenginsk. Lushnikov preserved Nikolay Bestuzhev's drawings and portraits, which are well known to everyone; his household held sacred the many things belonging to the Decembrists that were given him and that he acquired, some of which are currently located in Kyakhta's regional museum. Sergey Trubetskoy undoubtedly dropped in whenever he went to Kyakhta. Grigory and Aleksandra

Potanin would stop by between expeditions, and Aleksandra Viktorovna was brought there from China on her final journey, to be committed
to her native earth. Nikolay Przhevalsky[20] considered himself Lushnikov's friend, and his spirit, too, lives on in that house, probably cursing the inconveniences it is now forced to endure. There Kennan, the
American, was amazed at the free discourses of his host as he looked
about at the luxury surrounding him; Dmitry Pryanishnikov, the eminent scholar and agrochemist, was born inside those walls. Yadrintsev
and Kozlov,[21] Obruchev and Klements,[22] Legran and the writer Maksimov—many, many people were received, entertained, listened to, and
congratulated in the spacious living room on the second floor of that
house.

I could say a good deal about Aleksey Mikhaylovich Lushnikov,
about the patron, protector, and guardian of the learned and cultural
institutions in Kyakhta and the surrounding villages, about his exceptional mind and the pleasing inclinations toward the arts and sciences
that made him incline his capital in their direction, too, and that won
over the foremost people of that era. The reactions of his famous Siberian contemporaries and Mikhail Bestuzhev's warm memoirs have
come down to us intact. He was that outwardly lucky and inwardly fortunate type of Russian who attained everything, including knowledge
and honors, himself and who, in contrast to a European, who would
have been happy with that, was tormented all his life by the dissatisfac-
tion and exactingness of his soul, which neither education nor philan-
thropy could soothe. Interestingly, Aleksey Mikhaylovich's son, I. A.
Lushnikov, carried the idea of "guardianship" even further: from 1905
to 1907 he published the Kyakhta newspapers *Baikal* and *Our Voice*
[*Nash golos*], which were clearly revolutionary in content.

We walk up to the house through piles of trash and stand beside it
for a long time. The first floor, as the rich commonly built their houses,
was made of stone, with small, modest windows; the second story was
wooden, tall, and filled with light as it looked around at the distant,
open view. Now it looks nowhere or only inward, at its old age and
neglect. Two windows on the upper floor have been smashed out,
scraps of paper and rags sway back and forth in them with nettling triumph, the carved trim adorning the cornice has broken off, and the
wooden staircase with sagging railings that leads from the courtyard to

the loggia is barely standing. The majestic masonry gate, which now lacks walls, sticks up like a mausoleum structure. The Chinese-style summer house in the courtyard did not survive, but the servants' house and the outbuildings far to the rear remain partially intact and now look more significant and less out of place than the main house, a historic building of significance to the whole republic, which has consequently taken it under state protection. The authorities plan to create a museum there to honor Kyakhta's outstanding residents. I would like to believe that they'll actually do it, if the house doesn't burn down or collapse first: the Russian snail is in no hurry to recover its ethnic memory, oh, no hurry at all.

And this is probably part of our character, too: we have to wait for something to collapse or reach the brink of ruin and only then do we display a full-speed-ahead enthusiasm for restoration. We don't acknowledge an economical middle ground in anything.

A hawk hovers high in the sky over the border zone, looking for prey on both sides, and some guy with a carbine watches it from the ground, squinting because of the sun and the bottomless sky. The dry air, smacking of sand, is ever so slightly catching its breath from the overripe smells, stirring in a roundabout motion; the distant pine forests wreathe the hills with light green; the town floats in the yellow haze of blazing larch trees. In moments like these, time, fooling us with its warmth, seems to leave the earth, soaring to its own celestial heights, and we are left with neither past nor present, just traces of both.

No, we'd better head into town; everything there is in its rightful place.

Cows amble along Kyakhta's main street just as they did one hundred and two hundred years ago; old folks sit on benches basking in the sun. A rooster is singing loudly and triumphantly in a courtyard somewhere. A trickle of pedestrians passes unhurriedly under the arches at the entrance to the open-air market; three young women, officers' wives, wrapped in moderate, tasteful clothing stand near some new red Zhigulis, engaged in bored conversation. A local adolescent boy keeps an eye on the officers' wives from the high roof of the bakery where Nestor Kalandarishvili[23] lived during the civil war years, mentally giving pluses and minuses to his own adolescent lass. An announcement on a modest piece of paper has been stuck to the door of the House of

Culture, whose barnlike architecture next to Holy Trinity Cathedral would have resulted in floggings with a birch rod in former times:

Anyone who's not a coward
And whose spirits never droop,
We invite all ardent townfolk:
Come and join our drama group!

If the commercial colony was cruelly punished for its wealth, then the town, which lived more modestly, has remained mostly intact and has carried its patriarchal appearance down to the present; although marked here and there with new buildings, it still looks strong and dashing, as before.

Recollections of the past, of what has been lived through and is now over, are not true recollections but random memories, a restoration of what was that holds no discoveries. Full, deep recollection is the tracking down of something that wasn't but should have been, a sensitive, joyful reaction to a belated scene, an encounter with something kindred that got lost along the way. In this frame of mind we walked around Kyakhta, formerly Troitskosavsk, almost guessing what we would find around each corner and in the next courtyard, infallibly coming out at places where it was impossible not to stop awhile and see things we couldn't miss in order to form some kind of protective recollection.

You feel as though you actually should have been born there, in those streets, but for some reason this didn't work out and you were carried off to a different spot.

Kyakhta was lucky to have escaped devastating fires, while in recent decades it didn't have enough money to organize a mass demolition and give itself a new face. What might have happened is apparent from several stunning attempts. At this point the town fathers of Kyakhta might become indignant: we haven't been "lucky" at all! What about the apartment problem, and the dozens of small boiler rooms, and providing services and utilities, and staying up to date?! A falsely perceived up-to-dateness in the form of standardized high-rises has become a disease of epidemic proportions in our smaller cities, an affirmative value of their prosperity, a yardstick for competence. No, until we learn to build at a level equal to the architecture of the past, not destroying but developing and supplementing it in the look that took shape a long time ago, until the practice of shoddy construction disappears, it's better not to hurry. It's better to wait for the arrival of people capable of respecting the past and of not regarding our cities merely as places of residence for their own personal lives. I don't mean Kyakhta alone; Kyakhta, I repeat, was lucky. And unfortunately the title of historic town cannot always serve as a protection against destructive alteration. Irkutsk, which is ranked as a historic town and invested with protective rights and laws, did not preserve its age-old center, blotting it out with the alien geometry of self-styled modernism.

And as for those who pick up on our good intentions, see what they turn them into with memorials that, with few exceptions, look like monuments to monuments, like the tombs of anniversary celebrations standing here, there, and everywhere in the Siberian expanses that have been set aside as spiritual ground. Memorials have become a means of adding another modern convenience in which generous amounts of heavy concrete freeze and wall up rather than arouse the sensitive currents between past and present, between people and history. Is it our taste that fails us or did our memory-conducting channels prove to be cut off before this happened? The standards of memory indicate the standards of life and the standards of a generation; we are capable of justifying the primitiveness of urban architecture with pressing needs that demand apartments in any kind of walls, and our magnificent but cold symbols of memory attest to a wasteful poverty.

There is now also a memorial in Novoselenginsk, where Nikolay Bestuzhev, Mikhail Bestuzhev's wife and son, and Torson's[24] children are buried, that represents just such a vulgar concrete triumph, from which the modest old gravestones peep out awkwardly like weeds in a clean field that's been treated with weed killer. The mighty concrete encircling wall displays visual propaganda in the form of sculptured scenes from the lives of the Decembrists, with written propaganda beside them. All this is generously proportioned and on a broad scale, sparing nothing in terms of labor, money, and square meters, instead of simply the essential patch of earth that Nikolay Bestuzhev, one of the noblest and most impressive Decembrists, who did so much for the good of this region as well, finally entered and became. This instead of

Memorial to the Decembrists in Novoselenginsk

the patch of earth where the tear of a sensitive descendant might have fallen and from which the puff of reciprocated thanks that he awaited might have reached him. Now no tear will fall and nothing will reach him, but to make up for it, walk around on the hard surface without fear of getting your feet wet in bad weather, examine the inside-out, textbook-style pictures, and read the famous words about how "they'll write our names on the wreckage of despotism."[25]

Their names were written, all right, but surely there's more to it than that. People go to the graves of great citizens not to make their acquaintance or to fill in the gaps in their education but for spiritual enlightenment, for the sake of a few moments of perceptible contact, to be in a world of human upliftedness. They go to sense themselves in that world and that world in themselves, to divine educational aids that symbols cannot express, to comprehend the true values of being.

Everything at this site used to be simple, modest, and close to the departed. When Mikhail Bestuzhev left Siberia after the deaths of his wife and brother, friends of the Bestuzhevs—B. V. Belozerov from Petrovsky Zavod and Aleksey Lushnikov from Kyakhta—promised that the graves dear to him would not suffer from lack of care and attention.

In Petrovsky Zavod, where the Decembrists served out their terms of hard labor, they had artisans cast monuments and a little metal door for a fence, which they decided to face with masonry. And they put up a small chapel beside them. I must note that these grave markers were not in Novoselenginsk proper but five versts [about three and a half miles] away, in what is now an uninhibited spot but then was close to the Bestuzhevs' dwellings in the small settlement where the Decembrists lived. Today the area is a dump and goosefoot grows all over the site of their hovels. From a shallow hollow you get a good view of the Selenga flowing between bare banks; a white church stands on the opposite side—the sole reminder of old Selenginsk, the celebrated town on the way to China—and guards its eternal rest.

Everything else around there also breathes peacefulness and puts you in the mood for long-range thoughts. Cliffs tower like guards over the influx and efflux of the Selenga, woodless hills lie drowsily in the sun like burial mounds, silent witnesses to the westward marches of Ghengis Khan's forces and their descendants, and the air smells drily of wormwood and thyme. At this point it is an Eastern landscape existing within ancient outlines, almost aerial, the construction of different gods, the initial hieroglyphs of the great Asian philosophies. This is the land that Nikolay Bestuzhev loved and pondered at length in letters and conversations with his friends.

But let's return to Kyakhta, to the old part of town that has escaped destructive alteration. If nature conveys a sense of eternity, then human settlements should convey not the futility of human beings, who come into the world for only a short time, but the warmth that remains after they are gone. Memory is precisely that: the warmth given off by human life. Without warmth memory does not exist. It, like the kind of walls people lived in, can be used to judge what they lived by and whether their lives were a continuation of the tendencies of the common folk or a distortion of them.

When you walk around Kyakhta (Troitskosavsk), you'd better watch out. Suddenly you'll see, no, not a fairy-tale vision but something out of a *bylina*: thick-walled like a fortress, with windows as economical as embrasures and a heavy mossy roof. A solid fence made of horizontal planks stands parallel to the cottage and contains a gateway and a wicket with a spiral cast-iron ring under a little roof; a mighty larch tree rises out of the yard as if it hadn't grown there but was built to fit the general plan. Then twenty paces from the fort such showing off crops up in front of you that you'll just ooh and ah: tall, towerlike, multiwindowed and multichimneyed, gleaming, decorated with gingerbread trim, with a side balcony along the upper floor and intricate gutters ornamented at the corners with figures that look like Serpent Goryniches leaping onto the roof. You'll actually think an upstairs window is about to open and a capricious voice, mixing up time periods, will demand something or shout something enthusiastic. Of course the lacework of carved trim is riddled with holes, the wood has darkened and cracked, one of the windows, considered unnecessary, is boarded up, interrupting the bright musical phrase, the original frame of another window has been replaced with a false note, and the balcony has begun to rot, but even so, it's a picture of loveliness: you stand there and can't take your eyes off it. The house next to it is a little simpler but also out of the ordinary, somehow completely alive with a life all its own, sprightly and cocky, the property, judging by its appearance, of one of the merchants' assistants who struck it rich. You walk on, and suddenly the end of a majestic wall juts out into the street; neatly faced with masonry, well-groomed once and for all, this wall, descending step by step toward a courtyard, was built as a protection against fire and wind. The house it protected no longer exists, but the wall still stands, waiting and waiting for it to appear on its former site. On the other side of the street a merchant's small shop, now used for some household purpose, perhaps as a woodshed, catches your attention with the carved bar holding the door shut; above it, on the four-sided roof peeping out above the surrounding lineup, wooden openwork smokestacks perch on the chimneys like strange birds; and such a merry-go-round of trim appears on the sides of the high ridge beam, whose front end has been carved into the shape of a horse, that you are automatically drawn to examine it more closely. That's what it's like everywhere. And the courtyards, almost all of them, are made up entirely of the distant past: little cottages grown into the ground up to their windows, blackened, slightly decrepit barns, buildings for sleighs and wagons, sheds, workshops—the beginnings and the backyards of distinguished and undistinguished Troitskosavsk families, along with the assistants they employed in their work, which preserve to this day the order of a life that is gone forever.

During the 1960s some border guards were dismantling one of the old buildings and stumbled across a canvas. It turned out to be a painting by Mikhail Nesterov.[26] The picture now hangs in the regional museum, which also contains another find, by an unknown artist of the Italian school. In Kyakhta you can't help being surprised not at the discoveries but at the small number of them; the most valuable articles, which could have filled a museum of their own, probably perished along with the commercial colony. Just think how many paintings, drawings, and objects created by Nikolay Bestuzhev alone, whom the merchants repeatedly hired to paint portraits and icons, should have been preserved. Anything made by the Decembrist brothers was in extraordinary demand among Kyakhta's merchants precisely because it came from the Bestuzhevs' hands, immediately becoming a relic and a source of pride by dint of authorship. One of their inventions, the *sideika* (a two-wheeled carriage with springs), was used everywhere in Siberia; it was irreplaceable on the broken-down mountain roads, which the majority of ours were.

Nowadays people no longer travel by *sideika*, which required a horse; one of them stands in the museum as an exhibit, arousing curiosity. When the museum was still in the organizing stage, Mikhail Bestuzhev's writing desk/bureau was brought over from Lushnikov's house, which is apparently when the other Decembrist things were gathered together, including Nikolay Bestuzhev's pistol and several of his watercolors. Speaking of the museum, I must admit that Kyakhta's version of a regional museum is spacious and splendid, the only remnant of the town's former grandeur still intact. One hundred years have passed since the day it opened; the same amount of time has gone by since the appearance of a group of political exiles (Ivan Popov, Nikolay Charushin[27] and his wife, and others) started a new wave of social and educational activity in Kyakhta, which resulted in the museum and the Geographical Society and the public library. Dropping in at the present-day library, we found not a single item from the materials collected by the residents of Kyakhta back then: they had been hauled off somewhere—fine, as long as it wasn't to the dump—in disregard of the zeal and labors of enthusiasts who worked selflessly for the good of their town in the old days, too.

That seems to have been the last burst of cultural excitement in which an intelligentsia composed of political exiles still played the leading role. After that the excitement, growing and spreading, became revolutionary; for Kyakhta, as for the whole country, different priorities came to the fore. Kyakhta lost all commercial significance; over the years its resonance, more and more muffled as time went on, became a purely local sound. Now Kyakhta is nothing but a county seat, with all the inevitable attributes this rank entails, including the usual attitude toward a town of this sort from the outside and its own moods within. It did not end up on the register of historic places, and essential restoration projects have dragged on in imitation of an eastern steppe song that has no end.

You walk around Kyakhta with contradictory feelings, alternately joyous and bitter. It's as if two masters took up residence there long ago and have been warring with each other nonstop over the course of many years. One of them takes pains to help Kyakhta rise to its full and glorious historical height; the other bends it in the direction of blind servility to the present day. One opens new branches of the museum; the other, scattering the remains of gravestones, levels a cemetery to build a stadium on top of the graves and enjoys the sounds of the foul language coming from it. One watches to make sure that nobody burns Holy Trinity Church to the ground; the other, wearing an ironic smile, puts a public restroom right next to it and with calculated permissiveness converts the whole park into the above-mentioned place. One understands that morality cannot grow in just one upper layer; the other ruins even that layer with primitive, banal buildings.

Kyakhta isn't the only town that needs to be reminded of these perplexing problems; this misfortune afflicts many of our cities. But Kyakhta is a small town and therefore its contradictions are more noticeable than in others. They are so clearly neighbors, proclaiming their rights to citizenship with alternating success, that you automatically begin to ponder where the majority of us stand, on the side of paternal memory, on which the people's prosperity depends to a large extent, or on the side of a militant carelessness toward sacred things that we can't seem to outrgrow? Whom will we be with and whom will we be against when the cleansing period of sobering up finally sets in?

1987–91

7
❖❖❖

Russkoe Ustye

THE PEOPLE OF YORE

I heard about Russkoe Ustye [literally, Russian Estuary] too late. If I'd known about it, say, ten years earlier, I could then have managed to capture a lot of the things that now remain only in memory while they were still alive and functioning. The same airplane that brought me to Polyarny for the first time took Mikhail Ivanovich Chikachyov, Russkoe Ustye's last great storyteller, to the hospital. He never returned. During those ten years television has reached Russkoe Ustye, outsiders from the mainland have poured in, old-timers acquainted with the distant past have died off, crosses in the numerous graveyards along the Indigirka River have tilted and fallen over, and the local residents have begun to speak more and more "the way they do back yonder" [*"po-tamosnomu"*], the way we do, losing the archaic distinctiveness and marvelous resonance of their own language.

I came upon Russkoe Ustye at what I believe was the exact crossing point when the old days were becoming echoes of the old days, at the very moment when the villagers were bidding them farewell forever. The present, which had lagged behind the general flow of time there for so long, had finally caught up with it both in symbols and in pace. There, too, people have begun to divide up the twenty-four-hour cycle into hours and minutes, looking first at their instruments for keeping track of time and only then out the window or over their shoulders. And the universal mad rush has also penetrated those parts. The long arctic day still gives way to the long arctic night, as always; birds, following ancient instincts, migrate back and forth; the Indigirka River freezes over and opens up in due course; and after the white silence of the tundra comes its mysterious unsilence, dappled, undulating, and brownish green. But all this has a quality of something set apart and acquired—as if nature has been forced to acknowledge the power of human beings and, while following its age-old routine, changes course not on its own but in accordance with the calendar they have established. Nowadays, unlike at the beginning of the twentieth century, it can no longer be said of the inhabitants of Russkoe Ustye: "During the last 300–350 years the people who live there, in the domain of snow, ice, and the northeaster, have undergone a kind of anabiosis: they have become frozen solid in their thoughts, speech, and entire manner of life and so far have been unable to thaw out" (Vladimir Bogdanov).[1]

In the last two, at most three, decades they have not only thawed out but have also entered that single stage of human existence whose inner workings, for all the outer differences between South and North, East and West, are approaching a common standard for everyone. Standards are standards: they diminish color and sound and everything else. A single style of life is the same as a single battlefront in which everybody must fall in to maintain a straight line. This makes for a thriving style but an impoverished life.

Today precious little remains of Russkoe Ustye, of the past to which two interesting books attest: *The Age-Old People near the Arctic Ocean*[2] by Vladimir Zenzinov, a political exile, which appeared in czarist times, and Andrey Birkengof's *The Descendants of Pioneers*,[3] which describes Russkoe Ustye during the late 1920s. Their very titles allude to the uncommonness of the fate specially selected for the Russians living along the lower Indigirka, to their concentrated form of heredity through blood, spirit, faith, and primordial origin. Of particular value in both books are the authors' descriptions of local folklore and the glossaries they compiled based on old-timers' speech. There were other eyewitness accounts written before and after these, but they mention Russkoe Ustye only in passing and fall into the general ranks of memoirs, impressions, and scientific notes. These two books, however, are devoted mainly to Russkoe Ustye and are the most thorough. With their help it is not difficult to determine what is still alive and living out its final days and what has vanished into the deep underworld once and for all.

In Russkoe Ustye people speak as they did in the remote past, exaggerating not just twofold but threefold, saying not "deep underworld" [*preispodniaia*] but "triple-deep underworld" [*treispodniaia*], not "extremely bright" [*presvetloe*] but "triple-bright" [*tresvetloe*]. You will recall that in *The Tale of Igor's Campaign*[4] Yaroslavna exclaims, "Bright, triple-bright sun!" [*"Svetloe-tresvetloe solntse!"*].

Of all the losses suffered in Russkoe Ustye, the greatest is that Russkoe Ustye was almost dismissed for good. Forty some years ago (back when the concept of the "unpromising" village[5] was still being explored) workers' towns were set up in the Arctic region. At that time all the "households" [*"dymy"*] scattered along the Indigirka for dozens of kilometers that, taken together, made up Russkoe Ustye, including the actual settlement by that name, were collected into one encampment and, so as not to poison memory with history and without giving it much thought, the authorities named the result Polyarny [literally, Polar]. There are countless such Polyarnies up and down the seaboard, but in all the wide world there is just one unique Russkoe Ustye, which has, in addition, many of the kinds of things we ought to cherish as the apple of our eye. Only very recently was it given back its name.

But even after disappearing from the map, its original name, contrary to callous bureaucratic logic, still remained in current use. Residents bought plane tickets to Polyarny but lived in Russkoe Ustye. On certificates, directives, and reports it was called Polyarny, but in people's memories it was Russkoe Ustye, just as before. Polyarny was nearly washed away by the Indigirka, which pulled cottage after cottage into the water as it carried off hastily chosen chunks of the village's steep bank, but Russkoe Ustye came to life every summer along all three channels of the river when families dispersed to the "sands" [*"peski"*] (the fishing grounds along the Indigirka), because those "sands" are, as a rule, the very places where their grandparents and great-grandparents stood and where a good many of their graves still remain. Aviators and navigators, geologists and border guards knew it as Polyarny, but hunters and fishermen from the Yana River to the Kolyma knew and still know it as Russkoe Ustye. This was not simply the use of a long-standing name out of sheer habit. It was an inseparable part of a solidly created local world in which the human and the natural had grown together and become one.

While lamenting that I arrived in Russkoe Ustye at least ten years too late, I must point out that my tardiness was by no means complete and final. Many of the customs, beliefs, and rules of life in Russkoe Ustye had, of course, slipped away for good or had become hidden instead of apparent, but an attentive gaze could find many that also remained intact. They had retreated rather than stayed in place but could still be detected. I was too late to find them where they had lived for hundreds of years, but I could make them out as they slipped away, bidding farewell. Out on the tundra you can see for a very long way: it was still not hard to spot the figure of a little old man, sorrowful, ancient, and all worn out from work but carrying himself nobly and erect as he receded into the arctic night.

The figure was receding, but he didn't take everything with him all at once. What has been sifted and amassed over centuries could not be hauled off all at once, and what is left will still last for years, even decades. There I encountered paganism, always amazingly tenacious in Russians no matter where it is found, but there it seems to thrive in an utterly organic way, coming to life again every spring. I was probably primed to feel the mystery of the place, but I sensed a certain separate mystery about Russkoe Ustye so quickly that it must have been lying in plain sight. I sensed it in the faces of the Indigirka dwellers, in their tales of the past, in the labors that never change, and in their relationships with one another. And at last I heard their language. Lord, what a joyous messenger, what pleasure and good fortune (in the words and sounds by which it has come down to us in the present)—the Russian language in Russkoe Ustye!

PRILOG

We love mystery. We want there to be a Loch Ness Monster, and a Big Foot in the Pamir Mountains, and a mysterious *chuchuna* [a mythical beast held responsible for various kinds of misfortune] in the Siberian tundra, and "flying saucers." In an exposed and chill world where everything has an explanation, we feel cold and forlorn without it. Any news of something unknown stirs our imagination and offers hope that nature still has enough strength in reserve to resist our merciless, scalping minds. The majority of us seem to contain two people: one, the child of our education and the age we live in, agrees with a mechanistic structuring of the world, and the other rejoices every time the logic of the first is called into question. We are simultaneously passive and pushy, feeling and calculating, weak to some point of undetermined mightiness and strong to a dangerous degree of exhausting overexertion. People contradict themselves; the way they function in perceiving and interacting with the world does not fit into one orderly system.

To the scholarly mind, a mystery is merely something that remains to be solved. That which defies solution does not exist for such a mind, even if all of living nature were to rest on a mystery that cannot be unlocked. And according to this mentality, anything that has been forgotten or lost, that has fallen outside its time period and does not conform to the explanatory shorthand prevalent today, is nothing but a fawning reptile. How odd that as humankind became more and more familiar with new phenomena, as it delved into this knowledge and carried it to previously inconceivable heights and depths, it meanwhile lost whole continents, civilizations, mighty cities and laws more than once during the course of its history, but when some of these accidentally turned up, humanity could not find room for them among its structures: all the links in the moving chain were locked together and nothing could squeeze in anywhere. All the sciences love straight, focused movement; they have no use for parallel or winding routes that circle back.

The Russians of Russkoe Ustye have a *prilog* (a legend or traditional tale) according to which their ancestors arrived not from the south by rivers and portages, the way Siberia was colonized everywhere else, but from the sea, setting foot on Siberian soil considerably earlier than other settlers as they escaped in small, two-masted sailboats from the devastating oppression of Ivan the Terrible. Their ancestral homeland was northern Russia, the territories belonging to old Novgorod. We know that in 1570 Ivan the Terrible took sore savage reprisal against the Novgorod freemen. Waves of mass executions rolled across all their lands, forcing the survivors to flee to the four corners of the earth. Coast-dwellers from the White Sea region fled east, to the area they had been sailing to in search of fish and game since time immemorial and where they had spent more than one winter when their return routes were cut off by ice, thereby learning the local conditions and the lay of the land. Most likely they did not reach the Indigirka right away, in one crossing or in one year. Perhaps they did not even know about it at the beginning of their exodus but, moving from river to river, following rumors of more lucrative lands, and having resolved to escape the sovereign's surveillance altogether, they finally came out on the Indigirka from a western channel, which they later named the Russian Channel [*Russkii protok*], pushed deeper inland, and founded the settlement of Russkoe Zhilo [literally, Russian Habitation] about eighty versts [about fifty miles] from the sea.

One all-too-Russian detail supports the authenticity of this legend: when they stopped at the mouth of the Yelon River, a tributary of the Indigirka, the newcomers spent the first winter drinking themselves into a stupor and, considering that place unlucky, subsequently left it and moved to another one not far away. Ever since then, the original spot has in fact been called Gulyanka [literally, Outdoor Merrymaking]. Zenzinov, who spent almost all of 1912 in Russkoe Ustye, found the remains of an old graveyard still intact at the mouth of the Yelon that could have originated with seafarers.

My first visit to the Indigirka took place in the spring—late March, early April—when the tundra lay buried in snow and winter didn't shudder a bit at the emerging sun. The bitter cold held steady at about -40°C [-40°F], blizzards were expected, snow made the whole world perpetually white, night and day, and the heavy, endless drifts showed no sign of ever melting. I chose summertime for my second trip. We headed downstream from Chokurdakh, the county seat, in a cutter owned by the Fish Protection Service and entered the river's lower reaches, the domain of the old Russian settlements. We pulled up at Gulyanka late in the evening and found the nearby summer cabin of Pavel Cheryomkin, whom I had met during my first trip. His dogs, who were tied up outside, silently watched our cutter dock but started barking as soon as we set foot on the shore. Cheryomkin leaped out of a gully. Bearing one of the original surnames of Russkoe Ustye, this robust young man was known throughout the entire region for his prowess as a hunter. He had stuck in my memory as a clear exception to the belief that only silent types live in the Arctic. And now, too, no sooner had he made out who we were than he began describing what had just happened in a quick, excited manner, for he hadn't cooled down yet and still hadn't decided what to do. He'd gone away for four days with his son and nephew to repair *pasti* (snares for polar fox), while his wife and the other children had stayed in Gulyanka; when he'd returned that day no one was home and a note on the table said that some wild animal had killed one of the dogs. His whole team was there, fifteen strong, and now he had to go to town and get his family, who were afraid of the unknown animal, and it was dangerous to leave the dogs.

The dogs, shaggy, well-fed creatures with strong paws who had fallen silent as soon as their master began to speak, looked at us with that measure of curiosity and indifference that constitutes the dignity of any working being.

Up there people assure you that the Indigirka sled dog is the best in the world, and that seems to be true. Not for nothing did the explorers' first reports call it the Dog River. The death of a good dog is no small loss, and now, when hunters use Blizzard snowmobiles more often than dogs, they cannot always recoup such a loss. Cheryomkin is one of the few who still keeps a dog team. For him it is not simply a matter of calculating whether dogs are an advantage or a disadvantage; a snowmobile, for which you don't have to lay in a supply of fish, clearly has more advantages. For Pavel Cheryomkin, a proud man and the proven mainstay of the local professional hunters, a dog team is a mark of distinction denoting a native of Russkoe Ustye descended from a long line of hunters; it signifies loyalty to a tradition and gratitude to that tradition for having fed many generations of his clan.

I asked him about the old graveyard at Gulyanka. Cheryomkin had heard of it, but to the best of his recollection he had never encountered any crosses or graves. Most likely the Indigirka had swept them away. Every summer the river, changing the pressure of its current, attacks its banks with rust-colored water from the tundra and swallows up everything living and dead that stands or lies in its path. Just south of Gulyanka we'd passed a place called Yurtushki, where Pavel Cheryomkin's older brother, Konstantin, had a summer cabin; we'd noticed that an old log house already hung over the water and that its owner was putting up a new one some distance away without waiting for it to fall in.

The long arctic day was still in full force, the sun set for only brief periods, and you could see for quite a distance in the faint, incorporeal twilight. At Gulyanka the Indigirka turns sharply to the right, then swings back and goes to pay a call on the left side. As it flows across the flat land, where all routes lie open to it without impediment, it pokes into everything, producing such cloverleafs with its curlicues, channels, and temporary passageways that it seems to be not one river but a clump of rivers, like a clump of snakes that have come together and won't crawl away, eroding the boundless tundra.

After receiving the Yelon, the main channel turns to the right, and there Russkoe Ustye appears at last, with the crosses and one roofless building that are the sole remnants of that ancient refuge for the people of yore, where they remained for three hundred some years, if we can believe the legend . . .

If we can believe the legend . . . But what basis do we have for believing it? Or, on the contrary, what basis do we have for not believing it?

"The Indigirka River in the Yukagir territory" was discovered by the sovereign's men (detachments led by Fasting Ivan, Ivan Rebrov)[6] in the late 1630s. In their reports on the Yukagirs, on how soldiers could be fed and quartered in that region, and on how it might profit the sovereign, they made no mention of Russian settlements. Either there weren't any at that time, or some figure with a vested interest in keeping quiet about them exerted his influence, or the detachments had bypassed them by taking a different branch of the river. Anything could have happened. Let's not forget that even if Russians had settled there by then, they had fled Russia because of oppression and would hardly have hastened to make an appearance before servants of the government. The very reason they went into hiding so far away and at such peril was to keep from being found. After taking a look at Stanchik, an old settlement on the Kolyma Channel where a chapel still stood intact, we got lost on the way back in the countless waterways and reversals, straying for several hours even though our guides were local men who knew everything there inside out. What does this say for new arrivals? Even if they'd been the most experienced and well-informed frontiersmen, could they have drawn a complete and flawless map of the area amid the widespread, thoroughly tangled flooding of the Indigirka? This, of course, does not mean that Russians must have been there, but they could have been, and we should not discount this likelihood.

In his book, Zenzinov quotes an old man from Russkoe Ustye: "I've heard from the old folks, from very old people, that the river used to belong only to the Yukagirs. Then some Russians got together from different provinces and took to the sea in boats—they were trying to get away from this disease, from asthma. And Russia lost all track of them." It's quite possible that this thought more than anything warmed, strengthened, and united them in an inhospitable, naked, and frozen land: "Russia lost all track of them" and wouldn't find them in the middle of nowhere and break their backs physically and spiritually with evil, overbearing authority.

In 1831, when the Yakuts, claiming rights to the lower Indigirka, decided to have the Russians evicted, the latter defended their hereditary ownership with the following argument, among others: "Russian sailboats were the first to find this river."

Archaeological excavations on the eastern shore of the Taymyr Peninsula confirm the theory that such a journey could have taken place: in 1940 archaeologists found traces of a winter camp belonging to Russian coast-dwellers from the White Sea region that date from the very beginning of the seventeenth century. If Russians were sailing the seas in the early seventeenth century, don't we have to assume that they'd been doing so for some time? Several scholars refer to this with certainty. Boris Dolgikh's view, stated in "New Data on Russian Navigation along the North Sea Route in the Seventeenth Century,"[7] is well known: "Even before the Russian state annexed the seaboard of Eastern Siberia, Russian seafarers were sailing to that area by the North Sea route, skirting Taymyr. At that time Russians from the northern coastal regions of European Russia who were engaged in manufacturing and trade were probably already active at many points along the northern coast of Eastern Siberia."

Incidentally, a legend about the arrival of the first settlers in those parts by boat also existed on the Yana River, in the former Russian village of Kazachy. How do we know that at one point they didn't head east as a single party and then split up, with one group of seafarers remaining on the Yana, while the other sailed farther on and reached the Indigirka?

But why the Indigirka? As they passed river after river, was it really impossible, even in the Far North, to choose one less bleak and more favorable for habitation? What advantages could they have been seeking? Remote is remote, if that is where they saw salvation, but even as they sought remoteness they would not have gone too far without heavy incentive, and at that time this was precisely "going too far," for no one had as yet beaten any paths farther east. What actually drew the Russians to that particular place? What did they find there that could even partially make up for the homeland they had left behind?

Let's not, however, exaggerate the lifelessness and utter frigidity of those parts; they have already been exaggerated enough. In terms of harsh conditions, the northern zone of European Russia cannot compare with northern Asia, of course, but it didn't exactly weaken the local work ethic either, and the distant voyages that were always essential to the coast-dwellers had tempered it even more. If the Indigirka didn't scare them, it means that through long winter stays and close companionship they'd gotten used to being unafraid, plain and simple. Just so you'll know: the people who live downriver, near the Arctic Ocean, consider their region warm, and in comparison with continental Yakutia, which contains spots of record-breaking cold, this is actually true. What the river-dwellers fear most during the summer is hot weather capable of turning every drop of water into a breeding ground for mosquitoes, from which there is no escape for man or beast.

But incentives for the Russians to go and remain there did exist, of course, and had probably been ascertained in advance. First, there was an abundant supply of fish, birds, and reindeer, which hasn't run low to this day. If the supply isn't low even now, try to imagine what was in those lakes and catches of fish, in those hills and sea meadows three and four hundred years before us. The polar fox, thank heavens, hadn't been wiped out in those parts, and there was as yet no way to poison all the chir, the Siberian white salmon, or the muksun.[8] Yury Karachentsev, former manager of the trading post in Polyarny, told me that about two years ago someone from the town sent a complaint to Chokurdakh, possibly as a prank, about the lack of meat in the grocery store. Officials there were surprised, not because there was no meat but because there was no reason for the store to carry any. Responding to the complaint nonetheless, they sent over what beef happened to be on hand in Chokurdakh. It sat there for several months and, after it had lost all color and taste, they finally got rid of it; even the dogs would have turned up their noses at it. When the local residents need meat, a hunter climbs onto his snowmobile (every hunter has two or three Blizzards), drives a short distance into the tundra, and uses his binoculars to pick a spot where reindeer are likely to appear. When they come into view, he steps on the gas, heads them off with his iron dogsled, and has fresh game in just half an hour. People stack large fish (for human consumption) like logs in dugout refrigerators and pile small ones (herring to throw to the dogs) in heaps on the ice.

The ancestors of the Russians in Russkoe Ustye had no binoculars or snowmobiles, of course, but just as we don't suffer without the things that will exist three hundred years from now, so, too, did they calmly use the means they had at hand. Although they expended more physical effort than people do nowadays, they did an excellent job of obtaining the fish, meat, and furs with which they warmed and fortified their families, and they sent generation after generation out into the world from their newly fledged homeland.

But before carving out that new homeland, they must have taken a careful look around to see how they would live and to find out who their neighbors would be. Who their neighbors would be played a very large part in their decision. They well knew that their descendants would not remain in good health very long if confined to the small circle of new arrivals and that one way or another they would have to become related to the indigenous tribes. Nomadic Yukagirs and Lamuts (Evens) roamed those parts, and there were known to be Chukchi, who tended herds of reindeer on the other side of the Kolyma. At that time Yakuts hadn't moved into the lower reaches of the Indigirka yet, and the Russians of Russkoe Ustye were subsequently right when they claimed to be the first settlers. But there was enough land for everyone. Arguments over who would live where soon abated once and for all.

The Russians turned out to be situated closest to the Yukagirs, a people reared freely under the mighty tundra sky to be gentle, unselfish, and tidy. The same can be said of them as Baron Maydell,[9] who traveled all over northeastern Yakutia between 1868 and 1870, observed of the Chukchi:

It is remarkable that a people can exist without any rulers whatsoever. This can only be explained by the circumstances of the reindeer breeders' way of life, in which each person lives separately, by himself, a great distance from his nearest neighbor. Such a life makes it possible to avoid countless occasions for the arguments and misunderstandings so often encountered among settled peoples but found much more rarely among nomads. We do observe, however, that even nomadic peoples establish rulers, including peoples forced to lead as isolated a kind of life as has fallen to the lot of the Chukchi. For this reason the explanation for such a strange phenomenon cannot lie in isolation alone. In my opinion, it pays to note that from the very beginning the Chukchi never had to defend their land from hostile neighbors, and what's more, they themselves have never carried out any campaigns of conquest. Under ordinary circumstances the power of a paterfamilias is quite enough for the nomad living on his own; such figures also exist among the Chukchi, of course, and are perfectly capable of exacting obedience from their children and the other members of their households. But as soon as an enemy crowds the nomads, they must have a chief; this necessity is probably what produced the universal view that a ruling elite is essential.

Maydell did not note the same peculiarity among the Yukagirs that he observed in the Chukchi only because he wasn't studying them and rarely encountered them. In this respect there was actually no difference whatsoever between the two neighboring nomadic peoples.

No evidence remains as to whether the Russians immediately came into contact with the people that had sprung into being there or whether this took some time, but contact did occur, and eventually it became quite close. In certain families you can easily spot Asiatic features, mostly of Yukagir origin. But neither language nor customs nor memory suffered as a result. The community had probably resolved from the very start to keep its Russianness in a fortress and, despite centuries of ordeals and deprivations that we can only guess at, they preserved it so well that we can't help being astonished.

The first information about Russians living along the lower Indigirka dates from Bering's Great Northern Expedition. Lieutenant Dmitry Laptev, a member of that expedition who had pushed eastward from the Lena River in 1739, was forced to abandon his icebound boat, the *Irkutsk,* opposite the mouth of the Indigirka and spend the winter in Russkoe Zhilo. During that winter Russians from Russkoe Ustye helped

Laptev transport thirty poods [about 1,080 pounds] of provisions more than eighty versts [about fifty miles] to the Kolyma, and in the spring eighty-five local inhabitants chopped the *Irkutsk* out of the ice with heavy crowbars and hauled it to open water. Residents of Russkoe Ustye later picked up a small infantry detachment led by a seafarer named Nikita Shalaurov near Lice Creek [*Vshivaia rechka*] and transported them to the Yana.

We can't help seeing proof in these reports that Russians were firmly rooted in the northern soil. There were quite a few of them, they felt sure of themselves in that area, they knew the tundra far to the east and west, and they used Russian and family names to designate their surroundings: for example, the Yelon River (from *elan'*) [a clearing in the woods], the Golyzhensky Channel, Lice Creek, and so on. All this had undoubtedly taken a long time to evolve.

In *A Journey along the Northern Shores of Siberia to the Arctic Ocean Undertaken in 1820, 1821, 1822, 1823, and 1824*[10] by Ferdinand Wrangel, the famous Arctic explorer, we find the following lines: "The inhabitants of the Siberian tundras make long journeys covering several thousand versts of monotonous, unpopulated expanses using nothing but small, windswept ridges of snow to determine the proper direction. Here I must mention the guides' amazing art of adhering to and remembering a given course." Matvey Gedenshtrom speaks of the same thing with wonder in *Excerpts about Siberia*:[11] "Every year professional hunters travel to distant islands in search of mammoth ivory. They choose their route according to the positions of snowdrifts and walls of ice. Long-standing experience has taught them how to determine which direction to take in order to reach the islands they want."

Both authors passed through Russkoe Ustye and speak of Russian river dwellers. Gedenshtrom counted 108 men in three settlements in the early nineteenth century. A hundred years later, in Zenzinov's time, there were far fewer. The language of Russkoe Ustye still contains the expression "the Zashiversk filth" ["*zashiverskaia pogan'*"], referring to smallpox, which twice wiped out the town of Zashiversk, on the middle stretch of the Indigirka, where the residents of the river's lower reaches were also registered, and which made merry among them, too, we must assume.

All this, of course, does not constitute direct, documentary evidence in support of the *prilog*, the story of Russians reaching the Indigirka from Russia by sea. It is evidence that this "could have happened," and it outweighs the "could not have happened." Direct evidence will probably never come to light now because, I repeat, here we see a clandestine expedition of a handful of Russian people who did not appear at the same time and by the same route as those who took part in the mass, legitimate colonization of Siberia that occurred later.

And now let's ask ourselves why we are so suspicious of legends. Don't they, in the majority of cases, bring us true events from the most ancient epochs, even from Old Testament times? A legend is not folklore, hearsay, or a beautiful story; it is not an artistic but a historical recollection that for some reason was not or could not be written down. It is also generally very choosy about facts and picks significant, crucial facts that lend themselves not to embellishment but to transmission along a human chain. And in this case, when a group of people found themselves isolated far from their original ethnic milieu, a legend could not afford to yield to invention one bit. Acting as a support cable and embodying the first words about the exodus that were directed toward the future, it had to choose real life as the most durable and steadfast material. Our ancestors easily distinguished the voices of fact and fable; this legend, which seems beautiful now, was once prosaic in action and sound, having descended to earth not from the heavens but from a sailboat, and did not lend itself to such artistic forms of narration as the *bylina* or the tale. This is material of an ordinary, everyday cut, distinct from festive attire in its tatters and simple seams.

But why is it absolutely necessary to determine whether the legend is deceiving us or not? Out of love for the legend? Out of love for the truth? For both reasons, obviously, but most of all out of a desire to understand the unique, exceptional phenomenon of an old language and an old way of life that are still intact. The twentieth century, of course, has left its mark even on the people of Russkoe Ustye. Things are far different there now from what they were at the beginning of the twentieth century, when Bogdanov wrote: "An archaeologist would consider it his greatest good fortune if, after excavating a sixteenth- or seventeenth-century grave, he could then clothe the ancient skeleton in the appropriate garb of life with any sort of accuracy, give it a soul, and hear its speech. In Russkoe Ustye the archaeologist doesn't need to exhume ancient people. In Russkoe Ustye these ancient people stand before him as if they had never died." You certainly can't say this today, but what does remain preserved in "the garb of life" and especially in the language of the Russians there seems astonishing and makes you suddenly wonder, What century is this, anyway?

Scholars came up with a simple explanation: the Far North, the difficult conditions for subsistence, the remoteness from civilization, being surrounded by non-Russians, and the extreme isolation (for a long time the men of Russkoe Ustye didn't even have to serve in the military) were more conducive than anything imaginable to preserving all they had. In this regard the permafrost proved an excellent medium for conservation, leaving everything that ended up there in its original state for centuries. And we must take these reasons into account, for they are actually quite significant, but we need to regard them as conditions equally favorable for the preservation of forces that contained unbelievable powers of resistance and that set resistance as their goal from the very start. Let's not forget that while Russians were found all over the Arctic in virtually identical natural, non-Russian surroundings, the majority of those living next door to a strong people like the Yakuts became assimilated and lost half their native language. Half indeed! Maydell recounts how in one large Russian village in the Olekminsk Region, where he had traveled, not a single person understood Russian. The former Russians along the Kolyma called themselves Kolymans and those along the Indigirka a hundred versts [about sixty-five miles] south of Russkoe Ustye became Indigirkans, realizing that they were neither Russians nor Yakuts but something in between, that they'd been ground to a uniform consistency and mixed together, and that they belonged to a locality but not to a particular ethnic group.

The Russians of Russkoe Ustye did not succumb to the powerful influence of the Yakuts, Yukagirs, Evens [Lamuts], and Chukchi who surrounded and outnumbered them. They mastered only the most essential hunting, fishing, and household terms in the local languages, for things that did not exist in their former daily routines and thus did not have names. They didn't succeed in completely preserving the purity of their race—an admixture of Yukagir and Yakut blood is apparent—but this was unavoidable, for self-replacement from the

Modern Arctic dwellers

same small circle of people threatened them with degeneration. And yet roughly one out of every four inhabitants of Russkoe Ustye retains the regular contours of the Russian face, which in them seemed to bear traces of asceticism and self-sacrifice and looked somehow rather dry, as though seared from within by a piercing gaze. You still see such faces only in the oldest villages of Old Believer origin. And this pure-blood-ed type, along with the type of face that was once partially but not repeatedly affected by Asiatic intermingling, suggest that the first Russians arrived at the lower Indigirka in families, unlike the Cossacks, hunters, and fishermen who moved downriver from the south and who, practically without exception, had to take non-Russian wives. But they did not arrive in families as a result of the great religious schism; their exodus could only have taken place before the Schism because they had no recollections of it whatsoever.

The uncommon ethnic stability, the self-contained old way of life, the isolation of language and customs, the striking retentiveness of memory—all these taken together are evidence, far from groundless albeit indirect, that here we are dealing with an exception rather than with the rule, with something utterly separate and out of the ordinary. Just think: nearly half the language spoken in Russkoe Ustye has vanished everywhere else in Russia, but there, perhaps unconsciously, words that lost their connections to objects when transplanted to the new environment found other meanings not adverse to their original designations and continued to live on. There were no cattle, so they called dogs *cattle* and kennels *cowsheds*—and they didn't let the words die. Who among us now knows the meaning of *vich'*, *vadiga*, *golk*, *edoma*, *narva*, *svetsy*, and so on? We aren't the only ones who don't recognize these words—Russians living near the inhabitants of the lower Indigirka don't know what they mean either. Pronunciation there differed so drastically from the norm that even now when people from Russkoe Ustye switch to their own dialect it's almost impossible to understand them. The neighboring Indigirkans and Kolymans had trouble understanding them even a hundred years ago. Their pronunciation cannot be compared to anything else; it is an inseparable combination of human and natural intonations that have merged into a single muffled, whooshing stream of sound.

And, finally, we come to folklore. Russkoe Ustye is like an oasis in the drought of poetry surrounding it. How this oasis could have avoided withering, losing its voice, and freezing to death becomes one more insoluble riddle if we lump the Russians of Russkoe Ustye together with everyone else. Even Zenzinov was amazed to encounter variations of "What It Was Like in the Town of Astrakhan" [*Kak vo gorode bylo vo Astrakhani*], the folk song that Pushkin put down on paper. The different versions immediately suggest that the song could have been picked up on the Indigirka from a source other than Pushkin's text, that it could have arrived by some route of its own. During his stay there Zenzinov wrote down several historical songs, dance tunes, and a *bulia* (*bylina*) and also reconstructed a wedding with all its richness in ritual; even back then, however, he lamented that the folklore in Russkoe Ustye showed every sign of living out its last years. Fortunately he was mistaken, and the discovery and recording of folklore in Russkoe Ustye continued and still continues decades later. One expedition alone, which T. A. Shub led in 1946 and which included Nikolay Alekseevich Gabyshev,[12] then a teacher in Chokurdakh and later a well-known Yakut writer, brought back sixty-two tales, eleven *byliny*, and more than one hundred songs. Quite recently the Academy of Sciences' Institute of Russian Literature issued a sizable separate volume titled *The Folklore of Russkoe Ustye*,[13] which consists largely of Gabyshev's recordings, but which also contains research done before and after the 1946 expedition, including work from the last few years. Folklorists feel that, from their point of view, the main value of Russkoe Ustye as a haven for folk poetry is not so much the number of recordings as the uniqueness and original state of several historical songs and *byliny* that are no longer preserved anywhere else or that are preserved in later redactions.

Zenzinov was mistaken, but today there can be no mistake: the last folk song is now reaching its final refrain and the last tale is nearing its conclusion—they can't compete with television, with Valery Leontiev and Alla Pugachyova [contemporary popular singers]—and for a long time there has been no trace of the former communal fortress that was capable of making the right choice. Here it's important to note that for a gold mine of this sort to be preserved and carried all the way down to the present, it must have been kept not on scattered pages but in a communal, well-made book. Other material, of course, was added later: the Cossack songs and the urban romantic songs (no doubt imported by merchants, trade facilitators, and exiles) that took root there attest to this. Roads to Russkoe Ustye were marked out in the nineteenth century, and, whether involuntarily or of their own free will, many people came to call. Even before that, however, an occasional Cossack, hunter, or fisherman would enter the ranks of permanent residents, for Russkoe Ustye did not expand along the branches of the

Indigirka without an inflow from the outside, which brought along melodies, words, and habits that had only recently come into being. As time went on, Russkoe Ustye expanded and renewed itself, but it must have kept its former guiding heart and core, derived from the families who had arrived first. Otherwise the words of yore in songs and tales surely would not have survived.

Language, folklore, and tradition more than anything else helped those people hold out in a land long referred to as the outer limit of survival and made them appear completely Russian in the eyes of Russia, even more Russian in some respects than those of us who have remained within the ethnic body as a whole. And now, when they have come practically out of nowhere ("Russia lost all track of them") and joined us, instead of taking a close, careful look at them and finding out the source (finding out the reason) for their miraculous salvation, we ask Ivan the Terrible or Czar Alexis for information verifying how they arrived, by land or by sea, and whose trade or business led them there, those children of different regions and a different nature, and what their arrival signifies. "Rus is strange!" people in Russkoe Ustye would exclaim when something incomprehensible reached them from our quarter; now, too, they have every right to say with perplexity, "Rus is strange!"

Even if the legend could be proven true, nothing in the world, of course, would change. We would not grow more wheat, or mine more coal, or even catch more fish and polar fox on the Indigirka; our society's accumulation of material things would not increase as a result. And a separately filled page in the history of the settlement of empty Siberian lands would add nothing to the general view of the region's history. Nothing in the world would change. Except for one thing. A legend that has remained a legend would become fact, and we, then inclined to believe our ancestors' words, might regard our own words with greater responsibility.

And for some reason it just makes you feel good when a legend, like a promise, comes true. Let's visualize it this way: a legend hung wearily in the air in outline form for decades on end, growing fainter and fainter only because there was no one on earth to draw a likeness of it with which it could coincide and thus come to life. But now a likeness finally emerges . . . I'm not speaking here about our legend but about legends as a whole. Now a likeness finally emerges, what had been suspended in the air descends weightlessly onto it and matches up with it at every point, and a miracle occurs: out of nothing comes an intelligible, persuasive voice confirming that no truth and no action in the world is lost forever.

Concerning our legend, it had, has, and will always have a sufficiently large number of defenders. Here is what Sergey Azbelev, one of the collectors and compilers of *The Folklore of Russkoe Ustye*, writes in an article in that book:

Among the current place names in the Indigirka Delta are some going back to the names of several leaders of the Cossack expeditions that passed through there in the middle and second half of the seventeenth century. This fact indicates that some kind of Russian population already existed then. No one else could have bestowed those names and preserved them.

That's true, you know. How else could they have taken hold?

In recent years one group after another has outfitted itself for expeditions to the Arctic region and to the North Pole; some go by dog sled, some on skis, some on their own two feet. Newspapers write about every step they take, every little adventure; television chronicles these events as if broadcasting from a theater of military operations, and the voices of the announcers, interrupting each other, force us to follow the daredevils' fate with racing hearts. These expeditions have many objectives, but their main goal is to test the capabilities of the human body under harsh arctic conditions and at the same time to match the feats, under comparable circumstances, of the first pioneers who journeyed across land and ice. I am not suggesting that we recall yet another means of travel and head out with small, two-masted sailboats across the Obonezhskaya Territory of old Novgorod, Chudskoe Zavolochye, and Podvinye, then along the shores of the White and Kara Seas, sailing farther and farther east past the mouths of the great Siberian rivers. I am not suggesting this because I know what these expeditions mean for northerners. They are no better than a natural disaster. Border guards, aviators, radio operators, hunters, fishermen, geologists, meteorologists—all are taken away from their work and pressed into service

ensuring safety, supplying emergency assistance, and providing surveillance, escorts, warnings, and maintenance. In Polyarny residents have
given up their best dogs and prepared sleds and clothing, in Chokurdakh one party took a snowmobile from the Fish Protection Service
(they left money in return, but in the Arctic the problem isn't money;
it's where to get something for money), and in Chersky on the Kolyma
a fleet of arctic aircraft was converted into transport planes for ferrying
hordes of journalists, writers, and admirers to the ice floe that some
routine expedition was approaching so that they would be there in
time to greet the group with ardent embraces. And not only aircraft:
the whole huge Lower Kolyma District devoted itself to the fuss and
bother of receptions, rapturous publicity, and hospitality, which, I must
point out, ends up costing the local populace a great deal and takes its
toll on them afterward.

No one means to discount the courage of the participants in present-day polar expeditions: the Arctic is the Arctic, and it demands a
tremendous expenditure of physical, psychological, and superhuman
strength under any conditions, even the most ideal. But surely this cannot compare with what our ancestors experienced when they went off
in dog sleds and small sailboats across many thousands of versts to
places where no one was expecting them and no one met them, where
it was impossible to convey to anyone else in the whole world what
was happening to them, about which even their graves remained silent.
If this takes courage today, what did it take back then? This something,
which faced a greater degree of risk and effort than we can imagine,
was called simply patience. People of old were given not to words but
to action and know-how.

Just as you can't reproduce one person in another, you can't dupli-
cate events. You can cover the very same route with more than your
share of misfortune, but that misfortune is weighed on today's scale,
not yesterday's. In comparison with their ancestors, people today have
clearly declined in terms of physical stamina and spiritual uprightness.
We have excelled in other areas—in soccer and hockey, for instance—
that also demand stamina and uprightness but in different tendons. Yet
our ancestors wouldn't understand this either. They relegated *kulika*
(an old form of hockey) to childhood because they wanted to strength-
en their tendons, not wear them out.

The scientific concerns of the modern treks that follow in virgin footsteps are not capable, and indeed have no intention, of penetrating our ancestors' holy of holies and kindred of kindreds: their sense of ethnicity. This feeling must have been just as powerful as their physical hardiness and pioneering savvy, and it was especially necessary for achieving their goal in the place where they were carving out a new homeland. Duplicating their route to the Indigirka, whether by land or by sea, is probably feasible, but it's impossible to travel the same route using the same means of survival as our ancestors. This simply defies imagination; time and again the requirements for life out there exceeded human resources many times over. Members of polar expeditions know what it means to spend only one winter under conditions that even today are considered extreme, but for the first settlers those winters went on and on forever.

And doesn't the key, the secret to the uncommon fate of those people lie in what they emphasized right from the start by choosing the names *Russkoe Zhilo* and *Russkoe Ustye*? On the day they arrived they determined the only way of life and set of rules that could help them preserve the makeup of their group. We have to suspect that they did not simply speak Russian, the language given to them by nature, without being aware of it or putting any feeling into the usual questions and answers, but that they spoke it with joy, finding it a pleasure to listen to each other as well as to their ancestors through the poetic compositions of old. And they did not simply maintain traditions and observe rituals in order to fulfill an obligation, but rather regarded them almost with visceral satisfaction: what was a burden for the inhabitants of European Russia constituted just as great a necessity in Russkoe Ustye as food and sleep. That is why the Russians there have retained both talkativeness and a liveliness of feeling. After lighting a fire in the *chuval* (the fireplace), they would spend the long arctic night recalling tales, songs, and *buli*, reciting them together and taking turns, and then the older folks would make sure the younger ones didn't leave out a single word that had been brought from the old homeland. Folklorists have observed that the *byliny* and ballads in Russkoe Ustye match the original, definitive texts almost perfectly. Whoever deviated from them would be dismissed with displeasure by a wave of the hand: you don't know how. We mustn't think that this protective force operated for

centuries all by itself; no, it probably operated according to some seeing and unswerving will.

And this means that while the Russians on the Indigirka lived in
friendship and harmony with Yakuts and Yukagirs and Evens, the way
people who share a single land as neighbors ought to live, they always
felt themselves to be Russian and demonstrated this in every way.

311
✦✦✦

THE SENDUKHA

Few people in the Arctic call the tundra *tundra*. They call it the
sendukha, giving this archaic word spoken with a modern tongue an
authoritative ring. *Tundra* designates geography and pedigree; *sendukha*
is nature's primordial power, all-encompassing and almighty, which
punishes and rewards, a single breath of infinite extent. Geologists
work with instruments in the tundra and border guards keep watch
over it, dividing it into squares; the sendukha, where the *sendushny*,
chuchuna, and *chandala* roam, is also where Evens, Yukagirs, and
Chukchi, the true children of that land and that sky, make their home
and their living, as do the Yakuts and Russians who arrived later but
became entirely one with the sendukha. "Mother Sendukha, at whose
breast we are fed!" they all exclaim, praying and giving thanks to it
each in his own language. The tundra can be freely measured, studied,
and adapted for various purposes whereas the sendukha eludes everyone; you can fly in from Moscow a hero and vanish the next day without a trace, lost in a quagmire or snowbank at some unmarked point.
The sendukha is the essential force (*stikheia*, as the local folks say), the
single spirit that rules over land and water, darkness and light.

Nowhere does the sky press as closely to the earth as it does there.
Unlike the steep banks of the Kolyma or the Indigirka, where layers of
soil alternate with layers of pure ice in the places that have been torn
away, it doesn't rise from the edges to tower overhead but lies above the
great flat land in a smooth wide-openness that plunges below the earth
along the ring of the horizon. And likewise the horizon itself is not an
enclosure or an obstruction to the eye but a distant prospect that weak-
ens the gaze. Even before the astronomic and geographic discoveries of
the Middle Ages, people in the tundra must have drawn the conclusion

that the Earth is round: out there it revealed the curve of its surface without requiring any calculations.

And there under that low sky the Siberian rivers flow into the ocean, lending their names to the tundra and marking it off into the Lena, Yana, Indigirka, and Kolyma regions; the rivers are treeless and unadorned in those parts as they collect the turbid water of the tundra. Between them lie hundreds and hundreds of versts (it's somehow inappropriate to measure the sendukha in kilometers) covered with a dense patchwork of lakes, large and small laidas (lakes in the process of drying up), and *lyviny* and *viski* (channels). The land itself consists of *kaltus*, *veret'e*, and *edoma* with steep, broad gullies. All these words are Russian, but nowadays even the Russian ones have to be explained more often than not: a *kaltus* is a wetland, a *veret'e* is a somewhat higher and drier area, a *edoma* is a hill, and the gullies between them are called *razlogi*. For those who have lived in the countryside, who found the Russian language alive and as yet unfiltered through the sieve of radio and television, these words require no translation.

When you fly over the tundra in the summer, you can't tell whether there is more water or more land. Wherever you look you see nothing but a lacework of water, which seems uniform and artificially contrived: water is drying up in some places and showing through in others, which makes the pattern appear even odder and more intricate. The channels flowing out of the lakes and laidas look like canals dug with the aid of a ruler; they maintain the same width between their banks even where they turn, and, after rounding a bend, straighten out again and move along without the least bit of pushing and shoving from side to side. The laidas hung out along them are drying up, and vegetation appears immediately wherever they become partially dry. There are bright green patches, then brown splotches, then faded spots arranged like footprints, as if some gigantic animal had passed through, stamping out tracks.

And how beautiful the tundra is in the summer! Wintertime is another matter: in the winter it is cloaked in exhaustingly white snow, in a heavy, impassive monotony in which even the elevated spots, the *veret'e* and *edoma*, look like mere snowdrifts. In the winter beauty shifts to the sky, which becomes fierce and bright with stars, all the more so when the northern lights are flashing. But in the summer . . . Summer doesn't last very long: there is still snow on the ground in May, lingering at the base of small hills until more snow comes; the rivers aren't free of ice until the middle of June; then snow begins to fall again in August. Summer is extremely short, and you won't find orchards and oak groves flourishing on the tundra; the only trees are dwarf birches no bigger than a good-sized whortleberry bush and willows that get smaller and smaller as you near the ocean until they become stunted pickings for birds. White splashes of partridge grass and valerian lie among the mosses, along with a lot of swamp grass and a kind of mint comparable to dandelions except that it is sticky and has shaggy heads; there are also red cloudberries. And moss, moss, moss . . . Reindeer moss grows on drier ground, while the low-lying areas have a clean carpeting of young, green moss. Seen from above, this uniform speckledness looks like the shell of a huge turtle; from below it defies comparison—just watch out so you don't land in some water.

The closer you get to the ocean, the more lakes and laidas you find. The ground is littered with white reindeer antlers and covered with mounds of driftwood, timber washed out by the rivers and heaped up on the shore, which has been lying there for years, even decades; the piles of wood look like several lines of defense fortifications arrayed against the ocean. Judging from the driftwood, I'd say that the shore is advancing, pushing the ocean back little by little. Colonies of swans live beside the lakes, pacing about handsomely and pompously in pairs; there are lots of geese, although the local residents observe that in recent years their numbers have declined noticeably.

Huge black sandbars lie at the boundary between land and sea. There is no real boundary as such: in some places there is water, in others land, and in others the two are mixed into a sticky silt. Up there, generally speaking, water, earth, sky, shore, dry land, time, distance, and people all require special definitions. Water and earth argue endlessly over which will be what. Time taps out its increments not in dribs and drabs as it does everywhere else but on a large scale: the arctic day and the arctic night. The wind can start blowing so hard that if it doesn't stop in two days, it will keep on for a week. Until recently the units of distance were either the coast-dwellers' *dnishche* (one day's rowing) or the Yakuts' *kes* (roughly one hour's travel by dog sled). A unit of distance was a unit of time, whereas a unit of time was some

Driftwood

customary activity. Someone would say, "He rode until the teakettle came to a boil." And it was immediately clear how long a ride "a teakettle on the fire" meant; nobody needed a more precise explanation.

Under those conditions, with quantities and definitions all mixed together, people, too, had to represent something special. Not on a moral plane—that's another story—and not in outlook and occupation but somehow in physical makeup. They had no choice but to let the tundra enter them to the same extent that the land there let in water.

They not only took food and drink from the tundra, lived in it, bowed down to it, and obeyed its rules, but they also carried it inside themselves as part of their personality, along with winter's numbness, blizzards, and freezing cold and summer's impetuosity and welcomeness. As far as I know, few of those who went off to other regions ever became acclimated elsewhere. After five years, seven years, ten years they would go back, unable to restructure themselves, to alter their nature: their internal rhythm did not coincide with the external one, which led to a dangerous discord and confusion. I am now speaking of the Russian tundra-dwellers: what does this say for the Yukagirs or the Chukchi, the true children of that land? The outer limit of survival and sorrow (a novella by Wacław Sieroszewski, a Polish exile, has that very title, "The Outer Limit of Sorrow"[14]) had become the Promised Land. Here indeed is something to mull over when we discuss the concept of homeland and try to explain it.

We aren't the only ones who said, "The place where you were born is the place where you belong."

There are also examples of a different order. In recent times the Arctic coast has begun to attract people not only because of high wages or because they are running away from their wives as though fleeing Ivan the Terrible's bodyguards, so that "Russia would lose all track of them"; they are also going there to live permanently, choosing that life of their own free will. They can't be compared with the first inhabitants, for the distance between them is as great as the distance between the sixteenth and twentieth centuries: some houses in Chersky on the Kolyma and in Chokurdakh on the Indigirka now have hot plates and televisions and steam heat, and you can even find work close to home. You'll have to bend over backward if you want to exchange an apartment in Sochi [a resort town on the Black Sea] for one on the Kolyma in Chersky; northerners don't like to turn over living quarters obtained with great difficulty to temporary residents, who still make up the majority of those employed at construction sites, in aviation, at seaports, and at transfer points for cargo.

But people keep going there, and they go to stay. On my last visit to Polyarny I went to see some new arrivals who hadn't been there during my first trip. Pavel Nikolaevich Kovalyov and his wife, Nelli Nikolaevna, are no longer young; they're over fifty, and once past that threshold of age, people usually seek a refuge for eternity. Pavel Nikolaevich had helped build a school there about ten years earlier and, as he explains it, he got used to the sparse population. No matter where he lived after that, it always seemed noisy and crowded and he always felt drawn to return. And so he made arrangements by mail, lined up a job, and left the Big Land.

"That Big Land isn't back there—it's right here. There isn't even any land left back there, there's nothing to look at, nothing but soot and racket everywhere," he said.

"And do you feel calmer now?"

"Yes, I do. I'll go out into the sendukha, sit down on whatever I happen to find, and just sit there and look around and breathe. And I'm not afraid that somebody will come along and shove me aside or cuss me out."

Yury Karachentsev had lived in Polyarny for about fifteen years. For seven of those years he worked as a highly skilled hunter. In the Arctic you can readily become a medical technician, an electrician, a doctor, or a teacher and not experience any particular interruption in the pleasant course of life or any loss of the customary crutches. But to become a hunter, to have your own share of tundra with hundreds of snares and steel traps, to keep a dog team, to hunt for weeks at a time in solitude, to sleep in the snow when it's -40°C [-40°F]—not everyone has this capability. Open the gates and let the tundra enter you, acknowledge the existence of the *sendushny*, that spirit of the tundra and capricious protector of hunters, remember the *chuchuna* with its bow, that wild creature of fact and fiction that either was not granted or declined the honor of becoming a human being, look closely at the sky, get used to the smell of the wind, and heed the aching in your joints. Otherwise you won't be able to cope. Rely on yourself but don't forget about "faith"; there "faith" covers a whole collection of tundra rules and regulations, hidden and obvious, some of which do not reveal themselves to anyone and can be fathomed only if you have an exceptional knack. "Such is our faith," the people of Russkoe Ustye say enigmatically without giving any explanation—they would be unable to—as to which part of their "faith" pertains to the tundra and which to human beings, which to skills and precautions and which to the sparkling flashes from those other worlds of conjecture and premonition.

Karachentsev became a good hunter. He trapped plenty of fox and got lots of fish in his allotted catches, and he understood dogs, and he learned to read the tundra as well as anyone, and he didn't spare himself while hunting, and he was acknowledged by the local, native-born huntsmen as a full-fledged hunter. It wasn't easy for a native of other, warmer climes to reset his internal dial for the Arctic and, once there, to choose a life in the tundra, but he seemed to have familiarized himself with everything required of a hunter. He became familiar with everything, and yet not completely. That tiny, miniscule something that escaped him had nothing to do with experience or with the premonitions that make up for limited experience; it was linked to his being an outsider not deeply rooted there. He had picked up everything he needed to know for hunting, he could guess whatever had to be guessed, and when he had no choice but to trust his instincts, he trusted them; there was probably nothing more that he could have acquired. All he lacked were some special particles, some special salts, that only the local land can build up in you from birth. And, knowing everything, able to do everything, he still felt undersalted inside.

The incident that nearly cost Karachentsev his life took place several years ago, at the beginning of November. He had returned from his trapline to his hunting shack toward evening and hadn't unhitched his dogs or made a fire yet when suddenly a fox flashed by. The dogs got all excited; he jumped into the sled just as he was, in a quilted vest and light mittens, and started chasing the fox. Telling the story, he pronounced the word *chase* the way all the Russians in Russkoe Ustye do: *pogonil* instead of *pognal*. Catching the animal did not prove easy, in the heat of the chase he didn't turn back right away, and half an hour later a blizzard sprang up.

He spent seven days in the snow, buried in a snowdrift with his dogs. For seven days the tundra rocked like a tossing ship as the storm lashed and howled continuously. He had to get up every half hour or forty minutes and shake the dogs to keep them for getting buried so deeply that they wouldn't be able to crawl out later. I won't try to describe what a person might feel in this situation, for only those who experience it can know. On the fifth day he decided to eat the young dog that played more in harness than it pulled. He dragged it out from under the snow and . . . felt sorry for it. After that he put his carbine to his own chest. What kept him from pulling the trigger was the thought of his newborn son. Toward the end of a week he saw flashes of lightning in the sky, used them to get his bearings, shook his dog team awake, and headed north. He came out at one of his snares and found the road to his shack. The stove was all set up for a fire, but he couldn't light a match: his mittens had frozen to his skin. When somehow he finally got a fire started, he went outside so he wouldn't go crazy. The old folks said that if you looked at fire after you'd been in that kind of fix, you'd go out of your mind.

He never would have made it home by dog sled. The Polar Station was closer, so he went even farther north. The people staying there that winter sent for a plane. He didn't sleep for three weeks: the *neminia* (a *neminia* is a tornado or storm) was still whipping and roaring as before and he had to keep shaking the dogs awake. But once he did fall asleep. . . . They even fed him while he slept. A month after he left the hospital he found the place where he'd sat out the storm: on the ice of a lake. Falcon, the pup he had intended to eat, became his lead dog. One time, recalling what might have happened (he was certain that if he'd eaten the dog, he himself would have perished), he was deeply moved and stopped the sled, but Falcon barked, unhappy at having stopped too early, before the *poperdo*. A *poperdo* is a rest break for a dog team.

Pavel Cheryomkin, a native of Russkoe Ustye and one of the finest and most productive hunters on the state farm, patted the neck of his former lead dog, the "retired" Charcoal, and said, "He saved my life several times." Concerning Yury Karachentsev, his response was, "Good for him—he didn't panic. Only why did he run out into the sendukha half an hour before a blizzard was going to hit?! Up here you've got to keep your eyes open all the time." Innokenty Ivanovich Soldatov, describing the art of hunting handed down to him for life by his stepfather, old Golyzhensky, said proudly, "I've never spent a single night in the snow." But of his stepson and apprentice, Iosif Shchelkanov, who couldn't boast of the same, he said with certainty, "He doesn't have the knack."

Having the knack is valued there as a God-given talent, and God is viewed as a force in which the sendukha also plays a significant part.

TO SIT DOWN ON THE SNOW AND FALL ONTO THE GRASS

When I entered Russkoe Ustye in January of 1866, I couldn't for the life of me grasp where I was—granted, it was quite dark—or what was happening around me. I was apparently riding across a completely level spot without even a bush let alone a house standing out anywhere, and yet fiery columns appeared on all sides, rising from the ground. I even saw a cross that seemed to be sticking up out of the ground a short distance from my sled, which my driver told me was the cross of the chapel located in Russkoe Ustye. But then the sled stopped and a door opened way down below us—a ray of light shot up at me as if from a cave. I had to descend at a steep angle, and I found myself before the door of a little dwelling with a flat roof in which a fire was burning brightly and where it was very pleasant and cozy after the long ride in the cold. The mystery was cleared up the next day: the whole place was snowbound and each little house was encircled by a wall of snow that stood exactly as high as the building itself and about three feet away from it, thus forming only a narrow passageway. Every homeowner maintains a very steep path from his door to the wall of snow, which you reach by climbing the path, and only then do you realize that you are dealing not with a separate wall but with a solid mass of snow that covers the whole settlement like a flat hill. You see before you nothing but an endless snowy surface with quadrangular depressions here and there; these are the houses with their surrounding passageways. This is what Russkoe Ustye looks like in the winter. During the warm season the houses rise up out in the open, of course, but they are surrounded by the endless, monotonous tundra of the Arctic seaboard. Not a single tree or a single bush is visible anywhere, which also presents a fairly bleak picture.

This was Baron Maydell's impression of Russkoe Ustye. Many other travelers of the recent and distant past whose routes reached as far as the lower Indigirka formed roughly the same impression, of a cheerless and depressing place. The snow in winter and the water in summer

have not diminished over the centuries. This is what the original settlers' very first winter in Russkoe Ustye was like, and from then on "to
sit down on the snow" ["*sadit'sia na sneg*"] has meant to carve out a new
home in an uninhabited place. And "to fall onto the grass" ["*na
travushku upast'*"] means to be born into the wide world [literally, the
white world (*belyi svet*)], which there, for the most part, truly is white.

They arrived, they sat down on the snow, and then kids began
falling onto the grass. They brought their language, faith, customs, and
spirit with them; this load did not weigh very much, but it proved no
less useful than food and *lopot'* (clothing). Whether they came with
dogs or not is impossible to make out across the distance of the years,
but dogs apparently did not exist in the Arctic before Russians arrived.
If the Russians didn't master reindeer herding, it means that they never
engaged in that occupation and traveled by dog sled from the very
beginning.

Their whole life was hunting and fishing. Their whole world was
family and the tundra. There was no time to sit around *na razveziakh*
(nurturing doubts): the harsh land demanded a great deal of activity,
extremely sharp wits, and limitless strength. And when that same Maydell accused the Russians in Russkoe Ustye of laziness, everyone who
went there after him replied unanimously, Not true. We need no special proof to understand that survival under those conditions meant
they had to keep moving like a house afire, to be in a whirl summer
and winter as if someone had wound them up.

God's deer (wild reindeer) provided meat and hides; polar fox were
first used for barter and later traded for money. When a market developed for mammoth ivory, they began making special trips to search for
it, traveling all the way to the New Siberian Islands. The Indigirka supplied them with an abundance of fish and also brought driftwood logs
from its upper reaches, which they stockpiled for fuel and construction
material. But before heating with it, they used that same driftwood to
build cottages. The Russians, who loved beauty and a finished look,
probably did not give up their pitched roofs right away; only when
they realized that no peak could withstand the destructive winds did
they resign themselves to "modest" ["*stydkie*"] cheerless cottages as flat
as a box. Before they had mica or glass they made windows out of burbot skins, which they sealed in winter with a layer of ice. To this day

residents of Russkoe Ustye seal the windows of private homes with ice for warmth.

They started keeping *svetsy* (wooden calendars) so as not to lose any days or mix up weekdays and holidays, and, just like on our calendars, the big religious holidays that underlay everything were specially singled out and the work rhythm set accordingly. They were fated to get along without bread, without salt and milk, for many long decades, possibly even centuries, and—what else could they do?—they got used to it; scholars would later label them ichthyophagous. It's no wonder that, as Zenzinov writes, they didn't know what a wheel was and asked how flour grows. Trying to explain grain to them, he was forced to compare it to fish roe. It had gone out of use and the whole concept had vanished. When bread came back they didn't call it bread but *chernostriapano*, to distinguish it from *tel'no*, a kneaded fishcake, and *toptanik*, a loaf with fish filling inside a fish dough. There were no vegetables or cereal grains, and even berries were limited to cloudberries and bilberries. They substituted sourness for saltiness: they pickled fish and birds. To this day fanciers of that cuisine, young folks as well as old, prefer slightly spoiled goose, just as their ancestors did two and three hundred years ago.

But what about scurvy, avitaminosis, and so on? Were these illnesses simply looking the other way? Why, without green vegetables and salt, without milk and sugar, didn't they knock body and soul out of those cut-off and deprived people? Especially since they knock them out of us today despite our full complement of domestic and foreign vitamins, when we have plenty of everything, when everything is written out and we all know at which hour to take what, what to emphasize, and what to avoid, and yet we keep becoming less and less healthy.

Every natural habitat appears to contain the right juices for a full measure of life. As long as nature exists, that is. And it did exist in the Arctic, and for the time being still does. Our present satiety, our flirting with vitamins, is nothing other than a decorous tinkering with our own wires. As we kill nature, as we destroy water and air, forests, and the fruits of forests, water, and the land, how can we possibly not take care to put a good face on a sorry situation?! We are like the doctor who learned not how to cure but how to console, and when his own turn came, instead of administering drugs he told himself a lie, too, having forgotten that he wasn't some extraneous patient, and with that he departed for the next world without figuring out what had happened.

Northerners have always eaten raw fish. They call it *stroganina* [literally, shavings] (around Lake Baikal it is known as *raskolotka* [literally, splinters], for there they shave raw meat). At first glance the procedure for preparing *stroganina* seems rather crude: you grip a frozen fish, a chir or a white salmon, between your knees like a log and slice it into thin shavings, then salt and pepper it and pop it into your mouth. But even this uncomplicated procedure has its subtleties: northerners don't pile fish shavings on a plate in the same order in which they slice them but lay them out so that the tastiest piles, the fat belly pieces, come last, to build up greater and greater satisfaction. And this is true satisfaction! When people say that something melts in your mouth, they are trying to convey a sensation of bliss. That's just what happens here: the icy coating vanishes as soon as you put a piece into your mouth and the fish thaws out, melts with a butteriness that penetrates your whole body, is absorbed without being swallowed, and spreads gently and insistently throughout your entire system. Someone who has never heard of *stroganina* instantly finds it agreeable without any coercion (the fish is raw, after all) or pretense.

Stroganina satisfies and invigorates and warms you up. Thanks to it the residents of Russkoe Ustye don't know the meaning of scurvy. Everything else the body requires they obtained from meat, birds, sorrel, snakeweed roots, and fish oil. And from the water and air. In 1868 a pood [about thirty-six pounds] of fish oil cost thirty kopecks in Russkoe Ustye (according to Ivan Khudyakov's figures in *A Brief Description of the Verkhoyansk Region*).[15] By comparison a pound of tobacco cost up to five rubles. And this isn't the same foul-smelling fish oil we give to children; along the Indigirka it is exactly like butter—white, thick, and tasty.

To say that *stroganina* warms you up is not a slip of the tongue. One bright sunny day at the end of March we got ready to go out into the tundra with Yury Karachentsev, to display ourselves and to have a look at others. We put on fur hats and coats, hitched two sleds to his snowmobile, and headed out. And in the course of about three hours we actually did encounter almost the entire tundra population: hare and partridge and deer. We checked part of Karachentsev's trapline at the same time but didn't find any fox there and had to be content with its tracks; to make up for it, we got to watch him construct and set a *past'*, the kind of fox trap commonly used along the whole Siberian coast, from the Ural Mountains to the Pacific Ocean, since earliest times.

March is March and sunshine is sunshine, but the temperature was -22°C [-30°F] and, what's more, a breeze was tearing into us because of our speed. And we became chilled to the bone quite quickly. When you're freezing, you don't notice the crest of a *edoma* under the snow or the depressions of lakes or the small, windswept ridges of snow. You stop being amazed when what looks like a verst marker from several kilometers away becomes, up close, some sharp object sticking half a meter out of the ground, and the whole tundra blurs into an endless cold, bleached void. Noticing our silence, Karachentsev sensed our frame of mind and stopped the snowmobile.

"Now we're going to warm up."

Under such circumstances "to warm up," according to universal custom, means to break out a bottle. That is what we were prepared for. But instead of taking a bottle out of his bag, Karachentsev produced a chir, frozen rock hard, and began to shave off slices.

"Eat," he said as he offered us pieces. "Eat, eat, warm up."

We were already scarcely alive because of the cold, and then to swallow ice on top of it! That seemed tantamount to death.

The fish is fat and rich in calories, and it makes the body generate warmth like fuel thrown onto a hearth when the fire has died down. This is probably the best way to explain it. But hardly had I begun to perk up when for some reason a law of mathematics came to mind: a minus times a minus equals a plus. This happened very rapidly, as in mathematics or physics, and we continued on our way in good spirits, amazed at the miraculous change.

Northerners are so accustomed to *stroganina* that they can't go without it for a single day, winter or summer. What do they do in the summer? Nothing could be simpler: the whole tundra is one big freezer. Dig down a little way and you can preserve anything you like, even for centuries.

Zenzinov observed that, in addition to frozen fish, the Russians in

Russkoe Ustye ate unsalted strips cut from freshly caught live fish. They gnawed raw goose legs during goose season and reindeer tendons while hunting, and they did so without the slightest revulsion—on the contrary, with pleasure. We must assume that it was not because they had become savages, as an educated being will hastily surmise, but because they knew how to heed the call of their own flesh, which had not yet been sloughed off the body of nature for good. Now they have everything—green vegetables are brought in, and apples along with "applebet" soup, and all kinds of pickles and preserves—but just as in the past, a resident of Russkoe Ustye, glancing over his shoulder to see if anybody "from back yonder" ["*tamosnyi*"] is watching, will sink his teeth into the raw marrow of a reindeer leg, especially a frozen one, and savor it to his heart's content the way his grandfather did before they had apples and "applebet" soup. Isn't this why ripe old age is nothing rare in a place where you'd think all vital forces would be exhausted or frozen in no time?

We could probably try to imagine what life in Russkoe Ustye was like during those dark times that left no evidence behind, but all we could conjure up would be the round of cares and concerns linked to food and warmth. Relying on the echoes of tradition, of "faith," we can reconstruct the performance of rituals with some degree of accuracy, determining which part came when, what was spoken and sung, what was eaten and drunk. In addition we know that the people there gave up bread and salt, but was it easy for Russians raised on bread and salt to give them up? And to get used to the absence of forests, to the scarcity of "God's gifts" in the summer, to winter's universal numbness interrupted only when a *neminia* would spring up, whether on a whim or as punishment, and not leave them alone for weeks on end? And by casting our imaginations backward, can we really depict anything remotely like having a foreign region grow on you day after day and year after year or learn which words and concepts were derived from the tundra for this purpose? Were they the ones heard even today in the incantations "Father Fire-Czar! Mother Sendukha! Mother Indigirka!" or were there also others that fell out of use later on as the newcomers became acclimated and no longer needed them? Did the thoughts and feelings concerned only with survival, with a narrow circle of people and a narrow round of cares, grow dim? What was their greatest fear and their greatest joy? How did they maintain affectionate relations with each other, how did they guard against cursing each other (one of the most terrible curses was, "May you become constipated!" that is, let your constipation be my vengeance), and why did their moral standards calmly and even kindly tolerate "maiden" children [*"dev'i" deti*], those born out of wedlock? Who was the first to break away and establish a new "household" apart from the common "habitation" [*"zhilo"*]? And was that break voluntary or was it a punishment meted out by the old men who governed law and conscience? How did they get along with the Yukagirs and the Chukchi in the beginning without interpreters? Did they consider their exodus final?

Hunters, trappers, and fishermen who stayed only for the winter, who sat down on the arctic snow temporarily, were aided by the hope that if they just held out long enough, it would all come to an end and they would return with their fish and game to a normal life. In Russkoe Ustye it was forever. There the abnormal and the exceptional became the norm. And that process of acclimation rather than simply of survival, which drew on feelings, will, patience, and faith, is by now impossible for people of today to imagine. It has come and gone with as final an irreversibility as the era of Czar Alexis. People conform to their era not only in manner of thought but also in physical makeup, and the physical makeup of those times was capable of silently bearing burdens that somehow even defy comparison.

The Russians in Russkoe Ustye were not fussy: "What else do we need as long as God gives us some grub?" What today we call society's infrastructure wasn't exactly crawling out of the water and snow back in those days and didn't extend beyond what they could fashion with their own hands. Even if they'd had guns, such weapons would have been good for nothing but amusement without powder and shot. And so they made do without them. Khudyakov reports that during the second half of the nineteenth century "there were practically no guns in Russkoe Ustye; they used bows and arrows tipped with metal arrowheads." And what does this say about "tomorrow," "the day after tomorrow," and "the day after that" [*o "zakhtre," "poslezakhtre" i "natot-to"*] as we count backward through the centuries? They used spears to kill swimming deer from *vetki* (rowboats), shot birds with bows and arrows, set snares for them made out of horsehair, and also wove horsehair nets to catch fish and molting geese. That is how they started out and that is how they continued for a long time, until factory-made goods came into use and other foodstuffs became available. Gunpowder and shot were considered so precious that when flour began to appear, the Russians in Russkoe Ustye regarded powder and shot as a foodstuff because of their unavailability, the same category the old folks place them in even today.

The first order of business, along with "grub" ["*edishka*"], was warmth. In a frozen land without a single tree or bush, in a land with its own peculiar calendar, where spring, autumn, and winter were all winter, life itself depended on fuel. And there was only one choice: driftwood. Somewhere in the upper reaches of the Indigirka where there are forests, logs fall into the water along with chunks of the bank or the river washes down felled timber during floods and carries it off, transporting it hundreds of versts, stripping off its bark and bleaching it along the way, and up north all eyes are on the lookout to make sure nothing floats past. They built cottages out of driftwood, made and repaired snares with it, sheathed their boats with driftwood planks, and stockpiled firewood, firewood, and more firewood. They dragged it into the tundra to keep them warm in their cottages and hauled it with them in their sleds. Fire-worship is a long-standing practice there. Neither the old folks nor the young would forget to feed the fire, to throw pieces of food into it and thus win its favor. Incidentally, they don't forget nowadays either. Young people do it seemingly as a joke, but they still do it, keeping the superstition alive for the time when science will fail. For centuries it was "Father Fire-Czar, turn back this weather!" "Father Fire-Czar, give us a goose!" and "Father Fire-Czar, don't tell him" when it was necessary to conceal something from the *sendushny* or the bear.

Researchers link the worship of fire, the Indigirka, and the sendukha with popular beliefs taken from the local peoples, from the Yakuts and the Chukchi. But Slavs worshiped them, too, and to no less an extent. Aleksandr Afanasiev, whom we know as a collector of folk tales, described many of the practices found in Russkoe Ustye in his extremely valuable work *The Slavs' Poetic Views of Nature*.[16] Such beliefs did exist, living on for a long time side by side with the Orthodox faith.

Russians were prudent when it came to deities: Christianity was for the salvation of the soul, while the old religion was kept for maintenance of the belly (by the way, in Russkoe Ustye the word *zhivot* [stomach, belly] has not lost its original meaning of *life*). Out there, in the middle of nowhere, one faith was considered all the more insufficient. And besides, Christ didn't have time to bother with driftwood or molting geese, so the Indigirka dwellers apparently relieved him of worrying about such trifles.

For the Russians in Russkoe Ustye those were far from trifles. From the first day the Indigirka opened up until the day it froze over again they would "dig out" ["*kolupali*"] of the banks and lakes whatever timber the river had brought. They said "dig out" (this is not a borrowed phrase; it grew out of driftwood the same way *to fell timber* [*rubit' les*] arose in the taiga region) because they literally had to dig it out of the steep banks and the silt, using all their might. In Russkoe Ustye a log is called a *kolupok*. Thus the Indigirka provided not only fish but also warmth; it helped the river-dwellers catch fox and deer as well. And when the ice was being swept away the "Orthodox Christians" would go out onto the riverbank and bow down, to welcome the life and work that were unfolding. The first time they stepped into a boat after winter had ended they never failed to say, "Mother Indigirka, at whose breast we are fed, accept this little gift" as they threw colored scraps of cloth, *komochki*, into the water.

Their diet was and still is mainly fish. And what fish! Chir, muksun, white salmon, omul—all splendid and excellent. These are used for food, while the rest—pike, herring, and many others—are considered grub fit only for the dogs. It's hard to believe that they prepared a kind of porridge using fish roe [*ikra*], called it *ikranitsa*, ate it with a spoon, and made patties out of it. What didn't they make out of fish! I could start listing the various dishes, but the menu would be far from complete; I don't recall everything and didn't even sample everything. They have *shcherba, stroganina, tel'no*, dried fish, *ikrianka* (*shcherba* with roe), little pies called *pirozheniki*, fish hash (they also make goose hash), *tolkusha, baraban* (pancakes made with crushed roe), *borcha* (a smoked, crushed mixture resembling porridge), *varka* (crushed boiled fish), and so on.

But families weren't the only ones who needed fish. No one could go anywhere in the tundra without dogs, and only a few households kept just one team; more often than not they had two or even several teams. And they had to feed them fish. The horses in Russkoe Ustye could get by with foraging—if they survived, fine; if not, people could manage to live without them—but the dogs were looked after like children. Thanks to them, the word *broska*, meaning one meal for a dog, is still alive in the language spoken in Russkoe Ustye, but, surprisingly enough, the word *vich'* has also been preserved. In olden times, according to the *byliny*, *vich'* meant the daily ration for a *bogatyr'*, but in Russkoe Ustye it denotes the amount of food needed for a dog team. If a family of four had only one team, they figured they would need ten to twelve thousand small whitefish for the dogs and one thousand to twelve hundred "edible" ["*edomye*"] fish for themselves. And about four tons to use for bait in their fox traps. Modern times require an adjustment: now they must hand over two tons to the state farm. It's true that when the fish are running in June, they can catch up to one ton a day, for there are still plenty of fish. And then today they must also make one more adjustment: few people feed dog teams anymore, but snowmobiles need another kind of *vich'*, which is now being sought in the tundra more eagerly than life itself. And when it is discovered, the fish and the deer and the fox as well as the entire Mother Sendukha will be in for a bitter experience.

Fox are obtained the same way they were three hundred years ago. Some hunters, it's true, have tried steel traps, but the factories in our country slap them together any old way and they aren't much good. Pavel Cheryomkin, passionate and "fiery" ["*ozhignoi*"] about everything, howled at the top of his lungs when the talk turned to steel traps:

"You take a crate of them, sixty altogether—and you have to throw them all out. You can't press them back, you can't do—" Cheryomkin spent his term of military service on Sakhalin Island, where there was no ban on strong language, some of which he brought back with him. "The welded joints come apart in certain places, one right after another. They've started cluttering up the whole tundra."

Pasti, which existed in bygone days, are more dependable. What is a *past'*? The construction is just as simple as it is reliable: a log triggered by a *simka* (a horsehair or a fine thread) is suspended over a wooden platform and bait is strewn around it. When a fox takes the bait, it brushes against the *simka*, activating the trap, and the log kills the animal. The pelt is not damaged—as long as you retrieve it in time. If you delay, a fellow fox will leave nothing but clumps of fur.

A trapper would inspect his trapline from three to five times every winter. If the traps were far away each trip would take nearly a month. If he sang a song or howled like a wolf during those weeks, no one would respond; not a word or a sigh would second him. Only his dogs were nearby, and he had to keep his eyes glued to them so they wouldn't get all excited and take off after some animal racing by, leaving him to perish. How many times did that happen! Pavel Cheryomkin described how he once let his team get away from him and walked eighty kilometers—not walked but ran—back to town through the "arctic night" ["*poliarka*"] in a light sweater. Afterward they searched for the team by plane and almost didn't find it.

But the Russians of yore had no airplanes at their fingertips, and losing dogs had more dire consequences for them than for Cheryomkin, who today, to be on the safe side, also has a snowmobile. And what about losing the breadwinner? If a trapper doesn't return when he's supposed to nowadays, everything available on land and in the air is enlisted to search for him, but three hundred, two hundred, one hundred years ago a hunter had no one else to count on. His mother or wife would see him off, making the sign of the cross over him, then carry some wood chips into the house, set them down beside the fireplace, trying to conjure up a large number of fox or deer, and appeal to the tundra: "Mother Sendukha, protect our breadwinner." And that was all the help they had. Whether *khud'ba* (disease) struck them, or their dogs took sick, or they ended up in a *kuter'ga* (a blizzard), they themselves were their only hope.

And they lived like that for years, decades, centuries. Somewhere back yonder czars changed, wars were declared, reforms were carried out, academies and dumas opened their doors, views on the origin of the human race changed, and the greatest discoveries were made, but all this reached them, if it reached them at all, with the same dimness and delay as the light of distant stars. Life there remained subject in the same way, without any change, to the migratory routes of fox and deer, to the arrival and departure of birds, to the forming and melting of ice on the Indigirka. Fox traps and "fishing sands" were passed down from father to son, from son to son, and from his son on down. The measureless sendukha had long been divided into family tundras, it no longer contained any vacant, unclaimed land, the limitlessness found itself limited, and allotments increased only when they overlapped one another. Back yonder the latest philosophies were becoming firmly entrenched, while in Russkoe Ustye a newborn baby was still given two names: the parents would christen him Semyon but call him Ivan. "The evil eye" ["*porcha*"] would look for Ivan, but he was really Semyon. Or else they would try to confuse the Evil One by giving the child a dog's name, which was then actually transferred to a dog when the boy was a bit older and raising his own puppy, who, like a brother, never left his side.

They believed that the dead returned from the next world in the form of an infant. They would bore a hole in the coffin lid to make it easier for the deceased to get out. This return was called "coming back in reality" ["*priiti v"iavi*"]. But if they didn't want someone to return and repeat his bad qualities, they had no qualms about driving an aspen stake into his grave. Nowadays we would very likely be unnerved by such boldness. With our threadbare morality, which allows us neither to condemn nor to defend anyone based on his merits, we would allude to the notion that no one has the right to draw a final conclusion about the life someone else has led. In this instance the people of Russkoe Ustye, who seemed fashioned entirely out of prejudice, were quite open: Accept what you deserve until memory fades and don't plead for forgiveness, because that's how you were. When reflecting on the actions of today's "river-rerouting" father figures [*otsy-"perevorot-chiki"*], who are destroying our sacred national treasures up hill and down with the haste of an invading army, you involuntarily turn to this experience: it wouldn't be a bad idea for them to know that not everything is forgiven at the time of death. *To be forgiven*, incidentally, combined two meanings: a final sendoff and a release from blame, which the living would accept as their burden. And whatever could not be accepted would not be forgiven.

It's a great shame that we have no written *zavertushki* (word) from those rock-bottom days of earliest settlement as to what the Russians of Russkoe Ustye spake and wrought on arrival. Perhaps they were too busy with their strenuous labors to record anything, but most likely any written account simply vanished over time. The coast dwellers along the White Sea could read and write, as a rule; moreover, the legend explains that the founders of Russkoe Ustye were eminent people. And we should by no means hasten to attribute this to the embellishment characteristic of local legends. Let's not forget that if people were escaping the oppression of a supremely irate sovereign, it wasn't the simple folk who would have had to escape first. Simple folk could wait it out, whereas prominent families would have been better off taking to their heels.

The legend was nearly one hundred years distant from any eyewitness accounts when Zenzinov wrote it down for the first time. But even his transcriptions contain indications of actual direct testimony that he would not have found had he arrived a little later. In our time a native of Russkoe Ustye has turned up, quite by chance, who remembers a great deal, has seen a great deal with his own eyes, has questioned the old folks about many things, has taken part in many activities, and has collected a vast amount of material on the history, ethnography, way of life, religious beliefs, and thoughts of his compatriots. He is Aleksey Gavrilovich Chikachyov, a member of one of the oldest families in Russkoe Ustye and a former employee of the Communist party. Chikachyov's book on Russkoe Ustye, a firsthand account, as we call it, was recently published in Novosibirsk. While referring to old sources, which consist of the impressions, observations, and reactions of people who found themselves in that corner of the world temporarily or even accidentally, I am also pleased to cite the testimony, completed at long last, of a native of Russkoe Ustye himself, who probably had to restrain his pen when choosing those aspects of his fellow countrymen's life that might interest the reader. But everything in this book (called *The Russians on the Indigirka*)[17] is interesting: how they worked, how they worshiped, how they spoke and felt.

Yes, they worked, they worked hard, but it's also important to enliven this draft-horse conception with a few particulars. They knew not only how to work but also how to relax, laughing "till they dropped" ["*za khody zakhodit'sia*"]. Even nowadays the old folks recall that after the annual goose hunt, after they'd finished driving the molting geese into nets at the mouth of the river, they liked to hold their own brand of bridal inspection.[18] This is how Chikachyov describes it:

Immediately after the hunt they would organize rowing competitions (*khvasnia*), covering distances of eight to ten kilometers. Three prizes (*vesy*) were usually established, each consisting of a certain number of geese, to which some well-to-do resident would add two ounces of his own tea or a couple tobacco leaves. The winners were called oarsmen.

There were two kinds of oarsmen in Russkoe Ustye.

Pertuzhie oarsmen—long-distance rowers—could cover seventy to eighty kilometers in one day while rowing against the current. *Khlestkie* oarsmen rowed for short distances. People said that in the old days some of them could keep up with seagulls for two or three kilometers.

These are in fact the very same tests of mettle with which other Russians amused themselves in the Middle Ages, and they used identical terms. What chronicles and legends can't tell us turn out to be alive in the customs "of yore" [[*v "dosel'nykh" obychaiakh*]. *Kulika* (an ancient form of hockey) was popular, along with ball games, "greetings" ["*poklony*"] (conveying information with pieces of cloth, using color, length, and knots), and a great many more games that have been almost completely forgotten everywhere else.

And omens! What science could possibly get along without omens that, tested and retested, never failed?! If a horse yawns, bad weather is coming. If a dog buries itself in the snow, take shelter because a blizzard is on the way. If a goose flies high overhead, the weather will be warm; if it flies low, that means it will get cold. People will live there for another thousand years and for a thousand more years they won't give up omens, not as long as there are horses, dogs, and geese. But these omens aren't as amazing as those that existed in the past. Arctic dwellers even used to use mosquitoes as omens—they weren't scarce then and aren't likely to become rare any time soon—but one mosquito for making predictions is still not a lot to go on.

And so we must assume that at first the Russians of Russkoe Ustye lived in what we consider total darkness and then began peeping out on rare occasions, moving ever closer and more inevitably toward brighter days. But before they emerge into the light once and for all, let me cite one more eyewitness account of their twilight existence. It comes from Zenzinov and pertains to the year 1912, when he had just arrived in Russkoe Ustye:[19]

The door of my yurt banged constantly during the first days, and my guests watched with avid curiosity as I uncrated one unfamiliar object after another. News of each novelty quickly spread to all the cottages. A kerosene lamp—the first in Russkoe Ustye—produced the greatest effect. Observers related that "he took some kind of shiny teapot and put a glass dish over it." More news made the rounds that evening: "He lit it, he lit it!" And they kept coming to me for a long time after that (even from neighboring areas) specifically to look at the lamp, and they would ask, "What's burning inside?" This lamp made such an impression on the minds of the Indigirka dwellers that I'm certain they will regard it as the beginning of a new era here.

This would have happened in all likelihood had not a new era actually, and not merely figuratively, burst forth. Rumor of revolution and civil war did not reach the lower Indigirka quickly, and when it did, little changed at first. The Indigirka dwellers didn't know what revolution was, what you ate with it, and they continued to toil under their indestructible burden of life without any changes for several more years.

I must explain that under the czar, "the people of yore" were registered as members of the petty bourgeoisie. Neither their kind of work nor their way of life resembled that of the bourgeoisie, but they didn't precisely resemble any other class either. Therefore it made no difference to them: call us a pot if you want to; just don't shove us into the oven. They paid their taxes without fail, governed themselves through an elder and an elected representative, and resolved fundamental issues at meetings (assemblies). Once a year, sometimes less often, the district police superintendent would arrive from Verkhoyansk; once a year a priest would also show up, conducting all necessary religious rites in an hour's time. The merchants who brought in goods robbed everyone—Yakuts, Yukagirs, and Russians—alike. Gedenshtrom describes an incident (it dates back to 1810, but little changed during the next hundred years) in which "a member of the Indigirka bourgeoisie" had a merchant bring him a silver mounting for an icon of Saint Nicholas the Miracle Worker. It was valued at seventy rubles. The member of the bourgeoisie paid fifty-six foxes, at a rate of one ruble per pelt, which left him owing fourteen rubles. Over the course of the next seven years he gave the merchant another eighty-six pelts to pay off his debt, but according to the merchant's clever sliding scale, the debt had grown to 1,200 rubles. Had the authorities not intervened, the man would have been enslaved forever. And such things happened all the time.

At some point someone, probably an official, brought the word *republic* to Russkoe Ustye and explained it as confusion or disorder. The people of Russkoe Ustye, receptive to anything that might prove useful, liked the word. They applied *republic* to every kind of disorder—in a dog team, among women in the kitchen, or at the general assembly. Whenever something was slightly amiss, it was called a *republic*.

For Russkoe Ustye the new era began not in 1917 but in 1930, when collectivization was implemented. Even *republic* was insufficient to describe what happened then. The initial meeting was "a great battle," according to Birkengof, who was present and unwillingly took part. Before I quote from his *The Descendants of Pioneers*, it wouldn't hurt to remind the reader once more that the Russians in Russkoe Ustye had just barely emerged from the darkness of antiquity and hadn't even had time to rub their eyes before they were noticed and summoned to that great meeting of fate-bearing force.

An authorized government official announced the agenda. One item on the agenda, "the expropriation of property belonging to feudal lords," no doubt sounded to the local residents like lofty and incomprehensible wisdom from the people "back yonder." And at that point I, who had sufficiently mastered the language of Russkoe Ustye by then, had to step into the role of "interpreter" and explain to the assembly the meanings of incomprehensible and alien words.

Thus the meeting was called to order, members of the presidium were selected and took their seats, and the "interpreter" began to carry out his duties.

"Comrade Chairman, I ask that we get rid of this smoke!" said Afanasy Sivtsov, an agent with the government trading post in Yakutsk and a native of the Kolyma region, as he sternly surveyed the assembly. The presidium proposed that everyone stop smoking. This was also something new; it underscored the impending changes in what was customary and fixed, stressing the solemnity of the meeting and the importance of coming events. And unquestioningly, though not without regret, the audience, who had started puffing on their pipes, extinguished them with their fingers and put them away.

Then they read out a list of registered voters broken down "by the election committee into special groups." All eyes were fixed on me again; they were waiting for an explanation.

After my explanation there were several indignant and unexpected protests: people didn't want to be "classified" as poor peasants, regarding this designation as somehow insulting.

S. Varakin, a "sedentary non-Russian" ["*sidiachii inorodets*"] (this is what people in Russkoe Ustye sometimes still call Russified Lamuts and Yukagirs), arrived late and, on hearing the words "poor peasant" and "peasant of average means," he made a low bow to the audience and announced, "We've come to hear how you've registered us (meaning him) and to tell you what we own."

They tried to stop him. But when his turn finally came, Varakin vigorously attempted to prove that he belonged with the peasants of average means. "I have four houses, three hundred traps, and twenty-four nets, so I'm not a poor peasant. A poor peasant I am not!" Varakin said.

And he actually wasn't a poor peasant. But why did he so strongly resist being "classified" as one? Somebody, tired of Varakin's objections, made a proposal: "Oh, let him be a peasant of average means if he's so set on it."

Semyon Shulgovaty also protested with great passion, "I have a hundred and fifty traps, nets, boats, and a *karbas* [a large boat with high sides for transporting cargo]. I don't want to be put with them" (that is, with the poor peasants).

If the truth be told, the people of Russkoe Ustye lived in poverty but didn't know it.

What could they do? A whirlwind had descended. Their dogs, nets, and traps were collectivized; quotas were adopted "from above" ["*spushchennyi*" *plan*] and turned out to be a resounding failure that first year. The kulaks had to be deported, but where to? No one in Russia, or in the whole world, for that matter, lived any farther north than they did; even if a resident of Russkoe Ustye were sent to the Bear Islands, he wouldn't be at a loss there either. And yet the authorities did send them elsewhere, correctly reasoning that the main thing was to tear them out of their native environment and they would pine away no matter where they ended up, even at the Black Sea. Especially at the

Black Sea, where they would pine away all the faster. People did a lot of stupid things with those collective farms at the beginning of collectivization. Even now the old folks shake their heads when they recall the 1930s, covering their eyes in embarrassment: they went too far and did much more damage during that period than was ever done during the previous three hundred years.

Around 1936 a directive was apparently issued to Russkoe Ustye's Pioneer Collective Farm to immediately take up reindeer breeding. The Russians there had never kept reindeer, but a directive was a directive and had to be carried out. So they bought forty deer from the neighboring Yukagirs, found an Even in the tundra named Kabakhcha, and made him the herdsman. Kabakhcha took the deer out into the tundra, as he was supposed to.

At the end of August, the exact time when they usually killed wild deer swimming in the river, the herd suddenly appeared on the opposite bank and plunged into the water. Without thinking (*izlishne ne kataias' umom*), the men quickly jumped into their rowboats and slaughtered every last one. Kabakhcha turned up about ten days later and announced that he'd lost the deer. The farm managers got together and began passing judgment on the herdsman, threatening him with prison. Kabakhcha left the office with the firm intention of fleeing into the tundra while he was still alive. Not far from the village he stumbled across some sawed-off reindeer antlers and recognized the farm's herd by their markings. When he took the antlers back to the managers, one of them, a native of Russkoe Ustye for whom the world had turned upside down and still hadn't righted itself, simply couldn't understand why, when the men advanced with weapons, the herd hadn't give any sign that it belonged to the collective farm instead of to God.

But at that time the world still hadn't flipped over completely. It did an honest-to-goodness (*zabol'*) somersault when a woman, Larisa Chikachyova, was elected chairman of the village soviet. That was the absolute end. Beyond that point, in the view of the Indigirka dwellers, there was nowhere left to go (*taramgat'sia*). Ever since the days of old, women in Russkoe Ustye had been expected to know their place. Shortly after that, before they had a chance to collect their wits, the "households" along all the channels were raked into one heap and made into a settlement. The authorities named the result Polyarny.

Then they set up a branch of the Allaikhov State Farm in Polyarny.

E-E, BRA, POSHUKHUMA BAESH¹

I myself come from a part of Siberia that was originally settled by immigrants from the northern part of European Russia. For that reason many of the words that Zenzinov found necessary to decipher even at the beginning of the twentieth century are part of my mother tongue and constitute irreplaceable, living linguistic stock. When I was a child growing up on the middle stretch of the Angara River, anyone who substituted *to speak* [*govorit'*] for *to talk* [*baiat'*] had obviously succumbed to an urban oddity from "back yonder." In Russkoe Ustye no one had to explain to me the meaning of *lyva* (puddle), *mizgir'* or *sitnik* (spider), *galit'sia* (to make fun of, to mock), *lonis'* (last year), *lopot'* (clothing), *dospet'* (to make), *divlia* (good), *kruzhat'* (to stray, to get lost), *likhomatom* (quickly, loudly), *okolet'* (to be cold, to freeze), *ulovo*, *uros*, *shcherba*, *shmet'e*, and a great many other words. And now, translating from Russian into Russian, I can't help feeling guilty regarding my language because I must resort to this. But how could it be otherwise? Education leads not toward language but away from language, and in our country the natural process of renewing and augmenting vocabulary has developed into a passion for Newspeak.

My ancestors and the ancestors of the Russians in Russkoe Ustye came out of the same nest, but they left at different times and settled on different soils. When the future inhabitants of the Angara region moved away from their former homeland (our most widespread surnames are *Pinegin* and *Vologzhin*) [derived from the names of the Pinega and Vologda regions], a good deal of time had passed since the exodus of the future residents of Russkoe Ustye. Language provides the best proof. During those one hundred some years changes took place in the language and in the venerable old Russian lands of northern Russia, the area where the Novgorodskaya, Vologodskaya, and Arkhangelskaya provinces and a sliver of the Kirovskaya Province are now located. What had dropped out of the language there by the beginning of the eighteenth century never made it to our part of the Angara, and what existed before that can be glimpsed in Russkoe Ustye.

The following is not a scholarly attempt to establish proof. Rather, it is a comparison based on sound. While reading about Russkoe Ustye before my trip, I was amazed to find that many dialectal peculiarities are identical in both variants of the language. I saw an obvious kinship, which at first seemed close. But after visiting the Indigirka once and then twice, I realized that I had exaggerated this kinship. It exists, of course, but the connection is not as close as that of an older brother to a younger one. It is much more distant, like the relationship of a grandfather or great-grandfather to his descendants. If you compare pronunciation and manner of speech, the distance is even greater. But manner of speech deserves a separate discussion.

The main distinction is that the language spoken in Russkoe Ustye contains many more archaisms, words from bygone times. If you said to one of my countrymen, "*E-e, bra, poshukhuma baesh'!*", he wouldn't understand. Only one word would be familiar to him—*baiat'*. Where did *poshukhuma* or *shukhuma* (to no purpose, in vain) come from? I couldn't find it in any dictionary, no matter how much I dug around. From the looks of it, it couldn't have originated with the local languages either. *Bra* is a back-formation from *brat* [brother]. My compatriots were also experts at shortening words, but they, as a rule, swallowed vowels or economized on consonant clusters, whereas the Russians in Russkoe Ustye didn't spare their tongues and pronounced words in their entirety, even emphasizing their length.

Words that have eroded to the point of total decay almost everywhere else and that now exist only in literary texts have remained completely healthy and whole in Russkoe Ustye. There people continue to say *perst* (finger), *zaglumka* (smile), *ozoino* (cumbersome), *berdit'* (to be afraid), *vadiga* (a deep spot in a river), *guzno* (rear end), *golk* (a rumble or peal), *izuroch'e* (a rarity, a wonder), *kurzhevina* (hoarfrost), *mogun* (stomach), *patri* (shelves), *pokrom* (a strip of cloth for diapering a baby), *shigiri* (wood shavings), *sharkhali* (icicles), *korzhevina* (rust), *issel'noi* (genuine, real), *karga* (a ridge or peninsula), *klevki* (worms), and so on.

And while we have completely forgotten and lost the Old Church Slavic word *iveren'* (a part, piece, fragment), Bulgarian has *iver* and Czech *ivera* (woodchip or shaving). We have to turn to Bulgarian, Czech, and Slovak because they have best preserved the Slavic rootstock of their languages; and now we must make these leaps from

Europe to the far north of Asia in order to hear the precious similarity of sound from living lips. Bulgarian has retained *do povidan'ia* [good-bye], and so has the language of Russkoe Ustye. The same with *istok* (east); in Bulgarian, *izstok*. And *zhivot* [stomach, belly] has been preserved along the Indirgirka in the meaning of "life" or "property."

In our region, "to talk excessively, to jabber" was expressed by the word *travit'* and in Russkoe Ustye by the older *drevit'*. *Inde* lived on among us in the form of an intensifying particle; in Russkoe Ustye, as in all the oldest chronicles, it means "in another place."

It was not easy to track down why in Russkoe Ustye smart children [*shustrye deti*] are called "cloud children" [*oblachnye deti*]. What could the connection be, since *smart* and *cloud* are so far apart? Only by turning to the pagan period of the Slavs can you find the origin: cloud children, cloud girls were the mischievous ones who organized theatrical spectacles. In Afanasiev's *The Slavs' Poetic Views of Nature* we read:

The spectacles that took place on the Sunday before Whitsuntide [*rusal'naia nedelia*, literally, mermaid week] were accompanied by dancing, music, and dressing up in costumes, which symbolized the spirits of thunder and rain as they rose each spring and celebrated the renewal of life. Even mermaids, who belonged to this category of spirits, would clothe themselves in fleeces made of clouds and mingle with the devils and shaggy forest demons.

Or take the word *glinchina*, which among the Indigirka dwellers denotes a rotting tree. At first glance this looks like a reversal of sounds, *glin* for *gnil* [rotten, decayed]. And so it is, only the rearrangement is not accidental, for ease of pronunciation; in Old Russian *gnila* was both written and pronounced as *glina*.

And so forth. The examples of living linguistic antiquity (alive until quite recently and now dying out) could go on and on. In Ozhogino, another Russian village on the Indigirka but about one hundred versts [about sixty-five miles] upstream, where the first settlers unquestionably came by way of Yakutsk and where their descendants later intermarried heavily with the indigenous peoples, the local language can no longer boast of as many deeply distinctive marks, of similar chips and flakes of antiquity. But wait, you might think, a distance of one hundred versts in those vast expanses is nothing, yet even during the nineteenth century the difference in speech and customs was astonishing. Isn't this primary evidence of a special, separate exfoliation of Russians who populated the lowermost reaches of the Indigirka?

Both the natural world and the economic structure were different in many ways from those of the old North. The part of the language that adapted best and enriched itself the most concerned the "elements" ["*stikhei*"] of water and wind. There, too, a *shelonik* (a southwest wind) remained a *shelonik*; as is common everywhere along rivers, *verkhovik* means from the direction in which the current is flowing, while *nizovka* means from the same direction as it is headed. A northwest wind is called *lower west* [*nizhe zapadu*], an east wind is a *flow* [*stok*], a cold, sharp northeaster is a *bad flow* [*khudoi stok*], and a southeast wind a *warm flow* [*teplyi stok*] or *obednik*. But notice how the terminology designating wind expanded in relation to the river: a wind blowing in the direction of the current is called *downward* [*poniznoi*] and one against the current is *along a straight stretch* [*po plesu*]; a breeze blowing from your side of the river is called *pulled away* [*otdernyi*] and from the opposite bank, *breakers* [*priboi*]. In relation to a person's movements, there are *headwinds* [*protivnoi*], *tailwinds* [*posoboi*], and *crosswinds* [*bokovoi*].

Vadiga, iamarina (a hole in a river), *shiver* (a reef), *kur'ia* (a bay on a river), *osinets* (a chunk of ice), *michik* (thin ice), *karga* (a peninsula), *kuliga* (a bay), *erdan'* (an ice hole), *antiiakh, ogiben', ulovo, bystriad', kibas* (a sinker on a net), *niasha*—all these words were immediately applied to the Indigirka, to its banks and waters. In much the same way *kaltus* (a wet area), *veret'e, laida, zanovoloch'e* (an overgrown lake), *edoma, viska, taibola* (a remote, uninhabited spot), and *razlog* all depended on the tundra. Vocabulary depended even more heavily on the tundra than was warranted by the "bare bones" it provided for linguistic clothing: *elon'* or *elan'* means a clearing in the forest, but in Russkoe Ustye there was nothing to clear, and yet by some coincidence *elon'* took root anyway. Even *dubravushka* [a small oak grove] took root, becoming the designation for any kind of vegetation.

There were no cattle, as I've mentioned, so they began to call dogs *cattle*. Then a dog kennel became a cowshed. *To sweep the floor* means *to plow*. Bear cubs and wolf cubs became chicks. Zenzinov refers to the poverty of the language spoken in Russkoe Ustye, but judging only from the lengths the language went to, from the twists and turns it made not to lose in isolation its beauty and versatility, its basis in labor and ritual, and its precision, we have to regard the extent of its preservation as a miracle. Nearly half the man-made and natural objects in the river dwellers' former world vanished from their lives in their new surroundings and the words that designated them should have died out from lack of use; in turn, a new array of objects, phenomena, and sights that had names in the local languages should have joined the ranks of the mother tongue and occupied a legitimate place there, as happened everywhere else that Russians settled near non-Russians. Loan words do exist in the dialect of Russkoe Ustye. Roughly three or four dozen Yakut and Yukagir words became everlastingly entrenched in the Russians' native language. The very first words to take root during the initial naming were those seemingly dictated by the voice of northernmost nature: they referred to objects and actions concerning hunting and fishing and to certain utensils and articles of clothing. Another three or four dozen words might be thrown into a conversation but without any special weight, for substitutes are readily available. Generally speaking, we can only be astounded at how retentive, hardy, and strong the Russian language has shown itself to be in Russkoe Ustye, taking nothing from the outside without extreme need, holding out and fighting for its own down to the very last sound. Aleksey Chikachyov, the native of Russkoe Ustye mentioned earlier, says in his notes: "After adopting the fur clothing and hunting attire of the locals, the Russians gave them their own purely Russian names: *malakhai*, *sharovary*, *dunduk*, *brodni*, *shatkary*. And they preserved the dress of northern Russia at the same time: long jumpers with pinafores, a distinctive way of tying headscarves, skull caps, men's shirts and waistcoats." And this happened with everything.

From the standpoint of Zenzinov, an educated and bookish man of the twentieth century, their language probably did seem impoverished. The Russians of Russkoe Ustye, finding themselves sharing the same time and place with him apparently through no choice of their own, could not have had the loquaciousness and flexibility of thought that a political exile hungered for in social interaction. The Indigirka dwellers, accustomed to spending long periods of time all alone with the sendukha, expressed their feelings tersely. But this resonant terseness contained an accumulation of capaciousness and cheerfulness and talkativeness that were comprehensible only to those from the same circle. If the native tongue spoken in every family contains "birthmarks," all sorts of "artistry" with words and word formation that is unintelligible to others, then a closed community couldn't get along without them either. So what if they seem irritating and meaningless to outsiders!

In the old days anyone bound for Russkoe Ustye by way of Ozhogino on the Indigirka, Pokhodsk on the Kolyma, or Kazachy on the Yana, all of them Russian villages, would be warned, You won't be able to understand them up there on the lower Indigirka. Each of those towns cultivated its own accent, like the mellifluousness in Pokhodsk, for example, where they made do without *r*'s and sang out their *l*'s like short *i*'s [*i kratkoe*], saying *igoika* instead of *igolka* [needle]. People had their own manner of conversing everywhere, but in Russkoe Ustye their speech was altogether peculiar, unlike anything else. It was the same language, with an age-old stock of words restocked with new ones, but the instrument of articulation seemed to be constructed differently. In Chokurdakh I asked some Russians from Russkoe Ustye to get together and "talk a little" [*"pobaiat'"*]. For the first half hour I heard (understood) practically nothing, only isolated words; then I began to catch bits and pieces, and only toward the end of the evening did I gradually get used to their speech. And I adapted to it about as well as a fish lying in the sand when someone pours water over it: some of the water hits the mark and helps it breathe for a while, but most of it runs right off. Or like a bobber that keeps going under at every nibble, breaking your train of thought.

I don't know what their pronunciation can best be compared to. The people themselves, almost all of whom now also know the language commonly used "back yonder," call it "to speak with 'shibilants'" [*"shebarchet'"*]. Their speech actually does contain a lot of sibilants: whistling *s* and *z* have transformed themselves into muffled *sh* and *shch*, but not in every instance and with a certain freedom of choice that knows no rules. Regular patterns probably do exist, but that is the topic of the special studies that have been written and are still being written (by Aleksey Chikachyov, among others); if the rest of us ever dared set foot in those labyrinths, we'd never make it out in one piece.

Then what is this dialect like? The Russians in Russkoe Ustye speak rapidly, very rapidly, almost without pausing. Once they've unleashed the first word, their speech immediately takes off at a gallop. Filled with amazement, I paid special attention to the sibilants: there are lots of them, the dialect really is full of "shibilants," and yet it is also abrupt, a curt staccato like a wheel rolling down a coarse gravel road. It is abrupt and yet even, without any emotional ups and downs, and the endings are swallowed. This gives the impression that a word is never fully cooked, that it doesn't have time to sound forth completely before the pressure of the next word pushes it out of the way. When several people speak at once, they sound like excited geese cackling. Whether pronunciation changed drastically because of the magnetism of natural sounds or whether it came down this way from ancient times no one knows (how could we?!). But this pronunciation occurred nowhere else among all the tundra voices in the Far North, a result that, consequently, required a certain type of material to begin with.

We won't get into any linguistic labyrinths, but one more curious detail, which appears to be obsolete everywhere else, is worth mentioning: in Russkoe Ustye the particle *-to* continues to display gender.[20] *Sendukha-ta*, *izba-ta*, *more-to* exemplify feminine and neuter usage, while in masculine nouns it takes the reverse form: *muzhik-ot*, *veter-ot*. This, too, derives from the depths of antiquity.

Certain anomalies in agreement have been adopted from the Yakut language. But many purely Russian words, continually moving along in distorted pronunciation without correction, also became fixed in the language over time. And once a native of Russkoe Ustye gets something into his head, he'll stand by it doggedly. Aleksey Chikachyov believes that stubbornness and conservatism are the outstanding features of his fellow countrymen, but the Indigirka dwellers probably would not have survived without these qualities; traits that are annoying in other instances played a positive and strengthening role in this case. But what we're talking about now is unevenness and distortion in language.

Omolazhivat'sia [to rejuvenate] gradually became *omolakhtyvat'sia*. You won't instantly figure out that *pozavochchu govorit'* means *govorit' za glaza, za ochi* [to talk behind someone's back], or that *aviden'* is *v odin den'* [in one day] *adzhalo* is *odeialo* [blanket], *meledit'* is *medlit'* [to linger], *lenda* is *lenta* [ribbon], or *trobka* is *probka* [cork]. Immigrant words of foreign origin, brought in later by merchants, administrators, and expeditions, suffered the most. I know from my own background that such words seemed to stick crosswise in the throat and would invariably turn the long way—to avoid irritating the throat. *Pidzhak* [jacket] became *finzak*, *ad'iutant* [aide-de-camp] became *utitant*, and *observatoriia* [observatory] became *chervotoriia* [the root is similar to *cherv'*, meaning worm]. In the last example, the Russians of Russkoe Ustye did not stand on ceremony when they made a migratory word into something that would stay put. And when all this is mixed with Old Russian, which you don't expect to hear spoken, when words are uttered in an idiosyncratic manner with unusual subordinates and a rapid-fire delivery, you won't correctly comprehend the residents of Russkoe Ustye right away, even if you zero in on their speech and are all ears.

But when you begin to understand, when you learn to distinguish the scattering of linguistic seeds from the empty hulls, when the blood relationships of words ring in your ears, then you could listen to it forever, thirstily drinking in its precious repletion. And then you wish that others could hear and enjoy this speech before it's finally too late. For in a little while the sounds of bygone times will be heard no more and the valve will shut forever, that valve in Russians that rises slightly from time to time over the narrow, imperceptible opening through which we hear the coherent whispering of our ancestors, who know they will be understood. But as soon as there is no one left to understand them, nothing more will be said.

And what if one more of our senses were to die out? It's bad enough that we don't take care of this ability very well, that not everyone even knows of its existence, although it is made up of all the basic human senses: seeing, hearing, smelling, and touching something beyond our own lives.

Let's listen to the Russians of Russkoe Ustye some more, before they fall silent. How one hates to part with this speech! *Idti stup'iu* means to walk slowly; *oblai*, a rude troublemaker; *delat' nazgal*, *delat' v konets ruk*, to do something badly; *zaglumki davat'*, to smile; *za lishek zaiti*, to overdo it; *istok znat'*, to know the reason; *naperepuch'e*, so as to cross someone's path; *naidushka*, a find; *na ushuiu posadit'*, to deceive;

ne dai ne vynesi refers to a helpless person; *optopok* means worn-out footwear; *ogon' ugasit'*, to be left without a mistress of the house; *khoziaistvo po navil'nikam poshlo*, the household went to ruin; *paporotki otbit'*, to beat up (Chikachyov believes that this comes from *paporoz"*—a shoulder strap in Old Russian—but there is also *paporotok,* the joint in a bird's wing); *semilu bit'*, to fuss; *upaloi*, weak; *ukhul'nichat'*, to slander; *cherez govorit'*, to speak without respect; *sidet'do chuki*, to sit through to the end; *pereshchekaldyvat'*, to argue, to hinder conversation; *basnitsa*, a female gossip; *vara*, highly concentrated tea; *eres'*, a quarrel; *zhalet'*, to love; and *zarnost'*, greed (*zhalet'* and *zarnost'* have the same meaning today as they did in olden times).

We are fortunate that up there in the land of permafrost, where they still find mammoth carcasses and trunks of birch trees near the ocean, evidence of epochs with a different climate, the Old Russian language has also been splendidly preserved until very recently. And when you encounter it somewhere other than in chronicles and accidental echoes, when you hear it in reality, you can see with unusual clarity how many unjustifiable and irreparable losses, along with natural atrophy, the Russian language has suffered. In Russkoe Ustye these represented the last echo of Russia's ancient language and way of life. It's also a miracle that when they reached us, we remembered how to listen so that we could understand them.

WHAT IS BURIED IN OBLIVION, WHAT THE WATER WASHED AWAY

Having brought along the biblical tales of the creation of the world, the Russians of Russkoe Ustye lost no time expanding on them to include the tundra as well. Their legends about the origin of the sendukha and its inhabitants, about the appearance of nearby ghosts and spirits, of sins and vices in human beings themselves, their legends about the beginning of Russkoe Ustye and the family histories attached to them, the poetic details about birds and animals, hunting and other occupations, that folklorists have recorded (and how many disappeared before they could be written down?!)—I could read them aloud forever, one after another, those wise, beautiful creations composed by the community with the birds and animals themselves listening in. These legends, true stories, and tales contain so much harmony, learning, and soul.

Here is one appropriate to our discussion, called "About the Mammoth" (from *The Folklore of Russkoe Ustye*). P. V. Kochevshchikov recited it to N. M. Alekseev and T. A. Shub in Stanchik, on the Kolyma Channel, back in 1946:

Once there was thish flood. Water sho high everyt'ing drownt. Christ shaid, "Everyt'ing perishes. I'll keep one pair of eash animal," said Christ, "and Noah and hish whole family—the resht will die." All theshe animalsh agreet, but one beasht didn't agree—that beasht was the mammoth. "I can swim in the water for t'ree years," he says. He didn't want to be paired up, so they didn't try to forsh him. Noah built an ark and there he saved his family and one wife and one husband of eash animal. And so he sailed for t'ree years. And that mammoth swam in the water by himshelf. Going on the third year, the mammoth perished: he couldn't swim for t'ree years. The ones t'were on Noah's ark, they procreated, but that beasht perished for good, except for thoshe mammot' horns we find. God cursht him 'caush he wouldn't agree to be one of Noah'sh pairsh."

The moral couldn't be simpler or more direct: even if you are a Solomon, even if you are the very mightiest mighty "beasht," you will perish if you isolate yourself. And after a great length of time people will begin to guess at what strength you had only on the basis of your bones. And you didn't last only because you didn't know the limits of your strength, whereas those who knew how much strength they had, however miniscule, and preserved it weren't sent to their graves by fire or flood.

This has happened to events, civilizations, and entire peoples who scorned the truth that there is danger in greatness and ruin in excessive strength if we ignore memory and squander our strength through neglect.

But even this truth has no pride; it makes do with humankind.

At the beginning of August, on a cool day lit with streaks of sunlight, we went by boat to Stanchik, that very settlement on the Kolyma Channel where the legend of the mammoth used to be told. I'd heard about Stanchik because of its chapel. Aleksey Okladnikov referred to it,

intending to move it, along with the church in Zashiversk, to Novosibirsk to save it from neglect and ruin. Aleksey Chikachyov also sighed
over it. "I simply must try to save it before they burn it down, but how?
This isn't my district anymore." (He was working in the Kolyma region
at the time.) We saw it from a long way off as our boat spun around the
sharp bends in the river: a leaning tower beneath a cross. But as we
pulled out from behind the final point of land, the whole chapel came
into view on the low, steep bank, the last on the north end of several
buildings spread out along the riverbank.

The buildings were nothing but three cottages and two barns, also
not long for this world. Although the little chapel still towered above
them, it stood crookedly as though genuflecting before the river, star-
ing lifelessly into the expanses of water and verdure into which it was
casting prayers.

Is it any wonder that something abandoned to reality, to cold and
numbness, is capable of looking dead? The place had been deserted for
a long time. And deserted as if Mamay[21] had swooped down on it. The
rowboats and cargo boats left on the bank were full of cracks and holes,
a collapsed pit barely revealed the remains of an ice house, a rusty saw
had been tossed aside near one of the cottages, and a log lay across
some sawhorses, waiting to be sawn. Inside the walls objects of everyday life were scattered around, with blankets, mattresses, and hides
lying drenched beneath the gaping roofs and windows, there was rotted clothing in the barns. For some reason the inhabitants had abandoned in great haste everything they'd used to stay warm, fed, and
alive, and not a soul seemed to have set foot there ever since.

In Stanchik I experienced a depression as tangible as an annihilat-
ing pressure coming down from the sky. The weather also contributed
to my mood. The sky was raw, waves whipped its low dark edges, and
cold, isolated rays of sunlight filtered through every now and then.
And time after time a skua would cry out and swoop down, taking us
for fishermen. A ragged formation of crosses tilting on top of graves
turned away from the river in a single column and filed along it into
the distance. I made my way to the graveyard, getting my feet soaked
in a marshy spot. They actually had buried their dead in formation, on
a narrow, dry hillock, but no triangular wooden markers remained on
the sunken mounds any more and there were no names on the crosses,

Remnants of bygone days

no glimpse into the past, nothing to remember them by. Like in a forced labor camp. The previous week we'd been at the site of a huge camp at the mouth of the Kolyma where, alongside remnants of barracks and scraps of barbed wire, there stood the same sort of tilting stakes over nameless bones. But even though no one would visit them, the guilty and the innocent who had been driven there and thrown into the ground at least had numbers; for the people of Stanchik, however, this was their homeland, and tears had been shed at their funerals. But let's come down yet another notch with a justifying "whereas." Whereas no one lives beside those buried in Stanchik, you also see the same thing in all the inhabited places along the Indigirka and the Kolyma: dislocation, frigidity, abandonment.

And after this, what can be said about the little chapel, whose rightful place is in a museum? It was constructed artlessly but with beauty and inspiration, and it is also dying without pretention: the whole church is tilting, the cross has shifted, and the ceiling above the side altar sags. A small migratory bird had built a nest in the inner recesses of a rotting corner, managed to hatch its young, and was now teaching the fledglings how to take wing somewhere nearby; you could count the days until the Feast of the Holy Cross [August 14 (new style)], when the *plishechki* (small birds are lumped together in one word, *plishechki*) begin to migrate. Let the little chapel keep on serving this purpose; this is a service, too.

Tea would have tasted bitter there, so we got into the boat and crossed over to the left bank, from which we could see even more clearly what a convenient location, what a perfect spot Stanchik had occupied, favored even by the Indigirka itself, which puts no pressure on the right shoulder at this point and doesn't undermine the bank.

The Fish Protection Agency's cutter then took us into the river's lower reaches, toward Russkoe Ustye, Polyarny, and the most distant summer cabins belonging to residents of Russkoe Ustye, which stand near the ocean. At Chokurdakh we were joined by Aleksey Chikach-yov's brothers, Veniamin and Ivan, whose broad, dark faces displayed an ancient admixture to their Russian blood that gave them enviably strong bones and a vigorous overall bearing. The Chikachyovs' ances-tors on their father's side journeyed to the New Siberian Islands in search of mammoth ivory and fox (the Russians from Russkoe Ustye known as particularly skillful hunters at the beginning of the nine-teenth century were Ivan Portnyagin, Faddey Chikhachyov, Roman Kotovshchikov, and Ivan Rozhin). They accompanied Gedenshtrom's expedition to the same islands and, even earlier, helped chop Dmitry Laptev's vessel out of the ice. Another Chikhachyov, with the initials E. N., took part in Eduard Toll's expedition,[22] serving for three years as their guide; he excelled in finding the shortest routes to the ocean spits and was granted the highest possible reward. Pyotr Strizhov, the Chikachyovs' great-grandfather on their mother's side, sailed with Toll on the same expedition and made himself so useful that they named two islands after him. Yegor Chikachyov built the church in Stanchik, the very one we had just been sighing over. Their grandfather, Nikolay Gavrilovich, nicknamed "Gavrilyonok," whom Birkengof repeatedly mentions as a firm manager of his affairs, could read and write, a rarity among Indigirka dwellers in those times. Their father, Gavrila Nikolae-vich, was the director of the Pioneer Collective Farm during the 1930s.

This is no mean pedigree; it took shape during what were practically the crowning events of local history, and even dropped in occasionally on Russian history as a whole.

Their lineage began in the distant past: a Chukichyov (the name has followed a meandering course: Chukichyov, Chikhachyov, Chikachyov) is listed among the most outstanding members of Dmitry Zyryan's detachment, which sailed down the Indigirka from 1641 to 1642. And it continues today in full force: that summer Aleksey Gavrilovich was first secretary of the Nizhne-Kolyma Regional Committee of the Communist party, Veniamin Gavrilovich the vice chairman of the Allaikhov Regional Executive Committee, and Ivan Gavrilovich the chairman of the trade-union committee of the Indigirka trade organization. We could have had no better traveling companions, no better guides than the Chikachyov brothers, who knew where, what, when, and why things happened on the Indigirka tundra then and now.

Also joining us was Ivan Lukianovich Leshchenko, the "keeper" of the Indigirka, an employee of the Fish Protection Agency who glanced into more than a few ice houses and nets along the way, to see if there were any illegal seines or fish. Although not a native northerner, he seemed like one up there, as if the place were made to order for his disposition and physique. Local folk along the Indigirka are not terribly fond of "Varangians,"[23] but by the time I became acquainted with Ivan Lukianovich, he was already completely one of them and not subject to the humiliating humoring that is always noticeable in such cases. This was apparent from the way others treated him as well as from his own direct words and straightforward views on Indigirka life. While pondering how outsiders can take root in Siberia, wondering what kind of citizen this requires, I realized that he is a perfect example: someone who won't dilute the local inner core with emptiness but will add strength and prudence.

While digging around in the discarded junk at Stanchik, Ivan Lukianovich found a wide beltless caftan called a *malakhai* and an antique lamp for the regional museum in Chokurdakh.

To get to Stanchik we had turned off into the Kolyma Channel in a motorboat, leaving our cutter at a spit. After returning to the cutter, we came out on the Russian Channel toward evening of the same day. Boating on the Lower Indigirka, in contrast to boating on the waters of

Siberia's interior, requires almost a different kind of eye, one used to bare land and able to find joy in it.

Near Chokurdakh willow trees still clung to the low left bank, while hills, elevated in the local language to mountains, hunched over on the right, and my gaze didn't falter or run into nothingness, as it would later. I could see fishing shacks, some made of logs, some built like tepees. As soon as one vanished from view, another materialized as if floating down from the sky. Hugging the right bank, we squeezed into Semiruchye Creek and came to a waterfall: a steep ravine, loose rock, a slit with flowing, falling water, mushrooms, a berry bush—it was hard to believe that we were almost at the Arctic Ocean. Then back to the flood of murky water, runoff from the tundra. The left side was no longer bottomland but flat ground level with the river, the hills on the right receded into the interior, and the broad span of the river made us think we were entering the sea. Stormclouds hung low overhead, trailing loose strands; the oncoming wind was sluggish but cold; the earth's descent to sea level was increasingly noticeable; and more and more water surrounded us. In the midst of this boundlessness our cutter must have looked as powerless as a beetle swept along by the current.

We pulled up at Russkoe Ustye late that night, although it wasn't dark, arriving just as the sun briefly forced its way through the clouds to greet us. The deserted village stood on a cozy spot, where the Indigirka twists to form a peninsula. I noticed that the bank was undermined, but that two buildings—the cottage and barn of Gavriil Shelokhovsky, who'd lived there long ago—were still holding their own, just as they had been during my visit two winters earlier. The owner was long gone, and so was the last renter, a man named Sviyazov, who had maintained the spirit of habitation for many years in complete solitude and who, according to various stories, never turned off his loud-voiced radio day or night, to fend off depression. I saw the same metal plaque on the wall facing the Indigirka, which listed the names of famous scholars and travelers who had passed through Russkoe Ustye. But the cottage had been sturdier during the winter. We had crawled in through a window then, so as not to disturb an ermine fussing around in a pile of rags in the entryway. Now the ceiling had caved in, the sod roof that lay on the floor was overgrown with grass, and the stench of mold and rot poured out of it. A cargo boat and a rowboat were lying upside down on the bank just where they'd been two winters before; the same blackened barrels were scattered around. One of the Cheryomkin brothers had gathered some driftwood into a neat pile in order to haul it to the opposite bank.

If we can believe *The Book of Vles*,[24] the ancient Slavs had three worlds: Yav, the visible world; Nav, the other world; and Prav, the world of justice. The only remnants of Yav in Russkoe Ustye are those two collapsing buildings that belonged to Shelokhovsky and are now half-sunken in Nav, which begins and continues on an equal footing two dry steps away, at the cemetery. Not much meets the eye there: a cast-iron monument to Aleksey Kiselyov, whose family lived in Russkoe Ustye for generations—his well-to-do sons brought it from the greatest of distances in the early twentieth century—and what's left of the crosses and triangular markers erected over the graves. The cemetery receded into the depths of the bend in the peninsula, while the "habitations" extended for a hundred meters or so along the bank. The remains of the stoves from the cottages are still plainly visible to this day and, judging from the prosperity they indicated, even I, an outsider who had read and heard so much about Russkoe Ustye, could easily guess where the house of the wealthy Ivan Shchelkanov had stood and which one had belonged to "Gavrilyonok," the Chikachyov brothers' grandfather. Next to the Chikachyovs' ancestral hearth a memorial to Russkoe Ustye—a welded sheet of metal in the form of a sail on a medieval sailboat—stands out in lonely isolation, as a reward to Prav. The inscription reads: "Here stood the age-old settlement of Russkoe Ustye, founded by Ivan Rebrov in 1638." Aleksey Chikachyov took this information from an extant record stating that in that year Ivan Rebrov, coming from the Yana River, built winter quarters with a small wooden fort on the Indigirka as a base for collecting tribute.

And again a crushing depression, a feeling of futility and perishability: people lived there for three and a half centuries at the very least, and this is all that remains of them! We've grown accustomed to seeing the purpose of human existence in the products of our hands: in the cities we build, the fields we till, the machines we design and assemble. It's difficult to credit the age-old settlement with any of these things, for its inhabitants fed themselves with "God's gifts"—fox, fish, and meat—

which they also prepared for others, and even traveled along "God's" roads, which their feet had to create all over again every winter and spring. Everything they lived by on that riverbank for three hundred some years has faded, dried up, dispersed. And what has Russkoe Ustye become, besides a place of decay? Is there a just reckoning in the world that measures the benefit and futility of our existence? And if so, who establishes it? Can this be all that Russkoe Ustye finally deserves: a mournful country graveyard with a sail frozen in place above it as if on a medieval ship returning to its paternal boundaries?

353
+++

This is an injustice higher than human injustice. Time, perceptive and ruthless, keeps picking up and completing the actions toward which those who lived in it were inclined.

We use any occasion to repeat Lomonosov's words about Siberia, but we never bother to read them through to the end. The whole quotation states: "Russia's power will increase because of Siberia and the Arctic Ocean." We ought to immediately shift our emphasis to the Arctic Ocean. Let's not forget that before the Industrial Age this seaboard was, at the very least, visited regularly and divided up during the centuries of trade that marked the beginning of the region's development. The Russian settlements along the riverbanks near the ocean constituted the vanguard of labor and the military for hundreds of years. They were tiny islets of Russian culture, dotlike "birthmarks" on the canvas of the tundra, but they stood their ground, held out under conditions they were unaccustomed to, and displayed a dignity and wisdom in their dealings with the aboriginals that, above all else, say something about the heart and nature of the numerous Russian people, which make them great. Moreover, they also preserved their ancient inner core, with all its poetry and prose, so completely that we can only marvel.

And after all this we have only their graves to bow down to.

The abandoned bank seemed to stretch out and exert itself at the memory of people and was ready to offer us every knoll so that we would keep on walking down the untrod, marshy paths and keep talking, calling the bones in the graveyard by name. Even the sun seemed to find and cling to the only little window in the dam of clouds just to light our way. Everything that was still standing tilted, as if at half-mast. The remnants of the stoves we went up to gave off a smell of bitterness; forty years had passed since their owners moved away, and yet the spirit of habitation in the burnt, claylike residue persisted, continuing to seek and preserve something.

After we set sail the Chikachyov brothers remained silent for a long time, feeling guilty and depressed until they made tea on board the cutter and we began talking about how nowadays no one anywhere, in any land, is blameless. We all share some sort of universal guilt for the Earth as a whole and for each individual region desecrated by our evil civilization, which sheds no tears over anything out of the stubborn belief that might makes right. We are fervently led astray, then dismissed without repentance. Even the best of us have not escaped the temptation, sealed with a hasty "amen," to rush after those who can only look beyond the horizons without seeing anything at their own feet.

But now word has just arrived from the Indigirka region, which I gladly hasten to add to this finished text, that last summer the Chikachyov brothers, along with two other pairs of willing hands, hauled some construction material to Stanchik by barge, repaired the little chapel, practically picking it up from a state of collapse, and gave it at least a comely appearance if not a godly one. Hope requires so little—I instantly began to believe that in the Far North people have actually made and implemented a conscious decision not to yield to those who would reroute conscience as well as their native land.

And the other news from the Indigirka is that the Russians of Russkoe Ustye are preparing to celebrate the 350th anniversary of the founding of their town. Well, now, three hundred fifty years—that's quite a few. And if we add the remaining fifty years peeking around the aforesaid span, waiting in reserve and attracting us as the tastiest morsel, then all the better. It is certainly tempting to imagine that at roughly the same time that Yermak was taking the town of Isker on the Irtysh River away from the Tatars, approaching it from the west, Russians on the eastern extremity already held the other end of the encircling band in their hands—and all they had to do was tie the ends together. "All they had to do" sounds almost ironic. All they had to do was cross a huge landmass from one end to the other. But it also rings true that if this actually happened and if the same hands really did hold both ends, then tearing them apart would have been practically impossible.

The Russians of Russkoe Ustye, I must note, believe that they are exceptional. The expeditions studying folklore and dialects that frequented the Indigirka region until very recently along with the books and films about them encouraged this belief. They have an unpretentious but noticeably dignified attitude toward themselves: they compose songs about Russkoe Ustye and Zapolyarnoe and are even inclined, amid the mysterious sendukha, to poeticize their own activities. Visitors say they regard themselves with too much dignity, which can be stubborn and mercenary at times. They seem reluctant, for example, to share with new settlers the parts of the tundra and the "fishing sands" that their ancestors once owned. This is indeed true—they feel that "what was my family's is mine and will remain mine under any powers that be." Without dreaming of justifying this view, you can still understand it: their families toiled at difficult tasks on those tundras and "sands" and warmed that part of the earth for hundreds of years. In recent times the state farm has also tacitly approved the concept of inheritance, making only small, essential changes when remeasuring the area, and the hunters and fishermen have gotten used to ownership. But this is the exception rather than the rule: they sometimes had to share territory in the past, too, whereas now, as they begin to work more and more in teams, they will have no choice but to consider the land everyone's and not theirs alone.

But it was finally time to dock at Polyarny. Our cutter pulled in toward morning, when the light had grown heavy and covered the water and the sky with a uniform leadenness. As we drew near we heard a muffled, ponderous sound, as if the earth had settled. Ten minutes later the cause appeared before us: a huge chunk of land, as large as an island, had broken off and lay in the water with a ragged side as waves began to beat against the recessed wall of the bank, whose base was light blue with ice. Not far away a little cottage hung over the river like a bird's nest tacked on at an angle.

This was Polyarny, which used to begin right at the water's edge. At least that's where it had been during my winter visit when, after getting out of the plane, which had landed on the Indigirka, I'd had to climb a steep bank. After one full summer and half of another there was almost nothing left of the habitable bank. A narrow, terraced strip of land, serving only as a passageway, still held out between the Indigirka and

Shamanovka Creek, which made sweeping figure eights before flowing into the Indigirka. Later it, too, would be swallowed up, shortening the Shamanovka and turning the full force of the current directly at the bank where Polyarny stood.

The science of dynamics includes a concept called the Coriolis force (named after a French expert in mechanics), according to which the flow of the rivers in the Northern Hemisphere curves to the right; that's why right banks wash away, while flood lands form on the left. Polyarny stands on the left bank, but, contrary to Coriolis's law, the Indigirka is gnawing away at it nonetheless. If its appetite finds no reason to abate, the residents will still have a few years before they'll need to build a new town, but the old houses standing apart from the rest on an isolated hill, which affords a bleak and majestic view of the Indigirka on one side and a gentle picture of the flood plains beyond the Shamanovka on the other, seem doomed to go first.

Yegor Semyonovich Chikachyov's cottage had also vanished.

I recall how during my winter visit he had sent for me himself, to show me his dictionary of the language of Russkoe Ustye. This is just one more proof that the Russians there know their own worth as well as the value of their language, customs, and traditions. An unsteady hand had entered the ago-old words into a notebook, from which Yegor Semyonovich would pull out several at a time, syllable by syllable, and then, after extracting them, would look at me slyly: did I know what they meant or not? If I didn't know, his face, with its amazingly pure Russian features and an absence of wrinkles despite his advanced age, would beam with delight. This was an absorbing lesson/competition. A fire crackled in the stove, laundry was drying on some dogsled seats behind it, and the sparsely furnished cottage, with only the most essential pieces of furniture lining the walls, was warm, clean, and spacious. We sat across from each other at the table, which stood by a window through which nothing was visible but snow. Yegor Semyonovich, tenaciously grabbing the first part of an entry, would look it over from head to tail with some difficulty, then finally latch onto the whole thing, drag it out, shake it off, repeating it, and present it to me with the pride and excitement of a hunter.

"*Lyva!*" he declared.

"Puddle" [*luzha*], I translated with a similar Russian word.

Seated on a stool, he turned away from me, considering whether a *lyva* could be called a puddle, because different words really do carry different shades of meaning; no synonym is an identical twin of its counterpart. After giving it some thought, my examiner allowed the answer, granting that my guess was almost correct. I seemed to have scored a point. "*U rutu pena!*" he exclaimed, launching a new attack. I undoubtedly would have grasped the meaning of this phrase had I seen its written form, but with Yegor Semyonovich's pronunciation, which couldn't be called Russian, or anything else, for that matter, which was perhaps reminiscent only of the cry of some long-vanished bird, how could I have figured out that he was saying *u rta pena* [foam at the mouth]? But even if I'd recognized it, I would still have been stuck, for it meant "I have no time." I conceded. The same thing happened with *bakhtur*. It wasn't close to "watchman" [*storozh*, a synonym of *vakhter*], as Yegor Semyonovich triumphantly declared. "It's probably a Yakut word," I said, trying to get to the bottom of it. No. "Yukagir?" No again. It finally turned out that I had to look for the answer not in nearby regions but in Europe. *Bakhtur* is a mutilated form of *vakhter* [from the German *Wächter*]. A degree in philology would have been no help in this case; everything depended on linguistic instinct, which had to be turned loose without reins like a horse when you're lost.

And now, finding neither his cottage nor the land beneath it, I didn't count on locating Yegor Semyonovich himself in Polyarny either. We all know that every action, voluntary or involuntary, has a far-reaching reaction. But no, Yegor Semyonovich still lived there, in another cottage a bit more luxurious than the old one. When I walked in, a girl about twelve years old was "plowing the bridge" [*"pakhala most"*]—sweeping the floor. The head of the house got up, setting aside the object he'd been working on, recognized me, and smiled that simple-minded, crafty smile that only the word *zaglumka* can express. I asked about his old "villa" [*"khoromina"*]. "Mother Indigirka stole it," he explained without reproach, as if this had been inevitable. "When?" "*Lonis'*" [last year]. As usual, he spoke the language that was inside him, without substituting any words to help me guess his meaning but carefully enunciating whatever I asked him to repeat. He didn't hide his grief at the loss of his former "villa," which in other parts of the world would have been judged a hovel. Several times during our conversation he fondly referred to it as a "hospitable woman" ["*khle-bosolka*"].

Yegor Semyonovich had stopped recording words from the days of yore. As I understood it, he'd stopped when the old-timers' part of the settlement was "stolen." Polyarny now contains a good many people from back yonder. They've formed their own groups, tacking on the local youth as well. Those who have delved into antiquity, who form a link between the past and the present, lag behind. As their kind and the strangers grow together, they are less and less surprised by each other; "wise Rus" has appropriated even this piece of outlying land as part of its self-concept and one of its various marvels. Nowadays everything is cut to fit one size and constructed in one manner; even if you're a *chuchuna* captured in the sendukha, please be good enough to abandon your *chuchuna* ways so you can sit in front of the T.V. every night and utter such words as *intensifikatsiia* [intensification], *protuberantsy* [protruberance], and *uik-end* [weekend]. The culture of yore has become a memory, an oddity, an ancient old woman's wedding attire stored in a trunk: you can take it out and touch it lovingly, you can recall the ceremony with a quiet look back, but different voices and songs will inevitably break into your reminiscing.

And now the townspeople get together less and less often for the *omukanchik*, the ancient dance they once took to Moscow to demonstrate.

I saw the *omukanchik* performed in an unheated, half-empty recreation center. I had to conclude that the performance was incoherent because it had been arranged as a demonstration for a few outsiders, which aroused no enthusiasm whatsoever in the performers. Some showed up, some didn't. Even Omukan seemed to be played by the wrong man. But the musical accompaniment—not accompaniment but hallucination, audible sorcery, shamanism—fell to a withered little old lady sitting on the front bench who, using no instrument, raised her hands to her face and touched her lips with her fingers. Matryona Ivanovna Portnyagina touched her lips with her fingers and gave a sigh, squinting at the stage—and suddenly music began to sound forth, wild, life-giving, invocatory music unlike anything on earth. The first sounds were unhurried and soothing, at which point a young man named Omuk came out and began to conceal an animal; then the music began to hurry the hunter along and became stronger, more disturbing, more trumpetlike, as if a little old lady hadn't half risen from a bench, but tundra spirits were racing along, hungry for victory. And when victory came and the hunter began to circle his catch, her voice, dropping briefly, rejoiced along with him but belatedly, holding him back, curbing the young man's passion and calling him to passion of a different sort. Her voice was gentle now, undulating in light waves as if continuously backing away and returning, trying time after time to instill something in him. And Omuk heard this voice, heeded it happily and impetuously, and rushed toward his sweetheart, who was already making her exit. . . .

What the old woman had produced with her voice by fingering her lips, now strumming them, now pinching them, now slapping them rhythmically, was called *pripuvat'*. Her *pripuvanie* continued to echo in me for a long time, as if it had come from under the earth, a message from those who have already descended and are seeking kinship and joy from down below.

Surely this, too, will not be buried in oblivion?

I had the opportunity to compare seasons, and I can say that Polyarny looks better groomed and more exotic in winter. The dogs are tied outside to horizontal poles resting above their heads on criss-crossed supports; shaggy, quiet, half buried in snow, they stand up from time to time to shake themselves off and get warm. Deerskins covering the windows from the outside serve as protective shutters against the wind and bitter cold. Chunks of ice are stacked next to the walls of the houses like woodpiles; whenever you want water, just grab an armful and take them inside where it's warm. Firewood is piled up to dry in tall tepee-like formations whose interior space is used for cold storage. Seeing all this for the first time is both pleasant and unusual; it fulfills your expectation of novelty, and then some. If you stop by the state farm's workshops at this time of year, you'll observe the difficult, traditionally women's work of curing fox pelts by hand. After curing, they are sorted and sewn up in sacks—twenty-five to a sack—for shipment to the fur-processing center in Irkutsk. They're light as a feather but worth their weight in gold. In a good year twenty experienced hunters (there are inexperienced ones, too) along with two or three apprentices bring in more than three thousand pelts during one season. You can understand why the men of Russkoe Ustye were not even sent to the front during World War II: bringing in those platinum fur-bearing animals makes up for a lot. Hunters are well compensated for the difficulty of their work. They can't complain. This setup actually provides more than they need: each hunter has two or three snowmobiles and five to seven outboard motors. There is an old rule: a little extra won't put a hole in your pocket; it'll never wear out.

But this is beside the point.

In addition to fur shutters and woodpiles of ice, the town has one more wonder, which stands out winter and summer: raised above the ground, wrapped in an assortment of cloth and fur, and sheathed in wooden casings are pipes for steam heat. People also walk along them as if they were specially made pathways, staying above the mud and snow and deftly going around each other whenever they meet head-on. Two-story, eight-unit apartment houses are being constructed at a leisurely pace on the edge of town, away from the Indigirka, and are increasingly common. About three hundred people live in Polyarny; there was a time when Russkoe Ustye, with all its "households," numbered more than that. Some of the local folk are settling near the district offices in Chokurdakh; some are seeking their fortunes in other northern hamlets.

In winter the snow in Polyarny covers an uninvitingness that comes to light in warm weather and only increases with every passing year. In the summer the earth opens up and water from the permafrost seeps out everywhere, with wood chips, garbage, and waste sticking up and floating on top. Even the dogs watch their step, so they won't puncture their feet. This is that common, incurable Russian disease found at all our latitudes and longitudes—strewing everything under the sun around yourself and your dwelling, never thinking that tomorrow you will be the one to suffer because you so energetically toss things out. Throughout the entire glorious Arctic, in towns and around them, near summer cabins, overnight camps, stopping places, and even in corners that have never been inhabited there are thousands upon thousands of oil drums, enough to choke the incinerators of a steel-mill conglomerate. Refashioning them doesn't work; reproaching people doesn't help. The only consolation is that some day, motivated by the great poverty that, with our present wastefulness, is well-nigh upon us, human beings will start using sensitive instruments to hunt down those oil drums and dig them out of the frozen ground the way we now dig up mammoth tusks.

In the summer the appearance, the smell, and the mood of Polyarny all turn sour. Those residents acquainted with other regions rush off on vacation; they congregate in flocks like migratory birds, take wing, and depart to the sound of roaring motors, oppressed each year by the thought, Do we have to come back? Others, for whom the whole earth, the heart and core of everything, is right there, migrate like nomads to their summer cabins, where it's cleaner, where they find the spirits of their ancestors as well as fish, and where the wind blows away the mosquitoes and cuts through the heat. Some summers so much heat builds up that more water condenses from the existing water and breeds hordes of mosquitoes. Then it's bad news for man and beast. If the cargo ships have gotten through and the winter supplies are already in the warehouses, then people look forward to the snow and freezing cold as a relief. During the long arctic night they'll wait for the sun, the first sunshine will remind them of warm weather, the warmth will bring high water to the Indigirka, and then they'll look forward to frost and snow again.

That's how it was in the past, and that's how it will be in the future. Much is changing in that world near the very crown of the Earth, but this never changes. This anticipation of transitions according to the primordial cycle of nature stays the same, embodying both the meaning and the futility of life.

And what if we were to raise up the host of Russkoe Ustye's dead from beneath the tilting crosses and ask them, the descendants of White Sea coast dwellers and peasants, What was it all about when your eyes sought work and your hands performed it? Wasn't this the vanity of vanities, mere wood chips for the water to sweep away? Why did you spend over three centuries on end constructing and strengthening the fortresses of life if nothing remains after you now but neglected country churchyards?

And what would they reply? That no one lives for himself but merely continues to pave the way for the lives of others, constantly paving the way and not arguing with those ahead or behind, and in this tireless preparation lies the very meaning you seek? Or would they say that they put down strong roots and completed their labors in full—and haven't we grown up on those roots? Or would they nod toward the Indigirka, in the direction of the ocean, with reproach, asking, Whose shores are these? Aren't they Russia's? Or would they reveal some new truth unknown to us that would finally make everything fall into place, that would form, brick by little brick, a single, usefully constructed wall?

And when we pushed off from the pier in Polyarny, heading farther north toward the most distant summer cabins of Russkoe Ustye, which stretch almost to the very ocean, it seemed to me, after these nebulous thoughts, that figures were standing guard along the banks on both sides, peering at us and talking back and forth: Who can that be and what mission are they on? What kind of strange and witless folk have sprung up who do nothing but talk, talk, talk? What if they matched their words with deeds? How much simpler and sounder everything would be!

The sky cleared on the day we left Polyarny; you could see and hear for a long, long way.

1988

8

❖❖❖

Your Siberia and Mine

So what is Siberia today?

I'm not talking about vast areas and distances, or about the harsh natural conditions, whose harshness is greatly exaggerated, or about the resources, old, new, and eternal, or about all the things that immediately spring to mind and formed the first common conceptions of this region. Let's try to look into the heart of the matter and understand Siberia's place in our native country, within the framework of a kind of unified building where this great entity took up residence in one of the numerous wings, the largest and most disproportionately spread out and underpopulated. Let's try to divine Siberia's place in the fate of every person regardless of whether or not he thinks seriously about it, whether or not he feels the presence of its spirit inside himself even slightly. Let's try to put our finger on what Siberia means in our view of the present day and on what direction it is taking, how and in what way it stands out when we shift this view to tomorrow. What does it contain that has the power to influence and affect us? Why do people who have lived here two or three years, and often even less than that, then pride themselves for the rest of their lives on the period they spent in Siberia? All right, let's flatter them by presuming that they withstood ordeals, tempered their wills, as we say, or completed some professional school. But surely there is more to it than that. Even those who didn't pass any test, who weren't tempered or educated here, pride themselves on merely having been to Siberia the way people used to pride and congratulate themselves on making a journey to holy places. It is thus a question not only of material, professional, and physical gains, of all kinds of useful outgrowths brought back from Siberia, but also of something else that cannot be named in an instant or isolated in a simple, understandable way, yet that exists and constitutes no small part of our concept of "the Siberian attraction."

Some four hundred years have passed since Yermak's breakthrough into the Siberian expanses, and Tobolsk and Tyumen have celebrated their 400th anniversaries, but if we look at Siberian events of the sixteenth century from the heights of our time, the Russian Cossacks hadn't gotten very far from the Irtysh and the Ob by the end of that century and still had quite a hike ahead of them to reach the anniversary towns of Tomsk, Yeniseysk, and Krasnoyarsk. But the first Russian Siberians began to develop their distinctive character in the appropriated lands without delay. And skipping over them, rushing in after the Cossacks, came the first mowers and reapers of that which wasn't sown: the fanciers of furs and gold, the founders of a numerous and successful breed that matured more and more with time—a breed that robs this region blind.

Concerning the sequence of its events, Siberia's history is well known. Be it scanty, fragmentary, and often conjectural, a sketch has, however, been made and labeled by figures of the distant and relatively recent past, a sketch marked by periods of gradual awakening and animation. But it's a shame that no brilliant novelists turned up among the Siberian populace who could have described old Siberia with the same consistency and liveliness, the same artistry and passion that our contemporaries Valentin Ivanov[1] and Dmitry Balashov[2] display regarding old Rus. For Siberia did indeed have the space and the subject matter for a bold pen to go on a spree, especially during the first hundred years of strengthening its ties to Russia.

It was apparently back then that a certain attitude toward Siberia arose once and for all, an attitude which from the beginning accumulated a literature that helped people talk to death and conceal their true goals, but which has actually changed very little. It was back then that two differing views of Siberia began to form, two opposing approaches to its "appropriation" [*pribor*], which subsequently began to be called "development" [*osvoenie*]. The various expeditionary corps that alight in Siberia today trace their spiritual parentage to the past, and those first groups spawned descendants rich in reproduction. Siberians for whom this is their native land and seasonal workers for whom it is a place of temporary refuge, business turf, or a proving ground—this is how Siberia's population has long been divided, into permanent and fluctuating sectors, into a well-defined fortress and eroding waves that keep rolling in. It's not hard to guess which of these two forces gained the upper hand and who, while posing as a benefactor, knew no other approach to Siberia than removal and robbery.

During the second half of the nineteenth century a social and patriotic consciousness gradually began to arise and take shape among Siberians. At long last they began to talk about the abnormal position of this region; about the politics of the empire's mother country, which was depriving it of its future; about Russia's practice of squeezing out and hauling off all the best in Siberia while dumping its worst there, including human rejects, in return; about the humiliating bookkeeping, oversight down to the pettiest details, and so forth. And they didn't simply start talking about all this; Siberia's sighs and complaints had been heard before. They began talking simultaneously and energetically, appealing to wisdom, correctly linking the future of Russia with the future of Siberia, and forcing the government to pay attention to local needs. Thus Tomsk University was founded and the policy of banishing criminals to Siberia abolished.

It's interesting to take a look today at the fundamental issues that Siberia's passionate supporters (Yadrintsev, Potanin, and others) raised in order to improve the health of the social climate and to increase productive power. At first there were five: education, the abolition of banishment, economic relations with the mother country based on mutual advantage and equal rights, settlement of the region with high-quality people, and relations with the non-Russian minorities. It's also interesting to look at these topics now in order to compare Siberia's past and present positions in light of these specific issues: What was gained by raising them and where have they led during the course of a century?

Let's take education. Because of its intrinsic meaning [literally, formation (*obrazovanie*)], this word was justifiably not used in the nineteenth century; people said "enlightenment" [*prosveshchenie*]. This was considered the central poverty of Siberia and was linked to moral and economic well-being; the logical chain that started with enlightenment had an almost all-encompassing sphere of action: when you become literate, you'll be smart, you'll behave with fairness, you'll learn to be an efficient manager, and you'll devote yourself to the beneficial service of the region and the fatherland.

There is no doubt that only the light of enlightenment can lead Siberia out of the sad state that it's in. Only when, on one hand, the general level of intellectual development in Siberian society rises and people comprehend the impossibility of continuing to base economic management on the former destructive foundations and when, on the other hand, technical knowledge appears in Siberia and gives Siberians the ability to exploit the natural resources of their country rationally, only then will the period of chaotically plundering its productive forces and reserves come to an end and a period of correct and judicious economic development set in. (Aleksandr Kaufman,[3] 1892)

Unfortunately, the old Siberians were wrong. They wouldn't have been wrong if enlightenment had continued to be enlightenment in its former sense and within its former boundaries, with adjustments for the requirements of time and scholarship, and if it hadn't turned into training people according to opportunistic, self-contained standards that were cut out and put together hastily and badly and that cramped and curbed the mind. They wouldn't have been wrong if engineers had remained engineers as they knew them, and educators educators, and if professors of physics and chemistry had given some thought to the benefit of their subjects for humankind when they were taking charge of scientific interests. There is practically no trace of such concerns now. Nearly all even slightly big-sounding Siberian towns have universities these days, and there are ten times more technical and economic institutions of higher education than there were secondary schools devoted to math and science in the past, but these have become incubators for the mass breeding and bringing up of narrow specialists who aren't capable of looking into or understanding anything beyond their own specialties. Even the universities of today don't know what a well-rounded education is. And Siberia, which had just barely begun to rub its eyes in the nineteenth century and see its unlucky fate, which had started the difficult task of sowing the seeds of civic and humanitarian consciousness in its people, has now been thrown further back in this regard than it was one hundred years ago, and modern education played a primary role.

The ignorance, the lack of education could be explained one hundred years ago:

You can't help being struck by the absence of all foresight and the terrible ignorance of the population in every economic exploitation of Siberia. The inhabitants of Siberia act as if they have no intention of remaining there more than twenty-four hours, as if they're new arrivals, casual nomads who are here today and gone tomorrow, who haven't the slightest concern about how their sons, grandsons, and great-grandsons will live. They carelessly and indiscriminately grab the best of what they have at their fingertips and then, after grabbing, plundering, and disfiguring, turn to new speculative ventures. We attacked everything from gold nuggets to sable, which we slaughtered in our back yards, but as soon as persistent labor lay ahead of us, as soon as some effort and skill were required to create a solid culture and businesses not based on sheer chance, on blind luck, we retreated, disappeared, and complained about the niggardliness of nature in this virgin country. (Nikolay Yadrintsev, 1882)

Since then "ignorance" and "the absence of all foresight" have grown to such dimensions, leavened by the yeast of general education, by enlightenment deprived of light, that they would have deprived the former guardians of Siberia's prosperity of the gift of speech and of their last hope for a constructive result. We automatically adapt to reality, we live in it and don't fully take in the changes that occur, but if a clear head should appear today, someone who had missed the last three decades of Siberia's "development," he would conclude that out of some terrible necessity Siberia had been handed over to barbarians found somewhere on the planet so that they could pillage, desecrate, and destroy it, that Siberians had fled from them to avoid seeing their land disgraced, and that the fate of this region had been decided once and for all.

And what are the former rapacious exploitations and shocking behaviors in the far corners of Siberia compared to the present-day versions, which are joined together in one huge, mighty operation?! And what about Siberia's past dependence on the mother country? It can't hold a candle to the pressure exerted by government departments and ministries that get whatever they want in Siberia's hereditary estates (and not only in Siberia's), that keep local authorities on such a short leash that they won't utter a single word of defiance. Oh, if only we had the shocking old practices now! We ought to pray to God for them! The social and political commentators of former times certainly had reason to wax indignant: peasants too lazy to fertilize their plowed fields would abandon them as soon as they refused to produce a ten-fold yield and would tear up virgin land beside them; industrialists, skimming off the cream, would cover the rejected gold with slagheaps and carve out fresh mines; hunters and fishermen made no allowances for increasing the numbers of animals and fish; and immigrants started their new life by burning down forests to make fields. All this, of course, is far from praiseworthy and indicates a standard of economic management capable of growing into a habit, an attitude, a general rule; still, given the sparse settlement of Siberia and the short arms of Siberians back then, such things could not inflict great harm. The harm was more ethical: that wasn't the kind of worker Siberia's supporters wanted to see here; colonization of the region had been conducted all wrong. Siberians, like people everywhere, did not measure up to their ideal; perhaps Siberians fell even shorter of the mark because they were spoiled by the natural riches and not concerned enough about preserving them.

But today! Today we feel pity and embarrassment when we look back at our ancestors, who dug up Siberia with spades and hacked at it with axes. Why, in one year we spade (let's go ahead and use the usual verb [*perelopachivaetsia*]) more than a billion cubic meters of ground, making a whole landmass bristle. Now that's daring, that's scope! The Bratsk Dam alone flooded more than half a million hectares of the most valuable land along the Angara. And next to it are the Irkutsk, the Ust-Ilimsk, and the Boguchany Dams, then the Krasnoyarsk, the Sayano-Shushenskoe, the Novosibirsk Dams, and so on. How lovely the glow of Siberia's electricity must look from outer space, from which you can't see its gaping wounds! Of the great Siberian rivers only the Lena has remained inside its old banks, but it, too, will soon share the common fate. The dam builders moved from the great rivers to the medium-sized ones, from medium to small, then girdled the great ones a second, a third, a fourth time. The aluminum and cellulose smelted and turned into pulp at the expense of Siberia's rivers are sold for hard currency, which is used to buy grain—the same kind that was grown quite recently in these very river valleys. What can you do?! That's what the economy is for, that's the purpose of its gigantic wheel, whose paddles, growing longer and longer all the time, have to reach America, Australia, the ends of the earth. To do so they need Siberia's waters and mineral wealth, new capacities and raw materials to transfer elsewhere, raw materials, raw materials, raw materials . . . It's a vicious circle: the more that's transferred, the more million-year-old accumulations that are removed, the more common people that take part in this removal, the more we must import for their sustenance and satisfaction. And the more we import, the more we export. For every ton of goods imported to fill the gaps in products that Siberia used to have in abundance, ten times as many gaps go unfilled.

Just before the Trans-Siberian Railroad was built, Western Siberia alone had more than eleven million head of cattle. Siberia could produce enough grain for all of Russia. In 1898 it exported 149,000 poods [2,682 tons] of butter, while eight years later, in 1906, this figure rose to roughly three million poods [54,000 tons] (and what butter!), much of which went to Germany, England, and Denmark. You couldn't count all the poultry. The region had an abundance of game, fish, honey, and pine-nut oil, all products that fed people, and it could increase production, as with butter, several times over within a few years when there was a demand.

Today Siberia gets grain from Canada and Argentina, meat from France, poultry from Hungary and Australia, butter from Finland and Denmark, potatoes (a shame to admit, but a sin to hide!) from China, red currants (which until quite recently Siberians didn't even consider a berry because of their sourness) from Poland, and so forth. During just a few decades Siberia changed from a land of rich agriculture restricted only by the market into a land of risky, bankrupt agriculture, a parasite, a spendthrift that squandered its own share of nature's legacy with unprecedented ease and now steals what belongs to its grandchildren and great-grandchildren.

For several centuries, right up until about twenty years ago, Siberia was a land in reserve, a landmass of immense, untapped opportunities and unclaimed might. In the old days the czarist government let itself rush headlong into questionable ventures and, running short of money, traded away Alaska: Russia still had Siberia. Even when this was not written about and discussed openly, it was assumed to be the case. Siberia was a fortress where shelter could be found; a storehouse that could always be opened in case of need; a force that could be mustered; a bastion that could withstand any blow; and a glory destined to ring out someday. In the minds of everyone living in Russia, Siberia appeared as the continent of the future, to which they looked with confidence: whatever they might waste, squander, and use up in their own economic sphere today they would obtain in Siberia tomorrow; whatever they were sending ships to the four corners of the earth to bring back was kept in reserve for the time being right there, in Siberia.

Through Siberia, the Land of the Future[4]—that's how the great Norwegian Fridtjof Nansen titled the book he wrote about Siberia after making a trans-Siberian journey on the eve of World War I, first taking the North Sea route to the Yenisey River and then traveling by railroad from the Yenisey to the Pacific Ocean.

"I am immensely impressed by the boundless plains in the eastern part of Asia that still lie unnoticed and await human beings," writes Nansen.

And they waited until someone arrived. But who? It's as if others appeared before the ones they were waiting for, illegitimate imposters who were not prepared to work and not inclined to take either the demands of the present or Siberia's future into account, greedy, crude, impatient types who never learned how to take care of property and didn't know its true worth, nimble, cunning characters who appeared and laid claim to the land. And during a mere twenty to thirty years, like during the Thirty Years' War, when the carnage never ceased, these newcomers chewed it all up, turned it upside down, altered it, cut open Siberia's life-carrying arteries, and weakened it. They didn't so much take as scatter, spill, and destroy. Now rivers flow with oil, forests vanish underwater, and gas jets burn like eternal flames for the dead; where taiga once stood and wild animals roamed the woods have been cut down and half abandoned, left to rot; where there used to be yellow fields of grain and where cattle once grazed you see tall weeds, desertion, coldness, and homelessness; where towns and villages lived for centuries you find mobile camps that just discarded their wheels, sites populated with a new breed of nomad, with guest workers, seasonal workers, and raiders who move from place to place leaving behind either expanses made instantly lifeless or voracious monsters in the form of the world's largest industrial complexes and conglomerates, which gnaw out the taiga and the mineral wealth. If they'd been assigned the task of destroying Siberia as though it were a leper colony, they couldn't have done it faster and more reliably than under the present policy of "development."

Siberia's great expanses have retained only patches of virgin territory, some large, some small. But they, too, are being pressed from all sides by insatiable civilization and can find no salvation in the mountains or the marshes or the deciduous sections of the taiga. Here you have it: these far corners, quite recently considered dark and dense, and the encroachment of this civilization, which at the very first signs of sobering up can't avoid being called by the same phrase, "dark and dense," which is about as civilized as a monkey is human—here you have the meeting of past and present that casts Siberia's future into doubt.

It wasn't so long ago that the Siberian poet Omulevsky[5] wrote of the places through which the first railroad beyond the Urals passed:

There were flowers on the right, there were flowers on the left,
    As if I'd turned up in a garden gone wild.

But fifteen years ago Mikhail Dudin,[6] our contemporary, already observed a different Siberia:

Half-choked on gas, half-stifled, wheezing,
    Swimming in a swamp of oil,
Where are you rushing, where's your reason?!
Look inward with an eye of reason—
    Don't take the wealth all in one season,
    Leave just a bit for future toil.

The picture has not changed for the better during the last fifteen years. Far from it. It's merely gained momentum, stalked off in a huff, gone deep and wide with all its evils, driven by a whip—we be brave lads and true, who shall sing to ourselves of glory unprecedented, of unprecedented glory to our swashbuckling strength: like a mighty medieval army we've seized boundless Siberia itself, uncrossed by flight of bird, unspanned by cry of beast; we've trampled it beneath us and turned it loose in the wind.

Should we start singing glory to the "legendary heroes" [*"bylinnym bogatyriam"*] now or should we wait a little?

We can wait. This picture probably contains a certain amount of exaggeration, most likely explained by the narrowness of a native Siberian's view when he looks out from his own backyard. And can you see very far from your own backyard? All I see are desperate efforts to try to save Baikal; my native Angara, which no attempts can now succeed in saving, at which the dam builders/river tamers are throwing a fourth concrete lasso; I see wasteland in place of forests, which keeps growing and spreading as the quotas grow; I see plowed fields withering and shrinking, and with what narcotic passion chemicals are injected into them; I see how hastily and badly new cities are erected, like heaps of flophouses, and how solidly they are encircled with apartment complexes and smokestacks; I see the destitution of medicine, enlightenment, and culture and the increase of moral and physical ailments. Everywhere, looking around myself, I see outrages committed against the land and, along with corruption, outrages against human beings. And I don't see the purpose of it all. There is no well-being today, all the more so since there will be nothing to obtain it from tomorrow.

Knowing Siberia, I'm afraid that the view from neighboring backyards, whether they face east or west, is the same. Siberia didn't have enough plunderers of its own, so now we've started selling it off to foreign companies as fast as we can, for finished planks made out of our own pine trees, for a piece of meat, for all sorts of pumps. The merchants from our side are useless at striking deals; they've lost even this prowess. Others deceive us, but we'll agree to anything if only they'll do business with us, if only they won't abandon us to the mercy of fate in Siberia, where the economy has reached such a state that to be left alone amid our own looting is becoming somewhat terrifying.

That's what I see.

Yet I don't see that perhaps more remains underground than appears to the superficial glance inclined to gauge reserves by earthly order, by the towns and vales for whose improvement, if you follow primitive logic, the resources ought to be removed. Kuznetsk coal is expected to last for several decades. Tyumen oil and gas are also supposedly far from complete exhaustion, and there's still Yakutsk coal, which contains diamonds. Forests grow by themselves. Something else will turn up out there, you'll see. In short, we're a long way from impoverishing Siberia. It's too soon to write it off.

This is what the authorities are counting on: something like Tyumen oil or Yakutsk diamonds will be discovered, something is bound to materialize. Meanwhile look alive, like during the harvesttime rush every autumn when the crops are ripe, so you'll be able to gather everything in before the snow falls.

Siberians think about the likelihood of new mineral deposits with fear. Therein lies their final destruction. The only land that has escaped until now is what the geologists have passed over. Their prospecting work, whether they like it or not, is comparable to the splitting of the atom: in the wrong hands both bring equally dire results. But this matter has yet to reach the right hands, and no one knows if it ever will. Neither the Tyumen oil region nor the Kuznetsk coal region has any corners left where people might live without endangering their health; it's possible that sometime in the future, in about twenty or thirty years, they'll set up robots in the mines, in the rolling mills, and on the derricks that are capable of carrying out the same operations as human beings but that can stand any inferno. And will these robots actually become Siberians?! No one would like to see this, even from the gloomiest backyard.

Siberia needs to be developed. But it needs development, not the highway robbery concealed by this beneficial concept. The single fact that only one-tenth of the nation's population has settled on half its territory indicates underpopulation and opportunities for migration and ungrown crops. But it also indicates the prevailing attitude toward Siberia that, despite all the romantic attraction of past decades, it simply has never become a warmblooded land. The guest-worker system, no matter how many people it provides, is suitable for worthless territory unfit for habitation but not for Siberia, which deserves a better fate, which is capable of giving humankind an abundance of all the essentials. This method is appropriate for the moon but not for nearby Tyumen. Those who become guest workers are for the most part devil-may-care types to whom the laws of morality, as a rule, do not apply. This is the actual objective reality that determines consciousness. Money-hungry mercenaries, restless souls, a kind of modern Wild Field capable of anything—they value nothing here and love nothing, but this breed's keen sense of smell does an excellent job of sensing the ministry emissaries' frame of mind: come on, you guys, break and smash, don't spare anything, and don't listen to the whining of the local aborigines; we'll pay for everything.

Is this breed any better than the exiles of old, from whom Siberia suffered for centuries? If you judge them by the results of their comprehensive, destructive work, where morality and goodness never spend a single night, they are a hundred times worse.

Ah, yes, Siberia did not remain in a blissful state without criminals for long.

Minority ethnic groups in Siberia, who are inseparably rooted to the land of their ancestors through the entire spirit and structure of their existence, find themselves in the gravest position. What's the point of using the rights granted them for this, that, and the other if oil, gas, power plants, clear-cut forests, chemicals, and smoke drive them out of their ancestral territories and deprive them of their ancestral occupations?! This in itself dooms them to assimilation, to going out of existence. Will the descendants of the Voguls, Ostyaks, and Evenks be greatly consoled if a regional museum in some Oilville or Electrotown remembers the people that used to live there and displays the mournful remains of the tools they worked with?!

No, the primitive Siberians over whom the local boosters rightfully shed compassionate tears felt significantly safer under the czar than under the Ministry of Energy and the petrochemical industry.

Yes, Siberia's present is disturbing, its future uncertain. It's hard to say if it even has a future that hopes for a better lot, which people are accustomed to linking with tomorrow. After another one-and-a-half to two decades of rule like this, Siberia will vanish into thin air. Tyranny exists not only in relation to society but also in relation to the land. Rational utilization, comprehensive development, a cautious attitude toward Siberia's treasures large and small—all these concepts, inseparable from economics and morality, simply never became the law of life and action. *Sturm und Drang* did their job. Siberia continues to be viewed as a blushing bride whose entire happiness still lies ahead, yet she has become a feeble old women before her time. We intentionally or unconsciously continue to place our trust in Siberia's properties of self-preservation, hoping that little by little everything will be renewed by itself, will disperse and dissolve in the vast surroundings, will be healed on fresh soil. But these intrinsic recuperative powers have long been unable to cope with the increasing disembowelment.

One hundred years ago people regarded the establishment of broad-based self-government, a regional council capable of taking charge of land tenure, forest, mineral, and water resources, and planning and financing, as one of the main measures to ensure the judicious improvement of Siberia. Today the talk turns again to local government. One hundred years have passed just so that, after paving our road with wastefulness and endless mistakes, we can return to the very same thing. And is it a judicious person who throws away a whole century as a total waste?! We don't have another hundred years ahead of us. We've arrived.

The time has come to save Siberia. Immense and overstrained, majestic and powerless, many-tongued and disparate, a gold mine and a poorhouse, a land of bleakness that has been turned upside down, it waits quietly and secretly, perhaps losing hope, either for resolute help or for our last breath, so it can start all over again.

Siberia, in contrast to us, has not a few years ahead of it but millions.

As does the whole planet, which awaits the result of humanity's feeble efforts.

And yet why does Siberia draw people in with an irresistible and disquieting attraction? This attraction is often vague and not entirely identifiable, but it will persist until an inhabitant of Russia proper heads across the Urals and plunges into Siberia, whether carrying out an ancient, forgotten pledge or filling an aching emptiness inside that demands something like this, some kind of fulfillment and inspiration, as if diving into reality bared to the limit. And if reality doesn't fully correspond to his vision of it, we have only ourselves to blame. In any case life becomes easier for him whether or not he finds whatever he was looking for in Siberia: he acquires a palpable sense of being filled with a special spirit that exists only here and that afterward helps him understand himself and others better.

Perhaps these are merely idle conjectures and nothing of the sort happens in Siberia. But then how do you explain the self-confidence and tranquillity, akin to clarity of expression and self-discovery, that are so often encountered in people who have been to Siberia, qualities that were missing before? How do you explain the unintentional, innocent flash of joy on someone's face when he hears that you are from Siberia and then springs at you: "And I've been there, too, you know!" Nowadays going to Siberia is no great feat; it's not the moon or even Antarctica. Others have gone halfway around the world and suffered crossing half of Russia, but he doesn't want to know anything about all that; he's proud that he was here, that at one time he mustered the resolve to go, that he went, saw, and understood. If you ask him what he understood, he won't give you an answer. But a trace of the experience has remained, and he feels it inside himself like the working of a clock that noiselessly keeps track of soul-nourishing behavior.

He at least has been here, but why at the mere mention of the word *Siberia* do those living farthest away, who have never made it to Siberia, involuntarily perk up and pay attention: What's it like out there, in Siberia? What is it in them that responds to this sound? Joy or sorrow, some previous hope or disappointment, expectation or compassion? What has Siberia's all-pervasive vitality breathed into them? Don't they, with their vague notions and feelings, believe that we can tolerate strong-arm intrusion anywhere under the sun, only not in Siberia? Don't they feel that, having learned from the experience of other times and regions and as proof of our enlightenment, we were obliged to regard this young, fabulously rich land with joy and concern? And if we didn't, if we continue even now to destroy it, depriving our grandchildren of the last hope for a secure life anywhere on this planet, the legitimate and painful question arises: What's happening to the human race? Hasn't insanity become its fate?

Isn't this one more reason why people residing beyond its boundaries are drawn to Siberia, to feel in themselves the extent of the temporal and the eternal, the inconstant and the true, the ruined and the preserved?

This, too, can probably be observed better here, where everything in nature and in people is out in the open, than in any other place.

So then, does it have no past, present, or even a future? Is its lot for all time to be doomed and victimized, to experience, after the nomadism of the indigenous peoples in search of pastures and wild animals, the nomadism of hunters and gatherers of a different sort, who fly into Siberia in huge numbers seeking oil, gas, timber, coal, and gold, flying in and out like locusts that leave wastelands behind them? The nomadism of hundreds of thousands of strangers flying in and out, moving from place to place, and the inner, spiritual nomadism of millions of towns that resemble colossal, ungainly military camps, hostile and aggressive toward the rivers and vales that give them refuge? This is the present? Hundreds of years of recent time and thousands of years before that have passed in preparation for this? How can we look ahead when our eyes are clouded by today's picture? What can we see there to console us?

But something without a past, a present, or a future simply can't be. I'm not talking about those times, whose number is sizable, that today mechanically flow down through a narrow opening into a behind-the-back realm but about the times filled with reassuring pursuits, responsible people, and home building. Such periods did occur in the history of Siberia, when it truly woke up and saw the light, set about establishing order in its lands, and appealed to the protection of the law and the filial feeling of Siberians, but these periods, cropping up here and there amid the cupidity and the negligence, these beneficial times of sobering up were always like flashes on a dark horizon, like the light of sunrise, full of promise, that was soon dragged off into the twilight of highway robbery, which quickly returned to its usual spheres.

But it's also true, after all, that Siberia can't possibly submit to its humiliating and insulting fate forever. It simply hasn't ascended to a place befitting it and begun to shine with the light it deserves. Intelligent people, or as they still call themselves, civilized people, seem to have used their intellect for nothing other than proving the falseness and perniciousness of their civilization, which is based on undermining the principles that support life. Sooner or later it will leave the face of the Earth, as did all the abscessed societies before it, and the more speed it gathers and the more clearly it reveals its insatiability, the sooner this will happen. That's when a new kind of person might appear, individuals who, in view of the catastrophe with which our activities threaten them, will find saving, affirmative routes to take and won't confuse destruction with creation. How do we know that these new people aren't being prepared even today? How do we know that little by little their brain cells aren't being restructured in some different arrangement and that the spiritual principles we've awaited so long and prayed for so devoutly in order to attain the final resurrection aren't moving out ahead of everything else?

Siberia is waiting for just such people to be its saviors, builders, and guardians, tirelessly peering into the faces of all who ride and walk by, wondering if they aren't the ones, if they aren't bringing deliverance. And when, just beyond the Urals, birch groves and lakes come right up close to our road, when the remnants of a see-through ribbon of pine forest appear fleetingly and vanish, while birds congregate on the dips in the wires all along our route, when the steppe flies out powerfully on long wings and a curious boy with a suddenly quiet dog freezes like a little shepherd at the sight of its takeoff, when the taiga, stepping back a bit, stands sensitively in the twilight, catching and absorbing every smell and every sound, then Siberia itself is peering into us with hope and sorrow: What kind of people are these? What sort of souls are following the beaten path? What kind of work, what kind of service do they bring?

And when we pass the great rivers, the Ob, the Yenisey, the Angara, their names don't sound above the deserted waters any more—there's nothing left to designate by those names—but a call hums day and night, the call of an unfertilized land awaiting the seed that will finally produce action and soul-nourishing shoots.

And when storm clouds swell above the Altay and the Sayan Mountains and, drawn into the valleys, spill rain, the heavens inquire again and again: When will their moisture water those saving shoots and thunderclaps thunder out the fruitful results?

1984–91

379
+++

Notes

TRANSLATORS' INTRODUCTION

1. Valentin Rasputin, *Siberia on Fire: Stories and Essays*, selected, translated, and with an introduction by Gerald Mikkelson and Margaret Winchell (DeKalb: Northern Illinois University Press, 1989), 151.

2. *Siberia on Fire*, 150.

3. Valentin Rasputin, "Voprosy, voprosy" (Questions, questions) in *Chto v slove, chto za slovom?* (What's in a word? What's behind a word?) (Irkutsk: Vostochno-sibirskoe knizhnoe izd-vo, 1987), 177.

4. Valentin Rasputin, "V nekotorom tsarstve, v nekotorom gosudarstve" (In a certain kingdom, in a certain land), in *Chto v slove, chto za slovom?* 277.

5. "V nekotorom tsarstve, v nekotorom gosudarstve," 228.

6. Valentin Rasputin, "Chto v slove, chto za slovom?" (What's in a word? What's behind a word?), in *Chto v slove, chto za slovom?* 154.

7. Valentin Rasputin, "Iz glubiny v glubinu" (Out of the deep into the deep), in *Rossiia: dni i vremena: publitsistika* (Russia: days and times: essays) (Irkutsk: Pis'mena, 1993), 155.

8. Valentin Rasputin, "Veruiu, veruiu v rodinu!" (I believe, I believe in my homeland!), in *Chto v slove, chto za slovom?* 207.

9. "Voprosy, voprosy" in *Chto v slove, chto za slovom?* 175.

10. "Voprosy, voprosy," 177.

11. Valentin Rasputin, "Vremia i vremia trevog" (Time and a time for alarm) in *Chto v slove, chto za slovom?* 190.

12. "Veruiu, veruiu v rodinu!" in *Chto v slove, chto za slovom?* 184.

13. "Voprosy, voprosy" in *Chto v slove, chto za slovom?* 164.

14. "Voprosy, voprosy," 179.

15. "Chto v slove, chto za slovom?" 154.

16. "Veruiu, veruiu v rodinu!" 199.

17. "Voprosy, voprosy," 177–78.

18. "Voprosy, voprosy," 178.

19. "Veruiu, veruiu v rodinu!" 198.

20. "Veruiu, veruiu v rodinu!" 199.

21. "Chto v slove, chto za slovom?" 159.

22. "Chto v slove, chto za slovom?" 158.

23. Valentin Rasputin, "Sibir': i khram i masterskaia" (Siberia: both a temple and

Notes

a workshop), in *Dialogi o Sibiri: sbornik* (Dialogues about Siberia: a miscellany) (Irkutsk: Vostochno-sibirskoe knizhnoe izd-vo, 1988), 60.

24. Douglas R. Weiner, *Models of Nature: Ecology, Conservation, and Cultural Revolution in Soviet Russia* (Bloomington: Indiana University Press, 1988), 230.

25. "Voprosy, Voprosy," 169.

26. Anatole G. Mazour, *An Outline of Modern Russian Historiography* (Berkeley and Los Angeles: University of California Press, 1939), 75.

27. *Siberia on Fire*, 102–60.

CHAPTER 1

1. Vladimir Kalistratovich Andrievich (b. 1838), Russian historian; his major work is *Istoricheskii ocherk Sibiri po dannym predstavliaemym Polnym sobraniem zakonov* (A historical essay about Siberia based on data in The complete compilation of laws). 6 vols. in 8. (Saint Petersburg: 1886–89).

2. Aleksandr Nikolaevich Radishchev (1749–1802), Russian writer whose most important work, *Puteshestvie iz Peterburga v Moskvu* (A journey from Petersburg to Moscow) (1790), describes the condition of the Russian people in the late eighteenth century.

3. *"Slovo o Ermake"* is an excerpt from Radishchev's *"Sokrashchennoe povestvovanie o priobretenii Sibiri"* (A brief narrative about the acquisition of Siberia), found in vol. 2 of his *Polnoe sobranie sochinenii* (Complete works) (Moscow-Leningrad: AN SSSR, 1938–52), 146–47.

4. The Russian chronicles (*letopisi*) are historical works dating from the eleventh through the seventeenth centuries in which the narrative is divided into years. Most have survived as parts of chronicle collections, which combine individual entries, reports, tales, lives of the saints, and other material in one account. As chronicle writing in general declined during the seventeenth century, local chronicles began to appear, the most interesting of which come from Siberia. The best known of these are the Stroganov and Esipov chronicles. In addition to providing important source material for research in early Russian history, the chronicles are invaluable for the study of Russian literature and the Russian language.

5. Tokhtamysh (?–1400), Mongol strongman and khan of the Golden Horde who invaded Muscovy and ravaged Moscow in 1382.

6. Dmitry Ivanovich Donskoy (1359–89), grand prince of Moscow famous for his military victory over the Tatars at the Battle of Kulikovo Field in 1380.

7. Pyotr Andreevich Vyazemsky (1792–1878), Russian poet, literary critic, and statesman.

8. Rus, the most venerable, and now largely poetic, name for Russia.

9. In Russian, *Dikoe Pole*, the popular name for the extensive steppe along the southern border of the Muscovite state, so called because of the Crimean Tatars and other marauding groups who lived there and often made devastating incursions into Russian territory.

10. The Livonian War of 1558–83, a prolonged military conflict in which Russia unsuccessfully fought Poland, Lithuania, and Sweden for control of Livonia (the lands on the eastern coast of the Baltic Sea north of Lithuania).

11. The Tatars were first defeated by the Russians in 1380 but remained a serious threat well into the sixteenth century; Peter the Great ruled from 1689 to 1725.

12. Kuchum was the last ruler of the khanate of Siberia, who destroyed Yermak's forces in 1585 and continued to oppose the Russians until 1598, when he was finally defeated.

13. Ruslan Grigorievich Skrynnikov (1931–), Russian historian and author of numerous works on Siberia.

14. *Stroganovskaia lietopis'*, one of the earliest of the historical chronicles describing events in Siberia. It was composed sometime in the seventeenth century on one of the Stroganovs' patrimonial estates and draws on family archives, including correspondence between the Stroganovs and Yermak's detachment. Its author credits the Stroganovs with a leading role in organizing Yermak's campaign.

15. Kiprian Starorusennikov (?–1635), archbishop of Tobolsk from 1621 to 1624.

16. Stepan Timofeevich Razin (1630?–1671), Don Cossack and leader of the massive uprising that occurred on the Volga frontier of the Muscovite state from 1661 to 1671, after which he was captured and hanged in Moscow. Also known as Stenka Razin, he is the subject of many legends and has come to signify the essence of the Russian folk spirit.

17. Nikolay Mikhaylovich Yadrintsev (1842–94), Russian ethnographer, archaeologist, explorer of Siberia, and Siberian "regionalist" (*oblastnik*).

18. Ivan Yurievich Moskvitin, Cossack from Tomsk who explored the Far East, reaching the Sea of Okhotsk and exploring its shoreline until 1641.

19. In Russian, *sluzhilyi chelovek*, a person bound by obligations of service, especially military service, to the Muscovite state.

20. Semyon Ivanovich Dezhnyov (1605–1673), Russian explorer whose report on the strait he discovered remained buried in the archives in Yakutsk until German historian Gerhard Friedrich Müller found it in 1736, after Vitus Bering and others had also explored the area.

21. In Russian, *voevoda*, the governor of a town or province during the Muscovite period.

22. Sergey Nikolaevich Markov (1906–79), Russian writer whose literary themes draw on Russian history and who has written many articles and books on travel and on geographic discoveries, including *Podvig Semena Dezhneva* (The feat of Semyon Dezhnyov) (Moscow: OGIZ, Gos. izd-vo geogr. lit-ry, 1948).

23. *Stol'nik*, a rank five steps below boyar that was conferred on Russian courtiers from the thirteenth through the seventeenth centuries.

24. In Russian, "*zlatokipiashchaia*" *Mangazeia*, a town founded in 1601 on the Taz River as the point of departure for Russians advancing into Eastern Siberia by a northern route. It flourished in the seventeenth century as a wealthy fur-trading center before burning to the ground and becoming deserted after 1662.

25. *Sibirische Geschichte von der Entdekkung Sibiriens bis auf die Eroberung dieses Lands durch die russische Waffen*, 2 vols. (Saint Petersburg: Gedrukt bei der Kaiserl. Akademie der Wissenschaften, 1768).

26. Mikhail Aleksandrovich Bakunin (1814–76), Russian anarchist active in several European countries.

27. Afanasy Prokofievich Shchapov (1831–76), Siberian-born Russian historian, social and political commentator, and Siberian "regionalist" (*oblastnik*).

28. In Russian, *vol'nitsa*, runaway serfs, Cossacks, religious dissenters, and other "outlaws" in Muscovite Russia.

29. The Russian Orthodox Church split into two factions during the 1660s.

30. Stefano Sommier (1848–1922), Italian travel and nature writer whose works include *Un'estate in Siberia fra Ostiiacchi, Samoiedi, Siriéni, Tatári e Baskiri* (A summer in Siberia among Ostyaks, Samoyeds, Zyryans, Tatars, and Bashkirs) (Florence: Ermanno Loescher, 1885).

31. In Russian, *dekabristy*, the name given to the Russian dissidents, mainly military officers from the upper classes, who led an unsuccessful rebellion against the Russian government in December 1825. After the insurrection failed, 121 Decembrists were brought to trial, five were executed, thirty-nine were imprisoned, and the rest were banished to Siberia.

32. Semyon Yakovlevich Kapustin (1828–91), Russian government servant and expert on the peasantry who published a number of studies on the common people's means of existence and way of life.

33. In Russian, *kabala*, servitude by contract in which an individual promised service for life in return for a loan or other assistance from a landlord; *kholopstvo*, the system of slavery prominent in medieval and early modern Russia until it was merged with serfdom, *krepostnoe pravo*, under Peter the Great.

34. Russia has had two capital cities during its history. Moscow, the first and current capital, was superseded by Saint Petersburg from 1712 until 1918, during which time Moscow was considered the country's second capital.

35. A reference to a project conceived in the 1930s to divert northward-flowing rivers to arid regions in the southern part of the Soviet Union to provide water for irrigation and other purposes.

36. Serfdom was abolished in Russia in 1861.

37. Vasily Makarovich Shukshin (1929–74), Siberian-born author, actor, and film director.

38. Ivan Aleksandrovich Goncharov (1812–91), Russian novelist and travel writer.

39. Chekhov made a trans-Siberian journey in 1890, which he describes in letters and memoirs from that period and in a study of the penal system and the indigenous peoples of Sakhalin Island titled *Ostrov Sakhalin* (Sakhalin Island) (Moscow: Izd. red. zhurnala "Russkaia mysl'," 1895).

40. Goncharov took a world cruise from 1852 to 1855 as secretary for a Russian expedition on the ship *Pallada*, publishing a description of the journey in *Fregat Pallada* (The frigate Pallada), 2d ed. 2 vols. (Saint Petersburg: V Tip. Morskago minister-stva, 1862).

41. A town constantly ravaged and burned by the Tatars as they advanced toward Moscow.

42. In Russian, *Optina Pustyn'*, a fourteenth-century monastery visited periodically by Gogol, Dostoyevsky, and Tolstoy to consult with its elders. Desecrated and nearly destroyed during the Soviet period, it was returned to the jurisdiction of the Moscow Patriarchate in 1988 and has been restored.

43. Leo Tolstoy's estate.

44. The city where Dostoyevsky wrote *The Brothers Karamazov*, which is set there.

CHAPTER 2

1. *Byliny*, traditional Russian epic poetry transmitted orally from very early times.

2. Vladimir's Hill (*Vladimirskaia gorka*) and Beautiful Hill (*Krasnyi kholm*) are where the first buildings in each city (a cathedral in Kiev and a fort in Moscow) were erected.

3. In Russian, *ukrainy*, from which the name of the area's present residents, Ukrainians, derives.

4. Czarevitch Dmitry (1582–91), son of Ivan the Terrible and heir apparent. He died mysteriously in Uglich, possibly at the instigation of Boris Godunov, who was rumored to have arranged the boy's murder to ensure his own election to the throne.

5. Tobolsk was the chief city of Russian Siberia until 1764, when it became the capital of Western Siberia, sharing equal status with Irkutsk, the capital of Eastern Siberia. It was superseded by Omsk in 1839.

6. Pavel Ivanovich Nebolsin (1817–93), Russian historian, ethnographer, and geographer.

7. Nikolay Mikhaylovich Karamzin (1766–1826), Russian writer and historian whose major work, *Istoriia gosudarstva Rossiiskago* (A history of the Russian state), published in twelve volumes in 1816–29, reflects the most advanced historical thinking of his time.

8. Karacha was a Tatar nobleman and member of Kuchum's council who later ambushed and killed Ivan Koltso, Yermak's righthand man, and forty Cossacks.

9. *Murza*, a minor nobleman in Turko-Tatar tribes.

10. Matvey Meshcheryak, one of the four *sotniki* (commanders of units of one hundred men) in Yermak's army, who led the surviving Cossacks back to Russia after Yermak's death, subsequently returning to Siberia after joining forces with Voivode Ivan Mansurov.

11. Ivan Koltso, one of Yermak's *sotniki*, who was slain by Karacha after being sent to Moscow by his leader in 1582 to report to the czar the subjugation of the Siberian khanate to Yermak's Cossacks.

12. Mametkul, a relative, perhaps son, of Kuchum and leader of his forces.

13. A quotation from Aleksandr Vasilievich Suvorov (1730–1800), a Russian military commander noted for his achievements in the Russo-Turkish War of 1787–91 and in the French Revolutionary Wars, who never lost a single battle.

14. Danila Chulkov, military officer sent by the czar with many troops and artillery to occupy Siberia after the Tatars were driven out.

15. Pyotr Andreevich Slovtsov (1767–1843), Russian historian who produced the first important works on Siberian history and on the local lore of the peoples of Siberia.

16. Gerhard Friedrich Müller (1705–83), German historian, archivist, and archaeologist who took part in the Great Northern Expedition to Siberia and Kamchatka in 1733–43 and whose writings, in which Soviet scholars found "errors" in interpreting the origins of the Russian state, laid the foundation for the study of Muscovy's eastward expansion and colonization.

17. Johann Eberhard Fischer (1697–1771), German historian and philologist who traveled extensively throughout Siberia and published articles on the history, geography, and ethnography of Siberia and northern Russia as well as an abridged German edition of Müller's *Istoriia Sibiri* (A history of Siberia).

Notes

18. Vasily Borisovich Sukin, voivode who arrived from Russia in 1585 and helped found Tyumen, where he built the first Russian Orthodox church in Siberia and from which he dispatched Danila Chulkov to build a fort at the site of Tobolsk.

19. Seid-khan or Seydak, Tatar prince who deposed Kuchum, attacked Tobolsk unsuccessfully, and was finally captured by Chulkov and sent to Moscow.

20. In Russian, *O sport!—ty mir!*, the title of a Russian documentary film about the 1980 Olympic Games, which was released in 1981. The 1980 Summer Olympics were held in the Soviet Union.

21. In Russian, *Smutnoe vremia*, the period of political crisis leading to social and economic instability that followed the collapse of the Rurik dynasty in 1598 and ended with the establishment of the Romanov dynasty in 1613.

22. Dmitry Mikhaylovich Pozharsky (1578–1642), Russian prince, military leader, and folk hero who successfully led Russian forces against Polish invaders.

23. In Russian, *desiatinnaia pashnia*, a system of landholding popular in Siberia in which public land was cultivated by peasants, who then received allotments from the government for their own use, and by crown peasants as part of their obligation to the state. By the late seventeenth century some peasants had began to satisfy their obligations by paying an annual lump sum (called *obrok*), and in 1789 the government declared an end to the system, requiring the peasants to pay rent instead.

24. Yury Yansheevich Suleshov (1584?–1643), Russian boyar who served as voivode of Tobolsk from 1623 to 1625. He was one of the first rulers to take a census, and his methods of improving agriculture, increasing trade, and establishing order throughout the vast, newly acquired Siberian territories earned him the reputation of a completely honest man.

25. Yakov Kudenetovich Cherkassky (?–1666) and his son Mikhail Yakovlevich (?–1712), the last voivodes of Tobolsk, were noted for their conscientiousness and honesty.

26. Fyodor Ivanovich Soymonov (1692–1780), Russian hydrographer and cartographer who published atlases of the Caspian and Baltic Seas and who served as governor of Siberia from 1757 to 1763.

27. Mikhail Mikhaylovich Speransky (1772–1839), Russian count and close adviser to Alexander I who served as governor of Siberia from 1819 to 1821 and who drew up a plan for administrative reforms there.

28. Nikolay Nikolaevich Muravyov-Amursky (1809–81), Russian count and diplomat who served as governor of Eastern Siberia from 1847 to 1861, promoted study of the region, and led expeditions along the Amur River in 1854 and 1855.

29. Aleksandr Ivanovich Despot-Zenovich (1828–95), Polish exile sent to Eastern Siberia in 1848 who became governor of Kyakhta and, at age thirty-four, governor of Tobolsk, serving from 1862 to 1866 and becoming highly regarded by all levels of society for his honesty, his tireless struggle against lawlessness, and his improvements in education.

30. Denis Ivanovich Chicherin (1720?–1785), Russian general and governor of Siberia from 1763 to 1781 who built a highway from Tobolsk to Irkutsk and provided Tobolsk with such public services as a hospital, pharmacy, geodesic school, and trade school for exiles.

31. Matvey Petrovich Gagarin, Russian prince and first governor of Siberia, from 1711 until his execution in 1721.

32. Pavel was the metropolitan of Tobolsk and Siberia from 1678 until his death in 1692.

33. Fyodor Alekseevich (1661–82), czar from 1676 to 1682.

34. Semyon Ulyanovich Remezov (?–after 1720), Russian historian and cartographer who drew the first map of Tobolsk in 1683 and compiled the first Russian geographic atlas, *Chertezhnaia kniga Sibiri* (A sketchbook of Siberia). He also wrote *Istoriia Sibiri* (A history of Siberia) and *Khronologicheskaia kniga* (The chronological book), the latter an atlas containing diagrams of Tobolsk, descriptions of buildings, and maps of rivers and the surrounding steppe.

35. Philipp Johann von Strahlenberg (1676–1747), Swedish officer who became a prisoner of war after the Battle of Poltava in 1709 and lived in Siberia until 1730, when he returned to Sweden. During his exile, he made a map of Siberia based largely on Remezov's drawings and wrote a historical and geographical work titled *Das nord- und östliche Theil von Europa und Asia* (The northern and eastern parts of Europe and Asia) (Stockholm, 1730).

36. Juraj Križanić (1618?–1683), Roman Catholic priest, scholar, and writer of Croatian origin who advocated unity among the Slavs in order to eliminate the foreign domination and exploitation of Slavic nations. He went to Moscow in 1659, was exiled to Tobolsk in 1661 for unknown reasons, where he lived for fifteen years and wrote nine books, and left Russia in 1676.

37. A reference to a historical source known as *Cherepanovskaia sibirskaia lietopis'* (The Cherepanov chronicle of Siberia), compiled in 1760 by Ilya Cherepanov, a coachman from Tobolsk.

38. Filaret (1553?–1663), patriarch of Moscow from 1608 to 1610 and from 1619 until his death. In secular life, he was Fyodor Nikitich Romanov, father of Czar Mikhail Fyodorovich.

39. Boris Fyodorovich Godunov (1552?–1605), chief adviser to Czar Fyodor I (who reigned from 1584 to 1598). He was elected czar of Muscovy after the extinction of the Rurik Dynasty and ruled from 1598 to 1605.

40. Exiles were sometimes mutilated as a permanent indication of their status.

41. Pelym was the name given to the tribal union of the Mansi people, which existed from the middle of the fifteenth to the end of the sixteenth century on the Pelym, Sosva, and Lozva Rivers. It also included the Mansi on the Tavda River (the principality of Tabara), which was known to the Russians at that time as the Pelym State or the Pelym Principality.

42. Fyodor Mikhaylovich Lobanov-Rostovsky, voivode from 1592 to 1595.

43. Dostoyevsky lived in Staraya Russa from 1879 to 1880 while writing *The Brothers Karamazov*, which is set there.

44. Władysław IV Vasa (1595–1648), king of Poland from 1632 to 1648. When he was fifteen, his father, King Sigismund III Vasa, had him elected czar of Russia after Polish forces seized Moscow during the Time of Troubles, although he never actually assumed the Muscovite throne. His election was part of his father's unsuccessful plan to conquer Russia and convert the population to Catholicism.

Notes

45. Charles IX (1550–1611), king of Sweden from 1607 to 1611. To counteract Polish attempts to seize the Russian throne, he put forth his own sons, Gustavus Adolphus and Karl Filip, as potential czars.

46. Mikhail Fyodorovich Romanov became czar in 1613.

47. Jean Chappe d'Auteroche (1728–69), French astronomer who was sent to Tobolsk by the Paris Academy of Sciences in 1761 to observe the transit of Venus. He described his journey through Russia and Siberia in *Voyage en Sibérie, fait par ordre du roi en 1761* (A journey to Siberia, made by order of the king in 1761) (Paris: Debure, père, 1768), which contained so many critical remarks about Russia and Russian society that Catherine the Great felt compelled to respond by issuing a pamphlet, probably written by Ivan Shuvalov, titled "Antidote ou examen du mauvais livre superbement imprimé, intitulé: Voyage de l'abbé Chappe" (An antidote to or examination of the wicked book, superbly printed, entitled: The journey of l'abbé Chappe) (Amsterdam, 1771).

48. Anatoly Naumovich Rybakov (1911–), Russian writer and author of *Deti Arbata* (The children of the Arbat) (Moscow: Sov. pisatel', 1987), a novel depicting Russian life as experienced by young Muscovites in the 1930s, including arrest and exile to Siberia.

49. In anticipation of hosting the Summer Olympics in 1980, Soviet authorities rounded up prostitutes in the cities where the games would take place and sent them temporarily to Siberia.

50. A major Cossack and peasant uprising in 1773–75 led by Yemilyan Pugachyov.

51. Ferdinand Petrovich Wrangel, baron (1796–1870), Russian seafarer, explorer, and founding member of the Russian Geographical Society who completed the mapping of the northeastern coast of Siberia during an expedition in 1820–24 and after whom Vrangel Island is named.

52. Johann Georg Gmelin (1709–55), German naturalist who took part in the Great Northern Expedition and published his findings in the four-volume *Flora Siberica, sive Historia plantarum Siberiae* (Flora Siberica; or, A history of the plants of Siberia) (Petropoli: ex typographia Academiae scientiarum, 1747–69), which became a classic of botanical research. His *Reise durch Siberien, von dem Jahr 1733 bis 1743* (A journey through Siberia from 1733 to 1743) (Göttingen: A. Vandenhoecks, 1751–52), which was widely read throughout Europe, set a precedent for describing the Russian and indigenous peoples of Siberia as crude, ignorant, superstitious, and surly.

53. *Istoriia russkoi etnografii*, 4 vols. (Saint Petersburg: Tip. M. M. Stasiulevicha, 1890–92).

54. Elizabeth (Yelizaveta Petrovna) (1709–62), empress of Russia from 1741 to 1762.

55. In Russian, "v rabskom vide tsar' nebesnyi," a line from Fyodor Tyutchev's poem beginning "Eti bednye selen'ia . . ." (These poor settlements . . .), written in 1855.

56. Vasily Danilovich Poyarkov (?–1668), Russian explorer who led an expedition to the Amur region, expanding Russia's territorial holdings in the Far East and providing the first detailed description of the Amur area.

57. In Russian, *boiarskii syn*, a rank of Russian nobility between the boyars, the highest level of nobility, and government servants (*sluzhilye liudi*). Noblemen of this

rank composed the middle stratum of the military and administrative service sector. Despite the term's literal meaning, the title of boyar was not hereditary, and boyars' sons (*deti boiarskie*) usually attained their rank only after many years of service, which they normally performed in the provinces rather than in the capital.

58. Known as Kuznetsk until 1931, the city was renamed Stalinsk in 1932 and Novokuznetsk in 1962.

59. In Russian, this contraction is pronounced almost the same as *Sibiri*, the genitive case of *Sibir'* (Siberia).

60. Pyotr Pavlovich Yershov (1815–69), Russian writer and active participant in the cultural and social life of Siberia who lived in Tobolsk from 1836 until his death. His best work is considered the verse tale *Konek-Gorbunok* (The little humpbacked horse), first published in 1834 and a classic of nineteenth-century Russian literature.

61. Dmitry Ivanovich Mendeleev (1834–1907), Russian chemist who devised and published the periodic table of the elements in 1869.

62. Russian merchant and industrialist families who made fortunes in such industries as iron and gold and who also helped finance the exploration and economic development of Siberia, gave generously to charitable causes, and were patrons of the arts.

63. The current name for Chuvash Point.

64. Vasily Grigorievich Perov (1833–82), Russian portrait and landscape painter and graphic artist.

65. Grigory Nikolaevich Potanin (1835–1920), Russian traveler, ethnographer, and geographer who explored and described little-known areas of Siberia and Central Asia and who did much to develop the cultural life of Siberia by establishing learned societies, museums, and exhibitions.

66. Aleksey Pavlovich Okladnikov (1908–81), Russian archaeologist, historian, and ethnographer whose works treat the ancient history of Siberia, Mongolia, and Central Asia.

67. Aleksandr Aleksandrovich Alyabiev (1787–1851), Russian composer and conductor who was exiled to Tobolsk in 1828 for alleged complicity in a murder. On returning to his hometown, he organized a renowned orchestra of Cossacks and fellow exiles.

68. *Irtysh, prevrashchaiushchiisia v Ipokrenu.* The Hippocrene (Horse's Spring) is a spring in Greek mythology that appeared near the Muses' sacred grove when Pegasus struck a rock with his hoof. The muses would gather there to sing and dance, for its water was said to bring poetic inspiration.

69. Ivan Yakovlevich Bilibin (1876–1942), Russian painter and graphic artist known principally for his fanciful illustrations of Russian *byliny* and fairy tales.

70. *Subbotnik*, a day of "voluntary" unpaid labor, usually Saturday, often required by Soviet managers.

71. Clara Eissner Zetkind (1857–1933), German feminist and socialist who played a leading role after World War I in the new Communist Party of Germany and in the Comintern. Married to a Russian exile, Ossip Zetkind, and a personal friend of Lenin, she spent much time in Moscow and died in Arkhangelskoe.

72. One of Tobolsk's tourist attractions is a factory that produces decorative objects made of bone.

Notes

73. The House of Pioneers was the headquarters for the local branch of the national Communist organization for young children.

74. In Russian, "Umom Rossiiu ne poniat' . . .," the first line of an untitled four-line poem written by Fyodor Tyutchev in 1866.

75. In Russian, *Priamskoi vzvoz*, meaning the straightest, shortest route to the citadel.

76. The publication in 1790 of Radishchev's *Puteshestvie iz Peterburga v Moskvu* (A journey from Petersburg to Moscow), an indictment of serfdom, autocracy, and censorship, led to his immediate arrest and a death sentence, which was commuted to ten years' exile in Siberia.

77. "Opisanie tobol'skago namestnichestva" (1790–91?) and "Opisanie kitaiskago torga," originally titled "Pis'mo o kitaiskom torge" (A letter about trade with China) (1792), can be found in Radishchev's *Polnoe sobranie sochinenii* (Complete works) (Moscow-Leningrad: AN SSSR, 1938–52), 3:133–142, and 2:3–35.

78. The city's foundation was laid in 1703 and construction continued throughout the eighteenth century.

79. In Russian, *Baikalo-Amurskaia magistral'*, known as BAM, a second major railway running north of and parallel to the Trans-Siberian Railroad across Eastern Siberia, which drew workers from all over the Soviet Union during the 1970s and 1980s to help with construction but was never completed.

80. Ernst Johann von Biron (1690–1772), duke of Courland and chief adviser to Empress Anna Ivanovna, who reigned from 1730 to 1740. While holding no official administrative post, he became the central figure in the Russian government, leading a group of German adventurers who discriminated against the Russian nobility, exploited Russia's resources for their own benefit, and suppressed their opponents by having them executed or banished to Siberia.

81. "Istoriia Petra Velikago"; "Kratkoe iz"iasnenie astronomii"; "Izviestie o torgakh sibirskikh"; "Sibir', zolotoe dno"; "Opisanie Kaspiiskago moria"; and "Opisanie shturmanskago iskusstva," most of which appeared in the journal *Ezhemiesiachnyia sochineniia i izviestiia o uchenykh delakh* (Monthly writings and news of scholarly affairs). 10 vols. in 20 (Saint Petersburg: Pri Imp. Akademii nauk, 1755–64).

82. Dmitry Nikolaevich Bantysh-Kamensky (1788–1850), Russian historian, writer, governor of Tobolsk from 1825 to 1828, and governor of Vilna Province from 1836 to 1838.

83. *Slovar' dostopamiatnykh liudei Russkoi zemli* (Moscow: Izdan A. Shiriaevym, 1836), with a supplement (*Dopolnienie*) in 3 vols. (Saint Petersburg, 1847).

84. A paraphrase of a line from Mikhail Lermontov's 1837 poem "Borodino" that reads "Yes, there were real people in our day" ("Da, byli liudi v nashe vremia"), in which an aging Russian veteran of the Battle of Borodino looks down on the younger generation for lacking heroic qualities.

85. Mikhail Stepanovich Znamensky (1833–1892), Russian author and amateur historian who wrote a novel titled *Isker* (Tobolsk: Tip. Tobol'skago gub. pravleniia, 1891) and *Istoricheskiia okresnosti goroda Tobol'ska* (The historical environs of the town of Tobolsk) (Tyumen: Izd. A. A. Krylova, 1901).

CHAPTER 3

1. *Piatidesiatnik*, commander of a unit of fifty soldiers during the Muscovite period.

2. In Russian, *"proch'i sobach'i reki,"* so named because the main means of transportation in the Arctic at that time was dog sled.

3. "Rospis' protiv chertezhu ot Kuty reki vverkh po Lene i do vershiny i storonnim rekam, kotorye vpali v Lenu reku i skol'ko ot reki do reki sudovago khodu i pashennym mestam i rasprossnye rechi tungusskago kniaztsa Mozheulka pro bratskikh liudei i pro tungusskikh i pro Lamu i pro inye reki," originally published in *Dopolneniia k aktam istoricheskim* (Supplements to the historical documents), vol. 2 (Saint Petersburg: Arkheograficheskaia komissiia, 1846), 248–49, and republished in *Otkrytiia russkikh zemleprokhodtsev i poliarnykh morekhodov XVII veka na Severo-Vostoke Azii: sbornik dokumentov* (The discoveries of the Russian pioneers and arctic seafarers of the seventeenth century in northeast Asia: a collection of documents) (Moscow: Gos. izd-vo geogr. lit-ry, 1951), no. 23, 106–10.

4. Nicolae Milescu (known in Russia as Nikolay Gavrilovich Spafary) (1636–1708), Moldavian scholar, linguist, translator, and diplomat who spent most of his adult life in Russian service and was the Muscovite envoy to China from 1675 to 1678. One of his most valuable works is *Puteshestvie cherez Sibir' ot Tobol'ska do Nerchinska i granits Kitaia* (A journey through Siberia from Tobolsk to Nerchinsk and the borders of China) (Saint Petersburg: Tip. V. Kirshbauma, 1882).

5. Evert Ysbrandszoon Ides (b. 1660?), Danish merchant employed by the Russian government who lived in Russia from 1677 until his death sometime between 1704 and 1709. Peter the Great sent him to China to make commercial arrangements. His description of the journey in *Zapiski o russkom posol'stve v Kitai, 1692–1695*, (Moscow: Glav. red. vost. lit-ry, 1967), which includes a map of Siberia, greatly influenced West European scholarship.

6. Benedykt Dybowski (1833–1930), Polish zoologist and paleontologist who was exiled to Eastern Siberia from 1864 to 1877 for participating in the Polish Uprising of 1863. He was the first to describe Lake Baikal's physical features and fauna, publishing works in collaboration with fellow exile Wiktor Godlewski that laid the foundation for the scientific study of the lake.

7. Avvakum Petrovich (1620/21–1682), leader of the Old Believers, a conservative sect that split away from the Russian Orthodox Church under his guidance, for which he was banished to northern Russia and Siberia and eventually burned at the stake.

8. Mezen, a city in northwest Russia near the White Sea, to which Avvakum was exiled in 1664 and where he remained until 1665.

9. Dmitry Pavlovich Davydov (1811–88), Siberian-born Russian poet whose poem "Dumy begletsa na Baikale" (Thoughts of a fugitive at Baikal) became, with minor changes, the popular folksong "Slavnoe more, sviashchennyi Baikal."

10. Aleksey Ivanovich Martos (1790–1842), Russian writer and author of *Pis'ma o Vostochnoi Sibiri* (Letters about Eastern Siberia) (Moscow: V Univ. tip., 1827) whose memoirs, *Zapiski inzhenernago ofitsera Martosa (1806–1818)* (The notes of engineer officer Martos, 1806–1818), were published in the journal *Russkii arkhiv* (Russian archives), 1893, nos. 7 and 8.

Notes

11. Gleb Yurievich Vereshchagin (1889–1944), Russian hydrobiologist and head of the Baikal Limnological Station from 1929 until his death.

12. In Russian, *Shaman-kamen'*, a large rock formation where the Angara River flows out of Lake Baikal. In earlier times the Buryats revered the rock as a sacred place and their shamans performed incantations there. With the construction of the Irkutsk Dam on the Angara and the subsequent rise of the water level, most of the Shaman Rock is now submerged.

13. Ivan Dementievich Chersky (1845–92), Polish explorer of Siberia who was conscripted into the Russian army and banished to Omsk as punishment for participating in the Polish Uprising of 1863. After release from the army, he conducted geological research in the Baikal region and published a number of works on Lake Baikal.

14. Oleg Kirillovich Gusev (1930–), Russian biologist with the East Siberian branch of the Academy of Sciences and author of several books on Lake Baikal.

15. Gustav Radde (1831–1903), German naturalist and ethnographer who moved to Russia in 1852, where he participated in numerous expeditions, including one to Eastern Siberia from 1855 to 1860.

16. Wiktor Godlewski (1831–1900), Polish scientist exiled to Siberia for participating in the Polish Uprising of 1863.

17. Omul is an endemic subspecies of whitefish.

18. *Vizhu dno Baikala!* (Leningrad: Gidrometeoizdat, 1982).

19. The third line of the song "Glorious Sea, Sacred Baikal."

20. After trying for a decade to save the Stanislaus River Canyon in north central California and when legal action failed to stop the Army Corps of Engineers from constructing a dam there, Dubois prevented them from filling the reservoir by chaining himself to the bedrock in 1979. The Corps succeeded in flooding the canyon in 1982.

21. A musical comedy released in 1938 and directed by Grigory Vasilievich Aleksandrov, which features satiric episodes with much clowning.

22. *Za kujira: seikimatsu bunmei no shōchō* (The whale: symbol of civilization at the close of the twentieth century) (Tokyo: Bunshindō, Shōwa 58 [1983]).

23. On World Environment Day, June 5, 1984.

24. *Baikal v voprosakh i otvetakh* (Irkutsk: Vostochno-Sibirskoe knizhnoe izd-vo, 1984).

25. In Russian, "*sploshnaia likhoradka buden*," from Vladimir Mayakovsky's poem "Khorosho!" published in 1927, which celebrates the October Revolution: "Ia s temi, / kto vyshel / stroit' / i mest' / v sploshnoi / likhoradke / buden" (I am one of those / who came out / to build / and to sweep / in the unbroken / fever / of everyday life).

26. Leonid Maksimovich Leonov (1899–1994), Russian writer and member of the Soviet Academy of Sciences whose tragic or ambiguous views of moral and ethical problems in post-1917 Soviet society often brought him unfavorable criticism.

27. Mikhail Aleksandrovich Sholokhov (1905–84), Russian writer and member of the Soviet Academy of Sciences best known for his epic novel *Tikhii Don* (The quiet Don) (Moscow: Moskovskii rabochii, 1928–40).

28. In Russian, *Zmei Gorynych*, an evil character in Russian folklore that resembles a werewolf and that abducts and devours people.

29. Bottled water from Lake Baikal did in fact become available in the Soviet Union in 1991. On August 13, 1991, *Izvestia* reported that companies in Japan,

Taiwan, the United Arab Emirates, Britain, France, and other countries had expressed interest in buying lake water.

30. The Thirteenth Five-Year plan covered the period 1988–92.

CHAPTER 4

1. *Bogatyr'*, a larger-than-life hero in Russian folklore.

2. Ilya Sergeevich Glazunov (1930–), Russian landscape and graphic artist whose works include paintings based on themes from Russian history and from Dostoyevsky's novels.

3. From Gogol's 1831 article "Ob arkhitekture nyneshnego vremeni" (On contemporary architecture), vol. 6 of *Sobranie sochinenii v semi tomakh* (Collected works in seven volumes) (Moscow: Izd-vo "Khudozh. lit-ry," 1967), 75–[95].

4. Aleksey Petrovich Zholobov, who served as vice governor from 1731 to 1733, was beheaded for abuse of power in 1736.

5. P. N. Krylov was sent to Irkutsk by I. Glebov, chief investigating magistrate for the Russian Senate, and resided there from 1758 to 1760.

6. Speransky was appointed governor-general of Siberia in 1819 and instructed to reform the chaotic and corrupt administration of that region. His reforms, enacted in 1822, divided the area into Western Siberia, with the administrative center first at Tobolsk and then, from 1839, at Omsk; and Eastern Siberia, with Irkutsk as the administrative center. These and other measures transformed the way Siberia was ruled and laid foundations for administration that lasted into the twentieth century.

7. Ivan Borisovich Pestel (1765–1843), Russian government servant appointed governor-general of Siberia in 1806. After living and traveling in Siberia until 1809, he returned to Saint Petersburg and remained governor general until 1819, ruling from the capital through local governors.

8. Nikolay Ivanovich Treskin (1763–1842), vice governor of Smolensk whose lawlessness exceeded that of all his predecessors when Pestel appointed him vice governor of Irkutsk, where he served from 1806 until 1819, when Speransky dismissed him. After being stripped of rank and banished, Treskin died in poverty.

9. *Zapiski irkutskago zhitelia*, parts 1–3, *Russkaia starina* (Russian antiquity) 123, no. 7: 187–251; no. 8: 384–409; no. 9: 609–46 (all nos. 1905).

10. In Russian, *Bol'shoi kolokol v 761 pud*, which weighed approximately 27,400 pounds.

11. *Po Aliaske i Aleutskim ostrovam* (Novosibirsk: Nauka, Sibirskoe otd-nie, 1976).

12. Grigory Ivanovich Shelikhov (or Shelekhov) (1747–95), Russian merchant who started a fur-trading company that formed the basis of the Russian-American Company, founded in 1799. He also established Russia's first permanent colony in Alaska in 1784.

13. Konstantin Andreevich Ton (1794–1881), Russian architect whose most famous buildings, in the eclectic "Russian Byzantine" style, include the Big Kremlin Palace (*Bol'shoi Kremlevskii dvorets*) (1839–49) and the Kremlin's Armory (*Oruzheinaia palata*) (1844–51).

14. *Irkutsk: ego miesto i znachenie v istorii i kul'turnom razvitii vostochnoi Sibiri* (Irkutsk: its place and significance in the history and cultural development of Eastern Siberia) (Moscow: Tip. I. N. Kushnerev, 1891).

15. Aleksandr Andreevich Baranov (1746–1819), first governor of the Russian colonies in America (from 1790 to 1818). He also established commercial ties with California, Hawaii, and China.

16. I.e., Muravyov-Amursky. He received the title of Count Amursky for concluding the Aigun Treaty of 1858 with China, which set the border between Russia and China at the Amur River.

17. Mikhail Vasilievich (Butashevich) Petrashevsky (1821–66), Russian revolutionary, utopian socialist, and leader of a group of socialists who met secretly in Saint Petersburg in the late 1840s to discuss theoretical and political issues. Their discussions culminated in the formation of a revolutionary conspiracy in 1848, participation in which resulted in Dostoyevsky and other leading members of the circle, known as *petrashevtsy*, being imprisoned and banished to Siberia. Petrashevsky was sentenced to a life term of hard labor, which he served in the Nerchinsk mines near Lake Baikal. The *petrashevtsy* were granted amnesty in 1856, after which their leader spent the rest of his life in Irkutsk.

18. *Minuvshee i perezhitoe: Sibir' i emigratsiia: vospominaniia za 50 let* (The past and my experiences: Siberia and emigration: reminiscences covering fifty years), 2 vols. (Leningrad: Izd-vo "Kolos," 1924).

19. *Strel'tsy* (literally, "musketeers"), a military corps created by Ivan the Terrible that had developed into a hereditary military caste by the middle of the seventeenth century. Siding against Peter the Great in the struggle for succession that began in 1682, the *strel'tsy* were disbanded when Peter gained power and finally abolished in 1713.

20. Abram Petrovich Gannibal (1697?–1781), son of an Ethiopian prince who became a military engineer in Russia and later Peter the Great's valet and secretary. The great-grandfather of Aleksandr Pushkin, he was immortalized in the tale "The Black African of Peter the Great."

21. Aleksandr Danilovich Menshikov (1673–1729), comrade-in-arms of Peter the Great who in practice ruled the Russian Empire under Catherine I and was exiled to Beryozov under Peter II.

22. Artemy Petrovich Volynsky (1689-1740), Russian statesman and diplomat who served as a cabinet minister under Anna Ioannovna from 1738 until his execution as an opponent of her favorite, Count Ernst von Biron.

23. Nikolay Gavrilovich Chernyshevsky (1829–89), Russian revolutionary, writer, and literary critic who was exiled to Vilyuysk, a town in Yakutsk Province that became the home of many political exiles beginning in the early nineteenth century, where he lived from 1872 to 1883.

24. *Sibir' i katorga*, 3 vols. (Saint Petersburg: Tip. A. Transhelia, 1871).

25. Jaroslav Hašek (1883–1923), Czech writer best known for his satirical masterpiece *Good Soldier Schweik*. Drafted into the Austro-Hungarian Army during World War I, he was captured on the Russian front and made a prisoner of war. In Russia he became a member of the Czech liberation army but later joined the Bolsheviks, for whom he wrote Communist propaganda while living in Irkutsk.

26. Yekaterina Ivanovna Laval Trubetskaya (1800–1854), Russian princess and

the first Decembrist wife to follow her husband, Sergey Trubetskoy, into exile to the Lake Baikal region in 1826.

27. Aleksandr Vasilievich Kolchak (1874–1920), Arctic explorer and naval officer who during the Russian Civil War was recognized by the Whites as supreme ruler of Russia. After initial victories, Kolchak's forces were eventually routed by the Red Army and Kolchak moved his headquarters to Irkutsk. When captured by the Bolsheviks, he was summarily executed and his body thrown into the Angara River.

CHAPTER 5

1. Yegor Yegorovich Meyer (1820–67), Russian painter and landscape artist who traveled to Siberia and whose writings include "Poiezdka po Altaiu" (A journey to the Altay region) in *Otechestvennyia zapiski* (Notes on the fatherland), no. 11 (1834): 17–23.

2. Pyotr Aleksandrovich Chikhachyov (1808–90), Russian geographer and geologist who traveled throughout the Altay region and northwest China in 1842 and described the geographical and geological features of those areas.

3. Aleksandr Yefremovich Novosyolov (1884–1918), Russian writer known for his accurate and beautiful portrayals of the Old Believers' way of life.

4. During the Soviet period dams were usually built in flat areas and flooded vast amounts of farmland.

5. Nikolay Konstantinovich Rerikh (1874–1947), Russian painter, author, scholar, and world traveler.

6. Yevgeny Gennadievich Gushchin (1936–), Russian prose writer.

7. The Oyrats were a group of western Mongolian peoples, ancestors of the Kalmyks, who settled in Russia during the seventeenth century.

8. The name for Gorno-Altaysk until 1932.

9. Okladnikov headed numerous expeditions to the eastern Altay region beginning in the 1960s, where he discovered rock paintings from prehistoric times.

10. "Manzherok" is also the name of a current popular song.

11. Grigory Ivanovich Gurkin (1870 or 1872–1937), Russian painter and graphic artist born in Ulala (now Gorno-Altaysk) who studied icon painting in Saint Petersburg before returning to his homeland, where he lived in Anos from 1906 until his death.

12. Yekaterina Ivanovna Kalinina (1882–1960), party and government figure active during the Russian revolutions of 1905 and 1917 who received various assignments in industry and in the Soviet government and was a member of the Supreme Court of the Russian Republic. She was imprisoned by the secret police from 1939 until several days before her husband's death in 1946.

13. Mikhail Ivanovich Kalinin (1875–1946), participant in both Russian revolutions and leading figure in the Communist party who served as president of the Russian Republic and of the USSR and was a member of the Politburo from 1925 on. He was one of the few old Bolsheviks to survive Stalin's purges and to die of natural causes.

14. Vyacheslav Yakovlevich Shishkov (1873–1945), Russian prose writer whose main subject is Siberia's past and present.

15. The reservoir of the Bratsk Dam, for example, floods 179,000,000 cubic meters of land.

16. Vasily Vasilievich Sapozhnikov (1861–1924), Russian botanist and geographer who described his 1895 expedition in *Po Altaiu: dnevnik puteshestviia 1895 goda* (Travels in the Altay region: the diary from a journey made in 1895) (Tomsk: Tipo-lit. P. I. Makushina, 1897).

17. The collectivization of agriculture in the Soviet Union began in 1929, when millions of small farms were forcibly combined into thousands of large-scale socialist farming cooperatives. More than half of all peasant households were collectivized by the end of 1931.

18. Nikon (Nikita Minov) (1605–1681), patriarch of Moscow from 1652 to 1658 who introduced changes in church ritual based on Greek practices in an effort to unite the entire Orthodox Church, which led to the Schism of the Old Believers.

19. The same liturgical books had been used in Russia since the conversion of Rus to Christianity in 988.

20. A widespread precept among the Old Believers used to justify suffering in the name of the future.

21. Dzungaria is a region in northwestern China bounded by the Altay and the Eastern Tian-Shan Mountains.

22. Serafim Serafimovich Shashkov (1841–82), Russian historian, social and political commentator, and Siberian regionalist (*oblastnik*).

23. Akinfy Demidov (1678–1745), member of a famous family of mining industrialists who, by the end of his life, owned twenty-five mining works in the Urals, the Altay region, and central Russia and employed a total of 38,000 male peasants.

24. "Raskol'nich'i obshchiny na granitse Kitaia" in *Sibirskii sbornik* (The Siberian miscellany), no. 1 (1886): 21–47.

25. Until the emancipation of the serfs in 1861, Russian peasants were commonly conscripted for periods of twenty-five years, in effect for life.

26. The *volost'* was the smallest administrative district in czarist Russia.

27. Pyotr Mikhaylovich Golovachyov (1862–1913), Russian historian and ethnographer specializing in the colonization of Siberia.

28. "V gorakh Altaia" in *Sibirskii sbornik* (The Siberian miscellany), no. 4 (1897): 366–92.

29. Kerzhak is a regional term for Old Believer.

30. State farms (*sovkhozy*) developed from the private estates taken over by the Soviet government after the 1917 Revolution. They were organized like industries for large-scale production and paid workers wages. Collective farms (*kolkhozy*), introduced in the 1930s, paid workers a share of the profits. Many collective farms, the more prevalent form of agriculture, were converted to state farms during the 1950s.

31. See, for example, "Mesiats v Kedrograde" (A month in Kedrograd) and other essays in Chivilikhin's *Sobranie sochinenii v 4-kh tomakh* (Collected works in 4 volumes), vol. 2: *Proza i publitsistika* (Prose and social/political commentary) (Moscow: Sovremennik, 1985), 261–325.

32. In Russian, *kandidat*, a holder of the first graduate degree in the Russian system of higher education, which is roughly equivalent to an American Ph.D.

33. "Teletskoe ozero, kedrovniki i 'Kedrograd,' mify i real'nost'" (Lake Teletskoe,

the Siberian pine forests, and Kedrograd, myths and reality) in *Sibirskie ogni* (Siberian lights), no. 6 (1987): 131–40.

34. Scientists speculate that on June 30, 1908, the earth collided with a comet, which created a large strip of devastated forest near the Tunguska River.

35. *"Strannik na Zolotom ozere"* in *Sibirskie zapiski* (Siberian notes), no. 2 (1919): 2–7.

36. Gleb Aleksandrovich Goryshin (1931–), Russian writer born in Leningrad who worked as a laborer for geological expeditions in the Kola Peninsula, the Angara region, and the Sayan Mountains and whose stories describe Saint Petersburg and Siberia.

37. In Russian, *rabfak* (*rabochii fakul'tet*), a workers' school, one of many organizations established during the first years after the Russian Revolution to prepare workers and peasants for entering institutions of higher learning.

38. Mikhail Andreevich Suslov (1902–82), long-standing member of the Communist party who held many important party and government posts, including membership in the Politburo from 1966 until his death.

CHAPTER 6

1. Nikolay Aleksandrovich Bestuzhev (1791–1855), Russian officer sentenced to a life term of hard labor for his participation in the Decembrist Uprising of 1825 who, after working in the Nerchinsk mines, lived in a settlement near Selenginsk from 1839 until his death. A man of many interests and accomplishments, he was also an artist, creating ink drawings, watercolors, and portraits of great historical value that form a visual record of the Decembrists in exile.

2. Aleksandra Viktorovna Potanina (1843–93), the first Russian woman to explore Central Asia, participating in her husband's expeditions to Mongolia, northern China, and eastern Tibet. Author of several ethnographic works describing native peoples, she received a gold medal from the Russian Geographical Society in 1887 for *Buriaty* (The Buryats).

3. Savva Lukich Raguzinsky-Vladislavich (1670?–1738), a Serb who became a statesman and diplomat in the Russian government and carried out diplomatic missions in Turkey and China, heading a group that negotiated with China from 1725 to 1728.

4. Dmitry Ivanovich Stakheev (1840–?), Russian author who spent fourteen years in Siberia conducting business for his father, a merchant, and who wrote fiction and travel literature, including *Za Baikalom i na Amurie* (Beyond Lake Baikal and on the Amur River) (Saint Petersburg: Tip. K. Vul'fa, 1869).

5. Of the four Bestuzhev brothers who participated in the Decembrist revolt Mikhail Aleksandrovich (1800–1871) and Nikolay Aleksandrovich were both exiled to Selenginsk in 1839 after doing hard labor in the Nerchinsk mines.

6. Mikhail Vasilievich (1871–1943) and Sergey Vasilievich Sabashnikov (1873–1909) founded the publishing house of M. and S. Sabashnikov in Moscow in 1890 with an educational aim, issuing Russian and foreign literary classics, history

books, and works in the natural and social sciences. The press continued to operate independently until 1930.

7. Charles Frederic Worth (1825–95), Paris couturier born in England.

8. Possibly Antoni Navotni, a tailor in Saint Petersburg during the nineteenth century.

9. George Kennan (1845–1924), a journalist whose nephew became the American ambassador to the Soviet Union, was commissioned by the Century Company to make a 5,000-mile trip across Russia and Siberia in 1885 and 1886, after which he wrote *Siberia and the Exile System* (New York: Century, 1891).

10. Semyon Ivanovich Cherepanov (1810–84) wrote under the pseudonym "a Siberian Cossack." His works include *Puteshestvie sibirskago kazaka* (The travels of a Siberian Cossack) and *Vospominaniia sibirskago kazaka* (The memoirs of a Siberian Cossack).

11. Three Botkin brothers became famous: Vasily Petrovich (1811/12–69) was a writer and friend of Belinsky and Herzen; Mikhail Petrovich (1839–1914) was an engraver and landscape artist; and Sergey Petrovich (1832–89) was a therapist who helped found one of the first clinics for treating psychological disorders.

12. Nikolay Andreevich Belogolovy (1834–95), physician active in public life who wrote a biography of Sergey Botkin.

13. Dmitry Nikolaevich Pryanishnikov (1865–1948), Russian scientist and founder of agrochemistry who was born in Kyakhta and became a professor at the Petrovsky Agricultural Academy in 1895, where he remained until his death.

14. Maria Ivanovna Vodovozova (1869–1954), Russian publisher active in Saint Petersburg from 1895 to 1900 who published Lenin's *Razvitie kapitalizma v Rossii* (The development of capitalism in Russia) in 1899.

15. Ivan Vasilievich Shcheglov (1855–84), Russian historian who taught school in Yeniseysk, Krasnoyarsk, Irkutsk, and Troitskosavsk and whose main work, *Khronologiia istorii Sibiri 1032–1882 g.* (The chronology of Siberian history, 1032–1882) (Irkutsk: Izd. Vostochno-sibirskago otdiela I. Russkago geogr. ob-va, 1883), is a basic source for Siberian studies.

16. Dorzhi Banzarov (1822?–55), Orientalist and expert on Eastern languages who wrote a number of works on Mongolian languages and on shamanism.

17. Alexander Herzen (1812–70), Russian revolutionary, writer, and philosopher who published, with Nikolay Ogaryov, the first Russian revolutionary newspaper, *Kolokol* (The bell), in London (1857–1865) and in Geneva (1865–67).

18. Mikhail Nikiforovich Katkov (1818–89), Russian social and political commentator and publisher of *Russkii viestnik* (The Russian herald) (from 1856 until his death) and of *Moskovskiia viedomosti* (The Moscow gazette) (1850–55, 1863–67) who started his career as a reform-minded liberal and ended as an apologist for the government's reactionary counterreforms.

19. Ivan Ivanovich Gorbachevsky (1800–1869), Decembrist who was sent to work in the Nerchinsk mines in 1827 and who lived in a settlement in Petrovsky Zavod from 1839 until the amnesty of 1856.

20. Nikolay Mikhaylovich Przhevalsky (1839–88), Russian explorer of Central Asia during four expeditions between 1870 and 1885 who discovered a series of mountain ranges and lakes, assembled valuable collections of flora and fauna, and was the first to describe the wild camel, wild horse, and other species of vertebrates.

21. Pyotr Kuzmich Kozlov (1863–1935), Russian explorer of Central Asia who participated in Przhevalsky's expeditions and led his own expeditions to Mongolia and Tibet, collecting a large amount of geographic and ethnographic material.

22. Dmitry Aleksandrovich Klements (1848–1914), Russian revolutionary populist, archaeologist, and ethnographer who was banished to Siberia in 1881, where he continued his scientific work.

23. Nestor Aleksandrovich Kalandarishvili (1874 or 1876–1922), one of the leaders of the Russian partisans in Eastern Siberia during the Russian civil war, commanding forces in Yakutia from 1921 until he was killed in battle.

24. Konstantin Petrovich Torson (1790?–1852), Decembrist sentenced to fifteen years of hard labor who lived in Selenginsk from 1835 until his death.

25. The last line of Pushkin's 1818 verse epistle "Chaadaevu" (To Chaadaev).

26. Mikhail Vasilievich Nesterov (1862–1942), Russian painter who created poetic, religious images connected with the ethical questionings raised at the turn of the twentieth century.

27. Nikolay Apollonovich Charushin (1851–1937), Russian revolutionary populist who helped organize the first workers' circles in Saint Petersburg and who was sentenced in 1878 to nine years of hard labor.

CHAPTER 7

1. Vladimir Vladimirovich Bogdanov (1868–1949), editor of the journal *Etnograficheskoe obozrienie* (The ethnography review), who published the first study of Russkoe Ustye, "Russkoe Ust'e Iakutskoi oblasti Verkhoianskago okruga" (Russkoe Ustye in Yakutsk Province in the Verkhoyansk region) (1913, nos. 1 and 2) by Vladimir Zenzinov, and who wrote the introduction to the book version, *Starinnye liudi u Kholodnago okeana* (The age-old people near the Arctic Ocean), from which this quotation is taken (p. 4).

2. *Starinnye liudi u Kholodnago okeana* (Moscow: Tip. P. P. Riabushinskago, 1914).

3. *Potomki zemleprokhodtsev* (Moscow: Mysl', 1972).

4. *Slovo o polku Igoreve* is the story of the unsuccessful campaign undertaken by Prince Igor of Novgorod-Seversky against the Polovtsians in 1185, which was written anonymously between 1185 and 1187 and has now become a classic of old Russian literature.

5. In Russian, *"neperspektivnaia" derevnia*. To raise rural living standards, the Soviet government developed a plan to improve the cost-effectiveness of providing services to the countryside by increasing the size of villages, more than half of which contained fewer than one hundred people after World War II. To this end it classified all rural communities as either "promising" (villages selected for future expansion) or "unpromising" (those doomed to die, whether by liquidation or by withering away). Most "unpromising" settlements still existed as late as the 1980s, often deprived of basic services and inhabited mainly by old people. See "Living in the Soviet Countryside" by Judith Pallot in *Russian Housing in the Modern Age* (Washington, D.C.: Woodrow Wilson Center Press; Cambridge: Cambridge University Press, 1993), 211–31.

Notes

6. Ivan Ivanovich Rebrov (?–1666), Russian seafarer and Cossack from Tobolsk who explored several rivers in northern Siberia by sailing inland from the Arctic Ocean and who discovered the mouth of the Indigirka River around 1636.

7. "Novye dannye o plavanii russkikh Severnym morskim putem v XVII veke" in *Problemy Arktiki* (Problems concerning the Arctic), no. 2 (1943): 125–226.

8. Chir (*Coregonus nasus*) and muksun (*Coregonus muksun*) are types of whitefish.

9. Gerhard Maydell, baron (1835–94), author of *Reisen und Forschungen im Jakutskischen Gebiet Ostsibiriens in den Jahren 1861–1871* (Travels and observations in Yakutsk Province of Eastern Siberia from 1861 to 1871), 2 vols. (Saint Petersburg: Buchdr. der Kaiserl. Akademie der Wissenschaften, 1893–96), which was published in Russian as *Puteshestvie po sievero-vostochnoi chasti Iakutskoi oblasti v 1868–1870 gg.* (A journey through the northeastern part of Yakutsk Province from 1868 to 1870), 2 vols. (Saint Petersburg: Tip. Imp. Akademii nauk, 1894–96).

10. *Puteshestvie po sievernym beregam Sibiri k Ledovitomu moriu, sovershennoe v 1820, 1821, 1822, 1823 i 1824 g.* (Saint Petersburg: Tip. A. Borodina, 1841).

11. *Otryvki o Sibiri* (Saint Petersburg: V Tip. Med. departamenta Ministerstva vnutrennikh diel, 1830).

12. Nikolay Alekseevich Gabyshev (1922–), Yakut prose writer.

13. *Fol'klor Russkogo Ust'ia* (Leningrad: Pushkinskii dom, 1986).

14. "Prediel skorbi: poviest'," in his *Sobranie sochinenii* (Collected works), 2d enlarged ed., vol. 2 (Saint Petersburg: Izd. N. Glagoleva), 1905.

15. *Kratkoe opisanie Verkhoianskogo okruga* (Leningrad: Izd-vo "Nauka," Leningradskoe otd-nie, 1969).

16. *Poeticheskiia vozzrieniia slavian na prirodu*, 3 vols. (Moscow: Izd. K. Soldatenkova, 1865–69).

17. *Russkie na Indigirke* (Novosibirsk: "Nauka," Sibirskoe otd-nie, 1990).

18. In Russian, *smotriny*, the Russian folk rite of looking over a prospective bride.

19. After imprisonment in Yakutia for antigovernment activities, Zenzinov was banished to Russkoe Ustye, where he lived for nine months in 1912 until he escaped.

20. In modern Russian, the particle *-to* is genderless.

21. Mamay was a Tatar chieftain who invaded Russia during the thirteenth century.

22. Eduard Vasilievich Toll (1858–1902), Arctic explorer who led an expedition from 1885 to 1886 sponsored by the Saint Petersburg Academy of Sciences to study the New Siberian Islands.

23. Varangians were Scandinavian seafarers who established a dynasty in Russia in the ninth century.

24. *Vlesova kniha*, an early Slavic manuscript completed around 875 a.d. and discovered in 1919 near Kursk.

CHAPTER 8

1. Valentin Dmitrievich Ivanov (1902–75), Russian writer whose major works form a cycle of fiction devoted to Rus, including *Povesti drevnikh let: khronika IX veka* (Tales of ancient times: a chronicle of the ninth century) (1955), *Rus' iznachal'naia* (Primordial Rus) (vols. 1–2, 1961), and *Rus' velikaia* (Rus the great) (1967).

2. Dmitry Mikhaylovich Balashov (1927–), Russian writer and folklorist who collected and published ballads and tales from northern Russia. His historical fiction includes the tale *Gospodin Velikii Novgorod* (Mr. Novgorod the Great) (1970) and the novel *Marfa-posadnitsa* (Martha, the governor's wife) (1972).

3. Aleksandr Arkadievich Kaufman (1864–1919), Russian economist, statistician, and professor specializing in agrarian questions and population migration, whose works include *Krest'ianskaia obshchina v Sibiri* (Peasant communes in Siberia) (Saint Petersburg: Knizhn. mag. A. F. Tsinzerlinga, 1897).

4. *Siberien, ein Zukunftsland* (Leipzig: F. A. Brockhaus, 1914).

5. Innokenty Vasilievich Omulevsky (real name: Fyodorov) (1836 or 1837–83), Russian writer who attended high school in Irkutsk, where he was influenced by the Decembrists and the Polish exiles, and who wrote a cycle of poems about Siberia, including "Na beregakh Eniseia" (On the banks of the Yenisey), "Barabinskaia step'" (The Barabinskaya Steppe), and "Sibiriak" (The Siberian).

6. Mikhail Aleksandrovich Dudin (1916–), Russian poet from Saint Petersburg whose poems include "Tikhii vzdokh nad Sibir'iu" (A quiet sigh over Siberia), the last stanza of which appears in the text.

Selected Bibliography

The following bibliography is a topical ordering, arranged as follows:

Works about Siberia Cited by the Author

Works in English about Siberia
> *Antiquity*
> *Art and Architecture*
> *Bibliography*
> *Cities and Towns*
> *Commerce and Industry*
> *Description and Travel*
> *The Eastern Region*
> *Ecology*
> *The Economy*
> *Energy*
> *Ethnology*
> *Exile*
> *Forced Labor Camps (Gulag)*
> *History*
> *Lakes and Rivers*
> *Literature*
> *Natural Resources*
> *The Northern Region*
> *Railroads*
> *Religion*
> *The Southern Region*
> *The Western Region*

Works about Siberia Cited by the Author

Andrievich, Vladimir Kalistratovich. *Istoricheskii ocherk Sibiri po dannym, predstavliae-mym Polnym sobraniem zakonov* (A historical essay about Siberia based on data in The complete compilation of laws). 6 vols. in 8. Saint Petersburg, 1886–89.

Azbelev, S. N., and Meshcherskii, N. A., eds. *Fol'klor Russkogo Ust'ia* (The folklore of Russkoe Ustye). Leningrad: Izd-vo "Nauka," Leningradskoe otd-nie, 1986.

Bantysh-Kamenskii, Dmitrii Nikolaevich. *Slovar' dostopamiatnykh liudei Russkoi zemli* . . .

Selected Bibliography

(A dictionary of memorable people from the Russian land . . .). 5 vols. Moscow: Izdan A. Shiriaevym, 1836.

Birkengof, Andrei L'vovich. *Potomki zemleprokhodtsev: vospominaniia-ocherki o rus. porechanakh nizov'ev i del'ty r. Indigirki* (The descendants of pioneers: reminiscences/essays on the Russians living in the lower reaches and delta of the Indigirka River). Moscow: "Mysl'," 1972.

Chappe d'Auteroche, Jean. *Voyage en Sibérie, fait par ordre du roi en 1761: contenant les moeurs, les usages, des Russes, et l'état actuel de cette puissance: la description géographique & le nivellement de la route de Paris a Tobolsk . . .* (A journey to Siberia, made by order of the king in 1761: containing an account of the morals and customs of the Russians, and the present state of this power: A geographical description and surveying of the road from Paris to Tobolsk . . .). 2 vols. in 3. Paris: Debure, père, 1768.

Chekhov, Anton Pavlovich. *Ostrov Sakhalin: iz putevykh zapisok* (Sakhalin Island: based on travel notes). Moscow: Izd. red. zhurnala "Russkaia mysl'," 1895.

Chikachev, Aleksei Gavrilovich. *Russkie na Indigirke: istoriko-etnograficheskii ocherk* (The Russians on the Indigirka: an ethnohistorical essay). Novosibirsk: "Nauka," Sibirskoe otd-nie, 1990.

Chivilikhin, Vladimir Alekseevich. "*Mesiats v Kedrograde*" (A month in Kedrograd). In his *Sobranie sochinenii v 4-kh tomakh* (Collected works in 4 volumes), 2:261–325 (Moscow: Sovremennik, 1985).

Dolgikh, Boris Osipovich. "*Novye dannye o plavanii russkikh Severnym morskim putem v XVII veke*" (New data on Russian navigation along the North Sea route in the 17th century). *Problemy Arktiki* (Problems concerning the Arctic), no. 2 (1943): 125–226.

Fischer, Johann Eberhard. *Sibirische Geschichte von der Entdekkung Sibiriens bis auf die Eroberung dieses Lands durch die russische Waffen* (A history of Siberia from the discovery of Siberia until the conquest of this land using Russian weapons). 2 vols. Saint Petersburg: Gedrukt bei der Kaisrl. Akademie der Wissenschaften, 1768.

Galazii, Grigorii Ivanovich. *Baikal v voprosakh i otvetakh* (Questions and answers about Baikal). Irkutsk: Vostochno-Sibirskoe knizhnoe izd-vo, 1984.

Gedenshtrom, Matvei Matveevich. *Otryvki o Sibiri* (Excerpts about Siberia). Saint Petersburg: V Tip. Med. departamenta Ministerstva vnutrennikh diel, 1830.

Gmelin, Johann Georg. *Reise durch Sibirien, von dem Jahr 1733 bis 1743 . . .* (A journey through Siberia from 1733 to 1743 . . .). 4 vols. in 3. Göttingen: Verlegts Abram Vandenhoecks seel., Wittwe, 1751–52.

Golovachev, Petr Mikhailovich. "*V gorakh Altaia*" (In the Altay Mountains). *Sibirskii sbornik* (The Siberian miscellany), no. 4 (1897): 366–392.

Goncharov, Ivan Aleksandrovich. *Fregat Pallada: ocherki puteshestviia* (The frigate *Pallada*: travel essays). 2d ed. 2 vols. Saint Petersburg: V Tip. Morskago ministerstva, 1862.

Iadrintsev, Nikolai Mikhailovich. "*Raskol'nich'i obshchiny na granitse Kitaia*" (Old Believer communal societies on the Chinese border). *Sibirskii sbornik* (The Siberian miscellany), no. 1 (1886): 21–47.

404
+++

————. *"Strannik na Zolotom ozere"* (The wanderer at Golden Lake). *Sibirskie zapiski* (Siberian notes), no. 2 (1919): 2–7.

Ides, Evert Ysbrandszoon. *Zapiski o russkom posol'stve v Kitai, 1692–1695* (Notes on the Russian embassy to China, 1692–1695). Moscow: Glav. red. vost. lit-ry, 1967.

Irtysh, prevrashchaiushchiisia v Ipokrenu (The Irtysh turning into the Hippocrene). Tobolsk: Tobol'skoe glavnoe narodnoe uchilishche, 1789–91.

Ivanov, Kurbat. *"Rospis' protiv chertezhu ot Kuty reki vverkh po Lene i do vershiny i storonnim rekam, kotorye vpali v Lenu reku i skol'ko ot reki do reki sudovago khodu i pashennym mestam i rasprossnye rechi tungusskago kniaztsa Mozheulka pro bratskikh liudei i pro tungusskikh i pro Lamu i pro inye reki"* (An inventory based on sketches from the Kuta River upstream along the Lena to its highest point and along the side rivers that flow into the Lena River and how far by ship from river to river and how far across plowed areas and oral histories from the Tungus princeling Mozheulka about the Bratsk people and about the Tungus and about Lama and about other rivers). In *Otkrytiia russkikh zemleprokhodtsev i poliarnykh morekhodov XVII veka na Severo-Vostoke Azii: sbornik dokumentov* (The discoveries of the Russian pioneers and arctic seafarers of the seventeenth century in northeast Asia: a collection of documents) (Moscow: Gos. izd-vo geogr. lit-ry, 1951), no. 23, 106–10.

Kalashnikov, Ivan Timofeevich. *Zapiski irkutskago zhitelia* (The notes of an Irkutsk resident). Parts 1–3. *Russkaia starina* (Russian antiquity), 123, no. 7: 187–251; no. 8: 384–409; no. 9: 609–46. (All nos. 1905.)

Kaufman, Aleksandr Arkad'evich. *Krest'ianskaia obshchina v Sibiri: po miestnym izsliedovaniiam 1886-1892 gg.* (Peasant communes in Siberia: based on field research from 1886 to 1892). Saint Petersburg: Knizhn. mag. A. F. Tsinzerlinga, 1897.

Kennan, George. *Siberia and the Exile System.* 2 vols. New York: Century, 1891.

Khudiakov, Ivan Aleksandrovich. *Kratkoe opisanie Verkhoianskogo okruga* (A brief description of the Verkhoyansk region). Leningrad. Izd-vo "Nauka," Leningradskoe otd-nie, 1969.

Maksimov, Sergei Vasil'evich. *Sibir' i katorga* (Siberia and penal servitude). 3 vols. Saint Petersburg: Tip. A. Transhelia, 1871.

Markov, Sergei Nikolaevich. *Podvig Semena Dezhneva* (The feat of Semyon Dezhnyov). Moscow: OGIZ, Gos. izd-vo geogr. lit-ry, 1948.

Martos, Aleksei Ivanovich. *Pis'ma o Vostochnoi Sibiri* (Letters about Eastern Siberia). Moscow: V Univ. tip., 1827.

————. *Zapiski inzhenernago ofitsera Martosa (1806–1818)* (The notes of engineer officer Martos, 1806–1818). *Russkii arkhiv* (Russian archives), no. 7 (1893): 305–68 and no. 8 (1893): 449–68.

Maydell, Gerhard, Baron. *Reisen und Forschungen im Jakutskischen Gebiet Ostsibiriens in den Jahren 1861–1871* (Travels and observations in Yakutsk Province of Eastern Siberia from 1861 to 1871). 2 vols. Saint Petersburg: Buchdr. der Kaiserl. Akademie der Wissenschaften, 1893–96. Published in Russian as *Puteshestvie po sievero-vostochnoi chasti Iakutskoi oblasti v 1868–1870 gg.* (A journey through the northeastern part of Yakutsk Province from 1868 to 1870). 2 vols. Saint Petersburg: Tip. Imp. Akademii nauk, 1894–96.

405
+++

Selected Bibliography

Meier, Egor Egorovich. "*Poiezdka po Altaiu*" (A journey to the Altay region). *Otechestvennyia zapiski* (Notes on the fatherland), no. 11 (1843): 17–23.

Milescu, Nicolae. *Puteshestvie cherez Sibir' ot Tobol'ska do Nerchinska i granits Kitaia, russkago poslannika Nikolaia Spafariia v 1675: dorozhnyi dnevnik* (A journey through Siberia from Tobolsk to Nerchinsk and the borders of China by the Russian ambassador Nikolay Spafary in 1675: a travel diary). Saint Petersburg: Tip. V. Kirshbauma, 1882.

Müller, Gerhard Friedrich. *Istoriia Sibiri . . .* (A history of Siberia . . .). 2 vols. Moscow-Leningrad: Izd-vo AN SSSR, 1937–41.

Nansen, Fridtjof. *Siberien, ein Zukunftsland* (Through Siberia, the land of the future). Leipzig: F. A. Brockhaus, 1914.

Okladnikov, Aleksei Pavlovich, and Vasil'evskii, Ruslan Sergeevich. *Po Aliaske i Aleutskim ostrovam* (Travels in Alaska and the Aleutian Islands). Novosibirsk: Nauka, Sibirskoe otd-nie, 1976.

Podrazhanskii, A. M. *Vizhu dno Baikala!* (I see the bottom of Baikal!) Leningrad: Gidrometeoizdat, 1982.

Popov, Ivan Ivanovich. *Minuvshee i perezhitoe: Sibir' i emigratsiia: vospominaniia za 50 let* (The past and my experiences: Siberia and emigration: reminiscences covering fifty years). 2 vols. Leningrad: Izd-vo "Kolos," 1924.

Pypin, Aleksandr Nikolaevich. *Istoriia russkoi etnografii* (A history of Russian ethnography). 4 vols. Saint Petersburg: Tip. M. M. Stasiulevicha, 1890–92.

Radishchev, Aleksandr Nikolaevich. "*Opisanie tobol'skogo namestnichestva*" (A description of the region ruled by the governor-general of Tobolsk). In his *Polnoe sobranie sochinenii* (Complete works) (Moscow-Leningrad: AN SSSR, 1938–52), 3:133–42.

———. "*Pis'mo o kitaiskom torge*" (A letter about trade with China). In his *Polnoe sobranie sochinenii* (Complete works) (Moscow-Leningrad: An SSSR, 1938–52), 2:3–35.

———. "*Sokrashchennoe povestvovanie o priobretenii Sibiri*" (A brief narrative about the acquisition of Siberia). In his *Polnoe sobranie sochinenii* (Complete works) (Moscow-Leningrad: AN SSSR, 1938–52), 2:146–47.

Remezov, Semen Ul'ianovich. *Chertezhnaia kniga Sibiri* (A sketchbook of Siberia). Saint Petersburg: Izdano Arkheograficheskoiu kommissieiu, izhdiveniem P. I. Likhacheva, 1882.

Sapozhnikov, Vasilii Vasil'evich. *Po Altaiu: dnevnik puteshestviia 1895 goda* (Travels in the Altay region: the diary from a journey made in 1895). Tomsk: Tipo-lit. P. I. Makushina, 1897.

Shcheglov, Ivan Vasil'evich. *Khronologiia istorii Sibiri, 1032–1882 g.* (The chronology of Siberian history, 1032–1882). Irkutsk: Izd. Vostochno-Sibirskago otdiela Imp. Russkago geogr. ob-va, 1883.

Sieroszewski, Wacław. "*Prediel skorbi: poviest'*" (The outer limit of sorrow: A novella). In his *Sobranie sochinenii* (Collected works), 2d enlarged ed., vol. 2. Saint Petersburg: Izd. N. Glagoleva, 1905.

Sobanskii, Genrikh. "*Teletskoe ozero, kedrovniki i 'Kedrograd,' mify i real'nost'*" (Lake Teletskoe, the Siberian pine forests, and Kedrograd, myths and reality). *Sibirskie ogni* (Siberian lights), no. 6 (1987): 131–40.

Sommier, Stefano. *Un'estate in Siberia fra Ostiiacchi, Samoiedi, Siriéni, Tatári e Baskíri* (A summer in Siberia among Ostyaks, Samoyeds, Zyryans, Tatars, and Bashkirs). Florence: Ermanno Loescher, 1885.

Stakheev, Dmitrii Ivanovich. *Za Baikalom i na Amurie: putevye kartiny* (Beyond Lake Baikal and on the Amur River: travel scenes). Saint Petersburg: Tip. K. Vul'fa, 1869.

Strahlenberg, Philipp Johann von. *Das nord- und östliche Theil von Europa und Asia . . .* (The northern and eastern parts of Europe and Asia . . .). Stockholm, 1730.

Sukachev, Vladimir Platonovich. *Irkutsk: ego miesto i znachenie v istorii i kul'turnom razvitii vostochnoi Sibiri* (Irkutsk: its place and significance in the history and cultural development of Eastern Siberia). Moscow: Tip. I. N. Kushnerev, 1891.

Vlesova kniha (The Book of Vles). In Sergei Lesnoi, *"Vlesova kniga"—iazycheskaia letopis' doolegovskoi Rusi: istoriia nakhodki, tekst i kommentarii* (The Book of Vles—a pagan chronicle predating the reign of Grand Prince Oleg: the history of its discovery, with text and commentary). Winnipeg: S. Lesnoi, 1966.

Wrangel, Ferdinand Petrovich, Baron. *Puteshestvie po sievernym beregam Sibiri k Ledovitomu moriu, sovershennoe v 1820, 1821, 1822, 1823 i 1824 g . . .* (A journey along the northern shores of Siberia to the Arctic Ocean undertaken in 1820, 1821, 1822, 1823, and 1824 . . .). 2 vols. Saint Petersburg: Tip. A. Borodina, 1841.

Zenzinov, Vladimir Mikhailovich. *Starinnye liudi u Kholodnago okeana: Russkoe Ust'e Iakutskoi oblasti Verkhoianskago okruga* (The age-old people near the Arctic Ocean: Russkoe Ustye in Yakutsk Province in the Verkhoyansk region). Moscow: Tip. P. P. Riabushinskago, 1914.

Znamenskii, Mikhail Stepanovich. *Istoricheskiia okrestnosti goroda Tobol'ska* (The historical environs of the town of Tobolsk). Tyumen: Izd. A. A. Krylova, 1901.

WORKS IN ENGLISH ABOUT SIBERIA

Antiquity

Gryaznov, Mikhail P. *The Ancient Civilization of Southern Siberia.* Translated from the Russian by James Hogarth. New York: Cowles, 1969.

Jettmar, Karl. *The Altai before the Turks.* Stockholm: n.p., 1951.

Okladnikov, Alexei. *Ancient Population of Siberia and Its Cultures.* Russian Translation Series of the Peabody Museum of Archaelogy and Ethnology, Harvard University, vol. 1, no. 1. Cambridge: Peabody Museum, 1959.

Pfizenmayer, E. W. *Siberian Man and Mammoth.* Translated from the German by Muriel D. Simpson. London: Blackie and Son, 1939.

Rudenko, Sergei I. *Frozen Tombs of Siberia: The Pazyryk Burials of Iron Age Horsemen.* Translated from the Russian by M. W. Thompson. London: Dent, 1970.

Art and Architecture

Blaser, Werner. *Tomsk: Texture in Wood.* Basel: Birkhäueser, 1994.

Khabarova, M. V. *Narodnoe iskusstvo Iakutii* (The folk art of Yakutia). [Chiefly illustrations; summary in English.] Leningrad: "Khudozhnik RSFSR," 1981.

Martynov, Anatoly I. *The Ancient Art of Northern Asia.* Translated and edited by

Demitri B. Shimkin and Edith M. Shimkin. Urbana: University of Illinois Press, 1991.

Okladnikov, Alexei. *Ancient Art of the Amur Region: Rock Drawings, Sculpture, Pottery.* [Chiefly illustrations.] Leningrad: Aurora Art, 1981.

Ornament and Sculpture in Primitive Society: Africa, Oceania, Siberia. Translated from the German by Peter Prochnik. New York: October House, 1966.

Taksami, Ch. M., ed. *Kraski zemli Dersu: Fotorasskaz ob iskusstve malykh narodov Pria-mur'ia* (The colors of Dersu's land: a photo essay on the art of the minority peoples in the Amur River region). [Chiefly illustrations; summary in English.] Khabarovsk: Khabarovskoe knizhnoe izd-vo, 1982.

Tel'tevskii, P. A. *Velikii Ustiug: Arkhitektura i iskusstvo XVII–XIX vekov* (Ustyug the Great: architecture and art from the seventeenth through the nineteenth centuries). [Summary and captions in English.] Moscow: Iskusstvo, 1977.

Treasures of the Art Museum of Irkutsk. Foreword by Valentin Rasputin. Translation from the Russian by Valery Dereviaghin and Peter Meades. Leningrad: Aurora Art Publishers, 1989.

The V. P. Sukachev Art Museum, Irkutsk: Painting, Graphic Arts, Applied Arts. Artistic Treasury of Russia. Saint Petersburg: ARS Publishers, 1993.

Bibliography

Collins, David, N., comp. *Siberia and the Soviet Far East.* World Bibliographical Series, vol. 127. Oxford: Clio, 1991.

Cities and Towns

Hausladen, Gary. *Siberian Urbanization since Stalin.* Washington, D.C.: National Council for Soviet and East European Research, 1990.

Kotkin, Stephen. *Steeltown, USSR: Soviet Society in the Gorbachev Era.* Berkeley and Los Angeles: University of California Press, 1991.

Meisak, N., comp. *Novosibirsk.* [Chiefly illustrations.] Moscow: Progress Publishers, 1978.

Panov, P. G., ed. *Sverdlovsk.* New York: Research and Microfilm Publications, CCM Information, 1956.

Polivanov, S. N., comp. *Cheliabinsk: Gradostroitel'stvo vchera, segodnia, zavtra* (Chelyabinsk: city planning yesterday, today, tomorrow). [Chiefly illustrations; summary and captions in English.] Chelyabinsk: Iuzhno-Ural'skoe knizhnoe izd-vo, 1986.

Pristavkin, Anatolii Ignat'evich. *Bratsk.* Moscow: Progress Publishers, 1974.

Scott, John. *Behind the Urals: An American Worker in Russia's City of Steel.* Reprint of the 1942 ed. A Midland Book. Bloomington: Indiana University Press, 1989.

Sergeev, Mark. *Irkutsk: A Guide.* Translated from the Russian by Jan Butler. Moscow: Raduga Publishers, 1986.

Sverdlovsk. Moscow: Progress Publishers, [1968?]

Commerce and Industry

Fisher, Raymond H. *The Russian Fur Trade, 1550–1700.* University of California Publications in History. Berkeley and Los Angeles: University of California Press, 1943.

Foust, Clifford M. *Muscovite and Mandarin: Russia's Trade with China and Its Setting, 1727–1805*. Chapel Hill: University of North Carolina Press, 1969.

Hudson, Hugh D., Jr. *The Rise of the Demidov Family and the Russian Iron Industry in the Eighteenth Century*. Russian Biography Series, no. 11. Newtonville, Mass.: Oriental Research Partners, 1986.

Lied, Jonas. *Siberian Arctic: The Story of the Siberian Company*. London: Methuen, 1960.

Ross, Robert E., ed. *The Ross Register of Siberian Industry: A Guide to Resources, Factories, Products, Mines, Banks, and Stock Exchanges throughout Siberia*. Compiled by Eugene L. Posadskov et al. New York: N. Ross, 1994.

Swianiewicz, Stanisław. *Forced Labour and Economic Development: An Enquiry into the Experience of Soviet Industrialization*. London: Oxford University Press, 1965

Description and Travel

Bates, Lindon. *The Russian Road to China*. Boston: Houghton Mifflin, 1910.

Clark, F. E. *The Great Siberian Railway: What I Saw on My Journey*. London: Partridge, 1904.

De Weck, Christine. *Siberia, Outer Mongolia, Central Asia: Crossroads of Civilization*. New York: Vantage, 1993.

Dobell, Peter. *Travels in Kamchatka and Siberia*. Reprint of the 1830 ed. New York: Arno, 1970.

Gowing, Lionel F. *Five Thousand Miles in a Sledge: A Midwinter Journey across Siberia*. New York: D. Appleton, 1890.

Jenkins, Mark. *Off the Map: Bicycling across Siberia*. New York: HarperPerennial, 1993.

Kempe, Frederick. *Siberian Odyssey: A Voyage into the Russian Soul*. New York: Putnam's Sons, 1992.

Mowat, Farley. *The Siberians*. Boston: Little, Brown, 1970.

Nansen, Fridtjof. *Through Siberia, the Land of the Future*. Translated by Arthur G. Chater. Reprint of the 1914 ed. New York: Arno, 1971.

Sergeev, Mark, and Sergei Borisovich Shekhov, comps. *Siberia*. [Chiefly illustrations.] Moscow: Planeta, 1985.

Swenson, Olaf. *Northwest of the World: Forty Years Trading and Hunting in Northern Siberia*. London: Hale, 1951.

Vanderlip, Washington Baker. *In Search of a Siberian Klondike*. New York: Century, 1903.

Wrangel, Ferdinand Petrovich, Baron. *Narrative of an Expedition to the Polar Sea in the Years 1820, 1821, 1822 & 1823*. Reprint of the 1841 ed. Fairfield, Wash.: Ye Galleon Press, 1981.

Yevtushenko, Yevgeny. *Divided Twins: Alaska and Siberia*. [Chiefly illustrations.] Translated by Antonina W. Bouis. New York: Viking Studio Books, 1988.

The Eastern Region

Fedoseev, Grigory. *Mountain Trails*. Translated from the Russian by George H. Hanna. Moscow: Foreign Languages Publishing House, n.d. [1950s?].

Kirby, E. Stuart. *The Soviet Far East*. London: Macmillan, 1971.

Selected Bibliography

Krasheninnikov, Stepan Petrovich. *Explorations of Kamchatka, North Pacific Scimitar: Report of a Journey Made to Explore Eastern Siberia in 1735–1741, by Order of the Russian Imperial Government.* Translated by E. A. P. Crownhart-Vaughan. North Pacific Studies, no. 1. Portland: Oregon Historical Society, 1972.

Ravenstein, E. G. *The Russians on the Amur: Its Discovery, Conquest, and Colonisation, with a Description of the Country, Its Inhabitants, Productions, and Commercial Capabilities . . .* London: Trübner, 1861.

Rogers, Allan, ed. *The Soviet Far East: Geographical Perspectives on Development.* London: Routledge, 1990.

Stephan, John J. *The Russian Far East: A History.* Stanford: Stanford University Press, 1944.

———. *Sakhalin: A History.* Oxford: Clarendon Press, 1971.

Ecology

Bothe, Michael, Thomas Kurzidem, and Christian Schmidt, eds. *Amazonia and Siberia: Legal Aspects of the Preservation of the Environment and Development in the Last Open Spaces.* International Environmental Law and Policy Series. London: Graham and Trotman/M. Nijhoff, 1993.

Feshbach, Murray, and Alfred Friendly, Jr. *Ecocide in the USSR: Health and Nature under Siege.* New York: Basic Books, 1992.

Komarov, Boris. *The Destruction of Nature in the Soviet Union.* Translated by Michel Vale and Joe Hollander. White Plains, N.Y.: M. E. Sharpe, 1980.

Pelloso, Andrew J. *Saving the Blue Heart of Siberia: The Environmental Movement in Russia and Lake Baikal.* Bloomington: Indiana University, School of Public and Environmental Affairs, 1993.

Pryde, Philip R., ed. *Environmental Resources and Constraints in the Former Soviet Republics.* Boulder, Colo.: Westview Press, 1995.

Stewart, John Massey, ed. *The Soviet Environment: Problems, Policies, and Politics.* Cambridge: Cambridge University Press, 1992.

Turnbull, M. *Soviet Environmental Policies and Practices: The Most Critical Investment.* Aldershot, Hants, Eng.: Dartmouth, 1991.

Weiner, Douglas R. *Models of Nature: Ecology, Conservation, and Cultural Revolution in Soviet Russia.* Indiana-Michigan Series in Russian and East European Studies. Bloomington: Indiana University Press, 1988.

Wolfson, Ze'ev. *The Geography of Survival: Ecology in the Post-Soviet Era.* Armonk, N.Y.: M. E. Sharpe, 1993.

Ziegler, Charles E. *Environmental Policy in the USSR.* Amherst: University of Massachusetts Press, 1987.

The Economy

Conolly, Violet. *Siberia Today and Tomorrow: A Study of Economic Resources, Problems, and Achievements.* New York: Taplinger, 1976.

Dibb, Paul. *Siberia and the Pacific: A Study of Economic Development and Trade Prospects.* New York: Praeger, 1972.

Dienes, Leslie. *Soviet Asia: Economic Development and National Policy Choices.* Westview

Special Studies on the Soviet Union and Eastern Europe. Boulder, Colo.: Westview Press, 1987.

Hughes, James. *Stalin, Siberia, and the Crisis of the New Economic Policy.* Soviet and East European Studies, 81. Cambridge: Cambridge University Press, 1991.

Kaul, J. M. *Siberia and the Soviet Economy.* Calcutta: K. P. Bagchi, 1983.

Kirby, Stuart. *Siberia and the Soviet Far East: Resources for the Future.* London: Economist Intelligence Unit, 1984.

Krypton, Constantine. *The Northern Sea Route and the Economy of the Soviet North.* Westport, Conn.: Greenwood, 1976. (Originally published in 1956.)

Swearingen, Rodger, ed. *Siberia and the Soviet Far East: Strategic Dimensions in Multinational Perspective.* Hoover Press Publications, 336. Stanford: Hoover Institution Press, 1987.

Energy

Dienes, Leslie, Istvan Dobozi, and Marian Radetzki. *Energy and Economic Reform in the Former Soviet Union: Implications for Production, Consumption and Exports, and for the International Energy Markets.* New York: St. Martin's, 1994.

Dienes, Leslie, and Theodore Shabad. *The Soviet Energy System: Resource Use and Policies.* Scripta Series in Geography. Washington, D.C.: V. H. Winston, 1979.

Elliot, Iain F. *The Soviet Energy Balance: Natural Gas, Other Fossil Fuels, and Alternative Power Sources.* Praeger Special Studies in International Economics and Development. New York: Praeger, 1974.

Iurinov, D. M., ed. *Water Power and Construction of Complex Hydraulic Works During Fifty Years of Soviet Rule.* Translated from the Russian by A. Jaganmohan and G. Venkatachalam. New Delhi: Amerind, 1978.

Tsunts, Mikhail Zinov'evich. *Siberia's Hydro-power Projects.* Moscow: Foreign Languages Publishing House, 1957.

Ethnology

Donner, Kai. *Among the Samoyed in Siberia.* Translated by Rinehart Kyler. Edited by Genevieve A. Highland. New Haven: Human Relations Area Files, 1954.

Fitzhugh, William W., and Aron Crowell, eds. *Crossroads of Continents: Cultures of Siberia and Alaska.* Washington, D.C.: Smithsonian Institution Press, 1988.

Fitzhugh, William W., and Valerie Chaussonnet, eds. *Anthropology of the North Pacific Rim.* Washington, D.C.: Smithsonian Institution Press, 1994.

Forsyth, James. *A History of the Peoples of Siberia: Russia's North Asian Colony, 1581–1990.* Cambridge: Cambridge University Press, 1992.

Gogolev, Anatolii I. *Cultural History of the Yakut (Sakha) People.* Anthropology & Archeology of Eurasia, vol. 31, no. 2. Armonk, N.Y.: M. E. Sharpe, 1993.

Levin, M. G., and L. P. Potapov, eds. *The Peoples of Siberia.* Translated from the Russian by Scripta Technica. Chicago: University of Chicago Press, 1964.

Mayer, Fred. *The Forgotten Peoples of Siberia.* Zurich: Scalo, 1993.

Michael, Henry N., ed. *Studies in Siberian Ethnogenesis.* Anthropology of the North, no. 2. Toronto: University of Toronto Press, 1962.

Selected Bibliography

Simchenko, Yuri. *Winter Trek*. Moscow: Progress Publishers, 1990.

Slezkine, Yuri. *Arctic Mirrors: Russia and the Small Peoples of the North*. Ithaca: Cornell University Press, 1994.

Spiridonov, Nikolai. *Snow People (Chukchi)*. New Haven: Human Relations Area Files, 1954.

Exile

Chekhov, Anton. *A Journey to Sakhalin*. Translated by Brian Reeve. Cambridge: I. Faulkner, 1993.

Deich, Leo. *Sixteen Years in Siberia: Some Experiences of a Russian Revolutionist*. Translated by Helen Chisholm. New York: Dutton, 1903.

Desind, Philip. *Jewish and Russian Revolutionaries Exiled to Siberia, 1901–1917*. Jewish Studies, vol. 6. Lewiston: Edwin Mellen Press, 1990.

Gabel, Dina. *Behind the Ice Curtain*. Holocaust Diaries, vol. 4. New York: CIS Communication, 1992.

Hautzig, Esther. *The Endless Steppe: Growing Up in Siberia*. New York: Harper & Row, 1987. (Originally published 1968.)

Kennan, George. *Siberia and the Exile System*. 2 vols. New York: Russell and Russell, 1970. (Originally published in 1891.)

Mazour, Anatole G. *Women in Exile: Wives of the Decembrists*. Tallahassee, Fla.: Diplomatic Press, 1975.

Sukloff, Marie. *The Life-Story of a Russian Exile: The Remarkable Experience of a Young Girl, Being an Account of Her Peasant Childhood, Her Girlhood in Prison, Her Exile to Siberia, and Escape from There*. Translated by Gregory Yarros. New York: Century, 1914.

Sutherland, Christine. *The Princess of Siberia: The Story of Maria Volkonsky and the Decembrist Exiles*. New York: Farrar, Straus, Giroux, 1984.

Forced Labor Camps (Gulag)

Bacon, Edwin. *The Gulag at War: Stalin's Forced Labour System in the Light of the Archives*. New York: New York University Press, 1994.

Conquest, Robert. *Kolyma: The Arctic Death Camps*. London: Macmillan, 1978.

Doubassoff, Irene. *Ten Months in Bolshevik Prisons*. Edinburgh: W. Blackwood, 1926.

Ginzburg, Eugenia. *Within the Whirlwind*. Translated by Ian Boland. New York: Harcourt Brace Jovanovich, 1981.

Jakobson, Michael. *Origins of the Gulag: The Soviet Prison-Camp System, 1917–1934*. Lexington: University Press of Kentucky, 1993.

Lipper, Elinor. *Eleven Years in Soviet Prison Camps*. Authorized translation from the original German by Richard and Clara Winston. Chicago: Regnery, 1951.

Petrov, Vladimir. *It Happens in Russia: Seven Years Forced Labor in the Siberian Gold Fields*. London: Eyre and Spottiswoode, 1951.

Roeder, Bernard. *Katorga: An Aspect of Modern Slavery*. Translated from the German by Lionel Kochan. London: Heinemann, 1958.

Rossi, Jacques. *The Gulag Handbook: An Encyclopedia Dictionary of Soviet Penitentiary*

Institutions and Terms Related to the Forced Labor Camps. Translated from the Russian by William A. Burhans. New York: Paragon House, 1989.

Shifrin, Avrahan. *The First Guidebook to Prisons and Concentration Camps of the Soviet Union*. Uhldingen, Switzerland: Stephanus Edition, 1980.

Solomon, Michael. *Magadan*. Princeton: Auerbach Publishers, 1971.

Solzhenitsyn, Aleksandr I. *The Gulag Archipelago, 1918–1956: An Experiment in Literary Investigation*. Translated from the Russian by Thomas P. Whitney. New York: Harper and Row, 1974–78.

History

Armstrong, Terence, ed. *Yermak's Campaign in Siberia: A Selection of Documents*. Translated from the Russian by Tatiana Minorsky and David Wileman. Works Issued by the Hakluyt Society, 2d ser., no. 146. London: Hakluyt Society, 1975.

Black, J. L., and D. K. Buse, eds. *G.-F. Müller and Siberia, 1733–1743*. Translation of German materials by Victoria Joan Moessner. Russia and Asia, no. 1. Kingston, Ont.: Limestone, 1989.

Bobrick, Benson. *East of the Sun: The Epic Conquest and Tragic History of Siberia*. New York: Poseidon, 1992.

Connaughton, R. M. *The Republic of the Ushakovka: Admiral Kolchak and the Allied Intervention in Siberia, 1918–20*. London: Routledge, 1990.

Diment, Galya, and Yuri Slezkine, eds. *Between Heaven and Hell: The Myth of Siberia in Russian Culture*. New York: St. Martin's, 1993.

Dmytryshyn, Basil, E. A. P. Crownhart-Vaughan, and Thomas Vaughan, eds. and trans. *Russia's Conquest of Siberia, 1558–1700: A Documentary Record*. To Siberia and Russian America, vol. 1. North Pacific Studies Series, no. 9. Portland, Ore.: Western Imprints, 1985.

Fisher, Raymond H., ed. *The Voyage of Semen Dezhnev in 1648: Bering's Precursor, with Selected Documents*. Works Issued by the Hakluyt Society, 2d ser., no. 159. London: Hakluyt Society, 1981.

Golder, F. A. *Russian Expansion on the Pacific, 1641–1850: An Account of the Earliest and Later Expeditions Made by the Russians along the Pacific Coast of Asia and North America*. Reprint of the 1914 ed. New York: Paragon Book Reprint, 1971.

Ides, Evert Ysbrandszoon. *Three Years Travels from Moscow Over-land to China: Thro' Great Ustiga, Siriania, Permia, Sibiria, Daour, Great Tartary, &c. to Peking . . .* London: W. Freeman, 1706.

Lantzeff, George V. *Siberia in the Seventeenth Century: A Study of the Colonial Administration*. University of California Publications in History, vol. 30. New York: Octagon Books, 1972.

Lessner, Erwin Christian. *Cradle of Conquerors: Siberia*. Garden City, N.Y.: Doubleday, 1955.

Lincoln, W. Bruce. *The Conquest of a Continent: Siberia and the Russians*. New York: Random House, 1994.

Raeff, Marc. *Siberia and the Reforms of 1822*. University of Washington Publications on Asia. Seattle: University of Washington Press, 1956.

Remezov, Semen Ul'ianovich. *The Atlas of Siberia*. 's-Gravenhage: Mouton, 1958.

Selected Bibliography

Semenov, Yuri. *Siberia: Its Conquest and Development.* Translated from the German by J. R. Foster. Baltimore: Helicon, 1963.

Siberica [journal]. Portland: North Pacific Studies Center, Oregon Historical Society, 1990–

Snow, Russell E. *The Bolsheviks in Siberia, 1917–1918.* Rutherford: Fairleigh Dickinson University Press, 1977.

Treadgold, Donald W. *The Great Siberian Migration: Government and Peasant in Resettlement from Emancipation to the First World War.* Princeton: Princeton University Press, 1957.

Wood, Alan, ed. *The History of Siberia: From Russian Conquest to Revolution.* New York: Routledge, 1991.

Wood, Alan, and R. A. French, eds. *The Development of Siberia: People and Resources.* New York: St. Martin's, 1989.

Lakes and Rivers

Gusewelle, C. W. *A Great Current Running: The U.S.-Russian Lena River Expedition, with Lena Reunion.* Kansas City, Mo.: Lowell Press, 1994.

Haviland, Maud D. *A Summer on the Yenesei, 1914.* New York: Arno, 1971.

Jordan, Robert Paul. *Siberia's Empire Road, the River Ob.* National Geographic, vol. 149, no. 2. Washington, D.C.: National Geographic, 1976.

Lockwood, Nina. *Lake Baikal: A Selected Summary of Recent Literature, 1969–1979.* Rochester, N.Y.: Geological Sciences Library, University of Rochester, 1979.

Matthiessen, Peter. *Baikal: Sacred Sea of Siberia.* San Francisco: Sierra Club Books, 1992.

Sergeev, Mark. *The Wonders and Problems of Lake Baikal.* Translated from the Russian by Sergei Sumin. Moscow: Novosti Press Agency Publishing House, 1989.

Literature

Astafiev, Victor. *The Horse with the Pink Mane.* Translated from the Russian. Moscow: Progress Publishers, 1978.

———. *Queen Fish: A Story in Two Parts and Twelve Episodes.* Translated from the Russian. Moscow: Progress Publishers, 1982.

Dostoyevsky, Fyodor. *The House of the Dead.* Translated with a preface by Jessie Coulson. London: Oxford University Press, 1965.

Korolenko, Vladimir Galaktionovich. *Siberia: Three Short Stories.* Translated from the Russian by R. F. Christian. Liverpool: Liverpool University Press, 1954.

Lojkine, A. K., comp. *Siberia in Russian Poetry of the XIX Century: An Anthology.* Canterbury Readers in Russian Poetry, no. 12. Christchurch: University of Canterbury, [Department of] Modern Languages, 1978.

Rasputin, Valentin. *Downstream.* Translated by Valentina G. Brougher and Helen C. Poot. In *Contemporary Russian Prose*, edited by Carl and Ellendea Proffer. Ann Arbor, Mich.: Ardis, 1982.

———. *Farewell to Matyora: A Novel.* Translated by Antonina W. Bouis. Evanston: Northwestern University Press, 1991.

————. *Live and Remember*. Translated from the Russian by Antonina W. Bouis. Evanston: Northwestern University Press, 1992.

————. *Money for Maria and Borrowed Time: Two Village Tales*. Translated by Kevin Windle and Margaret Wettlin. Saint Lucia, Qld.: University of Queensland Press, 1981.

————. *Siberia on Fire: Stories and Essays*. Selected, translated, and with an introduction by Gerald Mikkelson and Margaret Winchell. DeKalb: Northern Illinois University Press, 1989.

Rytkheu, Yuri. *Old Memyl Laughs Last: Short Stories*. Translated by D. Rottenberg. Library of Soviet Short Stories. Moscow: Foreign Languages Publishing House, n.d.

Sartakov, Sergei. *Siberian Stories*. Translated from the Russian. Moscow: Progress Publishers, 1979.

Shalamov, Varlam. *Kolyma Tales*. Translated from the Russian by John Glad. New York: Norton, 1980.

Shukshin, Vasily. *Roubles in Words, Kopecks in Figures, and Other Stories*. Translated from the Russian by Natasha Ward and David Iliffe. London: Marion Boyars, 1985.

————. *Snowball Berry Red & Other Stories*. Edited by Donald M. Fiene. With translations by Donald M. Fiene et al. Ann Arbor, Mich.: Ardis, 1979.

Siberian and Other Folk-Tales. [Collected and translated by C. Fillingham Coxwell.] Reprint of the 1925 ed. New York: AMS Press, 1983.

The Sun Maiden and the Crescent Moon: Siberian Folk Tales. Collected and translated by James Riordan. New York: Interlink Books, 1991.

Vampilov, Aleksandr. *Duck Hunting; Last Summer in Chulimsk: Two Plays*. Translated by Patrick Miles. Nottingham, Eng.: Bramcote, 1994.

————. *Farewell in June: Four Russian Plays*. Translated by Kevin Windle and Amanda Metcalf. Saint Lucia, Qld.: University of Queensland Press, 1983.

Yevtushenko, Yevgeny. *Bratsk Station, and Other New Poems*. Translated by Tina Tupkina-Glaessner, Geoffrey Dutton, and Igor Mezhakoff-Koriakin. New York: Praeger, 1967.

Zalygin, Sergei. *The Commission*. Translated by David Gordon Wilson. DeKalb: Northern Illinois University Press, 1993.

Natural Resources

Barr, Brenton M., and Kathleen E. Braden. *The Disappearing Russian Forest: A Dilemma in Soviet Resource Management*. Totowa, N.J.: Rowman and Littlefield, 1988.

Budnikov, Gennady, comp. *Siberia, 65° East of Greenwich: Oil and People*. Translated from the Russian by Valery Kryshkin. Moscow: Progress Publishers, 1985.

Doyle, David S. *Siberian Natural Gas*. Air War College Research Report, no. 4899. Maxwell Air Force Base, Ala.: Air War College, Air University, 1973.

Gurkov, Genrich, and Valery Yevseyev. *Tapping Siberian Wealth: The Urengoi Experience*. Translated from the Russian by Sergei Sosinsky. Moscow: Progress Publishers, 1984.

Kirby, Stuart. *Siberia and the Soviet Far East: Resources for the Future*. London: Economist Intelligence Unit, 1984.

Selected Bibliography

Mote, Victor L. *The Baikal-Amur Mainline and Its Implications for the Pacific Basin.* Washington, D.C.: Association of American Geographers, 1980.

Osipov, V. *Siberian Diamonds.* Translated from the Russian by Xenia Danko. Moscow: Foreign Languages Publishing House, 1958.

Sansone, Vito. *Siberia, Epic of the Century.* Translated by Keith Hammond. Impressions of the USSR. Moscow: Progress Publishers, 1980.

Wallin, Thomas E. *West Siberia: The Key to Russia's Oil and Gas Future.* New York: Petroleum Intelligence Weekly, 1992.

The Northern Region

Armstrong, Terence E. *Russian Settlement in the North.* Scott Polar Research Institute Special Publication, no. 3. Cambridge: Cambridge University Press, 1963.

Bal'termants, Dmitrii. *Vstrecha s Chukotkoi: Glimpses of Chukotka.* [Text in Russian, English, and German.] Moscow: Planeta, 1971.

Neatby, L. H. *Discovery in Russian and Siberian Waters.* Athens: Ohio University Press, 1973.

Rytkheu, Yuri. *Reborn to a Full Life.* Moscow: Novosti Press Agency Publishing House, 1977.

Sauer, Martin. *Expedition to the Northern Parts of Russia.* Richmond (Surrey): Richmond Publishing Co., 1972.

The Soviet North. Translated from the Russian by David Sinclair-Loutit. Moscow: Progress Publishers, 1977.

Zenzinov, Vladimir. *The Road to Oblivion.* New York: R. M. McBride, 1931.

Railroads

Blackburn, Norman L. *The Baikal-Amur Railroad Mainline: Economic and Military Significance.* Garmisch, Ger.: U.S. Army Institute for Advanced Russian and East European Studies, 1978.

Marks, Steven G. *Road to Power: The Trans-Siberian Railroad and the Colonization of Asian Russia, 1850–1917.* Ithaca: Cornell University Press, 1991.

Meakin, Annette M. B. *A Ribbon of Iron.* Reprint of the 1901 ed. New York: Arno, 1970.

Newby, Eric. *The Big Red Train Ride.* New York: St. Martin's, 1978.

Shabad, Theodore, and Victor L. Mote. *Gateway to Siberian Resources (The BAM).* Scripta Series in Geography. Washington, D.C.: Scripta Pub. Co., 1977.

Shoemaker, Michael Myers. *The Great Siberian Railway from St. Petersburg to Pekin.* New York: Putnam's Sons, Knickerbocker Press, 1903.

Zhuravlev, V. *A Second Trans-Siberian.* Translated from the Russian by Yuri Shirokov. Moscow: Progress Publishers, 1980.

Religion

Avvakum Petrovich. *Archpriest Avvakum, the Life Written by Himself: With the Study of V. V. Vinogradov.* Translations, annotations, commentary, and historical introduction by Kenneth N. Brostrom. Michigan Slavic Publications, 4. Ann Arbor: Michigan Slavic Publications, University of Michigan, 1979.

Bawden, C. R. *Shamans, Lamas, and Evangelicals: The English Missionaries in Siberia*. London: Routledge and Kegan Paul, 1985.

Diószegi, V., and M. Hoppál, eds. *Shamanism in Siberia*. Bibliotheca Uralica 1. Budapest: Akadémiai Kiadó, 1978.

Jacobson, Esther. *The Deer Goddess of Ancient Siberia: A Study in the Ecology of Belief*. Studies in the History of Religions, vol. 55. Leiden: E. J. Brill, 1993.

Lupinin, Nickolas. "The Old Believers." Chapter 6 in his *Religious Revolt in the XVIIth Century: The Schism of the Russian Church*. Men and Movements in Religious History 1. Princeton, N.J.: Kingston Press, 1984.

Peskov, Vasily. *Lost in the Taiga: One Russian Family's Fifty-Year Struggle for Survival and Religious Freedom in the Siberian Wilderness*. Translated by Marian Schwartz. New York: Doubleday, 1994.

Shamanism: New Data from Central Asia and Siberia. Translated from the Russian. Soviet Anthropology and Archeology, vol. 28, no. 1. Armonk, N.Y.: M. E. Sharpe, 1989.

Thorpe, S. A. *Shamans, Medicine Men, and Traditional Healers: A Comparative Study of Shamanism in Siberian Asia, Southern Africa and North America*. Manualia Didactica, 21. Pretoria: University of South Africa, 1993.

The Southern Region

Curtin, Jeremiah. *A Journey in Southern Siberia*. Reprint of the 1909 ed. New York: Arno, 1971.

Egart, Mark. *The Ferry: Sketches of the Struggle for Socialism in the Altai Mountains*. London: M. Lawrence, 1932.

Elvin, Harold. *The Incredible Mile: Siberia, Mongolia, Uzbekistan*. London: Heinemann, 1970.

The Western Region

Atkinson, Mrs. Thomas W. *Recollections of Tartar Steppes and Their Inhabitants*. Reprint of the 1863 ed. New York: Arno, 1970.

Orlov, Vasilii Ivanovich. *Western Siberia: Study on Nature and Economy*. Saint Louis, Mo.: Linguistic Section, Western Area Branch, Chart Research Division, Aeronautical Chart and Information Center, 1964.

Sakk, V. *The Altai Sun*. Moscow: Planeta, 1979.

417
+++

Index

Page numbers for photographs are in italics

Index

Index

425
✦✦✦

Index

431

+++

Index

Index

Index

438
+++